365
Moments
to
Cherish

365
Moments
to
Cherish

by
Robert Strand

New Leaf Press

First printing: September 1997

Copyright © 1997 by New Leaf Press. All rights reserved. Printed in the United States of America. No part of this book may be used or reproduced in any manner whatsoever without written permission of the publisher except in the case of brief quotations in articles and reviews. For information write: New Leaf Press, Inc., P.O. Box 726, Green Forest, AR 72638.

ISBN: 0-89221-360-4
Library of Congress Number: 97-68955

All Scripture references are from the New International Version, unless otherwise noted.

Every effort has been made to locate the authors or originators of the stories contained in this book. Most are the result of conversations with pastors, while others were accumulated throughout the course of a 30-year radio and television broadcasting career.

Daily Bible Reading Calendar by:
        Irwin Printing Co., Inc.
        P.O. Box 9111
        Springfield, MO 65801-9111
        1-800-244-8654

Cover by Left Coast Designs, Inc., Portland, OR.

Presented to:

_____

Presented by:

_____

Date:

_____

To four wonderful people . . .
Marc, Kirk, Kent, and Cheriee
our children,
who in their own right
are each a special story in the making.

Introduction

Everybody is a story and everybody has a story! It is possible to re-write your own story as life is lived because it is a process which is subject to revision. What we do with our days and the kind of lifestyle we live is largely our response to the things which happen about us and to us. We can make choices . . . better choices.

A good life-story is sort of like a window letting in the light of revelation. It's like having a mentor who can be constantly referred to. A good story can open us up to new direction for living, it can challenge us to find some deeper reasons for living, it can present new possibilities which may never have entered your thinking, and it can be the trigger which allows permission to attempt something new and exciting.

"Cut a vital word and it bleeds" is simply another way of telling you that words have meaning and when words are strung together they live. Therefore, I have chosen to spend these next 365 days with you through stories. Hopefully, there are some that will touch a heartstring deep inside of your mind which will invite you to return to the inspiration of a particular story again and again. Perhaps other of these stories will inspire you to share them with others. Some are selected to cause you to re-think some area of living. Still others are here just for the fun of it, a chuckle with which to brighten your day. These next 365 days can be an adventure in building a new daily habit. The daily Scripture readings, found in bold print at the bottom of each page, will enable the reader to study the Bible in one year's time.

Why are stories so important? In my own personal life and ministry, stories, illustrations of truth, have become a vital part of my own personal daily devotions. A number of years ago I read Mark 4:34 with great interest, "He did not say anything to them without using a parable." It struck me . . . here was the greatest communicator who ever lived on the face of this earth who did not speak to people except in parables which are allegorical, stories, fables, myths, legends, homilies, apologues, folk stories, or illustrations of truth. If Jesus Christ chose to use this method of speaking truth, we had also better follow His example and speak in terms which people can understand.

Thomas Guthrie wrote, "By awakening and gratifying the imagination, the truth makes a deeper impression on the memory. The story, like a float, keeps it from sinking; like a nail, fastens it in the mind; like the feathers of an arrow, makes it strike; and like the barb, makes it stick."

The adventure ahead encompasses 365 stories which are designed to fasten truth into your mind and make it stick until it becomes an action! Build the daily habit of a devotional time into your schedule. It matters not what time of the day you may choose . . . just do it! Allow the Word of God and a human interest story to make your life a bit better. My prayer is that you will be blest and be better for having spent 365 days with others in story form and encouraged by the Word of God. Now . . . ENJOY!

January 1, New Year's Day — The Second Chance

On New Year's Day 1929, Georgia Tech played the University of California in the Rose Bowl. In that game, a man named Roy Riegels recovered a fumble for California. Somehow, he became confused and started running in the wrong direction with the ball. One of his team-mates, Benny Lom, overtook and tackled him 65 yards away, just before he was to score a touchdown for the opposing team. When Cal attempted to punt on the next series of downs, Tech blocked the kick and scored a safety which was to be the margin of victory.

That strange play came in the first half of the game and everyone who was watching was asking the same question: "What will Coach Nibbs Price do with Roy Riegels in the second half?"

The men filed off the field and went into their dressing rooms at the end of the first half. They sat down on the benches and on the floor, all except Riegels. He put his blanket around his shoulders, sat down in a corner, put his face in his hands, and cried like a baby.

If you have played football, you know that a coach usually has a great deal to say to his team during halftime. That day, Coach Price was quiet. No doubt he was trying to decide what to do with Roy Riegels.

The announcement came — three minutes before the second half was to begin. Coach Price looked at his team and said simply, "Men, the same team that played the first half will start the second."

The players got up and started out, all but Riegels. He did not budge. The Coach looked back and called to him. Still he didn't move. Coach Price went over to where Riegels sat and said, "Roy, didn't you hear me? The same team that played the first half will start the second."

Then Roy Riegels looked up and his cheeks were wet with tears. "Coach," he said, "I can't do it to save my life. I've ruined you. I've ruined the University of California. I've ruined myself. I couldn't face that crowd in the stadium to save my life."

Then Coach Price reached out and put his hand on Reigel's shoulder and said, "Roy, get up and go back, the game is only half over!" And Roy Riegels went back and those Tech men will tell you they had never seen a man play inspired football as he played that second half!

My friend . . . life's not over, yet! This New Year brings a new chance, a new beginning, another opportunity to start again! Let's get up one more time! God is the God of the second chance!

He who overcomes will inherit all this, and I will be his God and he will be my son (Rev. 21:7).

༅

Gen. 1-2; Ps. 1; Prov. 1; Matt. 1-2

It was during the war in Krakow, Poland. The basement of the cathedral in town had been turned into a hospital for the wounded. There in the very poor light lay hundreds of soldiers who were wounded, mangled, cold, and hungry. As they lay there, there was a steady stream of cursing and other epitaths from the men decrying their fate, anguished with pain.

There was only one doctor available to tend the wounded and he did his best. He moved as quickly as possible, attending to one after another of those whom he was able to help. The evening shadows lengthened as he was finishing his task. One more soldier lay in a corner, covered with some rags to keep him warm.

As the doctor approached, even in the dimming light it was apparent that he was too late. The man was already dead. But as the doctor drew a little closer he noticed something different about his hands. He asked the nurse for a candle to examine the dead soldier. There were wounds on his palms, and then the doctor gave a start. . . .

To protect some of the expensive statuary and other religious items in the cathedral above, many of those items had been moved to safer keeping. Before the doctor lay the form of Jesus Christ in a statue, covered by rags for protection.

Automatically he exclaimed, "Christ is here!"

As a pebble hits the water and its ripples extend, so this message passed from wounded to wounded, "Christ is here. Christ is here."

Soon a hush enveloped the wounded, their nurses, and the lone doctor. The cursing ceased. Even in the midst of this horror and devastation of war, "Christ is here!"

"Christ is here!" What a wonderful expression of caring. Christ is here to share. Christ is here to make a difference.

What a comfort the knowledge of the presence of Jesus Christ can make. From the Bible we have the promises that He is always present, but our problem seems to be a lack of that recognition. The disciples on the road to Emmaus were so blinded to His presence by their own grief that they were unaware of His walking and talking with them. When you hurt, He's there! When you are rejoicing, He's there! When you need help, He's there! Christ is here!

These are written that you may believe that Jesus is the Christ, the Son of God, and that believing you may have life in His name (John 20:31;RSV).

⟨◦⟩

Gen. 3-4; Ps. 2; Prov. 2; Matt. 3-4

January 3 — The Great Decision

A small boy was told by the family doctor that he could save his sister's life by giving her some of his blood. The six-year-old sister was near death, a victim of disease from which the boy had made a marvelous recovery two years earlier. Her only chance for restoration was a blood transfusion from someone who had previously conquered the illness. Since the two children had the same rare blood type, the boy was the ideal donor.

"Johnny, would you like to give your blood for Mary?" the doctor asked.

The boy hesitated. His lower lip started to tremble, then he smiled and said, "Sure, Doctor. I'll give my blood for Mary."

Soon the two children were wheeled into the operating room — Mary, pale and thin, and Johnny, robust and the picture of health. Neither spoke, but when their eyes met, Johnny grinned.

As the blood was siphoned into Mary's veins, one could almost see new life come into her tired body. The ordeal was almost over when Johnny's brave little voice broke the silence. "Say, Doctor, when do I die?"

It was only then that the doctor realized what the moment of hesitation and the trembling of the lip had meant earlier. Nine-year-old Johnny thought that in giving his blood to his sister he was giving up his own life! And in that brief moment he had made his great decision!

The doctor was caught up in the drama and the total commitment of that young man. He was choked up with the impact of the moment.

He paused a bit for his throat to clear before he answered, "Johnny, you will not die, but through your sacrifice your little sister will now live."

Now that is a touching story and it illustrates the much greater truth we find from God's Word. The Bible tells us that without the shedding of blood there can be no forgiveness of sin.

Think with me for a moment. Jesus Christ gladly went to the Cross, and there He willingly gave up His life that all who believe in Him shall never perish but shall have eternal life. He made a supreme sacrifice for all of us who might believe in Him and His sacrifice. What a gift!

Jesus Christ is the one who came; He came with the water of His baptism and the blood of His death. He came not only with the water, but with both the water and the blood. And the Spirit himself testifies that this is true, because the Spirit is truth (1 John 5:6;TEV).

⟨✥⟩

Gen. 5-6; Ps. 3; Prov. 3; Matt. 5

January 4 — Corrie's Rendition

My wife and I once had the happy privilege to travel to Milwaukee, Wisconsin, to hear Corrie ten Boom speak in person. We were at that time pastoring at Evangel Temple in Madison. It was an early spring day, and as we arrived the parking lot was nearly full. We had to sit about two-thirds of the way back in the auditorium.

We listened as she told her "flashlight" story and her famous story about being unable to forgive one of the guards in her prison camp. We had to strain to catch every word as she was very soft-spoken. She didn't look out at her audience very often, either. Then we began to notice . . . as she was speaking, she was also working on a piece of embroidery.

As she talked and worked her needle back and forth, she was describing the plan that God had for our lives. She talked about how her life had been lived in triumph and tragedy. She told about her prisoner-of-war camp experiences and the painful loss of her wonderful sister. It was touching and moving to watch and hear this lady who had been through so much. Her life was a challenge to all of us as we carefully listened so as to not miss one statement.

Near the end of her talk, she held up the piece of cloth on which she was working to display the back side. It was nothing but a jumble of colored threads, but she said that to us life often appears in a jumble. We can't seem to figure out what is happening or why God allows certain circumstances into our lives.

Then she flipped the cloth over to show us a beautiful picture of a crown. This, Corrie said, is what God sees and what He is working to complete in our lives. She concluded with the rendition of this poem:

My life is but a weaving, between God and me
I do not choose the colors, He worketh steadily.
Ofttimes He weaveth sorrow, and I, in foolish pride,
Forget He sees the upper, and I the underside.

Not till the loom is silent and the shuttles cease to fly
Will God unroll the canvas and explain the reason why,
The dark threads are as needful in the skillful Weaver's hand,
As the threads of gold and silver in the pattern He has planned.

And we know that in all things God works for the good of those who love him, who have been called according to his purpose
(Rom. 8:28).

☙

Gen. 7-8; Ps. 4; Prov. 4; Matt. 6

January 5 — Forgiving Father

On a cold winter evening a man suffered a heart attack and was admitted to the hospital. After being treated in the emergency room and taken to his room for the stay, he asked the nurse if she would please call his daughter. He explained, "You see, I live alone, and she is the only family I have."

The nurse went to phone the daughter. The nurse was immediately aware that the daughter was quite upset. As she almost shouted into the phone, the daughter said, "You must not let him die! You see, Dad and I had a terrible argument almost a year ago. I haven't seen him since. All these months, I've wanted to go to him for forgiveness. The last thing I said to him was 'I hate you.' "

There was a pause, then crying on the daughter's end. Then through the tears, "I'm coming now, I'll be there in about 30 minutes."

In the meantime, the patient slipped into cardiac arrest, and an alert was sounded. The nurse who made the phone call prayed, "Oh God, his daughter is on her way. Don't let it end like this."

The efforts of the medical team to revive the patient were fruitless. They had administered adrenaline, then attempted to shock the heart into action but to no avail. The patient died.

The nurse then noticed one of the doctors talking to the daughter outside the room. She could see the pathetic look on the woman's face and read the hurt that had surfaced. The nurse then stepped in, took the young lady aside, and said, "I'm so sorry."

The daughter responded, "I never hated him, you know. I loved him. And now I want to go in and see him."

The nurse thought, *Why put yourself through more pain?* But she took the young woman into the room. The daughter went to the bed and buried her face in the sheets as she sobbed her goodbye to her now deceased father.

The nurse, as she tried not to look at the sad farewell, noticed a scrap of paper on the table by the bed. She picked it up, read it, and then handed it to the distraught daughter. It read: "My dearest Donna, I do forgive you. I pray you will also forgive me. I know that you love me. I love you, too." And it was signed, "Daddy."

The tragedy of guilt and what could have been all come to mind. How much better if forgiveness had been offered sooner. Don't wait!

And when you stand praying, if you hold anything against anyone, forgive him, so that your Father in heaven may forgive you your sins (Mark 11:25;TEV).

‿

Gen. 9-10; Ps. 5; Prov. 5; Matt. 7-8

January 6 — The Failure

For more than 20 years, Robert Frost was a failure. He was considered a failure by friends, neighbors, and publishers. It was a lonely, frustrating struggle for recognition and publication, which never seemed willing to come his way. He often said that during this time he was one of the few persons who knew he was a poet.

The world has since mourned the passing of Robert Frost, and today he towers as one of America's greatest writers of verse. His poems have been published in 22 different languages at last count. The American edition of his poems has sold more than a million copies.

Frost was a four-time winner of the coveted Pulitzer Prize for poetry and had more honorary degrees thrust on him than any other man of letters. He was in constant demand to read his writings.

Robert Frost was 39 years old before he was able to sell his first volume of poetry to any publisher. He had been writing for more than 20 years. For these long years, his writing was received by an endless stream of rejection slips, yet he kept on composing poems and submitting his work. Finally his perseverance paid off. He was published and considered a poet. Today we can say that the world is a bit wiser and richer for the writings of Robert Frost.

An eminent psychiatrist, Dr. George Crane, recently listed various ingredients necessary for greatness. Among those qualities he noted are some you'd expect to find — talent, responsibility, etc. Then, surprisingly, he said that physical stamina is also necessary! He reasons that many men do not reach the apex of their life endeavors until quite late in life and, therefore, endurance is necessary. He cited Winston Churchill as a prime example.

What is true in the physical realm of life is also true in the spiritual part of living. If we are to reach the ultimate in what God wants us to be, there must be spiritual endurance. This quality is called "long-suffering" as well as "patience" in the Bible. The apostle Paul even lists long-suffering as a fruit of the Spirit.

In this journey on earth, it's the little things that drive us to despair. To reach your goal in life will take endurance, but it's worth the struggle. In the end, you'll be glad you didn't give up.

But he that shall endure unto the end, the same shall be saved
(Mark 13:13;KJV).

Gen. 11-12; Ps. 6; Prov. 6; Matt. 9

January 7 — Keep Going

The setting was a cold January morning in a little town in Northern Wisconsin on the southern shore of Lake Superior. It happened to be a Saturday when the town held the annual dog-sled race on the lake. A one-mile course had been staked out by sticking little fir trees in the ice. Because of the steep slope of the shore, those standing above the ice could easily view the entire course.

It was a youngster's meet, and the contenders ranged all the way from large boys with several dogs and big sleds to one little fellow, who was about six years old, with a tiny little sled and one dog.

They all took off at the signal, and soon the little fellow with his single dog was quickly outdistanced. He was so far behind it seemed as though he wasn't even in the race or was running one by himself.

All went well with the other racers until — about half-way around — the team that was in second place started to pass the team then in the lead. In the excitement of the race, the driver of the second-place team guided his dogs too close to the lead team, and the dogs got into a fight.

Then as each team came up, the dogs joined in the fight. None of the young drivers could seem to steer their dogs and sleds around the melee. Soon, the race had turned into a seething mass of dogs fighting, snapping, charging, growling, tumbling, and barking — all tangled up in sleds, boys, and harnesses!

The drivers of those sleds were in the middle, striking out at dogs, hitting, and trying to pull them apart! Whistling and shouting, the boys pulled with all their strength to free their full-grown, angry and growling Alaskan huskies. It was a total mess.

From the position of the spectators, what was once a race appeared to be just one huge, black seething mass of kids, sleds, and dogs.

Then they could see that little fellow with the little sled and the very little dog closing in on the fight. He simply guided his dog around the jumbled pile — the only one to manage it. He crossed the finish line amid the cheering of the crowd, taking first place and making him the only winner!

When he was interviewed at the finish line, he was asked how he did it. His reply was simple: "I just kept on going and kept my dog from getting into the fight. That's all!"

All men will hate you because of me, but he who stands firm to the end will be saved (Matt. 10:22).

～♋

Gen. 13-14; Ps. 7; Prov. 7; Matt. 10

January 8 — The Beggar King

Once there was a time, according to legend, when Ireland was ruled by a king who had no heirs. The king sent out his couriers to post notices in all the towns of his realm. The notices advised that every qualified young man should apply for an interview with the king as a possible successor to the throne. However, all such candidates must have these qualifications: 1) they must love God and 2) love fellow human beings.

The young man about whom this legend centers saw a notice and reflected that he loved God and also his neighbors. One thing stopped him . . . he was so poor that he had no clothes that would be presentable in the sight of the king. So the young man begged here and borrowed there and worked at odd jobs.

Properly attired, the young man set out on his journey and had almost finished the trip when he came upon a poor beggar by the roadside. The beggar was dressed in tattered rags, and he pleaded for help, "I'm hungry and I'm cold. Please, please help me . . . please?"

The young man was so touched by the beggar's plight that he took off his new clothes and exchanged them with the tattered rags of the beggar. He also gave him all the provisions he had left.

Now, somewhat hesitant, he continued on his way to the castle dressed in the rags of the beggar and no provisions for his walk back home. When he arrived, one of the king's attendants met him in the great hall. After a brief break to clean off some of the grime from the trip, he was finally admitted to the throne room where the king sat.

The young man bowed in reverence. When he looked up, he gasped in astonishment. "You . . . it's you! You are the beggar by the road."

"Yes," the king replied with a smile, "I was that beggar."

"But . . . bu . . . you are a beggar. You are the real king! Why?" he managed to stammer out after gaining some of his composure.

"Because I had to find out if you or any of the other young men really loved God and your fellow human being," replied the king. "If we met as we are now, I would never really know if you cared enough about others. So I used this ploy. I have discovered that you do sincerely love God and others. You will be the next king, you will be my successor. You will inherit this kingdom!"

A new command I give you: Love one another. As I have loved you, so you must love one another. By this all men will know that you are my disciples, if you love one another (John 13:34-35).

❧

Gen. 15-16; Ps. 8; Prov. 8; Matt. 11

January 9 — Joy and Laughter

Can you remember a time when your life was more joyful? I can! A recent study found that kids laugh an average of 150 times a day while adults laugh only about 10 times a day! What's happened to us? We have a laughter famine . . . especially in the church. We need to laugh at ourselves and with others.

John Updike, contemporary American novelist, describes his parents as "inclined to laugh a lot, and examine everything for the fingerprints of God!" Laughter is a great gift from God! Most of us tend to tackle every problem head-on without the release of laughter!

Grandmother and granddaughter, a precocious 10 year old, were spending the evening together when the little girl suddenly looked up and asked, "How old are you, Grandma?"

The woman was a bit startled, but knowing her granddaughter's quick little mind, she wasn't too shocked. "Well, honey, when you're my age you don't share your age with anybody."

"Aw, go ahead, Grandma . . . you can trust me!"

"No dear, I never tell anyone my age."

Grandma got busy fixing dinner and suddenly realized the little darling had been absent for about 20 minutes . . . much too long! She checked and found her upstairs in her bedroom. Her granddaughter had dumped the contents of her purse on top of the bed and was sitting in the middle of the mess, holding her grandmother's driver's license.

When their eyes met, the child announced, "Grandma, you're 76!"

"Why, yes, I am. How did you know that?"

"I found the date of your birthday here on your driver's license and subtracted that year from this year . . . so you're 76!"

"That's right, sweetheart. Your grandmother is 76."

The little girl continued, staring at the driver's license and added, "You also made an 'F' in sex, Grandma!"[1]

Somewhere between childhood innocence and NOW, life has become too grim! When did a well-exercised sense of humor and joy get sacrificed on the altar of adulthood? Who says that being a Christian means you must have a long face? To be joyful is a choice! To laugh is a choice! Let's choose to laugh and be joyful!

Though the fig tree does not bud and there are no grapes on the vines, though the olive crop fails and the field produce no food, though there are no sheep in the pen and no cattle in the stalls, yet I will rejoice in the Lord, I will be joyful in God my Savior
(Hab. 3:17-18).

❧

Gen. 17-18; Ps. 9; Prov. 9; Matt. 12

January 10 — Surprise Purchase

The very wealthy English Baron Fitzgerald had only one child, a son, who understandably was the apple of his eye, the center of his affections, an only child, the focus of this little family's attention.

The son grew up, but in his early teens his mother died. Fitzgerald grieved over the loss of his wife but devoted himself to their son. In the passing of time, the son became very ill and died in his late teens. In the meantime, the Fitzgerald financial holdings greatly increased. The father had used much of his wealth to acquire art works of the "masters."

And with the passing of more time, Fitzgerald himself became ill and died. Previous to his death he had carefully prepared his will with explicit instructions as to how his estate would be settled. He had directed that there would be an auction in which his entire art collection would be sold. Because of the quantity and quality of the art works in his collection which was valued in the the millions of English pounds, a huge crowd of prospective buyers had gathered, expectantly. Among them were many museum curators and private collectors eager to bid.

The art works were displayed for viewing before the auction began. Among them was one painting which received very little attention. It was of poor quality and done by an unknown local artist. It happened to be a portrait of Fitzgerald's only son.

When the time came for the auction to begin, the attorney read first from the will of Fitzgerald which instructed that the first painting to be auctioned was the painting of "my beloved son."

The poor quality painting didn't receive any bidders . . . except one! The only bidder was the old servant who had known the son and loved him and served him, and for sentimental reasons offered the only bid. For less than an English pound he bought the painting.

The auctioneer stopped the bidding and asked the attorney to read again from the will. The crowd was hushed, it was quite unusual, and the attorney read from the Fitzgerald will: "Whoever buys my son gets all my art collection. The auction is over!"

Whoever gets the son gets it all! Whoever gets Jesus, God's only Son, gets it all! It's that simple and that important. If you don't have the Son of God as part of your life, you really have nothing in the end! If you have the Son, you have all that God has to offer! All this and heaven, too! Whoever gets the Son gets it all!

And this is the testimony: God has given us eternal life, and this life is in His Son. He who has the Son has life; he who does not have the Son of God does not have life (1 John 5:11-12).

꙳

Gen. 19-20; Ps. 10; Prov. 10; Matt. 13

Everybody knows about angels . . . well, at least on some level. And it seems that more people are talking about angels than ever before. Today there are boutiques devoted to angels, and greeting cards, poetry, songs, and books portraying them in all their goodness. We even take these wonderful "angelic" qualities and apply them to a sweetheart, spouse, kids, or special people.

Billy Graham, in his popular book on angels, states, "Angels have a much more important place in the Bible than the devil and his demons."[2] The Bible is chock-full of dramatic angelic appearances . . . Abraham, Jacob, Moses, Joshua, Gideon, David, Elijah, Zechariah, Joseph, Mary, and Peter, along with others, saw angels. Angels in the Bible are seen in many roles . . . climbing ladders, wrestling with people, taming lions, lifting great weights, announcing births, recruiting leaders, warriors in battle, executioners, performing miraculous rescues, and comforting people.

Two angels are mentioned by name . . . Michael and Gabriel. Michael is depicted in three biblical books as the "Great Prince" or archangel; Gabriel is shown as presiding over paradise.

So what are angels? We know, according to the Bible, that they are created beings, dignified, majestic, and intelligent. They are personal beings who always represent God but are not omnipresent, which God is. Little is said of their appearance, but they can take on the physical form of a person and sometimes are mistaken for another human being. The word "angel" simply means "messenger." They are seen as protectors, messengers ordered by God to minister in a myriad of ways in the Bible.

Some things to note: At no time should an angel or angels be worshiped! The Bible is very clear that only God is to be worshiped. Second, we are not to pray to angels! You might ask God for help in an emergency, but we are never to pray to angels. Let's open our eyes and ears of understanding and ask God to help us develop a healthy balance in regard to His angels.

I believe that angels exist!

For by Him all things were created: things in heaven and on earth, visible and invisible, whether thrones or powers or rulers or authorities; all things were created by Him and for Him (Col. 1:16).

❧

Gen. 21-22; Ps. 11; Prov. 11; Matt. 14

January 12 — A Hallmark Story

More than a few of the townspeople who paused to survey the burned-out ruins of the Hall brothers' Kansas City greeting card warehouse on January 12, 1915, must have commented on the poor luck of the young owners of the business. The fire that swept through the building the night before had destroyed thousands of cases of Valentine's Day cards that were soon to be shipped, bringing in money that 23-year-old wholesaler Joyce Hall and his brother, Rollie, were counting on to pay off creditors. Now, with their entire inventory lost in the blaze, the brothers would be unable to meet their $17,000 debt.

Coming when it did, the loss was particularly heartbreaking for Joyce Hall, who was just beginning to establish himself as a successful businessman after years of struggle and poverty. The Norfolk, Nebraska, native had been working since the age of nine, when his father, an itinerant preacher, abandoned the family, leaving Joyce and his two older brothers to provide for their semi-invalid mother. Young J. C. (as he preferred to be called) peddled perfume door-to-door and later went into business selling greeting cards. Seeking brighter opportunities, he took a supply of cards to Kansas City, where he began wholesaling them to local druggists. Soon he added a line of imported Christmas and Valentine's Day cards, and within a year he was joined by his brother Rollie. They gradually expanded their sales territory into nearby cities and states before the fire wiped them out.

"If you want to quit, that's a good time to quit. But if you are not a quitter, you begin to think fast," J. C. said later of the calamity. Rising to the challenge, the young businessman borrowed more money and purchased a local engraving firm so that he and Rollie could replenish their stock quickly and cheaply by printing their own greeting cards. Their first two original designs were ready in time for Christmas 1915. Sold in midwestern drugstores, the tiny (2-1/2" X 4") hand-painted Yuletide greetings were a success with holiday shoppers, providing a badly needed inflow of cash to the Halls' devastated firm.

At the time of J. C. Hall's death in 1982, his namesake firm (Hallmark) was turning out 8 million greeting cards a day! Among them is still the very first everyday card, carrying a friendship theme by Edgar Guest: "I'd like to be the kind of friend you've been to me."

Friendship is really about perseverance, and isn't it fitting that the "hallmark" of friendships is still around after these many years?

Lazy hands make a man poor, but diligent hands bring wealth
(Prov. 10:4).

❧

Gen. 23-24; Ps. 12; Prov. 12; Matt. 15

In Oceanside, California, in Mr. Alter's fifth grade class, it was almost impossible to tell which boy was undergoing chemotherapy! Nearly all the boys were bald. Thirteen of them had their heads shaved so a sick buddy wouldn't feel out of place.

"If everybody has their head shaved, sometimes people don't know who's who. They don't know who has cancer, and who just shaved their head," said 11-year-old Scott Sebelius, one of the baldies at Lake Elementary School.

For the record, Ian O'Gorman is the sick one.

Doctors removed a malignant tumor from his small intestine, and he started chemotherapy to treat the disease called lymphoma.

Ian decided to get his head shaved before all his hair fell out in clumps. To his surprise, his friends wanted to join him.

"The last thing he would want is to not fit in, to be made fun of, so we just wanted to make him feel better and not left out," said ten-year-old Kyle Hanslik.

Kyle started talking to other boys about the idea, and then one of their parents started a list. Last week they all went to the barber shop together.

Their teacher, Jim Alter, also shaved his head.

"You're showing the country and the world what kids can do. People think kids are going downhill. This is the best," Alter said.[3]

To be a compassionate friend is sharing the feelings of sympathy, even sorrow for the hurt and suffering of somebody else. But it goes even beyond these feelings. It has as its reason for compassion the desire to alleviate some of the pain or even to remove its cause. What a wonderful kind of a friend — Ian had 13 of them! Other peers who had enough feeling, humanity, and heart to sacrifice their hair, too. When I am hurting, give me more of that kind of people.

The good Book tells us that in order to have friends, one must be friendly, first. One of the major keys to enjoying a wonderful life is to be a friend and have friends. While you are young is the time to begin establishing those friendships which will last you a lifetime. Who of your friends needs some compassionate understanding in their living?

A man of many companions may come to ruin, but there is a friend who sticks closer than a brother (Prov. 18:24).

᷍

Gen. 25-26; Ps. 13; Prov. 13; Matt. 16-17

January 14 — Praying Hands

The famous "Praying Hands" picture was created by Albrecht Durer, the son of a Hungarian goldsmith. He was born in Germany in 1471 and died in 1528. As is the case with nearly all men of genius, fact and fiction become interwoven and created the legend of the artist as we know him today.

It is said that while studying art, Albert, as he was called, and a friend roomed together. However, the meager income they earned on the side as they studied did not prove to be enough to meet their needs for rent, food, clothing, and other living expenses. Albert suggested that he would go to work to earn the necessary income for both of them while his friend pursued and finished his art studies. When finished, the friend would then go to work to provide support while Durer would finish his studies. The friend was pleased and happy with the plan, except that he insisted that he be the first to work and that Albert continue his studies.

This plan was followed and in time Albert Durer became a skilled artist and engraver. Returning to his room one day, Albert announced that he was now ready to assume the burden of support, while his friend studied art. But, as a result of his hard labor, his friend's hands were so swollen that he was no longer able to hold and use the paintbrush with skill. His career as an artist was ended.

Albert was deeply saddened by this disappointment which his friend had suffered. One day when he returned to their room he heard his friend praying and saw his hands held in a reverent attitude of prayer. At this moment, Albert received the inspiration to create the picture of those wonderful "praying hands." His friend's lost skill could never be restored but in and through this picture, Durer felt that he could express his love and appreciation for the self-sacrificing labor which his friend had performed for him. Durer also had another thought that such a picture could inspire a like appreciation on the part of others who may also be willing to sacrifice and give on the behalf of someone else.

The story is now legend. I cannot verify if this is factual or not, but it sounds wonderful. Self-sacrificing is a brand of love that is not too often seen in our too-busy kind of a world. Yes, in the act of sacrificial love we have identity as being part of the body of Jesus Christ, otherwise known as the Church. Humble giving and prayer are keys to open Heaven's door.

By this all will know that you are My disciples, if you have love for one another (John 13:35;NKJ).

꩜

Gen. 27; Ps. 14; Prov. 14; Matt. 18

❧

A good father will leave his imprint on his daughter for the rest of her life.

James C. Dobson

❧

January 15 — A Letter to a Sister

Salem, Jany, 15, 1767

Dear Sister,
Your kind letter I receiv'd today
and am greatly rejoiced
to (hear) you are all so well.
I was very uneasy
at not hearing from you,
indeed my dear Sister
the Winter never seem'd
so tedious to me in the World.
I daily count the days
between this and the time
I may probably see you.
I could never feel so comfortable as
I at present do,
if I thought I should
spend another Winter here.
Indeed my Sister
I cannot bear the thought
of staying here so far from
all my Friends if
Mr. Cranch can do as well nigher.
I would give a great deal
only to know I was
within Ten Miles of you if I could not see you.
Our children will never
seem so natural to each other
as if they liv'd where they could see
one another oftener. . . .

(This letter was written from Mary Smith Cranch to her sister, Abigail Adams.)

Everyone who quotes proverbs will quote this proverb about you:
"Like mother, like daughter." You are a true daughter of your
mother . . . and you are a true sister of your sisters (Ezek. 16:44-45).

❧

Gen. 28-29; Ps. 15; Prov. 15; Matt. 19-20

January 16 — Baptized by Socrates

There's an old story about a proud, arrogant young man who came to the noted philosopher Socrates asking for knowledge. He proudly walked up to the muscular philosopher and said, "O great Socrates, I come to you for knowledge."

Socrates, recognizing a pompous, thick-headed, numbskull when he saw one, asked the young man to follow him through the streets of Athens to the shores of the Mediterranean Sea. Together they waded out into the water, chest deep. Then he turned to the young man and asked, "What do you want?"

"Knowledge, O wise Socrates," said the young man with a smile.

Socrates put his strong hands on the pompous young man's shoulders and pushed him under and held him. Thirty seconds later, Socrates let him up. "What do you want?" he asked him again.

"Wisdom, O great and wise Socrates," the young man sputtered, without the smile this time.

Socrates crunched him under again . . . this time a little longer. Then he let him up, again. The young man was gasping for breath. "What do you want, young man?" Socrates asked again.

Between heavy, heaving breaths the young man wheezed, "Knowledge, O wise and wonder. . . ."

Socrates jammed him under again. This time he counted to 50 before he pulled him up out of the water. "What do you want?"

"Air!" he screeched. "I need air!"

"When you want knowledge as you have just wanted air, then you will have knowledge," said a smiling Socrates.

We live in what is called the "Information Age," or a time when information and knowledge is bought and sold. Inside information can be your ticket to wealth and prestige and position. Knowledge doesn't come easily . . . it is a learning process, it takes scholarship, the application of intelligence. It's a cultivation of the mind, it's a gathering of data, it's becoming aware, it's a sharpening of perception, it's honing the memory, and comprehension as to how it can be applied. Knowledge is today's commodity! Knowledge can be your ticket to an exciting future! So . . . bottom line: How much do you really want or need knowledge? When it becomes as important as your next breath you will have it or at least the beginning of knowledge!

If any of you lacks wisdom, he should ask God, who gives generously to all without finding fault, and it will be given to him (James 1:5).

⌐∾ᵔ

Gen. 30; Ps. 16; Prov. 16; Matt. 21

January 17 — Bigger Than Winning

They are remembered simply, sadly, as "The Falls." They are among the most poignant moments of Olympic history.

During the 1988 Winter Games in Calgary, Dan Jansen, a gold medal favorite, came out on the ice to skate the 500 meters only hours after learning that his sister had died of leukemia. As he rounded the first turn, the weight of the agonizing news seemed to crush him to the ice. Four days later Jansen tried again in the 1,000 . . . and again he fell, this time on a straightaway.

"It was very hard realizing that all my accomplishments didn't seem to matter, that all I would be known for was falling in the Olympics," he says. He needed time just to believe "that it wasn't going to happen again."

Since then Jansen has matured and married . . . and emerged, ready for another run for the gold.

Since winning the 1988 World Sprint Championships on his home turf (ice) in West Allis, Wisconsin, he's been America's most consistent male speed skater. In 1991-92 Jansen skated stride for stride in the 500 with defending Olympic gold-medalist Uwe-Jens Mey and broke the German's world record.

Yet Calgary forever altered his life perspective. Jansen soberly said, "Losing a sister was a lot bigger deal than winning a medal could ever be. Winning the gold can never again be the most important thing in my life."[4]

The 1994 Olympics from Norway are now history, and it appeared to be deja vu over again as Dan Jansen fell in the 500 meter event, then it happened again in the 1,000 meters sprint. There was only one event left for Dan to skate in . . . 1,500 meters. This was not his best sprint distance. Remember, he was the world record holder in the 500. It was to be his last race in his last Olympic competition! We were riveted to our TV sets as the drama unfolded for us. The gun sounded. Dan, as he had promised, gave his very best . . . setting a time which held up to win his last race! It was one of those special times!

On the awards stand, as the gold medal was placed around his neck, we watched the emotion. As our national anthem was played there were tears . . . then a salute given heavenward. This race was in honor of his sister . . . and we recalled his life-priority, "Winning the gold can never again be the most important thing in my life."

Do you not know that in a race all the runners run, but only one gets the prize? Run in such a way as to get the prize (1 Cor. 9:24).

❧

Gen. 31; Ps. 17; Prov. 17; Matt. 22

January 18 — Out of the Pens of Babes

After Christmas vacation, a teacher asked her small pupils to write an account of how they spent their holidays. One youngster wrote about a visit to his grandparents in a life-care community for retired folks:

"We always spend Christmas with Grandma and Grandpa," he said. "They used to live here in a big red house, but Grandpa got retarded and they moved to Florida. They live in a place with a lot of retarded people. They live in tin huts. They ride big three-wheel tricycles. They go to a big building they call a wrecked hall, but it is fixed now. They play games there and do exercises, but they don't do them very good. There is a swimming pool and they go to it and just stand there in the water with their hats on. I guess they don't know how to swim.

"My grandma used to bake cookies and stuff. But I guess she forgot how. Nobody cooks — they all go out to fast food restaurants.

"As you come into the park, there is a doll house with a man sitting in it. He watches all day, so they can't get out without him seeing them. They wear badges with their names on them. I guess they don't know who they are.

"My Grandpa and Grandma worked hard all their lives and earned their retardment. I wish they would move back home but I guess the man in the doll house won't let them out."[5]

Well, I guess, eventually, if we live long enough, this might happen to all of us. And it's refreshing to look at this and other things of life through the eyes of little people. What a different world, delightful. And let's face it, teachers have an opportunity to see a slice of life that few others do — to see and listen and be part of kids up close and personal. What fun to be a part of molding this potential. There is such an innocence and wonder at all of life through the eyes of children. Our challenge is how to maintain this excitement, yet encourage the development of their gifts. It's to direct and not thwart. It's to encourage and not dampen. It's to challenge and not overwhelm. Teaching may be the highest calling of all, because teachers work on eternal lives.

It would be better for him to be thrown into the sea with a millstone tied around his neck than for him to cause one of these little ones to sin. So watch yourselves (Luke 17:2-3).

⌒ᗚ

Gen. 32-33; Ps. 18:1-15; Prov. 18; Matt. 23

January 19, Martin Luther King Day —
Just an Ordinary Woman

Rosa Parks is just a very ordinary woman, a seamstress in one of the Montgomery, Alabama, department stores. Now her story: On December 1, 1955, she made history! She boarded her bus for the ride home after work. The "black" section in the back of the bus was full. The center section was available to blacks as long as no whites needed those seats. Rosa took the lone remaining seat of the center section. The bus continued . . . three stops later some whites were picked up, just enough to fill each remaining seat with one white man still standing. The bus driver informed Parks and three other black riders that they must vacate the center section so this white man could take his "rightful" seat.

Parks tells us in her word what happened next: "When the driver first spoke, didn't any of us move; but then he spoke a second time with what I call a threat, because he said, 'Ya'll better make it light on yourselves and let me have those seats.' At that point the other three stood up . . . the driver looked at me and asked me if I was going to stand up. I told him, 'No, I wasn't.' He said, 'If you don't stand up, I'm going to have you arrested.' I told him to go on and have me arrested. He didn't exchange any more words with me."

Rosa was arrested and spent the night in the Montgomery jail. Forty of the pastors of Montgomery churches pledged to lead a boycott of the city bus service. A new young pastor among the 40, the Reverend Martin Luther King, Jr. was selected to lead the boycott. Later he delivered one of the most exciting speeches ever given. It was electrifying. "I Have A Dream" resounded through the halls of legislatures and in Washington, D.C., as he led the modern day movement to do away with segregation. For his efforts, he was shot, martyred for the cause.

Rosa was convicted in court and fined $14. It was appealed to the U.S. Supreme Court which overturned this lower court decision. A lethal blow was struck which toppled all segregation laws and what had been any legal foundations justifying such laws.

Rosa . . . your life has spoken! Here's a lady who was willing to take a stand and be counted. She became the catalyst, in a very extraordinary way, to make life better for a whole lot of God's people everywhere!

For if you remain silent at this time, relief and deliverance for the Jews will arise from another place, but you and your father's family will perish. And who knows but that you have come to royal position for such a time as this? (Esther 4:14).

෴

Gen. 34-35; Ps. 18:16-36; Prov. 19; Matt. 24

January 20 — The Test

His name was Lt. John Blanchard, a soldier in basic training in Florida during WWII. One evening he wandered into the post library and found a book to read. The feminine handwriting in the margins intrigued him, so he turned to the front of the book and found the name of the previous owner . . . a Miss Hollis Maynell.

Blanchard did some research and found her address in New York. The following day he was shipped overseas. For 13 months the two corresponded by letter and began to open their hearts to each other. He asked for her picture, to which she refused by saying that if he really loved her it wouldn't matter what she looked like.

Finally the day came when they were to meet in Grand Central Station, New York City. She had instructed, "You'll recognize me by the red rose that I'll be wearing on my lapel."

Let's let the young soldier tell you what happened:

A young woman was coming toward me, beautiful, trim, blonde, eyes were blue as flowers, and in her pale green suit she was like springtime come alive. I started toward her forgetting that she was not wearing the rose . . . and then I saw Hollis Maynell! She was standing behind the girl. A woman with graying hair. BUT she wore a red rose on the rumpled brown lapel of her coat. So deep was my longing for the woman who's spirit had captured me that I approached her. There she stood, face was gentle and sensible and her gray eyes had a twinkle. I didn't hesitate. My hand gripped the small worn blue leather book which was to identify me to her.

I squared my shoulders and saluted and held out the book to the woman while choking back the bitterness of disappointment. "I'm Lt. John Blanchard and you must be Miss Maynell. I am so glad to meet you. May I take you to dinner?"

The woman's face broadened into a smile. "I don't know what this is about, son," she answered, "but the young lady in the green suit who just went by, asked me to wear this rose. And she said if you were to ask me out to dinner I should tell you that she is waiting for you in the large restaurant across the street. She said it was some kind of test!"

Apparently Lt. John Blanchard passed the test! Would you?

But the fruit of the Spirit is love, joy, peace, patience, kindness, goodness, faithfulness, gentleness and self-control (Gal. 5:22-23).

✺

Gen. 36-37; Ps. 18:37-50; Prov. 20; Matt. 25

January 21 — Handicapped?

Tracy MacLeod hates the word "handicapped!" She may use it when she's making jokes about herself to her teammates at Canada's Brandon University, but beyond that, the word does not apply to her. After all, what person with a real handicap would have returned to play basketball only three months after having half of her lower right leg amputated? What person with a real handicap could score 20 points and grab 10 rebounds in 20 minutes of playing time, as the 21-year-old MacLeod did recently against the University of Regina team?

Last season, MacLeod, a 6'-1" center, was averaging 11.2 points and 6.2 rebounds on two healthy legs.

But that was before one mis-step under the basket launched her into a medical nightmare. While attempting a lay-up in a home game against Winnipeg in January 1993, MacLeod landed awkwardly on her right leg. The crack of her tibia and fibula was so loud that several players covered their ears and turned away.

The leg was set and cast — within 24 hours circulation problems began, necessitating the first of nine operations over the next five months. They weren't successful, and finally the choice was facing a lifetime of corrective surgeries and a misshapen leg, or amputation.

In June of 1993 her leg was amputated eight inches below the knee. She went home walking nearly limp-free on a prosthesis 2-1/2 weeks later. MacLeod's doctors told her that a return to her former level of play at any time was an unrealistic expectation.

"I took what the doctors said and just kind of laughed," says MacLeod. "I wasn't about to let anyone put limitations on me. I just wanted to get back to my normal life and basketball was a big part of that life. I didn't know if I could play, but I had to try."

She is a step slower and can't jump as high as before but she moves remarkably well in the paint and still has the best shooting touch on the team. "Her comeback is amazing," says teammate Andrea Brown. "It is a real motivator to see her out there. It makes you think about what you take for granted and how much stronger you could be."

Opponents give her more respect than sympathy. "We play Tracy as tough as we always did," says rival coach, Tom Kendall, of Winnipeg. "If we don't, she scores."

"If they play slack defense, they're going to pay," says MacLeod. "He who hits first, wins. Usually, that's me!"[6]

"If you can?" said Jesus. "Everything is possible for him who believes" (Mark 9:23).

෴

Gen. 38-39; Ps. 19; Prov. 21; Matt. 26

January 22 — I Saved Nobody but Myself

Many years ago, a 25-year-old nephew of Dr. Gansaulus, a famous Chicago preacher, admitted his distress because he could find no purpose for his life. His uncle talked with him of the need to give himself for others as a means whereby such purpose could be found.

As he left the office the young man noted that the old Iroquois Theatre was burning. He saw several people trapped in an upper-story window. Quickly he found a plank, climbed to a level in the next building where he placed the plank across the window and helped several to safety. Unfortunately, a falling beam struck him and knocked him to the pavement far below. Dr. Gansaulus was called and arrived just before his nephew died. The young man looked squarely into his uncle's eyes and whispered, "Now I know why I was born."

Several years later Dr. Gansaulus was talking with another traveler in a hotel in Europe. A casual remark about Chicago so excited this man that he babbled unintelligibly; whereupon his companion led him away, explaining later to the minister that the man had been in the old Iroquois Theatre in Chicago on the fateful day it burned. He had managed to get out only by crawling and clawing his way over many screaming, fear-crazed, panic-stricken people. Ever since, at the slightest reference to Chicago, he would tremble and mutter, "I saved nobody but myself. I saved nobody but myself."[7]

The fire we're talking about happened in 1903 when Eddie Foy was there in a huge extravaganza. The place was packed with people. Fire broke out and seemed to explode as it filled and enveloped the building. Panic struck immediately! People jammed the aisles in a desperate struggle to get to the doors. Hot gases and smoke filled the place, turning it into a death chamber. A total of 590 people died. It was an awful scene.

Mainly because of this fire, public buildings were required to clearly mark their exits and install panic bars on doors that always swung outward. Fire-retardant materials were encouraged from that time as well.

There is an analogy here. Someday this world and world system will be under the judgment of fire according to the Bible. The only place of real safety is in Jesus Christ. As Christians we have found a place of refuge and safety, but how many of our friends still need our help to lead them to Christ? Life must be lived with an eye toward eternity.

For anyone who wants to save his life will lose it; but anyone who loses his life for my sake will find it (Matt. 16:25;JB).

⌒∽

Gen. 40-41; Ps. 20; Prov. 22; Matt. 27

January 23 — This First Grade Teacher Is Blind

Marjorie West was born with sight but has been progressively going blind. "Retinitis pigmentose" attacks the retina and in turn causes night blindness, the loss of depth perception, and the loss of peripheral sight. At age 46 she was declared legally blind.

"The Lord and I have proven the doctors wrong several times," she says. "I was told my retina wouldn't let me teach beyond 50, but here I am still going strong." Marjorie, seven years later, can still see a bit . . . like looking through a soda straw. She still keeps up with more than 20 rambunctious first grade students. All by herself? Not really. If you visited her first grade classroom of the Glennon Heights Elementary School in Colorado you would find Rush, her seeing eye dog, resting under her desk.

You would notice her full-time assistant, Karen Taylor, who has loaned her eyes since 1987 to be the look-out to help maintain order in this classroom. There is really only one more distinctive sign allowing for Marjorie's blindness . . . it's the way in which the kids identify themselves when responding orally.

It's been tough. Back in 1987 when the school board was told by Marjorie about her progressive disability, she was ready to fight for her job at all costs! She, with confidence, made her appeal to be allowed to be a contributor in the Jefferson County district. She offered to be re-trained, if they deemed it necessary. Also, there were laws which the district had to follow in making reasonable accomodations for the handicapped, provided her performance was good. Her excellent reputation preceeded her, which was also a help.

Today she is thought of as friendly, an overcomer, nurturing, committed, and professional. Outstanding could also be added to this list, as well as a teacher who has continued to learn.

She sums up her life this way: "The process of going through loss myself . . . not only my eyes, but divorce, giving up driving, my father's death . . . helped me become more sensitive to the needs, the fears, the feelings, and all the things kids bring to school with them." Her physical weakness has become an asset!

But he said to me, "My grace is sufficient for you, for my power is made perfect in weakness." Therefore I will boast all the more gladly about my weaknesses, so that Christ's power may rest on . . . I delight in weaknesses, in insults, in hardships, in persecutions, in difficulties. For when I am weak, then I am strong" (2 Cor. 12:9-10).

꩜

Gen. 42; Ps. 21; Prov. 23; Matt. 28

January 24 — The Messenger

This story begins in the early 1970s, in Rockford, Illinois, as Pastor Don Lyons led his church to purchase some farm land on which to build a church and a Christian radio station. They built a small house for the station's home, if they could get it launched. Pastor Lyons knew they needed a special person to manage the start up. As the pastor prayed about it . . . in his mind, he could see the name "Tietsort" spelled out. An unusual name. He dismissed it.

One day at a special pastor's meeting at which the churches in Rockford hosted a meeting, Pastor Lyons was greeting some of the guests when a young man walked up . . . the pastor stared at his name tag, "Ron Tietsort"! He was a pastor and had a radio/TV background in Sioux City, Iowa. Soon Ron accepted the job of station manager and moved his family.

His wife, Millie, became the bookkeeper, receptionist, and occasional programmer. Then in the winter of 1975 reality had to be faced. Despite all their efforts and a growing listener base, WQFL was in trouble. In order to catch up and keep it going, WQFL needed just over $3,000 and needed it like right NOW!

It might as well have been three million! Millie sat looking out the window on a new snowfall as she prayed, "God, we really thought You wanted the station to succeed. Did we misread You? Please tell us what to do now."

The front door opened and a middle-aged man walked in, carrying a scaled envelope. Millie was startled . . . she'd heard no car in the drive, no footsteps on the porch. Perhaps the snow had muffled the sounds. "Give this to Ron. Use it for the station." Before Millie could offer him a receipt for tax purposes he was gone. Strange.

She walked to Ron's desk, he slit the envelope open and gasped, "Millie, look!" Inside was more than $3,000 in cash! Ron leaped from his chair, raced to the front of the house, and flung open the door to call the man back so he could thank him or meet him.

BUT there was no car in the drive, no tire tracks in the driveway . . . none coming from the road and none going back. Then Ron looked down on the fresh snow of the porch which hadn't been shoveled yet, no tracks! No footprints on the white carpet anywhere!

Today WQFL and WGLS are still operating . . . and Ron and Millie never saw the stranger again. But they remember!

And my God will meet all your needs according to His glorious riches in Christ Jesus (Phil. 4:19).

✑

Gen. 43-44; Ps. 22:1-21; Prov. 24; Mark 1

January 25 — How High Can It Fly?

Do you remember your first helium-filled balloon? Did it happen at the fair, or carnival, or on the streets of your city, or was it at a parade? You clutched it with joy, maybe it was tied to your wrist. It was fun! It wanted to always go up. What fun with a balloon! Then . . . somehow, it slipped out of your hand, maybe you cried, as it went up . . . up . . . up, until it finally went out of sight, taken by the wind. Could it have been your first physics lesson learned the hard way? Now . . . did you ever wonder how high up that balloon really could have gone?

There is an answer provided for us from the "National Scientific Balloon Facility" located in Palestine, Texas. That little latex balloon would have eventually reached a height of approximately 18,000 feet! As it climbed, expansion would have taken place. At the 18,000-foot level, the helium inside would have expanded to about 80 percent more than its original volume. This is about the absolute limit of the latex to expand, and that little balloon would have burst!

What if you wanted to sail a balloon beyond that height? There are specially designed experimental balloons that can reach heights of more than 120,000 feet! These balloons have been designed with ducts which vent off the expanding pressure of the gases as the balloon rises.

So what's the difference in a plain ordinary latex balloon and an experimental balloon that can soar to unbelievable heights? The balloons we cherished as kids have a limited ability to expand and adapt while the others are designed for expansion.

It's much the same thing in life . . . some of us might be destined to blow apart with only a little pressure. But there are others who have prepared themselves for new heights, and because of the adaption and design will be able to withstand the pressures of life on the climb.

Life holds out fantastic possibilities for those who are willing to make preparation. Nobody plans to fail. Based on life insurance industry statistics you can take 100 people who are now in their late teens and look ahead to age 65 making these predictions:

1 will end up independently wealthy

4 will have all the money they need and be comfortable

5 will still be working to earn their living

36 will have died

54 will depend on family, friends, or the government for a living.

One thing I do: Forgetting what is behind and straining toward what is ahead, I press on toward the goal to win the prize for which God has called me heavenward in Christ Jesus (Phil. 3:13-14).

⌒◡〜

Gen. 45-46; Ps. 22:22-31; Prov. 25; Mark 2

January 26 — It Makes a Difference

It was early in 1945. As United States forces pushed deep into Okinawa they came across a village unlike any they had ever seen. Here at Shimabuku they were met and welcomed by two old men who invited the troops in as "fellow Christians."

Correspondent Clarence W. Hall described the hamlet like this: "We'd seen other Okinawan villages, uniformly down at the heels and despairing; by contrast this one shone like a diamond in a dung heap. Everywhere we were greeted by smiles and dignified bows. Proudly the old men showed us their spotless homes, their terraced fields, fertile and neat, their storehouses and granaries, and their prized sugar mill."

Searching for an answer as to why this one village was so different from all the rest, Hall uncovered an incredible story. Some 30 years before, an American missionary on his way to Japan had paused at Shimabuku and stayed only long enough to make two converts and leave them a Japanese translated Bible. These new converts, with only instructions to read the Bible and live by it, began sharing their faith with neighbors. Before long the whole town had accepted Christ and for 30 years had been following the Bible completely.

They had adopted the Ten Commandments as their legal code, the Sermon on the Mount as their guide in social conduct. In their schools they taught the Bible, and in their courts made decisions on what God's Word said.

Hall noted that they managed to create a Christian democracy at its purest. The result was that there were no jails, no bars, no drunkenness, no divorce, and a high level of happiness!

The war correspondent was so moved by the experience, he later requisitioned a jeep and investigated this town more fully. He attended a primitive but deeply spiritual service and came away more impressed.

After the war came to an end, Hall began to wonder what had happened to the tiny hamlet. Fifteen years later he went back there to find that while modern civilization had swallowed Okinawa, the spiritual influence of Shimabuku remained.

On leaving the town many years before, his jeep driver had said, "So this is what comes out of only a Bible and a couple of old guys who wanted to live like Jesus." Then with a glance at a shell hole, Hall recalled the driver murmuring, "Maybe we're using the wrong weapons to make this world over!"

And He said unto them, Go ye into all the world, and preach the gospel to every creature (Mark 16:15;KJV).

⌒∽⌒

Gen. 47-48; Ps. 23; Prov. 26; Mark 3

January 27 — Angels Unaware

In 1937 the Japanese began a full-scale invasion of China. In 1938 Dick and Margaret Hillis were missionaries for the China Inland Mission. By January of 1941 the Japanese were advancing toward their home in Shenkiu. Their city was soon to be the center of fighting. They had two small babies . . . two months and just over a year. In the midst of this Dick had an appendicitis attack with the closest doctor 115 miles away. What to do.

Miraculously, God had kept them safe and the Japanese did not invade this city. Dick packed them into two rickshaws to head for Shanghai. They were stopped at the Sand River by the Chinese army. They asked for permission to pass through the lines but the commander told them they were crazy. Eventually the commander gave them a written note of permission to go through the lines. As they were leaving the officer's headquarters, they were spotted by the son of a Christian they knew who recognized Dick. He was an opium smuggler, black sheep of the family, who offered them a place to sleep, a boat to cross the river, and a guide. God's first angel had come as a smuggler.

In the "no-man's land" they were approached by three Japanese officers. The one in the center was a two-star general. In perfect English he addressed Dick, "Where in the world did you come from?"

Dick was astonished . . . then quickly told his story of illness and the need for a hospital, rest, and milk. "And may I ask you, sir, where did you learn such perfect English?"

Without hesitation the officer informed them that he had attended the University of Washington in 1936. "General," Dick said, "give me the pleasure of introducing you to one of your fellow alumni. My wife was also at the University of Washington in 1936.

The General's face beamed. He greeted Margaret warmly and promised to fulfill each of their requests. "In the morning I will give you a pass to take you through Japanese lines. You will find milk at the little church, for the former missionary there owned a cow."[8]

And so God supplied three angels, who themselves, no doubt, were unaware of their role in guiding God's servant family to safety in a great time of trouble.

The angel of the Lord encamps around those who fear Him, and He delivers them (Ps. 34:8).

❦

Gen. 49-50; Ps. 24; Prov. 27; Mark 4

January 28 — If You Were Born Before 1945 . . .

We are survivors! Consider some of the changes we have witnessed: We were born before television, penicillin, polio shots, frozen foods, Xerox, plastic, contact lenses, frisbees, the pill, radar, credit cards, split atoms, laser beams, ball-point pens, pantyhose, dishwashers, clothes dryers, electric blankets, air conditioners, drip-dry clothes, computers, and before anybody walked on the moon!

We got married first and then lived together! How quaint!

In our time, closets were for clothes, not for "coming out" of, bunnies were small rabbits, and rabbits were not Volkswagons. Designer jeans were scheming girls named Jean or Jeanne, and having a meaningful relationship meant getting along well with our cousins.

We thought fast food was what you ate during Lent, and outer space was the back of the Bijou Theater. We were before house-husbands, gay rights, computer dating, dual careers, day care centers, group therapy, and nursing homes. We never heard of FM radio, CDs, computers, cellular phones, artificial hearts, word processors, yogurt, and guys wearing earrings. For us . . . time-sharing meant togetherness, not computers or condominiums; a "chip" meant a piece of wood; hardware meant screws and nails, and software wasn't even a word!

In 1940, "Made in Japan" meant junk and the term "making out" referred to how you did on your exam.

We hit the scene when there were five and dime stores, where you actually bought things for five and ten cents. Snelgrove's or Farr's sold ice cream cones for a nickel or a dime. For one nickel you could ride a streetcar, buy a Coke, or enough stamps to mail one letter and two postcards. You could buy a new Chevy coupe for $600, but who could afford one? A pity, too, because gas was 11 cents a gallon!

In our day grass was mowed, coke was a cold drink, and pot was something you cooked in. Rock music was Grandma's lullaby.

We were certainly not before the difference between the sexes was discovered but we were surely before the sex change; we had to make do with what we had. And, we were the last generation that was so dumb as to think you needed a husband to have a baby!

No wonder we are so confused and that there is such a generation gap today.

BUT WE SURVIVED!!!!

WHAT BETTER REASON TO CELEBRATE?

You have made my days a mere handbreadth; the span of my years is as nothing before you. Each man's life is but a breath (Ps. 39:5).

⟡

Exod. 1-2; Ps. 25; Prov. 28; Mark 5

January 29 — What Is Success?

In 1923, a group of the world's most successful financiers met at a Chicago hotel. Among those present were the president of the largest independent steel company in the world, the president of the largest utility company, the most successful commodity speculator, the president of the New York Stock Exchange, the president of the Bank of International Settlements, and the head of the world's greatest monopoly at that time.

Together these tycoons of the business world controlled more wealth than the treasury of the United States (remember that we were on the gold standard at that time). For years the media had been printing and talking about the success stories of these wealthy men. They had been held up as examples for all to follow, especially the youth of our nation. These men were at the very pinnacle of success in their world.

Let's take another look and see what happened to these men twenty-five years later.

Charles Schwab was the president of the largest independent steel company in the world. Twenty-five years later, he was living on borrowed money and died penniless. Incidentally, he was the first man in American history to draw an annual salary of $1 million.

Arthur Cutten, the greatest and most successful of commodity speculators, died abroad in dire poverty.

Richard Whitney, the president of the New York Stock Exchange, was sentenced to serve a term in Sing Sing Prison.

Albert Fall, who was a member of the president's Cabinet, was pardoned from prison so he could die at home.

Leon Fraser, president of the Bank of International Settlement, ended his life by committing suicide.

Ivar Kreuger, the head of the world's then-greatest monopoly, put an end to the misery of his life by committing suicide.

All of these men, considered at one time the very epitome of success, had learned how to make money — and lots of it. I'm sure they saved, studied, worked long hours, disciplined themselves, and set their goals to reach the top of their chosen fields. But in the final analysis, not one of them had really learned how to live. Life is much more than accumulating riches or material things.

Jesus still has the right perspective on life.

Beware! Don't always be wishing for what you don't have. For real life and real living are not related to how rich we are
(Luke 12:15;LB).

❧

Exod. 3-4; Ps. 26; Prov. 29; Mark 6

January 30 — I'm Here!

The Rogers are devout Christians who have built a strong family. The father has a special interest in the spiritual condition of each of his children and often would quiz them in order to know if they were sure of their salvation. Occasionally he would ask them to share in their own words about their relationship with Jesus Christ

One day it was seven-year-old Jimmy's turn to express how he knew he had eternal life. Jimmy told his version: "I think it will be something like this in heaven. One day when we all get to go to heaven, it will be time for the big angel to read from the big book the names of all the people who will be there. He will come to the Rogers family and say 'Daddy Rogers?' and Daddy will say, 'Here!' The angel will call out 'Mommy Rogers?' and Mommy will say 'Here!' Then the angel will come down to call out 'Susie Rogers?' and 'Mavis Rogers?' and they will both say 'Here!' "

He paused, took a big deep breath and continued, "And finally that big angel will read my name, 'Jimmy Rogers?' and because I'm little and maybe he'll miss me, I'll jump and shout real loud, 'HERE!' to made sure he knows I'm there."

Just a few days later there was a tragic accident. A car struck down little Jimmy Rogers as he made his way to catch the school bus. He was rushed by ambulance to the hospital, and all the family was summoned. He was in critical condition.

The little family group gathered around the bed in which little Jimmy now lay with no movement, no consciousness, and no hope for recovery. The doctors had done all that was in their power. Jimmy would probably be gone by morning.

The family prayed and waited. Late in the night the little boy seemed to be stirring a bit. They all moved closer. They saw his lips move; just one word was all he uttered before he passed from this life. But what a word of comfort and hope for a grieving family he was to leave behind. In a clear voice of a little boy, loud and clear enough so all could hear and understand, little Jimmy Rogers said the one word: "HERE!" And then he was gone to another life beyond this world where a big angel was reading the names of all those written there.

Say, my friend, is your name written there, too?

He who overcomes will, like them, be dressed in white. I will never blot out his name from the book of life, but will acknowledge his name before my Father and his angels (Rev. 3:5).

༺~༻

Exod. 5-6; Ps. 27; Prov. 30; Mark 7

There was a little, old cleaning lady, humble, clean, but she had to live on the "wrong side of the tracks" because of her meager earnings. She attempted to become a member at the fashionable "First" church. The pastor was not eager to have a seedy-looking lady in faded, out-of-style clothing sitting next to any of his wealthy, up-town members.

Her efforts at attempting to join this church had gone on for over a year . . . but she was persistent. So she called again, the seventh time, to set an appointment to discuss membership and her joining. The pastor put her off once more. "I'll tell you what to do," the pastor said in his most pious-sounding voice. "You just go home tonight and have a talk with God about it. Really pray about it. Then, later, you can tell me what God said to you about your membership in our church."

Weeks went by until they became months. He saw no more of her. No more attempts to set an appointment. He did allow as to the fact that his conscience bothered him a little. Then one day as he was on his way to an appointment downtown, he noticed her. Here she was in her uniform, scrubbing the floors in the foyer of this office building.

He stopped when he recognized her and felt that he should at least ask. "Did you ever have your little talk with God about church membership, Mrs. Pettibone?"

"Oh, my, yes," she replied, "I talked with God as you suggested."

"Ah . . . and just what did He tell you?"

"Well, Preacher," she paused, brushed away a couple of wisps of hair with her work-worn hand, put her hands on her hips and replied, "God told me not to be discouraged, but simply to keep on trying for my membership. He also said that He himself has been trying, without success, to get into your church for more than 20 years!"

Oh . . . oh, big trouble in River City! Honesty with a punch! Wow! What about your church? Is God on the outside looking in? Maybe, even more importantly, what about you and your life? Is God at home on the inside or is He still standing outside and seeking entrance?

It's so easy to fill our lives with the urgent and forget about the really important! We get so busy doing "religious things," "churchy things," but where is the Lord in all of our busyness? Outside, or on the inside? Too many of us like to keep God in a Sunday-kind-of-box. It's nice to go to His House . . . but to take Him home with us may be a bit too close for comfort. His presence may cramp our style.

Here I am! I stand at the door and knock. If anyone hears my voice and opens the door, I will come in (Rev. 3:20).

༄

Exod. 7-8; Ps. 28; Prov. 31; Mark 8

February 1 — It's All in Your Attitude

Extravagances and luxuries did not exist for my mother. The one exception to her frugality was a frilly nightgown which she had never worn. She explained, "I have that nightgown so that if I ever have to go to the hospital, I'll still look nice."

Many years later, my mother began to suffer from a mysterious disease. On a winter day just before her 69th birthday, she packed up her nightgown and checked into the hospital for tests.

The physician confided with me over the final test results. My mother had only a matter of weeks to live. I agonized for days over whether to tell her the news. Was there any hope I could give her?

I decided not to tell her . . . not just yet. I resolved instead to lift her spirits on her birthday by giving her the most expensive and beautiful matching nightgown and robe I could find. At the very least she would feel like the prettiest person in the hospital, dignified as she lay dying.

After unwrapping the present, my mother said nothing. Finally, pointing to the package she asked, "Would you mind returning it to the store? I don't really want it." She then picked up a newspaper and pointing to an ad for a summertime designer purse, she explained, "This is what I really want." Why would my ever-frugal mother want an expensive summer purse in the middle of winter?

Then I realized . . . my mother was asking me how long I thought she would live . . . if she would make it to summer. Maybe, if I thought she'd live long enough to use the purse, then she really would. When I brought the purse to her in her hospital bed, she held it tightly against her, with a smile on her face.

Many years later, that particular purse is long worn out, as are half a dozen others. Next week Mother celebrates her 83rd birthday! My gift to her? The most expensive purse I can find. She will use it well![9]

Yes . . . it is in attitude! That's not the only reason why we live or die . . . but it effects our living and when we die. One surgeon told me, as I stood by the bedside of his next patient, "I'm glad to see you, Reverend. It really helps my patients to have a support system. The people that pray recover sooner and I've found they live longer than people who don't pray." Now that's not scientific . . . but personal observation from a doctor-surgeon. It's in your attitude!

Finally . . . whatever is true, whatever is noble, whatever is right,
whatever is pure, whatever is lovely, whatever is admirable . . . if
anything is excellent or praiseworthy . . . think about such things
(Phil. 4:8).

ew

Exod. 9-10; Ps. 29; Prov. 1; Mark 9

February 2 — Angels on Assignment

This happened in 1956 during the Mau Mau uprisings in East Africa and is told by Phil Plotts, son of missionary Morris Plotts:

A band of roving Mau Maus came to the village of Lauri, surrounded it and killed every inhabitant including women and children . . . 300 in all. Not more than three miles away was the Rift Valley School, a private school where missionary children were being educated. Immediately upon leaving the carnage of Lauri, they came with spears, bows and arrows, clubs, and torches to the school with the same intentions of complete destruction in mind.

Of course, you can imagine the fear of those little inhabitants along with their instructors housed in the boarding school. Word had already reached them about Lauri. There was no place to flee with little children and women. So their only resource was to go to prayer.

Out of the darkness of the night, lighted torches appeared. Soon there was a complete ring of these terrorists around the school. Shouting and curses could be heard coming from the Mau Maus. Then they began to advance. All of a sudden, when they got close enough to throw spears, they stopped! Then began to run! A call had gone out to the authorities and an army had been sent but arrived after the Mau Maus had run. The army then spread out searching, which led to the capture of the entire band of raiders. Later, before the judge at their trial, the leader was called to the witness stand. The judge questioned: "On this particular night, did you kill the inhabitants of Lauri?"

"Yes."

"Was it your intent to do the same at the missionary school in Rift Valley?"

"Yes."

"Well, then," asked the judge, "why did you not complete your mission? Why didn't you attack the school?"

Remember . . . this was a heathen person from the darkness who had never read the Bible or heard about angels. The leader of the Mau Maus said: "We were on our way to attack and destroy all the people and school . . . but as we came closer, all of a sudden, between us and the school there were huge men dressed in white with flaming swords, and we became afraid and ran to hide."

For He will command His angels concerning you to guard you in all your ways; they will lift you up in their hands, so that you will not strike your foot against a stone (Ps. 91:11-12).

❧

Exod. 11-12; Ps. 30; Prov. 2; Mark 10

A country preacher was preaching very pointedly to his congregation one Sunday morning.

He said, "Now let the church walk!"

Deacon Jones said, "AMEN, let it walk!"

The preacher then said, "Let the church run!"

Deacon Jones said, "AMEN, Parson, let it run!"

"Let the church fly!" shouted the preacher.

"AMEN, brother, let it fly!" shouted Deacon Jones.

"Now it's going to take a lot of money to let it fly, brother," shouted the preacher.

"Let it walk, then," said Deacon Jones, "let it walk."

Preachers can be funny people. I'm one myself, and know quite a few other preachers. Most have discovered that it helps to develop a sense of humor. Many times we are caught in situations when nothing works. It's at such times that it helps to laugh.

There was a small town preacher who rushed to the railroad station every afternoon to watch the 3:08 train go by. Members of his congregation thought his pastime was too juvenile and so his church board asked him to give it up.

"No, gentlemen," he said firmly. "I preach your sermons, teach your Sunday school, bury your dead, marry your young people, run your charities, and am chairman of every drive it pleases you to conduct. I pray at every function you have. I won't give it up, this seeing the train every day. I love it! It's the only thing that passes through this town that I don't have to organize or push or pull!"

And there was a young, rookie preacher who was quite flattered when someone described him as a "model" preacher.

His pride soon vanished when he turned to his dictionary and found the definition of "model:" A small imitation of the real thing.

He used a bit more caution the next time. On being described as a "warm" preacher, he turned to his pocket dictionary which read: "Warm . . . not so hot."

The next time you see your pastor, how about praying for him? In fact, how about doing it now? No one in your community sees as thin a slice of life as your local preacher. He needs your support as well as your presence in church.

It was He who "gave gifts to men;" He appointed some to be apostles, others to be prophets, others to be evangelists, others to be pastors and teachers (Eph. 4:11;TEV).

༺༻

Exod. 13-14; Ps. 31; Prov. 3; Mark 11

∽

One father is worth more than
a hundred schoolmasters.

George Herbert

∽

February 4 — Life's Most Embarrassing Moment

Grady Nutt, preacher and humorist, now deceased, told this story about a young family who invited the new pastor and his wife over for a get-acquainted Sunday dinner. The mother of the home was quite concerned that this be a perfect affair. She drilled the children days in advance about their proper behavior, what forks to use, when to use them, how to hold a napkin, and other important aspects.

Finally, the day arrived and the meal was prepared, and at exactly the right time everyone was invited to come into the dining room where the table was formally set with a white lace table cloth, the best china, good silverware, centerpiece, candles, and everything. They all sat down at the beautiful, formal table and the father said the blessing and when the blessing was over, their little nine-year-old daughter reached for her glass of iced tea and knocked it over!

The little brother jumped to get out of the way of the spilling tea and knocked his glass over, too! There was an awkward moment of silence as everybody sort of looked to the mother, realizing how disappointed she must be. She had gone to so much trouble and now there was this huge spreading stain in the middle of the white lace tablecloth.

But before anybody could say anything, the father flipped his glass of tea over, and began to laugh. The preacher caught on and flipped over his tea and started to laugh. The pastor's wife knocked over her glass of tea and joined the laughter. Then . . . everybody looked to the mother and finally with an expression of resignation she picked up her glass and just dumped it out in the middle of the table and everybody around the table roared with laughter.

And the father looked down at his nine-year-old daughter, right beside him, and he winked at her. And as she laughed embarrassedly, she looked up at her father and winked back, but as she did, it flicked a tear onto her cheek and it rolled down her face. She continued to look up, almost worshipfully, at a father who loved her enough to be sensitive to save her from one of life's most embarrassing moments.

One more time . . . love comes to the rescue! Love does not embarrass another. Such behavior should not be a part of our living together . . . whether directed to a spouse or children or extended family or any other friends! Love does not embarrass someone else! To embarrass another is to send a very mixed signal. How can you show love and at the same cause embarrassment?

Dear friends, since God so loved us, we also ought to love one another (1 John 4:11).

❦

Exod. 15-16; Ps. 32; Prov. 4; Mark 12

February is a unique month on our calendar. It's the only month that will vary in the number of days. Every fourth year it has an extra day, the twenty-ninth. But it's also unique in that it commemorates the birthdays of famous men: Abraham Lincoln, St. Valentine, and George Washington. Let's add to that another great man: Dwight Lyman Moody, whose birthday is on February 5.

Moody grew up in the tiny town of Northfield, Massachusetts, on the bank of the Connecticut River six miles south of the New Hampshire-Vermont border. With less than a high school education, the 17-year-old Dwight headed for Boston to make his way in a bigger world.

He succeeded as a shoe salesman but far more as a soul winner! Denied membership in one church because of his ignorance of the Bible, he rented a pew in another and filled it with street people. Moody proved tireless in his efforts to see people put their trust in Jesus Christ. His approach was simple and most direct.

"Are you a Christian?" he would ask.

Unless the prospect could respond promptly with a convincing answer, he would find Moody in quick pursuit. "Why not?"

Moody's reputation spread. One day on a street in Chicago a stranger handled Moody's stock question with a sharp retort: "That's none of your business!"

"Oh, yes, it is!" Moody snapped back.

The man eyed him warmly. "Then you must be D.L. Moody."

Perhaps the turning point of his life happened when he was a young man. A friend, whose name is unknown, said to Moody, "The world has yet to see what God can do with a man totally committed to Him."

Moody is reported to have thought a moment and then exclaimed, "By God's grace, I'll be that man!"

As a result of his life and vision, more than twenty-three thousand former Moody students minister full-time across the United States and in other countries around the world. Nearly six thousand alumni missionaries' names appear in the foyer of the Moody Bible Institute's auditorium. Twenty of these have been martyred for their faith in Jesus Christ!

They that be wise shall shine as the brightness of the firmament; and they that turn many to righteousness as the stars for ever and ever (Dan. 12:3;KJV).

❧

Exod. 17-18; Ps. 33; Prov. 5; Mark 13

February 6 — The Other Jonah

The Bible contains the story of Jonah being swallowed by a "great fish" . . . real, or just an ancient fish story? There is record of a man who lived to tell the story after being swallowed by a whale. Here it is:

In February 1891, a young English sailor named James Bartley was a crew member of the whaling ship, *Star of the East,* which ranged in the waters off the Falkland Islands in the South Atlantic, searching for these marine leviathans. One day about three miles offshore the whalers spotted a sperm whale that later proved to be 80 feet long and weighed some 80 tons! Two boats with crew members and harpooners — one of them was Bartley — were sent out to get the whale. As they closed in, one harpooner catapulted his eight-foot spear toward the whale. The instant it struck, the whale twisted and lashed out with its huge tail. The tail slammed into one rowboat, lifted it into the air, and capsized it. But the sailors soon subdued and killed the wounded mammal.

When the rowboat was righted, Bartley and another crewman were missing and written off as drowned. The crew pulled the carcass of the whale alongside the ship and worked until midnight removing the blubber. The next morning, using a derrick, the sailors hoisted the whale's stomach on deck.

According to M. de Parville, science editor of *The Journal des Debats,* who investigated the incident, there was movement inside the whale's belly. When it was opened, Bartley was found on the inside, unconscious. He was carried on deck and bathed in sea water. He was confined to the captain's quarters for two weeks, because he was acting like a lunatic.

Within four weeks, Bartley fully recovered and related what it had been like to live in the belly of the whale. For the rest of his life, Bartley's face, neck and hands remained white, bleached by the whale's gastric juices!"[10]

Quite a fish story, a whale of a story, in fact. What an experience for Bartley! If he had had this experience in our day, he would be on the speaking circuit making big money, drawing huge crowds, hitting all the large churches, and writing his own book! Other than that . . . is there a moral? An application? Simply that the Bible is more than a story book. This story has been confirmed by a human experience. But how much of God's Word must be taken at face value and by faith? Without faith, the Bible says, it's impossible to please God.

The Lord provided a great fish to swallow Jonah, and Jonah was inside the fish three days and three nights (Jon. 1:17).

❧

Exod. 19-20; Ps. 34; Prov. 6; Mark 14

February 7 — Why Are We Here?

Corrie Ten Boom writes: One day in the concentration camp, I was very encouraged because I was told I was free to go. I stood before the gate and I knew: as soon as this gate opens, I am free. In this concentration camp I had been able to bring the gospel to many women. A great number died with the name of Jesus on their lips. The Lord had used my sister Betsie and me to show them the way.

And here I was standing before the gate. My sister had died about two weeks earlier. While I stood there waiting, somebody came to me and said: "Corrie, I must tell you something. Today Mrs. de Boer and Mrs. de Goede both died."

Then I looked at this cruel concentration camp for the last time, and I said: "Thank You, Lord, that You brought me here, even if only for these two women who were saved for eternity. You used Betsie and me to that end. Lord, if it were only for these two women, it was worth all our suffering, even Betsie's death."

It is worth living and dying if we are being used to save others for eternity. You and I can be used, whoever we are.[11]

So once again, we are faced with the question: Why are we here? If you are a Christian, the plan for your life is quite simple and clear. We have been commissioned to share — the challenge reads like this: "You are the salt of the earth. . . . You are the light of the world. . . . Go and make disciples" (Matt. 5:13-14, 28:19).

How does one become a Christian? The Bible challenges you to believe in your heart and confess with your mouth. The promise was expressed by Jesus Christ in John 3:16 when He said that God so loved this world that He sent His only Son as a sacrifice to take away the sins of the world, including yours.

God has planned that this world would have an ongoing witness. People who reflect the person and presence of the Lord Jesus Christ to others. He wants to live through each of us in such a way that others are also challenged to live for Him and change the world. Perhaps your commission will be to take this message of the gospel to your sister if she is not a believer, to live it for your sister, to pray for your sister, to sacrifice for your sister, to love your sister into the kingdom of heaven.

Why are we here? To become part of the family of God and to share the good news that it is possible for others to also become part of God's family. This is the family relationship that lasts for eternity!

Again Jesus said, "Peace be with you! As the Father has
sent me, I am sending you" *(John 20:21).*

☙

Exod. 21-22; Ps. 35:1-16; Prov. 7; Mark 15

February 8 — The Comforting Angel

Blanche and Anne ministered as a team of two single ladies in many of the churches of the upper midwest. Blanche was the singer and preacher . . . Anne was the piano player, accompanist, and gal "Friday." They went wherever they were invited — to storefront churches, struggling churches, and large churches, and enjoyed an excellent reputation and were a positive benefit to people wherever they ministered. They traveled back in the days of the extended, protracted meetings . . . two weeks and longer. They were humble, had simple tastes, and were so grateful for all that was done for them in return.

Life was wonderful, ministry was exciting, they were useful and fulfilled in their ministry. BUT that all came to an abrupt halt! Anne was struck down with a stroke! Over a period of time, with rehabilitation she was able to get about with a cane. But the use of her left hand and arm was out of the question . . . no longer could she play the piano, care for herself, or be a contributing factor in ministry.

This left Blanche in a deep quandry. She was frustrated. What to do with life and ministry? How would she support herself? How would Anne support herself? Questions that didn't have answers.

One night Blanche was lying in bed — reading, pondering, praying, and questioning what God was doing with her and her co-worker's life. She was looking up toward the corner of her bedroom when a small, bright, brilliant, white dot of light appeared. She was drawn to it . . . fascinated. Soon she was able to make out a figure . . . clothed in pure white garments which seemed to shimmer in the light. The figure came closer and closer until it stopped at the foot of the bed. Heavenly! She was awestruck! It simply looked at her with great kindness and exuding love for a period of time, she didn't know how long, and then it was gone!

Later as she reflected on this appearance . . . she was remembering how she seemed to have been flooded with a great sense of well-being. No questions were left to be asked because they were all answered in this personal appearance! Blanche says she has never questioned the happenings nor change of direction for her life as well as Anne's.

The songwriter has penned a simple line, "One glimpse of His dear face, all sorrows will erase. . . ."

Our mouths were filled with laughter, our tongues with songs of joy. Then it was said among the nations, "The Lord has done great things for them." The Lord has done great things for us, and we are filled with joy. Restore our fortunes, O Lord (Ps. 126:2-3).

❧

Exod. 23-24; Ps. 35:17-28; Prov. 8; Mark 16

February 9 — The Cipher in the Snow

It started with tragedy on a cold February morning. I was driving behind the Milford Corners bus, it veered and stopped at the hotel, which was not a regular stop. A boy lurched out of the bus, reeled, stumbled, and collapsed on the snow bank at the curb. His thin, hollow face was white even against the snow. "He's dead," the driver whispered.

It didn't register. I glanced at the scared young faces in the school bus. "A doctor! Quick! I'll phone from the hotel!"

"No use. I tell you, he's dead." The driver looked at the still form. "He never said he felt bad, just tapped me on the shoulder and said, real quiet, 'I'm sorry. I have to get off at the hotel.' That's all."

At school the news went through the halls. "I'd appreciate you going out to tell the parents," the principal told me. "They haven't a phone. I'll cover your classes."

"Why me?" I asked, "Wouldn't it be better if you did?"

"I didn't know the boy, and in last year's sophomore personalities column I noticed you were listed as his favorite teacher."

I drove down the bad road to the Evans' place. His favorite teacher! He hadn't said two words to me in two years!

The ranch kitchen was clean and warm. I blurted out my news somehow. Mrs. Evans reached for a chair, "He never said anything about bein' ailing."

His stepfather snorted, "He ain't said nothin' about anything since I moved in here."

I was to write the obituary for the school paper. "Cliff Evans, never legally adopted by stepfather, five half-brothers and sisters." Meager information and the list of D grades were all. Cliff Evans had silently come in the school door and left in the evenings and that was all. No clubs, teams, nor offices, he had been a nobody, nothing, zero.

How do you make a boy into a zero? The school records showed some of the answer. "Cliff won't talk. Uncooperative. Slow learner," from the third grade teacher. But his third grade IQ was listed at 106 . . . the score didn't drop under 100 until the seventh grade. Even timid children have resilience. It takes time to break them.

How many times had he been chosen last? How many had told him, "You're a nothing, Cliff Evans." Then it hit me . . . when there finally was nothing left at all for Cliff Evans, he collapsed on a snow bank and went away.

The King will reply, "I tell you the truth, whatever you did for one of the least of these brothers of mine, you did for me" (Matt. 25:40).

❧

Exod. 25-26; Ps. 36; Prov. 9; Luke 1

February 10 — Standing on the Promises

In the earlier days of our country, a weary traveler came upon the banks of the Mississippi River near the Minnesota and Wisconsin border. It was early winter, and the surface of this mighty river was covered with ice. With no bridge in sight, the woman, who was a stranger to this part of the country, faced a dilemma. Would she dare make a crossing? What about the thickness of the ice? Would this ice hold her weight? She couldn't turn back.

Night was almost upon her, and it was important that she reach her destination on the other side of the river. She really didn't know what to do. Finally, she convinced herself that there was a way she might be able to cross safely. If she got down on her hands and knees, she would distribute her weight over a larger surface.

With much fear and more hesitation, she began her long, cautious crawl across the broad Mississippi. All the while she was hoping and praying that she would make it to the other side without any kind of mishap.

About halfway across, she heard the sound of loud singing and the thunder of a team of horses. Out of the dusk appeared a man with an eight-horse-hitch pulling a huge load of coal. When the wagoneer came to the edge of the river, he didn't even slow down and drove his team right onto the ice and across, singing at the top of his lungs!

Suddenly feeling foolish on her hands and knees, the woman stood to her feet and walked with no fear the rest of the way across the frozen river. As she listened, the driver and his horses disappeared into the distance!

Too many of us are creeping through life with extreme caution on the promises of God! We are afraid and fearful that what God has promised might not be sufficient for our need. We step out in faith, lightly. The promises of God are not fragile and about to cave in with you standing on top of them.

We are to stand on the promises, just like the songwriter has challenged us to do. We are to appropriate them, use them, and stand firmly on them! They are foundational! They will not break with your need. It's God we're dealing with, and God is God! Believe what the Word of God says! He has promised that you can be an overcomer!

And this is what he promised us . . . even eternal life (1 John 2:25).

꙰

Exod. 27-28; Ps. 37:1-22; Prov. 10; Luke 2

February 11 — Premonitions

Over the past few decades, there has been a great deal of interest in the topic of prophecy.

One related topic is that of premonitions. The following is an account of interest by Abraham Lincoln during his last days, as told to Ward Lamon, related in the book *The Face of Lincoln.*

> About ten days ago I retired very late. I could not have been long in bed when I fell into a slumber and soon began to dream. There seemed to be a death-like stillness about me. Then I heard subdued sobs, as if a number of people were weeping.
>
> I wandered downstairs, but the mourners were invisible. I went from room to room, the same mournful sounds met me as I passed. I arrived at the East Room, which I entered. There I met a sickening surprise.
>
> Before me was a catafalque, on which rested a corpse wrapped in funeral vestments. Around it were stationed soldiers who were acting as guards and there was a throng of people, some gazing mournfully upon the corpse, whose face was covered, others weeping pitifully.
>
> "Who is dead in the White House?" I demanded of one of the soldiers.
>
> "The president," was his answer. "He was killed by an assassin!"
>
> Then came a loud burst of grief from the crowd, which awoke me from my dream. I slept no more that night, and although it was only a dream I have been strangely annoyed by it ever since.

Was Lincoln's dream a premonition or a prophecy? All of us want to have the privilege of looking into the future.

What would you do if you were to receive such a dream? Ignore it? Laugh at it? Act upon it? Or simply forget about it?

God does not always give us human beings an opportunity to look ahead. We are admonished to live a day at a time, making sure that we are ready to face death and the time of judgment that is to follow. What of your death? If you want to make heaven your eternal home, you must make an advance reservation.

> *Just as man is destined to die once, and after that to face judgment, so Christ was sacrificed once to take away the sins of many people . . .* (Heb. 9:27-28).

❧

Exod. 29; Ps. 37:23-40; Prov. 11; Luke 3

February 12, President Lincoln's Birthday — Abraham Lincoln's Creed

Abraham Lincoln, born in a log cabin in Kentucky on February 12, 1809, obtained his elementary education by the light of the fireplace. Later, he worked at the hardest type of labor as a farm hand and rail splitter. In 1834 he was elected to the Illinois Legislature. He became an able lawyer, and in 1846 was elected to Congress.

Although efforts to become a United States senator ended in defeat, he was elected president in 1860 and re-elected in 1864. On April 14, 1865, Lincoln was shot by an assassin and died the next day.

Many people consider Abraham Lincoln the greatest man of the nineteenth century. He rose from lowly beginnings to the highest office and led our republic through a crisis that might have destroyed it.

Here are a few quotes attributed to the man:

I remember a good story when I hear it, but I never invented anything original; I am only a retail dealer.

Let the people know the truth and the country is safe.

I don't think much of a man who is not wiser today than he was yesterday.

What constitutes the bulwark of our own liberty and independence? It is not our frowning battlements, our bristling seacoasts. Our reliance is in the love of liberty which God has planted in us. Our defense is in the spirit which prizes liberty, in all lands everywhere.

Let us have faith that right makes might; and in that faith let us to the end dare to do our duty as we understand it.

One thing is very significant thing about Lincoln: Our interest in him is not limited to his lifetime only. To this day there is still an intense curiosity about how he lived his life, how he handled his disappointments, and how he overcame difficulties.

We look for the secret of Lincoln's life and the impact it has had on forming our nation's history. For that answer we turn to his creed and discover it to have included these statements: "I believe in God, the Almighty Ruler of nations, our great and good and merciful Maker, our Father in heaven, who notes the fall of a sparrow and numbers the hairs of our heads. I believe in His eternal truth and justice."

Abraham Lincoln lived it as he wrote it.[12]

For the Lord knoweth the way of the righteous: but the way of the ungodly shall perish (Ps. 1:6;KJV).

◦◦◦

Exod. 30-31; Ps. 38; Prov. 12; Luke 4

February 13 — A Sympathetic Ear

A soldier in the Union army during the Civil War was a youngest son who had already lost his older brother and father in the terrible fighting. As the only male left in his family, he desired to go Washington, D.C., to see President Lincoln and ask for an exemption from military service. His mother and sister needed him to help with work on the farm.

After receiving a leave from the military in order to plead his cause, he made his way to the White House. The young man approached the doors and asked to see the president.

He was told by the guard on duty, "You can't see the president. Don't you know there's a war on? The president's a very busy man. Now go away, Son! Get back out there and fight the Rebels!"

So the young man left, discouraged and downhearted. He stopped to sit on a park bench and a little boy came up to him. The young lad said, "Soldier, you look unhappy. What's wrong?"

The soldier looked at this young boy and began to spill his heart about his situation and how his father and older brother had died in the war. He explained that as the only male left in the family, he was desperately needed back at the farm for spring planting. The child listened to his entire story.

Then the little boy took the soldier by the hand and led him around to the back of the White House. They went through the kitchen door, past the guards on duty, past all the generals and high ranking government officials who were in the White House. All of these officials stood at attention as this little boy took the private by the hand through the rooms of the White House. The young soldier didn't understand all that was happening.

Finally, they arrived at the presidential office itself, and the little boy didn't even bother to knock; he just opened the door and walked in. There was President Lincoln with his secretary of state, looking over a map of battle plans on his desk.

The president looked up and said, "What can I do for you, Todd?"

And Todd said, "Daddy, this soldier needs to talk to you." The soldier pleaded his cause and received his exemption.

We, too, have access to the Father through the Son. Jesus intervenes on our behalf with, "Daddy, here is someone who needs to talk to You!"

This then, is how you should pray: "Our Father in heaven, hallowed be your name" (Matt. 6:9).

❧

Exod. 32-33; Ps. 39; Prov. 13; Luke 5

February 14, St. Valentines Day —
The First Valentine

The story of Valentine's Day begins in the third century with an oppressive Roman emperor and a humble Christian martyr. The emperor was Claudius II, the Christian was Valentinus. Claudius had ordered all Romans to worship 12 gods and he had also made it a crime punishable by death to associate with Christians or worship their God. Valentinus was dedicated to the ideals of Christ and not even the threat of death could keep him from practicing his beliefs. He was arrested.

During the last weeks of Valentinus' life a quite remarkable thing happened. The jailer asked if it would be possible for him to bring his daughter, Julia, for lessons, for teaching. Julia had been blind since birth and was a beautiful girl with a quick mind. Valentinus read to her stories of Rome's history . . . he described the world of nature to her . . . he taught her mathematics . . . and told her about God. She, for the first time, began to see the world through his eyes, trusted in his wisdom, and found a special comfort in his quiet strength.

"Valentinus, does God hear our prayers?" Julia asked one day.

"Yes, my child, He hears each one," he replied.

"Do you know what I pray for every morning and every night? I pray that I might be able to see. I want so much to see everything you've told me about!"

"God does what is best for us if we will only believe in Him," Valentinus said.

"Oh, Valentine, I do believe," Julia said intensely. "I do!" She then knelt and grasped his hand.

They sat quietly, she kneeling, he sitting, each praying. Suddenly there was a brilliant light in the prison cell! Radiant, Julia screamed, "Valentinus, I can see! I can see!"

On the eve of his death, Valentinus wrote a last note to Julia, urging her to continue her learning and encouraging her to stay close to God. He signed it, "From Your Valentine!"

His death sentence was carried out the next day, February 14, 270. He was buried at what is now the Church of Praxedes in Rome. Legend tells us that Julia herself planted a pink-blossomed almond tree near his grave. Today, the almond tree remains the symbol of abiding love and friendship. On the anniversary of his death, February 14, St. Valentine's Day, messages of affection, love, and devotion are exchanged.

And now these three remain: faith, hope, and love. But the greatest of these is love (1 Cor. 13:13).

Exod. 34-35; Ps. 40; Prov. 14; Luke 6

The day was brilliantly sunny. A snowstorm had passed . . . the phone rang. The news was not good. My father was in the hospital. He'd had a stroke. It was like a replay of that awful day six years earlier when I'd received the news about Mommy.

Daddy slipped into a coma and never regained consciousness. With a little smile on his face as though he were going to meet his dear Tass, Daddy died on February 15, 1983, a month short of his 58th birthday.

This time the undertaker did not suggest that we hire pallbearers but simply assumed that Donald's daughters would carry him to his grave as we had carried our mother.

Could we manage it? We were older. Daddy was heavier. We resolved our doubts the same way we had before, by telling one another, "Women can do anything they put their minds to."

Gathered in the house that Daddy'd built and we'd grown up in, we talked about what we wanted to say at his service. Here we were: Betty, a nurse; Donna, a court reporter; Linda, a dentist; Rita, the head of the science department in a private school; Jeanette and I, both doctors. Independent women, women capable of taking care of themselves.

"How did he do it?" I mused aloud. "How did Daddy turn out six women like us?"

"Daddy was the bow and we were the arrows," someone said. "And he aimed high."

It called to mind the gospel according to Daddy, starting with: "If you're a musician, they can break your fingers. If you're an athlete, they can break your kneecaps. But . . . " Here he always paused dramatically. "***But,*** if you are educated, once you've got something in your head, it's yours as long as you live."

And there was: "If the door doesn't open, climb through a window. If the window is closed, try to get in through the cellar. If that's locked, go up on the roof and see if you can get in through the chimney. There is always a way if you keep trying."

We spoke most of his single-minded devotion to family. "If loving my family is wrong," he often said, "then I don't want to be right."

He was right, with a wisdom all his own.

At the cemetery we lifted the flag-draped coffin. As determined then as during his life not to let our father down, the ditchdigger's daughters delivered him, without a stumble, to his grave beside Tass, his beloved wife.[13]

I can do everything through him who gives me strength (Phil. 4:13).

❧

Exod. 36-38; Ps. 41; Prov. 15; Luke 7

February 16, President's Day — The Fantastic Catch

One spring some time before the Civil War, a young man in search of work came to Worthy Taylor's prosperous Ohio farm. The farmer knew nothing much about the young man except that his name was Jim. Still he gave him a job for the summer.

Jim spent the summer cutting wood for the stove and fireplace, milking the cows, putting up hay, helping with the harvest, and anything else Mr. Taylor asked him to do. He ate in the kitchen and slept in the haymow.

Before the summer was over, Jim had fallen in love with Taylor's daughter. The farmer refused to let him marry her, telling Jim bluntly that he had no money, no name, no job, no vocation, and the prospects for his future and the future of his daughter, if married to him, were poor indeed. So the farmer said "NO" emphatically.

Jim got the message. Sadly he packed his few belongings into his old carpetbag and went on his way, never to be heard from again by the farmer or his daughter.

Thirty-five years passed, and the farmer Taylor decided to tear down his old barn to make way for a new and larger barn. When they got to removing the rafters above the old haymow, he discovered that Jim had carved his full name in one of the beams. That name was James A. Garfield. He was now the president of the United States of America!

Farmer Worthy Taylor missed the finest catch for his daughter that she could have had. The problem was compounded by the fact that Taylor's daughter had indeed married a man with his permission and blessing. Now 30 years of heartbreak had proven the husband to be a no-good bum!

Have you ever been offered a "fantastic catch" only to have turned down the opportunity? What compounds the situation is to have lived long enough to regret that mistake in judgment or choice.

Jesus Christ offers the most fantastic catch anyone can ever make — the opportunity to accept Him as Lord and personal Saviour! That decision can develop into the most exciting and growing relationship any human being could ever have.

How about you? Have you taken this step of faith? How about family members, friends, relatives, or neighbors? Farmer Taylor lived to regret his hasty decision. Don't you leave this life with regrets.

How shall we escape if we ignore such a great salvation? This salvation, which was first announced by the Lord, was confirmed to us by those who heard him (Heb. 2:3).

᷍

Exod. 39-40; Ps. 42; Prov. 16; Luke 8

February 17 — Deferred Decisions

Former President Ronald Reagan learned the need of making a decision early in his teens. A kind aunt had taken him to a shoemaker to have a pair of shoes custom-made just for him. The shoemaker asked, "Do you want a round toe or a square toe?"

Young Ronald couldn't make up his mind. So the cobbler said, "Come back in a day or two and tell me what you want."

A few days later the shoemaker saw Ronald on the street and asked what he had decided about the shoes. "I haven't made up my mind yet," the youth answered.

"Very well," said the shoemaker, "your shoes will be ready for you to pick up tomorrow."

When Reagan picked up the shoes . . . one had a round toe and the other a square toe. Says Reagan, "Looking at those shoes taught me a lesson. If you don't make your own decisions, somebody else makes them for you."

Decisions . . . decisions! Life is made up of decisions both large and small and everything in between. And while you are a teen, some of life's greatest choices must be made. Will I just finish school and get a job or do I go on to college or vocational school or trade school? Who will I live my life with? What kind of a life will I live? Will I embrace the drug culture? Will I become part of the armed services? Choices . . . decisions . . . and they just keep coming for the rest of your life.

In Guyana, 60 miles up the Essequibo River there is a village, Bartica, which serves as the supply center for the miners and prospectors working in the mountains further up the river. In the center of this village of a few thousand people there is a huge white monument placed on a concrete slab. It's impressive. Walk around the base and there is no inscription. Ask any of the citizens, and nobody knows why the monument was erected. Old-timers can't remember. Strange — a monument to nothing! A memorial that has no memory or meaning.

Could anything be more useless? Will your life become a momument to nothing? Right decisions will play a very important part in how useful your life will be . . . how meaningful your life can become. I want my life to count for something . . . how about you?!

> *But if serving the Lord seems undesirable to you, then*
> *choose for yourselves this day whom you will serve, whether*
> *the gods of your forefathers served beyond the River, or the gods*
> *of the Amorites, in whose land you are living. But as for me*
> *and my household, we will serve the Lord* (Josh. 24:15).

Lev. 1-3; Ps. 43; Prov . 17; Luke 9

February 18 — Pillars

Famed English architect Sir Christopher Wren designed a large dome for a church that was so unique he became the object of much criticism among his colleagues. During the construction of this dome they created so much fuss that the authorities demanded Wren add two huge supporting pillars to keep the dome from collapsing. Wren bitterly objected, insisting on the strength of his structure and the wisdom of his new architectural innovation. Besides, it would ruin the beauty and asthetics of the church. But the opposition was well-organized and powerful. The two pillars were added to the design over Wren's objections.

Fifty years passed since the construction of the controversial dome. It was now time to repaint the interior of the church, as well as the dome.

When the painters had erected their scaffolding to begin the painting they made the startling discovery that the two added pillars did not even touch the dome! They were short by two feet!

Sir Christopher Wren had such confidence in his work that he made sure the offending pillars were freestanding. The authorities, during his lifetime, came to make their inspection from the floor, saw the pillars, and assumed they reached the roof. They now felt secure, even though the pillars were freestanding and didn't support anything! Wren went to his grave with his little secret well-kept. I believe he may have had the last laugh at their expense. What a great little story!

Man has built many pillars to support his little world and to keep things from falling in on him. Often they seem strong and are able to stand the stress of time. But often they are just as useless as architect Wren's false columns.

Some have constructed pillars of religion, beautiful in structure and they seem strong enough. But religion is totally meaningless without the person of Jesus. Pillars of religion are freestanding without Christ and have no hold on eternity.

Others have erected pillars of intellectualism, money, pleasure, or philosophy. Lest we despair, there is a structure that is ample for the ultimate crisis of life. As Wren had confidence in his architectural creation, so can you have confidence in the structure God builds!

I am sending Christ to be the carefully chosen,
precious Cornerstone of my church, and I will never
disappoint those who trust in him (1 Pet. 2:6;LB).

⌖

Lev. 4-5; Ps. 44:1-8; Prov. 18; Luke 10

The small moment is the carrier
of God's most enduring gift.
It must not be permitted to
slip away unsavored
and unappreciated.

Gerhard E. Frost

February 19 — Ten Commandments for a Successful Marriage

Everybody from "Dear Abby" on down through just about any publication you want to read will have some kind of a version of "Ten Commandments for Women" or "Ten Commandments for Men." Well ... since we are on an equal footing, being partners in living, how about this version, the same set of commandments for both genders:

I. Put your mate before your mother, your father, your son and daughter, for your mate is your lifelong companion.

II. Do not abuse your body with excessive food, tobacco, drugs, or drink, so that your life may be long and healthy, in the presence of those you love.

III. Do not permit your business or your hobby or your recreation to make you a stranger to your children, for the most precious gift a parent can give his or her family is the gift of time.

IV. Do not forget that cleanliness is a virtue.

V. Do not make your mate into a beggar, but willingly share with him or her your worldly goods and possessions.

VI. Remember to say, "I love you." For even though your love may be a constant, your mate yearns to hear those words from you more than any others. Say it often.

VII. Remember always that the approval of your mate is worth more than the admiring glances of a hundred strangers, so remain faithful and loyal to your mate, and forsake all the others.

VIII. Keep your home in good repair, keep your marriage alive, for out of it come the joys of old age, together.

IX. Forgive with grace. For who among us does not need to be forgiven and often?

X. Honor the Lord your God all the days of your life, and your children and grandchildren will grow up and also bless you.[14]

Well ... there you have them. Not only interesting reading, but a plan of action! Words do us no good until they have been translated into an understandable language.

Maybe we should add #11 as well: You shall not hit your mate over the head with these commandments, but the keeping of these will be a willing act of love.

Submit yourselves unto such, and to every one that helpeth with us, and laboureth (1 Cor. 16:16).

༄

Lev. 6-7; Ps. 44:9-26; Prov. 19; Luke 11

February 20 — One Chance in a Million

Maybe you remember February 20, 1962? If not, I will refresh your memory by telling you that an American astronaut climbed into a space capsule and was hurtled more than a hundred miles into the sky. This capsule went into space orbit and circled the earth three times in the following four hours. Then, with its lone, brave passenger still cocooned in safety, splashed down in the Atlantic Ocean at precisely the spot which had been pre-selected by the crew of people who had sent it aloft.

Millions of people worldwide marveled at such an accomplishment of our scientific thinkers. How is it possible to plan such wonders? Today, it's old hat — we've had men walk on the moon and sent up our re-usable space shuttle many times. How is it possible to predict and plan the exact orbit of our space vehicles?

Much of the credit for such accomplishments has to go to a man whom you nor most Americans have never heard about. This man was born with three strikes against him. John Kepler was born prematurely in the year 1571. He was so tiny and premature at birth that the attending physician gave him only one chance in a million to survive! Somehow he survived!

At the age of four he was stricken with smallpox which left him crippled in both hands and with very weak eyes. Some time later, both of his parents were declared insane and placed in an institution.

He determined to amount to something in spite of the unhappy lot life had dealt him. He would become an astronomer. This is the man who discovered the "three laws of motion" of the planets. He discovered the concept of the convex lenses which make possible the giant telescopes of our day which scan the heavens. That's not all — this man also discovered the foundations upon which the science of calculus is based!

Without John Kepler and his discoveries — laws of planets in motion, the convex lense, and calculus — America's space program would have always remained on the ground! There never would have been a space program. And Kepler, in humility, always acknowledged that God was the source of his life and knowledge and discoveries!

Endure hardship with us like a good soldier of Christ Jesus (2 Tim. 2:3).

✎

Lev. 8-9; Ps. 45; Prov. 20; Luke 12

February 21 — My Best Friend

The late Dr. W. L. Stidger, while pastoring a church following World War II, asked a young man from his congregation, a returning naval officer this question: "What was your most exciting adventure during the war?" And here is the reply:

We were cruising through a submarine zone in the North Atlantic and knew that a wolf pack of enemy subs was near. Naturally we were all alert to the danger. It was early morning and not my watch, but I was up much before dawn on that fateful morning. I felt that I just wanted to be on the bridge, because I was also afraid. We were a troopship carrying 10,000 soldiers on their way to Europe. I had a great sense of responsibility for those American G.I.'s and their safety.

About half an hour after I went up on the bridge with the captain, the sun just barely began to come up out of the east horizon. We watched in fascination. It was beautiful. As we were looking at it through our glasses, we both spotted it at the same time! We watched the white wake of a torpedo headed straight for our ship! It was a terrorizing thing! We couldn't dodge it . . . we had no time to maneuver our cumbersome ship out of its path. The captain turned to me, thinking of those 10,000 boys asleep down in the holds and said, "This is it."

My heart stood still. Of course, the captain called all hands to their battle stations, but it seemed like such a futile gesture.

Then . . . suddenly, something happened which none of us had even considered. There was a destroyer riding to our port, battling the waves. The skipper of that smaller ship had seen the same thing that we had seen from our bridge . . . the enemy torpedo out of that Nazi wolf pack of subs headed straight for the middle of our ship.

That young skipper instructed his engine room: "All engines ahead flank!" This headed his destroyer straight into the path of that torpedo. It struck full impact and sank in less than 10 minutes with most of her crew going down with her, including that young skipper. He knew when he gave that order that he and his crew would be lost . . . but he didn't hesitate a single second. He willingly gave himself for more than 10,000 others.

That young skipper? He was my best friend!

Greater love has no one than this,
that he lay down his life for his friends (John 15:13).

∽

Lev. 10-11; Ps. 46; Prov. 21; Luke 13

February 22 — George Washington's Birthday

George Washington, our first president, set a standard of quality for all Americans since his birth. Our beautiful country has seen many great men, heroes, excellent citizens, and people to be admired. But as we look back from our vantage point in history there has been no other, with the possible exception of Abraham Lincoln, who has been a living example of what we think great Americans should be.

He gave us a quality of leadership and living that was seen in the cherry tree incident of his childhood. He confessed his wrongdoing and went on to a special kind of maturity.

As I look back at history I see a man who was eager for life in a new nation, a nation that was forming and was still seeking an identity. The imprint of this man's life is still with us. Our nation's capital was named for him.

Here is a man who loved life as it was given to him. At the tender age of 20 he became the heir to Mt. Vernon and spent the next 20 years of his life in pursuit of the good life, in the social whirl, enjoying the power of his wealth.

We are told that on his fortieth birthday he went to a part of the vast lawn of Mt. Vernon overlooking the Potomac River and meditated, dreamed, and prayed about his future. It was at this moment that he gave himself to God and pledged his life to this new country. He started his public service in a humble position, that of adjutant in one of the five military districts of Virginia.

He left the comforts of home when he was called upon to serve his country. We next see him in the bitter winter of Valley Forge sharing the hardships with his men, providing them the standard. One of the most touching scenes is watching him kneel in the snow in the quiet of the woods, and there call upon God to aid his suffering, oppressed people.

Victory became his and then he was summoned once more to serve, as our first president. We see him walk away after giving two terms which could have become another Imperial kingdom, all without pay or any kind of remuneration. Thank you, George Washington, for setting a high standard for us!

He has showed you, O man, what is good. And what does the Lord require of you? To act justly, and to love mercy and to walk humbly with your God (Mic. 6:8). Washington's favorite verse of Scripture, which he quoted in a letter written on June 8, 1783, containing his prayer for the 13 states.

᠙

Lev. 12-13; Ps. 47; Prov. 22; Luke 14

February 23 — The Sermon in Shoe Leather

One afternoon in 1953, reporters, officials, dignitaries, and the welcoming committee gathered at the Chicago railway station awaiting the arrival of the 1952 "Nobel Peace Prize" winner. There was naturally anticipation and excitement, even in Chicago. The train came to a halt and he stepped off the train — a giant of a man, just over six-feet-four-inches, erect in posture, with a thatch of bushy hair, a large moustache, and dressed simply in a cotton khaki suit and tie. The only thing missing was his trademark pith helmet.

Cameras flashed, city officials approached with outstretched hands. They presented him with a key to the city and began telling him how honored they were to meet him. It was a formal kind of occasion.

He expressed a polite thanks, then paused, as he was looking at something catching his attention over their heads. He looked at them and asked if he could be excused for a few moments. He then made his way through the waiting crowd with quick, firm strides until he reached the side of an elderly black lady who was struggling as she attempted to carry two rather large and heavy suitcases. No one had offered to help and everyone was focused on the man who had just departed the train.

He nodded to the lady, picked up those two suitcases in his big hands, carried them to the open luggage compartment where the bus driver placed them on the rack, and with a smile escorted the lady to the waiting bus on which she apparently was making her way home following her train ride. Then he helped her aboard the bus, helped her find a seat, and wished her a safe journey and that someone would be at the other end to help her with her load.

Meanwhile, the crowd had tagged along behind him, observing this scene, and maybe all feeling a bit guilty for not having offered to help. He turned to them and said, "Sorry to have kept you waiting."

And the welcoming continued, but almost in hushed tones of greeting. Almost as though something spiritual had taken place — it was sensed and not easily written about. The lesson was obvious.

The Nobel Peace Prize winner was the world-famous, missionary-doctor, Albert Schweitzer. A man who had spent his life helping the poorest of the poor in Africa. One of the members of the official reception committee turned to one of the *Chicago Times* reporters and said: "That's the first time I ever saw a sermon walking."

And if anyone gives a cup of cold water to one of these little ones because he is my disciple, I tell you the truth, he will certainly not lose his reward (Matt. 10:42).

❦

Lev. 14; Ps. 48; Prov. 23; Luke 15

February 24 — Nothing Could Beat Me

This happened in the 10,000 meter race at the Olympics in Munich, Germany. Entered in this race was a young man from Finland by the name of Lasse Viren. Nobody expected him to even place in this race. He wasn't listed among the top 15 runners in the world. He was literally a nobody when it came to this distance. But he had trained for the Olympics and committed himself to this grueling event.

Over 85,000 people were present in the stadium. The gun went off signaling the start, and 75 men took off to run 25 laps — about 6 1/2 miles. Lasse Viren took off with the pack for this greatest race of a lifetime. It was his big chance! About 2 1/2 laps into the race, with elbows and legs flying, the man who was expected to win was hit and thrown off the track. When he was hit he was knocked unconscious. In his fall he also knocked Viren to the track, head over heels. How would you like that? Ten years in training and then an accident like that in the biggest race of your life.

Viren, however, jumped back up to his feet and with confidence began running to catch up with the pack. The crowd sensed the drama unfolding before them and was soon on its feet shouting encouragement. They could not believe what they were seeing. Viren kept on running. He caught the last man, and kept running until he caught up with and passed the leaders in the pack to cross the finish line first to set a new Olympic record in the 10,000 meter race!

Later, Lasse Viren was interviewed by the press and he told them he found out that if he could be knocked down and win, nothing could beat him!

I believe the reason he won was because of the shock of being knocked down. It's like a shock treatment! Under the stress of the race and the double tragedy of the fall, he used reserve energy that would have been released in no other way. What does falling or failure do to you or in you? Do you go down to stay or do you bounce back for another try?

I love the courage of attitude as shown to us by a little old lady. She was frail, too. And she had lost the sight of one of her eyes which had to be removed. When it was to be replaced with a false eye, she said to her doctor, "Young man, when you select that new eye for me, be sure and choose one with a twinkle in it!" I love it, don't you?

Be strong and take heart, all you who hope in the Lord (Ps. 31:24).

❦

Lev. 15-16; Ps. 49; Prov. 24; Luke 16-17

February 25 — If You Want to See the Angels

Have YOU ever seen an angel? Dr. S. W. Mitchell, a Philadelphia neurologist, thought he had. After one very tiring day he retired early, but was awakened by a persistent knocking at the door. It was a little girl, poorly dressed and deeply upset. She told him that her mother was very sick and needed his help. Even though it was a bitterly cold, snowy night, Mitchell dressed and followed the girl.

He found the mother desperately ill with pneumonia. After treating her, Dr. Mitchell complimented the sick woman on her daughter's persistence and courage. The woman said, "My daughter died a month ago. Her shoes and coat are in the closet there."

Dr. Mitchell went to the closet and opened the door. There hung the very coat worn by the little girl who had been at his front door. The coat was warm and dry and could not possibly have been out in the wintry night!

Have YOU ever seen an angel?

One night the king of Syria sent his army under cover of darkness with lots of chariots and horses and horsemen to surround the city and cut off all escape routes. When the prophet and his servant got up early the next morning and checked around outside, they discovered troops, horses, and chariots everywhere! The servant, obviously frightened, asked, "Now what are we going to do?"

Elisha the prophet answered in so many words, "Don't be afraid because our army is larger than theirs!" Then, Elisha prayed, "Lord, open his eyes and let him see." And when the Lord had opened the young man's eyes he saw horses of fire and chariots of fire everywhere on the mountains surrounding the army which had surrounded them!

Have YOU ever seen an angel? Maybe we just need our eyes to be opened!

And Elisha prayed, "O Lord, open his eyes so he may see." Then the Lord opened the servant's eyes, and he looked and saw the hills full of horses and chariots of fire all around Elisha (2 Kings 6:17).

⤳

Lev. 17-18; Ps. 50; Prov. 25; Luke 18

February 26 — Painful Memories

As an English medical doctor in Africa for 30 years, Helen Rosavere wondered about the problems facing the developing African nations all around her. Trouble began when insurgents from bordering countries started a rebel movement in Helen's area. Some rebels, high on drugs, attacked the village where Dr. Rosavere was staying. They took over the hospital, seized Helen, and held her as a hostage.

At the time, Helen was in her fifties and had never been married. She had given her life to the people of Africa. The rebels repeatedly raped Helen. In the midst of it all, at the blackest moment of the violent incident, Helen cried out, "Why, Lord? How can You let this happen?"

But the answer came quickly, "Thank you, Helen, for giving Me your body years ago. You see, Helen, they aren't raping you. They are raping ME!" At that moment she felt the peace of God, but she still had to deal with the awful memories.

A few months after her release, Helen came to the United States to address some medical students at a university. When she was introduced, Helen walked up to the podium and noticed two girls sitting in the front row on the left side. Both were too young to be medical students. One of the girls stared intently at Helen, making her feel somewhat uncomfortable.

As Helen began her speech, God impressed upon her to tell the audience what had happened to her in Africa. Helen resisted because it had nothing to do with her delivery, but again she was impressed to relate the story about when she was raped. She began to tell of the incident as if it was a part of her presentation. Then she went on to finish her address.

When the lecture was over, Helen went to the back of the podium and noticed again the two girls on the left side. One approached Helen and said, "Doctor, I'm sorry to bother you, but my 15-year-old sister over there was raped five weeks ago and hasn't said a word or made a sound since then. She has seen ministers and psychologists, and none have helped. Could you talk to her for a few minutes?"

Helen looked up and walked toward the girl. When she was about halfway, the girl stood up and ran toward Helen. When they reached each other, they embraced so hard that they crashed to the floor, crying.

After an hour of crying, the girl talked non-stop for two hours. She had found someone who could identify with her hurt.

Perfect love casteth out fear (1 John 4:18;KJV).

෴

Lev. 19-20; Ps. 51; Prov. 26-27; Luke 19

February 27 — It Took More Grace

A large, prosperous downtown London church had three mission churches it had started under its care. On the first Sunday of the new year all the members of the mission churches came to the downtown mother church for a combined communion service. From those mission churches, which were located in the slums of the city, had come some outstanding cases of conversions — burglars, thieves, drunks, and so on. All knelt side by side at the common communion rail to share in this special service.

On this particular occasion, the pastor saw a former burglar kneeling beside a judge of the Supreme Court of England — the same judge who had sent the burglar to jail for seven years. After his release, this thief had been converted and become an excellent Christian worker in the church. Yet, as they knelt there, the judge and the former convict, neither one seemed to be aware of the other.

After the service, the pastor was walking home with the judge who said to him, "Did you notice who was kneeling beside me at the communion rail this morning?"

The pastor replied, "Yes, but I didn't know that you noticed." The two walked along in silence for a few more moments.

Then the judge said, "What a miracle of grace."

The pastor nodded, "Yes, what marvelous grace."

Then the judge said, "But to whom do you refer?"

And the pastor said, "Why, to the conversion of that convict."

The judge said, "I don't refer to him. I was thinking of myself."

Now the pastor turned in surprise, "You were thinking of yourself? I guess I don't understand."

"Yes," the judge replied, "it did not cost that burglar much to get converted when he came out of jail. He had nothing but a history of crime behind him. When he saw Jesus as his Saviour, he knew there was salvation and hope for him. And he knew how much he needed that help. But look at me. I was taught from infancy to live as a gentleman; that my word was my bond; that I was to say my prayers, go to church, take communion, and so on. I went through Oxford, earned my degrees, was called to the bar, and eventually became a judge. Pastor, nothing but the grace of God could have caused me to admit that I was a sinner on a level with that burglar. It took more grace."

For it is by grace you have been saved, through faith — and this not from yourselves, it is the gift of God — not by works, so that no one can boast (Eph. 2:8-9).

❧

Lev. 21-22; Ps. 52; Prov. 28-29; Luke 20

February 28 — I'm Tired

Don't know about you . . . but as for me, I'm tired! For many years I've been blaming it on middle age, old age, or just plain aging, iron poor blood, lack of vitamins, air pollution, saccharin, obesity, dieting, underarm odor, dandruff, plaque on my teeth, lower back pain, greying hair, and a dozen or more other problems that really make you wonder if life is worth living after all.

But I've just found out, tain't that at all! I'm tired because I'm overworked, I've found out that there are just too few people working, so it's because of overwork!

Consider that the population of our country is about 250 million and about 114 million are retired. That leaves about 136 million to do the work.

There are 95 million in school which leaves 41 million to do the work. Of this total there are 22 million employed by the government. That leaves only about 19 million to do the work!

Of this total 4 million are in the armed forces of the U.S. This leaves us only about a remaining 15 million to do the work! Now subtract from that total the 14.8 million who work for the state, city, and county governments and that leaves only 200,000 to do the work!

We must not forget that our country has 188,000 people at any one time in hospitals so we now have only 12,000 people left to do any work!

On most days, there are about 11,998 people serving time in our prisons! Subtract that total and that leaves only TWO people to do the work! And it looks like it's YOU and ME!

And you're sitting down to read this! That leaves only ME . . . no wonder I'm tired!

And isn't it fun to play games with numbers and nonsense. The bottom line is that work is a very important part of life and living! We're of the generation which had a strong work ethic. We were told, and have found it to be true, that God helps those who help themselves. We've created a world of wealth by jobs and hard work and creativity and perseverance and the entreprenuerial spirit! But have we done a good job in passing along these principles to the next two or three generations who are following us?

Whatever you do, work at it with all your heart, as working for the Lord, not for men (Col. 3:23).

◌◌

Lev. 23-24; Ps. 53; Prov. 30-31; Luke 21

February 29 — A Fractured Parable for a Fractured Day

February 29 occurs every fourth year. Why? So that our calendars can be adjusted to keep the rest of the year working on time. It's a bonus day for all the bonus babies born on this day who only get an opportunity to celebrate a birthdate once every four years. So let's have a bonus story with a bit of humor in it.

A man began attending a church and he made application for membership. The committee was examining him and one of the questions asked was: "What part of the Bible do you like best?"

Back came the reply: "I like the New Testament best, sir."

To which the questioner asked, "What book?"

The man answered, "The book of the parables."

The questioner went on, "Would you be so kind as to relate one?"

So he started, "Once upon a time a man went down from Jerusalem to Jericho and fell among thieves and the thorns grew up and choked him. And he went on and met the Queen of Sheba and she gave that man, sir, 1,000 talents of gold and silver and 100 changes of rainment. And he got in his chariot and drove furiously. And when he was driving under a tree, his hair got caught in a limb and left him hanging there. And he hung there many days and many nights, and ravens brought him food to eat and water to drink. One night while he was hanging there asleep, his wife, Delilah, came and cut off his hair and he dropped and fell on strong ground and it began to rain. And it rained 40 days and 40 nights. And he hid himself in a cave. He went on and met a man that said, 'Come and take supper with me' but he said 'I can't come, for I have married a wife.' And that man went out into the highways and byways and compelled him to come. He went on and came to Jerusalem and saw Queen Jezebel sitting high up in a window and when she saw him she laughed and he said 'Throw her down' and they threw her down 70 times 7 and of the fragments they picked up 12 baskets full. Now whose wife will she be in the day of judgment?"

End of parable! It sounds like this man needs to get into a solid and systematic Bible study group. It's sad . . . but there are many people who have only a smattering of biblical knowledge . . . just enough to be dangerous. Your best defense against errors in biblical teaching is a thorough knowledge of God's Word. If you do not attend a good Bible teaching church, find one. God has answers for today and every day!

Do your best to present yourself to God as one approved, a workman who does not need to be ashamed and who correctly handles the word of truth (2 Tim. 2:15).

March 1 — It's in the Message

A number of years ago, a young man was seeking a job as a "Morse code" operator. He found an ad in the local newspaper and went to the office address that was listed. When he got there, he found it was a large, busy office with lots of hustle and bustle, including the constant chatter of a telegraph key in the background.

As he made his way into the office, a sign directed all the applicants for the position of telegraph operator to take a seat and wait until they were summoned into the inner office. About a dozen applicants were sitting, waiting ahead of him for their instructions. This was a bit discouraging, but the young man figured he had nothing to lose so he sat down along with the others to wait his summons.

After two to three minutes this young man stood back up, walked over to the door where the sign was hanging and walked right on through to the inner office. Naturally, all of the other applicants perked up and started looking at each other and muttering. It was only about another five minutes when the young man appeared at the door, this time with the employer also.

The employer looked at the dozen other applicants and said, "All of you gentlemen may go now. Thanks for your interest. The position has been filled by this young man."

At this, several of them grumbled again, and one of them spoke up and said, "Sir, I don't understand. He was the last one of us to come in, and we never even got a chance to be interviewed. Yet he got the job. I don't think that's really fair."

The employer said, "I'm sorry, but all the time you've been sitting here the telegraph key has been ticking out a message in Morse code. This is the message: 'If you understand this message in Morse code, come right in. This job is yours.' None of you heard it. He did. The job is his!"

It's easy to become so absorbed in achieving success or getting that coveted position that we fail to hear the still, small voice of God speaking to us. Are you so deafened by the roar of this world that the real message about Jesus Christ is being drowned out? Stop for a moment, and listen to your heart. God may be speaking to you if you will only be open to hear His voice.

We preach Christ crucified: a stumbling block to Jews
and foolishness to Gentiles, but to those whom God has
called, both Jews and Greeks, Christ the power of God
and the wisdom of God (1 Cor. 1:23-24).

꙳

Lev. 25; Ps. 54; Prov. 1; Luke 22

March 2 — Train Number 8017

Train Number 8017 wound its way through Salerno, Italy, without anyone giving a thought to the disaster its passengers faced in a few short hours on a rainy evening on March 2, 1944. The train did not collide with anything nor was it derailed, burned, or damaged in any way. Yet it brought death to more people than any other rail disaster in history. What happened?

The silent killer in this train was the low grade coal used to fire the locomotives. Shortly after 1:00 a.m. the heavy train with 600 passengers lumbered into the tunnel called "Galleria delle Armi." What went wrong nobody really knows.

When the two locomotives pulling the train reached mid-tunnel, the drive wheels apparently began to slip. Sand was then sprayed on the tracks, but that didn't help. The wheels lost traction, and the train stopped. All else is speculation as both engineers died at the controls. Carbon monoxide snuffed out more than 500 lives.

Ironically, when authorities began clearing out the bodies, they found the leading locomotive was unbraked with its controls set in reverse. The second engine was unbraked with its throttle full speed ahead! Apparently when the train stopped, the two engineers had different ideas about what to do — it proved fatal. They were pulling and pushing against each other. It was believed that if they had both been clear in their direction, either front or back, that all the passengers would have survived! But there they were, straining against each other and filling the tunnel with deadly poison.

Powerful forces are at work in our lives! We, too, have two engineers vying for direction. Lusts pull one way, our conscience the other. Intellectualism tugs at our minds; our spirits draw us toward God.

How often in our frustration have we felt that we really were opposing ourselves? Many times we come to a stop until we can sort out which direction to move. Real freedom to move in the right direction comes in your life when Christ is invited — not to take sides — but to take over.

In our world of increasing tension, it is reassuring to know that Christ can control the individual. He can help us bring these inner wars to a cease-fire. When we relinquish the controls of our living to Him, His terms of peace are always on our side.

In all these things we are more than conquerors through him that loved us (Rom. 8:37;KJV).

❦

Lev. 26; Ps. 55; Prov. 2; Luke 23

March 3 — To Feed the Birds

About 20 years ago, Los Angeles residents were shocked and saddened to learn that one of their own was starving himself just to be able to feed the birds in two different city parks. Newspaper reporters learned of the strange story and reported it nationally. Retired Raymond Lopez, 80, gaunt, sick, and feeble, explained, "I don't care about myself anymore. I'm only interested in helping all things that suffer and all things that are hungry."

Most of Lopez's social security check and small pension went to pay the delivery man who came every Tuesday with 2,000 pounds of feed for his fine-feathered friends. The bill came to about $150 per week. Many of his friends had encouraged Lopez to take a trip, to relax, or to enjoy other material things of this life. To such suggestions he merely replied, "I'd rather go hungry myself than let my birds go hungry."

A good many of us would question the wisdom of the bird lover's actions. Still, the elderly Californian has learned one of the more valuable lessons of life. I believe he discovered that it is more blessed to give than to receive.

This world seems to be divided into two camps of people — the givers and getters. We could also call them the eternalist and the materialist. Jesus dealt a lot with these two philosophies of life and firmly positioned himself on the side of the givers.

The taker, the getter, is one who believes he/she must take all, even from the weak and helpless. This person fares quite well until another comes along who is stronger and takes what the getter has been taking. Some have labeled this concept as "the survival of the fittest." It's part of Darwin's theory of life.

Take the giver — this eternalist believes in ultimate accountability before God and knows he is placed on earth not as a taker but as one who is called upon to help, to give, to love, and be a positive influence for good. Most of the world laughs at the giver. Still, this is the only person who really endures. This person has placed treasures where earth's fickle circumstances cannot touch them.

It is important that we find a cause to live with and for, that is larger than who we are. Let Mr. Lopez of bird-lover note be a challenge to all of us as we live. Are you a getter or a giver?

Seek ye first the kindom of God, and His righteousness; and all these things shall be added unto you (Matt. 6:33;KJV).

～୨

Lev. 27; Ps. 56; Prov. 3; Luke 24

March 4 — Heavyweight Angels

My mother told me this story about another ministry couple who were contemporaries of theirs, the now deceased Pastor and Mrs. Bennie C. Heinz. At the time of this happening, the Heinz family was pastoring a North Dakota church.

Pastor and Mrs. Heinz and another couple made their way to a springtime fellowship meeting quite a distance away in the town of Dickinson. If I recall correctly, he was one of the speakers. This was one of those all-day affairs . . . morning service, lunch, afternoon service, minister's business meeting, dinner, and finally the evening rally/service. When they left it was approximately 10:30 p.m. as they drove away from the church. Weather in North Dakota can be very unpredictable in the springtime. They turned north on Highway 85 towards Williston and it started to rain/sleet/snow all at the same time.

They started down into the last valley and the icy mixture continued to fall, but with more intensity. It started to accumulate on the highway making driving very treacherous. They had no snow tires or chains on the car. Mrs. Heinz began to pray, "Help us Lord, help our car, keep us safe."

As they began the climb from the valley floor, the car began to lose traction and soon they came to a complete stop. No matter what was tried the car would spin out of control, no traction. Nothing to do but prepare to spend the night huddled in the car. About that time a car drove up behind them with six husky young men in it. They stopped behind the stalled car and one of them asked if they could be of help. Pastor Heinz said, "A push would help us but we really need more traction on the rear end, perhaps more weight would help."

The pastor started the car and five of these young men began to push the car up the steep road . . . after it got rolling they all jumped up on the trunk . . . two were hanging over the sides, the other three were sitting with their feet on the rear bumper. They easily made it.

At the top of the hill, Pastor Heinz stopped the car to get out to thank these kind heavyweight strangers. When he stepped out of the car to go to the rear to speak with the men . . . they were all gone! Disappeared! Not a trace! Not a track! Not even of the car in which they had come!

But you have come to Mount Zion, to the heavenly Jerusalem, the city of the living God. You have come to thousands upon thousands of angels in joyful assembly, to the church of the first born, whose names are written in heaven. You have come to God (Heb. 12:22-23).

༄

Num. 1-2; Ps. 57; Prov. 4; John 1

ALL I REALLY NEED TO KNOW about how to live and what to do and how to be I learned in kindergarten. Wisdom was not at the top of the graduate-school mountain, but there in the sandpile at Sunday school. These are the things I learned:

Share everything.
Play fair.
Don't hit people.
Put things back where you found them.
Clean up your own mess.
Don't take things that aren't yours.
Say you're sorry when you hurt somebody.
Wash your hands before you eat.
Flush.
Warm cookies and cold milk are good for you.
When you go out into the world, watch out for traffic, hold hands, and stick together.
Live a balanced life . . . learn some and think some and draw and paint and sing and dance and play and work every day some.
Take a nap every afternoon.
Be aware of wonder. Remember the little seed in the styrofoam cup: the roots go down and the plant goes up and nobody really knows how or why, but we are all like that.
Goldfish and hamsters and white mice and even the little seed in the styrofoam cup . . . they all die. So do we.
And then remember the Dick-and-Jane books and the first word you learned . . . the biggest word of all . . . LOOK.

Everything you need to know is in there somewhere. The Golden Rule, love, and basic sanitation. Ecology, politics, equality, and sane living. Think what a better world it would be if the whole world had cookies and milk at 3:00 every afternoon and then laid down with our blankies for a nap. Or if all governments had a basic policy to always put things back where they found them and to clean up their own mess.

And it is still true, no matter how old you are — when you go out into the world, it is best to hold hands and stick together.[15]

The fear of the Lord is the
beginning of knowledge (Prov. 1:7).

෬ා

Num. 3; Ps. 58; Prov. 5; John 2

❧

Strange that I did not know him then,
That friend of mine.
I did not even show him then
One friendly sign. . . .
I would have rid the earth of him
Once, in my pride.
I never knew the worth of him
Until he died.

Edwin Arlington Robinson

❧

March 6 —Shocking Generosity

The story goes that while Robert Smith was taking his afternoon walk as part of his therapy in recovering from a massive heart attack, the phone rang and his wife Delores answered. The call was from the Reader's Digest Association Sweepstakes in New York. They were calling to inform the Smith family that Robert had just won $1,500,000. Well, as you can imagine, Delores was absolutely ecstatic. Now all those dreams would come true!

But then she remembered, her husband was just getting over his heart attack and the doctor had said no excitement over anything. Delores was afraid that if she told him they had just won such a large sum, he would have another heart attack and die. After some thought, she decided to call their pastor and ask his advice because he had had some experience in breaking difficult news to families.

Delores dialed, "Hello, Pastor Baldwin . . . this is Delores Smith."

The pastor replied, "Hi, Delores. How are you? And how is Bob?"

"I'm fine, thank you. And so is Bob. He's recovering nicely. But, I've got a problem and I need your advice."

"Sure, if I can help, I'll be glad to," the pastor replied.

"Well, Pastor, I just got a call from The Reader's Digest Sweepstakes informing me that Bob has just won $1,500,000!"

"That's great!" said the pastor, "But what's the problem?"

"Well, I'm afraid that if I tell Bob, he'll get so excited that he will have another heart attack and drop dead. Can you help me?"

"Well, Delores, I think I can. Hold on, I'll be right over."

So in about an hour, Bob is now back from his walk and he and Delores and Pastor Baldwin are in the den. The pastor leans toward Bob and says, "Bob, I've got a problem and need your advice."

"Sure, Pastor, if I can help, I'll be glad to," Bob said.

The pastor takes a deep breath and goes on, "It's a theoretical situation regarding Christian stewardship. What would a person — take you for instance — do if all of a sudden you found out you had won $1,500,000? What would you do with all that money?"

"That's easy," Bill replied, "I'd start by giving $750,000 to the church."

Whereupon, Pastor Baldwin had a heart attack and dropped dead!

Give, and there will be gifts for you: a full measure, pressed down, shaken together, and running over, will be poured into your lap; because the amount you measure out is the amount you will be given back (Luke 6:38;JB).

〰️

Num. 4; Ps. 59; Prov. 6; John 3

March 7 — An AIDS Mistake

At 18, Kaye Brown was ready for the world! The bubbly honor student was looking forward to life in the army. Last March, she signed up at a recruiting office in Houston and took a mandatory AIDS test. One week later she learned she was HIV-positive and the world was no longer a sure thing! "I was really, really angry," she says. "My career had been snatched away from me."

Though doctors estimated that she had contracted the virus recently, they recommended that she tell anyone she had had sex with in the previous year. The list was long. "It was easy for me to list the guys I had slept with," she says, "but when I counted 24, I was like, gosh!"

One former partner said, "But you don't look like you're that way."

Brown shot back, "What is that way? HIV doesn't mean that I'm dirty or low. It just means I made a mistake."

Brown blames only herself. "It makes me angry that I allowed this to happen," she says. "Choices I made have stolen away the choices that I might have had in the future."[16]

Not only will her choices be gone but her life will be taken . . . if AIDS takes its normal course of development. She has about two to four years to live, if she is fortunate and has some excellent health care.

The virus that causes AIDS is known as the human immunodeficiency virus or HIV. We do know that this virus is less infectious than others such as the virus for hepatitis B. However, once contracted there is no known cure and the result is death. From June through September, last year, there were 912 new cases among 13 to 19 year olds. There is a caution . . . these numbers are just the visible tip of the iceberg. They only include those who are in the final stages of infection with HIV. It is estimated (CDC) that between one and two million Americans are now infected with the virus. The CDC also estimates that as many as 30 percent of all AIDS-related deaths are never reported. Scary! Deadly!

We have a choice! Certain behaviors are the major cause of spreading AIDS, among them is sexual promiscuity. Let's make a choice not to indulge but to abstain . . . and the old message from God himself is to wait until marriage. Make virginity your choice! Take the moral high ground! You'll be glad you did.

It is God's will that you should be sanctified: that you should avoid sexual immorality; that each of you should learn to control his own body in a way that is holy and honorable, not in passionate lust like the heathen, who do not know God (1 Thess. 4:3-5).

◦∽◦

Num. 5-6; Ps. 60; Prov. 7; John 4

March 8 — The Freedoms of Abstinence

Bernice Krahn and Rita Salvadalena, volunteers at the Crisis Pregnancy Center, Everett, Washington, use the following "freedoms" in teaching teens to say "NO" to sexual temptations. These freedoms have been adapted from Teen Aid curriculum, by Steve Potter and Nancy Roach. Here they are:

1. FREEDOM from pregnancy and sexually transmitted disease.
2. FREEDOM from the problems of birth control.
3. FREEDOM from the pressure to marry too soon.
4. FREEDOM from abortion.
5. FREEDOM from the pain of giving your baby up for adoption.
6. FREEDOM from exploitation by others.
7. FREEDOM from the guilt, doubt, disappointment, worry, and rejection that comes with a sexual affair.
8. FREEDOM to be in control of your body.
9. FREEDOM to get to know your dating partner as a person.
10. FREEDOM to plan for the future and for the kind of life you want to live.
11. FREEDOM to respect yourself.
12. FREEDOM to be unselfish: not taking pleasure in sex at the expense of your boyfriend or girlfriend.
13. FREEDOM to look forward to marriage and to be chosen by the kind of person you want for the mother or father of your children, without worrying about his/her learning about your sexual past.
14. FREEDOM to enjoy being a teenager, with many friends and boy-girl relationships.
15. FREEDOM from severe pain when you break up.
16. FREEDOM to form a strong marriage bond with one person only for life. Such couples can trust each other to be sexually faithful in marriage because both of them have practiced resisting sexual temptation before marriage.
17. FREEDOM to later remember your high school/college dating experiences, after you're grown up, with pleasure and happy memories, and no shame.[17]

That really says it all. You make the decision to abstain and if you ask, God will give you grace and strength! Abstinence is the answer!

Flee the evil desires of youth, and pursue righteousness, faith, love and peace, along with those who call on the Lord out of a pure heart (2 Tim. 2:22).

Num. 7; Ps. 61; Prov. 8; John 5

March 9 — The Delany Sisters

Sarah and A. Elizabeth Delany, 104 and 106 (in 1994; Sarah has since passed away), have taken the public by storm. It was their surprise bestseller, *Having Our Say: The Delany Sisters' First 100 Years* that elevated them to become "America's grandmas." Charming, candid, witty, and wise, these sisters struck something in the souls of Americans that kept them on the *New York Times* best-seller list for 28 weeks! "Twenty-eight weeks on the *New York Times* best-seller list . . . not bad for two old inky-dinks over 100 years old!" Bessie is fond of joking.

As a result of all that attention the letters have come pouring in from readers crammed with questions. People want their advice on all kinds of subjects . . . what to do was a problem. One day it dawned on them that they could write another book which would not give their life story but their secrets of old age. So in 1994 another book was released, *The Delany Sisters' Book of Everyday Wisdom* (with Amy Hill Hearth).

What is the secret of attaining old age? According to Sadie: "So you want to live to be 100. Well, start with this: No smoking, no drinking, no chewing. And always clean your plate. We get up with the sun, and the first thing we do is exercise. God gave you only one body, so you better be nice to it. Exercise, because if you don't, by the time you're our age, you'll be pushing up daisies."

According to Bessie: "I have gotten smarter about a few things in my old age, things like taking chances. Now, I know there are folks who are afraid to try anything new, and that's a big problem for them. But me, I was never afraid of anything. I mean, I was always absolutely fearless! Naturally that meant that I didn't always have good sense."

And from them both: "For about the last 35 years, things were mighty quiet. We had a pleasant life, working in the garden, going to church, visiting with friends and neighbors. We took good care of ourselves, doing exercises every morning . . . except Sunday . . . and eating carefully. We eat a whole lot of vegetables and fruits and take vitamin supplements.

"Now it seems like the whole world has been writing to us . . . it seems that a lot of folks, especially young ones, don't know how to live right. We're as old as Moses, so maybe we have learned a few things along the way, and we'd like to pass them on. We hope you find them useful."[18]

"Honor your father and mother" — which is the first commandment with a promise — "that it may go well with you and that you may enjoy long life on the earth" (Eph. 6:2-3).

Num. 8-9; Ps. 62; Prov. 9; John 6

SADIE: For us there was never a time when we did not believe in God. There's a lot in this world you can't see that you still believe in, like love and courage. Well, that's the way it is with faith. Just because you can't hold it in your hand doesn't mean it's not there. A person who has faith is prepared for life and to do something with it.

The Word of God . . . was the center of our home. The Bible is where we go for guidance. God's wisdom is at work in the words, but you can also get plenty of practical advice in the Bible. After all, mankind hasn't changed that much.

BESSIE: When we walk into our house . . . whether we're coming back from a long trip or just from seeing the neighbors . . . the first thing we say is, "We're home. Praise the Lord." We do that to honor Him, to thank Him for watching over us.

I think God understands that I'm only human. He gave this mouth, He gave me a temper, and so I'm bound to err. I'm sure I must be getting credit for trying! But every once in a while, just to keep on His path, I try to take in an old-fashioned fire-and-brimstone sermon. I'm an Episcopalian, and I appreciate the thoughtful preaching in my church . . . but there's nothing like fire and brimstone to set me straight. Fight fire with fire, I always say!

SADIE: I can't get over the litter on the ground in New York City. People eat a sandwich, they throw the wrapper on the ground. You might think that's a little thing to be provoked about, but it's not a little thing. It shows a lot about the character of the person, that he doesn't care about any one else. It's plain bad manners!

We hate bad manners. By "manners" I don't mean using the right fork or spoon at the dinner table. All I'm talking about is performing simple acts of consideration, which sounds easy . . . and it is easy, but too few people even bother to try.

BESSIE: When you get older, it's natural to look back on your life. And like most folks, I have a few regrets. The main regrets I have from 100 years of living come from when I haven't treated someone as well as I could have.

Mama used to tell me, "Bessie, someday you're going to have to account for every mean thing you've ever said." That's what's got me so worried. If I had to do it all over again, I'd hush up once in a while.

Listen to your father, who gave you life, and do not despise your mother when she is old (Prov. 23:22).

❧

Num. 10-11; Ps. 63; Prov. 10; John 7

March 11 — Natural Instincts

Two brothers wished very much to receive a generous inheritance from their aged grandfather. Both spent many, many hours tending to his every whim in order to gain his favor and have the inside track.

One day, the old man, a bit weary of the whole thing, asked them a question: "Is a child born well-mannered and considerate, or is it something that one must be taught?" As chance would have it, each brother took one side of the argument, hoping that would be the opinion of their grandfather. The two brothers began to argue and debate . . . this went on for days, loudly and insistent. Finally, their grandfather said, "Bring me proof to back up your argument. One year from today, I will give the larger inheritance to the one of you who can bring me positive proof to back up your point of view on this issue."

One year later to the day, the two brothers returned. Both claimed to have proof. The first brother barked out this command: "Please bring my dear grandfather a cup of coffee." To the amazement of the elderly gentleman, a cat wearing a tiny apron walked in from the kitchen carrying a steaming cup of coffee, a creamer, and sugar on a silver tray. The cat was something else. This brother had trained the cat to walk on hind legs and balance the tray with the front paws. After placing the tray on the coffee table, this cat bowed low and stood at full attention.

The grandfather said, "Never have I seen anything like that!" The implications were so obvious. . . . "If you can train a cat like that, then a person can be trained to behave respectfully," continued the grandfather. He was about to promise this grandson a huge inheritance.

"Just wait a moment, Grandpa," protested the other brother, "you have not given me my opportunity to present my proof."

This brother had been aware of the extraordinary cat his brother had trained and for months he was in deep despair fearing he would lose his inheritance to a trained cat. What should he do? On this day he was ready. From his pocket he produced a small box and said, "In this box I have the proof that one cannot change the way one is born." With a flourish, he placed the box on the floor, tapped on the top of the box, and opened the lid. Out popped one small mouse which scampered across the floor in front of the cat! The cat forgot all his training, and still dressed in the small apron followed in hot pursuit!

At the moment of crisis, natural instincts surfaced . . . the cat was not a trained butler. It was still a cat. What it needed was a new nature!

Jesus declared, "I tell you the truth, no one can see the kingdom of God unless he is born again" (John 3:3).

⟨∽⟩

Num. 12-13; Ps. 64; Prov. 11; John 8

March 12 — Going Home

An old Civil War veteran of the Confederate army told the following story of how he got home after the long, sad years of war. He and a group of other young soldiers from Mississippi struck out for home. They had no horses, almost no clothes, no shoes, and their feet were bleeding, frostbitten, and tied up with gunny sacks.

Through a wretched Southland, they trudged their way. Finally, they were within a few miles of home, footsore, tired, and weary.

The other gaunt soldiers wanted to lie down and sleep and go on the rest of the way in the morning, but Bill said, "I am on familiar ground; just a few more miles, and we will be home for breakfast."

The others said, "We are too tired; let's sleep."

But Bill said, "No, I am going home — I'm going to eat breakfast at home in the morning!"

He left the group, dragged on through the night, and when the first break of day came, he stood on the last hill from home! He saw the smoke from the chimney; his mother was getting breakfast.

He forgot he was tired; forgot his bleeding feet. He quickened his pace and ran, coming to the foot of the hill and the lane leading up to the house. His younger brother, Jim, sitting on the rail fence, happened to look his way and saw him. Jim shouted to those in the house, "Yonder comes Billy! Yonder comes Billy!"

Out came dad and mom and all the family! The slaves and all came running — whites and blacks together struck out down the long lane. They grabbed the tattered soldier, hugged him, carried him up to the house, and took off his rags. They bathed him and gave him clean clothes, and all together shouted and laughed and praised God for Billy's homecoming!

Homecomings have a special place in the course of human events and human relationships. When you have been gone for a period of time, nothing compares with the emotions of going home.

Have you given any thought to the heavenly homecoming? One of these days there will be a great homecoming when all the saints of the ages will be gathered to a heavenly home. It's promised to be an unexpected event so, in order to be a participant, each of us must always be prepared. It's like a sudden knocking at the door — it can come at any time! Are you ready and watching?

Nothing impure will ever enter it, nor will anyone who does what is shameful or deceitful, but only those whose names are written in the Lamb's book of life (Rev. 21:27).

~◠◡~

Num. 14; Ps. 65; Prov. 12; John 9

March 13 — The Great Unknown

San Francisco has had more than its share of colorful characters. Among those of the last century was a strikingly handsome man who was called the "Great Unknown." He was tall, erect, slender, with jet black hair, and was clean-shaven at a time when most men wore beards or mustaches. His dress was absolutely impeccable. He wore a top hat that was always brushed and clean. His boots were always polished. He was aloof, mysterious, and never talked with anyone. Nobody knew his name, his origin, his occupation, or where he lived. Rumor had it that he was an exiled nobleman or former diplomat, but no one knew.

One day he was missed from his normal afternoon appearance in the downtown district. His habit was to walk through the downtown district for about two hours each evening and then disappear.

Some days later, his body was found in a tiny loft by the waterfront. He lived humbly, and it was discovered that he made his living by stuffing pillows and mattresses. The room was sparse but absolutely clean.

His clothing was still immaculate. His boots were arranged in military fashion. On his dressing table was a wig of jet black hair. On the crude bed was the body, his handsome face frozen by death. His hair and beard were snow white. Whatever his secret, it died with him and he remained the "Great Unknown." He was buried in a pauper's grave with no one claiming the body.

Why? Did he attempt to be somebody he was not? Was he afraid that people might reject him as a pillow stuffer? Did he have some deep, dark, ugly secret about his past that he wanted to keep hidden? Did he crave recognition?

All of us want to be accepted and admired, but we know ourselves better than anyone else. How many of us have lived a deception? How many of us have secrets we'd rather keep to ourselves?

Jesus Christ came to set us free from deception! He came to make us sons and daughters of the King. No longer are we slaves to the past or servants to a secret. We have been accepted by Jesus Christ himself! For the first time we can look at others without suspicion or fear or deception or defense. In Christ we can be free to love and experience the great joy of living that comes from a clean conscience!

Know ye that the Lord he is God: it is he that hath made us,
and not we ourselves; we are his people,
and the sheep of his pasture (Ps. 100:3;KJV).

᷂

Num. 15-16; Ps. 66; Prov. 13; John 10

How do I know that my youth's all spent?
Well, my get up and go has got up and went.
But in spite of it all, I am able to grin
When I recall where my get up has been.
Old age is golden, so I've heard it said,
But sometimes I wonder, when I get into bed.
My ears in a drawer and teeth in a cup,
My eyes on the table until I wake up.
The sleep dims my eyes, I say to myself . . .
"Is there anything else I should lay on the shelf?"

And I am happy to say as I close my door,
My friends are the same, perhaps even more.
When I was young, my slippers were red,
I could kick up my heels right over my head,
When I grew older my slippers were blue,
But still I could dance the whole night through.
Now I am old, my slippers are black.
I walk to the store and puff my way back;
The reason I know my youth is all spent,
My get up and go has got up and went!

But I really don't mind,
When I think with a grin
Of all the grand places my get up has been.
Since I have retired from life's competition,
I busy myself with complete repetition.
I get up each morning, dust off my wits,
Pick up my paper, and read the "Obits,"
If my name is missing,
I know I'm not dead.
SO I EAT A GOOD BREAKFAST AND GO BACK TO BED![19]

Praise be to the Lord, who this day has not left you without a kinsman-redeemer. May he become famous throughout Israel! He will renew your life and sustain you in your old age (Ruth 4:14-15).

❧

Num. 17-18; Ps. 67; Prov. 14; John 11

March 15 — Old Hickory

He's called "Old Hickory" because of his grit! His mother named him Andrew on March 15, 1767, when she gave birth to this independent rebel. He was not interested in school. He was wild, quick-tempered, and answered the call for soldiers at age 13.

Shortly after becoming a soldier, he was taken prisoner. While a captive, he refused to polish an enemy officer's boots and was struck with a saber. This was Andrew's first introduction to pain.

He carried that mark for the rest of his life, but his disposition never changed. Andrew was a fighter to the core. He chose to settle arguments in duels and lived most of his life with two bullets painfully lodged in his body.

After his battlefield heroics, his name became a household word for courage. When politics called, "Old Hickory" accepted the challenge. He was voted to the United States Senate, then there was the nomination for the presidency. It was then he experienced a different kind of pain — he lost a narrow race to Quincy Adams.

Four years later, Andrew ran again and won! But two months before he was to take the oath of office, he lost his beloved wife, Rachel. Grief-stricken and ill, the president-elect carried on and was sworn in as our seventh president as he fought the raging fever caused by an abscess in his lung. Later, one of the bullets in his body was surgically removed — without benefit of an anesthetic!

Even his political career was painful at times. A nasty scandal split his cabinet, allowing critics to have a field day at his expense. However, he weathered that storm and was one of the very few presidents to leave the office more popular than when he came.

I believe it was pain that drew the qualities of greatness out of Andrew Jackson! Pain can humble the proud; it can soften the stubborn; it can melt the hard; and the heart alone knows its own sorrow. This message can be communicated to statesmen, presidents, servants, preachers, and prodigals. By staying, pain refuses to be ignored; and by hurting, it reduces the victim to anguish. It's at this point that the sufferer submits and learns. Here is developed either maturity of character or self-pity of soul. Every strong-willed person who has become great knows the meaning of pain.

He said unto me, "My grace is sufficient for you, for my power is made perfect in weakness." Therefore I will boast all the more gladly about my weaknesses, so that Christ's power may rest on me (2 Cor. 12:9).

❧

Num. 19-20; Ps. 68:1-18; Prov. 15; John 12

Dale Carnegie was what we would call a "late bloomer." He had some early success as a salesman for correspondence courses, then became an outstanding salesman for Packard automobiles, along with a brief stint as an actor. He came to a turning point in his life — he had the vague feeling that all was not right, that there might be more in life for him. So Carnegie began to evaluate himself, to take a look at where he was headed with his life. Among the things he valued was a teacher's certificate, but he didn't know what to teach. What should he do next with his life?

In his evaluation he reached the decision that the most important and valuable thing in his education was that he had learned public speaking. He put together a proposal which he presented to the YMCA and their schools in New York that he should teach courses in public speaking to local businessmen. The YMCA administrators thought so little of the idea that they refused to pay him the $2 per night which he had requested. They would allow him to teach and use their facilities and contact their clientele, but no salary of $2 per night. However, instead, they agreed to give him a percentage of the net profits from these courses. In less than three years, these courses taught by Carnegie became so popular that soon he was receiving $30 and more per night. Word spread. Enthusiasm built a demand for this information. Soon he was besieged with offers to teach public speaking in many other U.S. cities and even in Europe.

Out of these courses came the first of many wildly successful, best-selling books, *How to Win Friends and Influence People, Public Speaking* and *Influencing Men in Business,* and more best sellers. Also as an outgrowth, the Dale Carnegie Institute was established which still conducts seminars on a worldwide basis.

There is a story about P.T. Barnum and how he became a victim of his own success. So many people were crowding into his shows that huge lines were forming outside the tents. To facilitate and speed up the turn-around, he placed large signs inside the tent exit which read: "This way to the egress." People, gullible, thinking that "egress" meant another attraction, would eagerly file outside following the show.

So it's my hope that you will find a new adventure outside your tent.

He who was seated on the throne said, "I am making everything new!" Then he said, "Write this down, for these words are trustworthy and true" (Rev. 21:5).

❦

Num. 21-22; Ps. 68:19-35; Prov. 16; John 13

March 17 — The Power of Friendship

As a part of an assignment for a doctoral thesis, a college student spent a year with a group of Navajo Indians on a reservation in the Southwest. As she did her research she lived with one family, sleeping in their hut, eating their food, working with them, and generally living the life of a twentieth-century Navajo Indian.

The old grandmother of the family spoke no English at all, yet a very close bond formed between these two. In spite of the language difference, they shared the common language of love and understood each other. Over the months the student learned a few phrases of Navajo, and the grandmother picked up a little of the English language.

When it was time for the student to return to the campus the tribe held a going-away celebration. It was marked by sadness since the young woman had become close to the whole village and all would miss her.

As she prepared to get up into the pickup truck and leave, the old grandmother came to tell her goodbye, personally. With tears streaming from her eyes, she placed her gnarled, weathered hands on either side of the young woman's face, looked directly into her eyes, and said in her broken, halting English, "I like me best when I'm with you."

And isn't that just the way we feel when we are in the presence of good friends? Friends see us as worthy and valuable when we spend time together. Friends help overlook the hurts, the cares, the disappointments of our lives. Friends are spirit-lifters. Friends help each other's self-esteem. Friends place great value on each other.

Edwin Markham, poet, was asked which of his poems he valued the most. He replied, "How can you choose between your own children?" He then went on to voice his opinion that his four lines called "Outwitted" might have the best-lasting qualities because love lasts:

> He drew a circle that shut me out.
> Heretic, rebel, a thing to flout.
> But Love and I had the wit to win:
> We drew a circle that took him in!

To be conformed to the image of Jesus Christ, the greatest of all friends, is to hopefully generate in others the old Indian grandmother's response: "I like me best when I'm with you."

And the scripture was fulfilled that says, "Abraham believed God, and it was credited to him as righteousness," and he was called God's friend (James 2:23).

Num. 23-24; Ps. 69:1-15; Prov. 17; John 14-15

March 18 — Jackie's Angel

Jackie is a beautiful girl of 17 with shining black hair and sparkling brown eyes. A delightful glow sets her apart from other beautiful young girls.

Three years ago Jackie faced a painful tragedy. Doctors had discovered a tumor on her cheekbone . . . the kind of tumor usually found only on a long bone such as an arm or leg. It had spread its deadly tentacles throughout the entire cheek region of her attractive face. Surgery offered the only hope to save Jackie's life. The doctors would be making an incision along the nose area and down through the upper lip. All of her teeth on the left side of her face would have to be removed as well as the cheekbone, the nose bone, and the jaw bone. Needless to say, an operation of this immensity, performed on the face of a lovely, at that time 14-year-old girl, was a grim prospect. Many tears were shed.

Several days before the surgery, lying in her hospital bed, she thought about what it would mean to go through life so terribly scarred, if indeed she even lived through the operation. She was frightened, she desperately wanted to live. She wanted to experience all that life held for her. As she tossed on her pillow in lonely fear that night, she began to pray. With tears of anxious apprehension, she asked God to help her.

About two o'clock in the morning Jackie was awakened. She didn't know what woke her up; she only knew she was awake and alert. She saw a glowing light at the foot of her bed, and the silvery form of an angel appeared. The presence was very powerful and totally loving. An aura of stillness filled Jackie like the warmth of a summer day. She felt enfolded by the presence and a sense of incredible wonder touched every part of her body.

A voice filled with sunshine said, "Do not be afraid, Jackie. You are going to be all right." And then the angel presence was gone.

The following day, Jackie was taken to the X-ray room for preoperative X-rays. To the utter astonishment of the doctors, every trace of the tumor and its deadly tentacles was gone!

That was three years ago. Now here she is, this beautiful daffodil princess. Her lovely face is unmarred, and she remains very much aware of God's miraculous touch upon her life![20]

But the angel said to them, "Do not be afraid. I bring you good news of great joy" (Luke 2:10).

❧

Num. 25-26; Ps. 69:16-36; Prov. 18; John 16-17

March 19 — The Winning Attitude

Kelley Roswell, age 11 (at this time), is a Little League softball player. She plays shortstop and pitcher for the Grand Mesa Major girls all-stars. She loves softball. She can hardly wait for springtime to roll around so she can get back on the field to play.

That's not all. Kelley is an outstanding student in school and refuses to settle for anything less than an "A" in any of her classes.

Kelley is young, and normally people this young don't deserve the label of "hero," but in my estimation she is very deserving. I don't think she can be considered an ordinary girl.

Kelley Roswell, age 11, has leukemia.

Since it was diagnosed in March of 1988, she has been in a life-and-death battle with the disease. She has "ALL," otherwise known as "Acute Lymphocytic Leukemia (commonly known as childhood leukemia). As a result, she traveled to Denver, Colorado, and spent weeks in the Children's Hospital in earnest battle for her life. She had to return to Denver from Grand Junction (500 miles round trip) every week for a time. This was reduced to a return trip every six weeks. The four-hour trips, injections, transfusions, and pills . . . all have been taken in stride by Kelley, without complaint. Normally, chemotherapy has the side effects of vomiting and nausea, but according to her father, Steve, she's had no major problems; she has yet to get sick from the treatment.

Mother Joanne said, "As a mother, I could be weepy, but Kelley hasn't allowed that. God gave us Kelley and we've learned that the time we have with her is special. God's had His hand on Kelley. God gives us children as gifts and they belong to Him. We get them for only a certain amount of time."

The Roswells are a committed Christian family. Prayers have been a great help in this battle. The church and community have been sources of strength and support.

Even leukemia didn't slow Kelley in playing her beloved softball. For example, during the summer of 1988, she just didn't slow up; she's a real star, pitching and hitting her team to a second place finish! Any way you look at it, Kelley's a winner.[21]

And . . . I can tell you, Kelley beat her cancer! She's disease-free, today! How do I know? I was her pastor during this ordeal. She's really a winner any way you look at it!

That is why, for Christ's sake, I delight in weaknesses, in insults, in hardships, in persecutions, in difficulties. For when I am weak, then I am strong (2 Cor. 12:10).

Num. 27-28; Ps. 70; Prov. 19; John 18

March 20 — B.C. Fully Described

There are many versions of this little story . . . the original source is lost someplace in antiquity. Enjoy:

My friend is a rather old-fashioned lady, quite elegant and delicate, especially in her choice of language. She and her husband were planning a week-long camping trip, so she wrote to a campground for reservations. She didn't quite know how to ask about toilet facilities. She didn't want to write "toilet" in her letter. After much deliberation, she thought of the old-fashioned term, "Bathroom Commode." But, when she wrote it down she thought she was being too forward, rewrote the entire letter and referred to the bathroom commode as the B.C. "Does your campground have its own B.C.?" she asked in her letter.

Well, the campground owner couldn't figure out what she was talking about. The "B.C." business had him stumped. After giving it much thought the owner decided that she must be asking about the location for the local Baptist Church, so he wrote the following reply:

Dear Madam: I regret very much the delay in answering your letter but I now take the pleasure of informing you that the B.C. is located six miles north of the campground. It is capable of seating 250 people at one time. I will admit that it is quite a distance away if you are in the habit of going regularly. No doubt you will be pleased to know that a great number of people take their lunches along and make a day of it. The last time my wife and I went was six months ago and it was so crowded that we had to stand up the whole time. Right now, there is a supper planned to raise money for more seats. It will be held in the basement of the B.C. I would like to say that it pains me that I am not able to go more regularly, but it is not for lack of desire on my part. As we grow older, it seems to be more of an effort, especially in cold weather.

If you do decide to come to our campground, perhaps I could go with you the first time that you go, sit with you, and introduce you to all the other folks. Remember, that this is a very friendly community.

The Campground Owner

Oh, well . . . what more can be added than to tell you that it's okay for couples to share a good laugh together! And do it often!

A cheerful heart is good medicine,
but a crushed spirit dries up the bones (Prov. 17:22).

❧

Num. 29-30; Ps. 71:1-16; Prov. 20; John 19

March 21 — Brotherhood

This story was told by Bob Tuttle, professor at Fuller Theological Seminary, and is alleged to be a true story that happened to the son of the Rev. Reuben Job, a United Methodist minister:

The boy (let's call him Billy) was attending his first day at junior high school. It began with an assembly, one feature of which was the introduction of all the homeroom teachers.

First to be introduced was Miss Smith, and the ninth graders, knowing Miss Smith to be an easy grader and not much of a disciplinarian, all began to cheer: "Yea, Miss Smith! Right on, Miss Smith!"

The next to be introduced was Mr. Brown, who was a young and popular teacher, a special favorite. This time the eighth graders joined in the thundering approval: "Yea, Mr. Brown! Hurrah for Mr. Brown!"

By the time the next teacher was introduced, even the ignorant seventh graders were getting into the spirit of the thing. Then they introduced Mr. Johnson, an older teacher who was reputed to be the hardest grader and least sympathetic teacher in the school as well as a strong disciplinarian. The cat calls began: "Booo, Mr. Johnson! Hiss . . . Mr. Johnson!"

The pain was evident on old Mr. Johnson's face. Suddenly Billy stood up in the middle of the bleachers and shouted, "Shut up! He's my father!" The noise died as they clearly got the message . . . *"Cool it, Johnson's son is here."*

That afternoon when school was out, Billy raced home. His father met him, "Son, what's wrong?"

"Dad, I've got to talk to you. I told a lie in school today."

So Billy told the story. When he was through, his dad put his arm around him and said, "It's all right, son. You didn't really tell a lie . . . you just got the family members mixed up. Mr. Johnson's not your father; he's your brother."

Brotherhood . . . have you given much thought to this concept lately? There is a common bond because we are all human beings . . . but beyond that? Do we really care enough to stand up and be counted on when it comes to helping a friend, a neighbor, a sister, or a brother?

Keep on loving each other as brothers. Do not forget to entertain strangers, for by so doing some people have entertained angels without knowing it (Heb. 13:1-2).

෴

Num. 31-32; Ps. 71:17-24; Prov. 21; John 20-21

March 22 — The Dignity of the Robe

A seminary president tells this story: In our particular denomination, when candidates are ordained into the ministry, they each have one thing assigned to them to do in that particular ordination service. The services are solemn, dignified, impressive, and meaningful.

At the conclusion of the worship/ordination service this candidate was to stand, walk up the steps into the chancel, turn, and pronounce the benediction. This was to be his very first official act as a newly ordained minister.

The time arrived, the candidate solemnly stood, approached the steps, and ascended. But on the first step, he stepped inside the hem of his clerical robe. This poor candidate/ordainee kept climbing up the steps . . . all the time walking up the inside of his robe. Each step made him smaller as he was forced to "duck walk" up the inside of his own robe.

Finally, at the top of the steps, looking like some kind of a dwarf in a white tent, he turned around. His robe could not turn with him, since he was standing inside it. The act of turning placed the left arm of his robe right in the center of his chest and the right arm was somewhere between his shoulders. All he could move was his left wrist from the center of his chest, arms pressed tight against his body by the constriction of the robe. With a wave of his wrist he pronounced the benediction, solemnly, not missing a word.

When he was finished, unable to take another step from his duck walk posture inside his robe, he was helpless. Two husky ushers came forward, picked him up by his armpits and carried him off like some piece of furniture.[22]

I wish I could have been there! How about you?

Ministry is so wonderful . . . the humor is explosive and subtle and so unexpected!

Do you ever think what might have happened to the Sermon on the Mount if Jesus had to speak through a sound system? Use a tape system that didn't tape? A faulty organ with a late organist? Use word processors that don't process? It's amazing that the Church still marches on in spite of technology and what we do to it ourselves. Oh, well!

Then he said to them, "Go your way, eat the fat, drink the sweet, and
send portions to those for whom nothing is prepared; for this day is
holy to our Lord. Do not sorrow, for the joy of the Lord is your
strength" (Neh. 8:10;NKJV).

ᕙᕗ

Num. 33-34; Ps. 72; Prov. 22; Acts 1

March 23 — Friends Understand

Bob Weber, former president of Kiwanis International, tells the following story. He had been the special guest speaker to a Kiwanis club in a small town and was spending the night with a club member who was a farmer, on the outskirts of the town. He and the farmer had just gotten comfortable on the front porch when a newsboy delivered the evening paper. The boy noticed the sign: PUPPIES FOR SALE! He got off his bike and asked, "How much do you want for the pups, mister?"

"Twenty-five dollars each, son."

Bob Weber said the boy's face dropped. "Well, sir, could I at least see them anyway?"

The farmer whistled and in a moment the mother dog came bounding around the corner of the house followed by four of the cutest puppies you would ever see, wagging their tails and yipping happily. Finally, another pup, a straggler, came around the house, dragging one hind leg. "What's the matter with that puppy, mister?" the boy asked.

"Well, son, that puppy is crippled. We had the vet x-ray her. There's no hip joint and that leg will never be right."

To the amazement of both men, the boy dropped the bike, reached for his collection bag and took out two quarters. "Please, mister," the boy pleaded, "I want to buy that pup. I'll pay you 50 cents every week until the 25 dollars is paid. Honest I will, mister."

The farmer replied, "But, son, you don't seem to understand. That pup will never be able to run or jump. She is going to be a crippled dog forever. Why in the world would you want such a useless pup as that? I'll be glad to give her to you, she's not worth anything, anyway."

The boy paused for a moment, then reached down to pull up his pant's leg, exposing a leg brace. The boy answered, "Mister, that pup is going to need someone who understands her to help her in life!"

And . . . don't we all?! I don't know of a person in this world who doesn't need friends and someone to understand and to care and to love! Do you? We all need to build our life on relationships and good times with good friends.

The greatest Friend in this world is the friend above all others. A friend who willingly laid down His life for you and me. He set the pattern for human friends and relationships. His name is Jesus Christ, known as the "friend of sinners."

A man of many companions may come to ruin, but there is a friend who sticks closer than a brother (Prov. 18:24).

❧

Num. 35-36; Ps. 73:1-14; Prov. 23; Acts 2

March 24 — Attack!

Supposedly this is a true story . . . but the source has been lost or misplaced. Could it have been one of those "Paul Harvey" stories? It is reported to have been written up in a small town newspaper.

There was a burglar who was casing the homes in one particular neighborhood, trying to find his next target. He especially was looking for houses that would be left unguarded by people leaving for vacation. He slowly cruised until he saw a family loading their suitcases and goodies into their family van. He parked a block away and watched until everything had been loaded and the van packed with kids and luggage pulled out of the drive.

He left and returned after dark and approached the front door and rang the bell. Of course there was no answer, but he was just checking. Then the burglar neatly picked the lock and let himself in. He called into the darkness, "Is anybody home?"

He was absolutely stunned when he heard a voice reply, "I see you and Jesus sees you."

Terrified, the burglar called back, "Who's there?"

Again the voice came back, "I see you and Jesus sees you."

Deciding to not run so quickly, the burglar switched on his flashlight and aimed it in the direction of the voice. To his great relief, his light revealed a caged parrot reciting the refrain, again, "I see you and Jesus sees you." The burglar laughed out loud. "I see you and Jesus sees you."

The burglar heaved a sigh of relief, his heart slowed down, he caught his breath. Then the burglar reached over and switched on the light. THEN he saw it! Beneath the parrot's cage was a huge Doberman Pinscher, mouth open, softly growling.

Then the parrot said, "Attack, Jesus, attack!"

The story was revealed by the burglar himself from the emergency room of the local hospital where extensive stitches were used to close up the many wounds.

We chuckle and think of the poetic justice meted out, "Serves him right!" Funny, yes . . . but there is a truth here, too. At all times we are being observed by others, yes; but even more closely by God. Even the darkness can't hide us from His omniscience. It makes you think. Not only are we being observed, but we will be asked, someday, to give an account of how we have lived this life.

Where can I go from your Spirit? Where can I flee from your presence? If I go up to the heavens, you are there; if I make my bed in the depths, you are there (Ps. 139:7-8).

❧

Deut. 1; Ps. 73:15-28; Prov. 24; Acts 3

March 25 — Does It Represent You?

In a particular church they had experienced such growth it demanded that they enlarge their facilities. It represented quite a step of faith. After much planning, praying, and working together, they decided on a new church building. It would be adequate for their expanded ministry. It was an exciting moment as together they came to the moment to begin raising funds for this multi-million dollar project.

The pastor and church board made their projections, along with their appeal to the congregation to share in this need by sacrificial giving. Everyone was challenged to be part of this expansion project.

After the service was over a lady came to the pastor personally and handed him a check for $50, asking at the same time if her gift was satisfactory. The pastor immediately replied, "If it represents you." There was a moment or two of soul-searching and she asked to have the check returned to her. She left with it.

A day or two later she returned to make an appointment to see the pastor. This time she handed the pastor her check for $5,000 and again asked the same question, "Is my gift satisfactory?"

The pastor gave the same answer as before, "If it represents you." As before, the truth seemed to be sinking deep into her mind. After some moments of quiet hesitation she took back the check and left. Now the pastor was beginning to get a bit worried. Perhaps he had been too bold and had offended her. He also wondered if she would ever return.

About two weeks later there was a phone call at the church office asking for another appointment with the pastor. It was the same woman. As before, she came with a check in hand and a big smile on her face. This time the check was for $50,000. As she placed it in the pastor's hand she said, "After earnest, prayerful thought, I have come to the conclusion that this gift does represent me, and I am most happy to give it to the church for our new project."

Money and giving are always touchy subjects to many people. Why? Do we have guilt in this area of our Christian living? Are we too selfish about the material things in our living? Giving and living are two things that go together in the Christian lifestyle. The Bible talks about sacrificial giving as well as cheerful giving. Just another question: Will your giving this week really represent you?

> *On every Lord's Day each of you should put aside*
> *something from what you have earned during the week,*
> *and use it for this offering. The amount depends on how*
> *much the Lord has helped you earn* (1 Cor. 16:2;LB).

❧

Deut. 2-3; Ps. 74:1-11; Prov. 25; Acts 4

March 26 — A Potpourri on Sisterhood

I can't think I had much of a sense of humor as long as I remained the only child. When my brother Edward came along after I was three, we both became comics. We set each other off, as we did for life, from the minute he learned to talk. A sense of the absurd was communicated between us probably before that. — Eudora Welty

All older children feel that they are "not good enough" when a younger sibling is born. Not, somehow, "up to snuff." They come to feel that somehow they were born a "Ford Pinto," and are in effect being "recalled by the manufacturer." Maybe you tried to look closely at the face of your sister at birth, and it looked like a stewed grape, and you thought, *This is an improvement?* — Stephanie Brush

Not being kissed at 16 was harder for me to endure than it otherwise would have been because Ramona, my 12-year-old sister, had been. She had had boy friends since she was 10. She had big boys of 15 hanging around her from whom I would have been proud to have a glance. They treated me like Ramona's old-maid aunt. My brother Neddie was only 16 months younger than I. When we were together where people didn't know us, I sidled up to him in a way I hoped onlookers would think romantic. To this day, Neddie still sits across the room from me when we visit. That year of sidling has made him permanently wary. — Jessamyn West

But however you might rebel, there was no shedding them. They were your responsibility and there was no one to relieve you of them. All your life people called you Sis, because that was what you were, or what you became — big sister, helpful sister, the one upon whom everyone depended, the one they all came to for everything from help with homework to a sliver under the fingernail. — Wallace Stegner

Celestine and Hortense had been drawn closely together in affection since they had come to live under the same roof, and they formed virtually one household. The two sisters-in-law stayed at home and looked after their children together, and this had created a bond between them. They had come to be so close to each other that they spoke their thoughts aloud. They presented a touching picture of two sisters in harmony — one happy, the other sad. Perhaps the contrast between them contributed to their warm friendship: each found in the other what she lacked in herself. — Honor'e de Balzac

Naomi said to Ruth her daughter-in-law, "It will be good for you, my daughter, to go with his girls, because in someone else's field you might be harmed" (Ruth 2:22).

⤜⤚

Deut. 4; Ps. 74:12-23; Prov. 26; Acts 5

Newspaper columnist and minister George Crane tells of a wife who came into his office full of hatred toward her husband. "I do not only want to get rid of him, I want to get even. Before I divorce him, I want to hurt him as much as he has me!"

Dr. Crane suggested an ingenious plan: "Go home and act as if you really love your husband. Tell him how much he means to you. Praise him for every decent trait. Go out of your way to be as kind, considerate, and generous as possible. Spare no efforts to please him, to enjoy him. Make him believe you love him. After you've convinced him of your undying love and that you cannot live without him, drop the bomb. Tell him you are getting a divorce. That will really hurt him."

With revenge in her eyes, she smiled and exclaimed, "Beautiful! Beautiful! Will he ever be surprised!"

And she did it with enthusiasm. Acting "as if." For two months she showed love, kindness, listening, giving, reinforcing, sharing. . . .

When she didn't return, Dr. Crane called, "Are you ready now to go through with the divorce?"

"Divorce?" she exclaimed. "Never! I discovered I really do love him!"[23]

Is it really possible that actions can change feelings? From this story it appears so, but more than that, it's also a life concept. It's called the "as if" principle. This was first discovered and encouraged by Dr. Will James early in this century. It simply means that when you act "as if," you are enthused (for example), soon, feelings will follow your actions.

Let's try this definition for what love is and does: Love is an action directed to another person that is motivated by our relationship to Jesus Christ and is given freely without a personal reward in mind.[24]

Love, when applied to life situations, is the factor which makes our home operate smoothly. Love is always the oil in any kind of human relationship. Love is the key to making your home a much more pleasant place in which to live. You may not always "feel" like loving or being loving . . . but remember that your actions of love can change the feelings and emotions of love! Let your loving actions lead the way in your living!

Let us not love with words or tongue
but with actions and in truth (1 John 3:18).

❧

Deut. 5-6; Ps. 75; Prov. 27; Acts 6

March 28 — Costly Friendship

This story comes out of World War II and details one particular bombing run over the German city of Kassel. Here's the story as told by Elmer Bendiner:

Our B-17 (the Tondelayo) was barraged by flack from Nazi anti-aircraft guns. That was not unusual, but on this particular occasion our gas tanks were hit. Later, as I reflected on the miracle of a 20 millimeter shell piercing the fuel tank without touching off an explosion, our pilot, Bohn Fawkes, told me it was not quite that simple.

On the morning following the raid, Bohn had gone down to ask our crew chief for that shell as a souvenir of unbelievable luck. The crew chief told Bohn that not just one shell but 11 had been found in the gas tanks . . . 11 unexploded shells where only one was sufficient to blast us out of the sky. It was as if the sea had been parted for us. Even after 35 years, so awesome an event leaves me shaken, especially after I heard the rest of the story from Bohn.

He was told that the shells had been sent to the armorers to be defused. The armorers told him that Intelligence had picked them up. They could not say why at the time, but Bohn eventually sought out the answer.

Apparently when the armorers opened each of those shells, they found no explosive charge. They were as clean as a whistle and just as harmless. Empty? Not all of them!

One contained a carefully rolled piece of paper. On it was a scrawl in Czech. The Intelligence people scoured our base for a man who could read Czech. Eventually, they found one to decipher the note. It set us marveling. Translated, the note read:

This is all we can do for you now.[25]

A story like that can give you goose bumps! Incredible! Little acts can amount to something as large as saving another's life. I wonder if the unknown Czech munitions worker ever got found out? Were more involved in this act of bravery? What a fantastic contribution nameless people can accomplish when they persevere in small acts of kindness. Another lesson learned in building friendships that last and are meaningful . . . if you put nothing into it, don't expect to get something back.

All the saints send you greetings, especially those who belong to Caesar's household (Phil. 4:22).

❦

Deut. 7-8; Ps. 76; Prov. 28; Acts 7

Some people are "gifted" lovers. They know how to make folks around them feel love, especially the love of Christ. The principles are the same in families as well as in churches or anyplace people meet.

LOVERS smile a lot. Something caring and contagious flows through them. It's inviting, warm, gentle, and kind.

LOVERS treat you as someone really special. Warmth and welcome quickly turn into genuine friendship. They like you as a wonderful person and do not hesitate to say so.

LOVERS' faces light up every time they see you. Their hugs, handshakes, and personal words make you feel totally accepted. Quickly they invite you into their conversation, group, or home. Instinctively you know that you have a place in their hearts.

LOVERS make knowing Jesus and living in Him so attractive. If coming close to Him is something like coming close to them, it has to be wonderful.

LOVERS know God. You sense that they tap into the true source of love often and regularly. The overflow of their lives show that the fruit of the Spirit is love.

LOVERS are generous with compliments from the heart, quick to see your strengths, and tender with your weaknesses.

LOVERS have flaws. Sometimes their weaknesses hurt us more than those of others from whom we expected so little.

LOVERS sometimes become victims of our rising expectations. We, and so many others, want to treat them like close friends. No one can keep up with the demands of true friendship for so many people. We can easily expect lovers to do more for us than is reasonable.

LOVERS need to be loved, too. Weddings, birthdays, anniversaries, even funerals, say something significant.

LOVERS have many who will rise up and call them blessed. And rightly so. They have blessed so many for so long that it only seems right to give them a little gratitude and appreciation in return.

LOVERS do incredible good to all within their sphere of influence. It's little wonder then that the most often repeated commandment in the New Testament is "love one another."

LOVERS are made and not born. To become a lover is a matter of decision, attitude, and commitment to become and be a lover for the rest of life.[26]

This is the message you heard from the beginning: We should love one another (1 John 3:11).

༺～༖

Deut. 9-10; Ps. 77; Prov. 29; Acts 8

❧

*You can't think how I
depend on you, and when
you're not there the colour
goes out of my life. . . .*

Virginia Woolf

❧

March 30 — Little Sisters

"Wanna play dress up, Cheriee? I'm gonna be the mommy and the television model and be real rich and famous."

"Then I wanna be a doctor, a baby doctor, and have a hospital and lots of nurses and have lots of babies."

"Okay. You get to wear the all-white dress 'cause I wore it last time. Those shoes aren't doctor shoes, those are too high. You'll only fall down. Try these. These are much gooder, these are white."

"Then, Susan, you live in a mansion with a pool and butlers. I live in a brick house. I'm gonna get in my convertible and drive over to visit you."

"You should fly 'cause you got lots of money. And you're flying to visit me 'cause we're sisters and we need to visit and we haven't done it in a long time and we're unhappy 'cause we miss each other 'cause sisters get together and talk real often. An' it's always fun to watch other people watch you hug."

"I'll fly in a big jet and we'll meet at the airport and we'll give each other big hugs, because sisters always hug, 'specially at airports and things. It makes me feel good when I hug you and you hug me."

"But, Mommy hugs are better. Sister hugs are next."

"Susan, that's not fair. We're kids and sisters and we're playing grown-up. No fair. We will be mommies some time, but not now."

"But Mommy is a grown-up, you're a kid, and I'm a kid. That doesn't mean I don't like your hugs, either."

"Then I don't like your hugs, either, silly."

"Oh, silly. I like and really looove your hugs. See, now, I'm hugging you real tight."

" I'm tired of playing models and doctors and dress up."

"Now I get to choose. Let's play house."

"No. You always get to be the mommie."

"Then, let's play shopping."

"No, 'cause you always make me push the cart and carry the groceries and things. You always get to pay the money."

"Okay, then, now, let's have a tea party."

Treat younger men as brothers, older women as mothers, and younger women as sisters, with absolute purity (1 Tim. 5:1-2).

❧

Deut. 11-12; Ps. 78:1-20; Prov. 30; Acts 9

March 31 — A Simple Principle

It was a one-room schoolhouse in the mountains where severe discipline was applied to keep the rowdy, uninterested pupils in check. In fact, physical punishment could be used for almost any transgression.

On this particular day, the school recess had been marred by the disappearance of yet another student's lunch. Periodically, it seems, one lunch would come up missing. It got to be a serious matter. Who was responsible for the theft? It had gone on too long — something drastic must be done.

The noon recess was ended, and the teacher was interrogating the class with regard to the disappearance of Sally Jane's lunch. After a few minutes of drastic, verbal threats and demands, a sob was heard. It came from little Billy, a thin, undernourished, neglected little boy. His family was the poorest of all those in that part of the mountain.

"Did you take Sally Jane's lunch?" demanded the teacher.

"Yes, sir," mumbled Billy through his tears. "I was hungry."

"Nevertheless, you did wrong to steal, and you know the punishment for stealing. You must be punished," declared the teacher.

As the teacher removed the leather strap from its place on the wall, little Billy was ordered to the front of the room and told to remove his shirt. As he slowly unpinned the pins where buttons should have been, the students all noticed how skinny Billy was. Every rib on his back could be counted. The arm of the teacher was now raised over the bent and trembling form of the small boy.

"Hold it, Teacher!" shouted a husky voice from the rear of the room. It was Big Jim. He was the biggest and toughest of all the kids in the school. As he made his way down the aisle, he was removing his shirt as he came. When he got to the front, he looked the teacher in the eye and said, "Let me take his whoopin'."

The teacher was taken back, but knowing that justice must be demonstrated, he consented and laid the belt to the back of Big Jim with such force that even the stronger, larger boy winced and his eyes watered as he took the whipping. It was quite a scene. But little Billy never forgot the day that Big Jim took his place.

The principle is simple. Jesus Christ stepped forward in time and took our place. He died for our sins! He was perfect, yet He took the punishment that should have been ours.

When they came to the place called the Skull, there they crucified him, along with the criminals — one on his right, the other on his left (Luke 23:33).

Deut. 13-14; Ps. 78:21-33; Prov. 31; Acts 10

April 1 — Ten Million Dollar Caper

Imagine, if you can, that you have sent in your entry for the "Publisher's Clearing House" contest for the ten million dollar grand prize... and you are notified you have won! While we're on this subject, if I were a gambling person I'd be willing to bet that most of us are diligent about sending back the entries for those delectable grand prizes. Well, we can at least dream. Back to our story.

Larry Whitaker, who is the advertising director at the Springfield, Missouri, *News Leader* (daily newspaper), was interrupted one morning at the office with the presentation of a huge TEN MILLION DOLLAR check from Publisher's Clearing House. There were official check presenters, they had arrived in the official van with the "prize patrol" insignia on the side, reporters were present along with TV cameras! What a happy occasion! TEN MILLION DOLLARS! And Larry Whitaker was already mentally spending the check. The activities had proceeded from inside the office to outside on the front sidewalk of the *News Leader* building. A small crowd was looking on and enjoying the good fortune of one of their own!

Then his wife, Charlene, mysteriously appeared, holding a huge bouquet of flowers, and walked over to Larry with a huge smile, grabbed him around the neck, and whispered in his ear, "April Fool!"

All of this was just one huge April Fools' Day prank which had been perpetrated by the *News Leader* publisher, Fritz Jacobi, and many friends who pitched in, along with wife Charlene. Fritz Jacobi said, "We just felt the ultimate prankster deserved the ultimate payback, and he got it!" And the two later played three hours of golf together.

"So we're still talking," Whitaker said, "but it's going to be fun getting even!"[27]

Into the life of every couple . . . some fun must fall! Life without a laughter break once in a while can get pretty grim. It's okay to laugh! In fact, it should be made a requirement for each couple to learn to laugh together.

To "laugh" is to chuckle, giggle, roar, chortle, guffaw, snicker, titter, cackle, break up, roll in the aisle, howl, make merry, be joyful, belly laugh, and to split one's side! And in today's world there is a laughter dearth! Over time, chuckling this much also lowers blood pressure and heart rate, reduces pain, strengthens the immune system, and cuts down on stress-creating hormones. Biggest problem: finding that many things to laugh about!"

The One enthroned in heaven laughs (Ps. 2:4).

❧

Deut. 15-16; Ps. 78:34-53; Prov. 1; Acts 11-12

April 2 — God's Special Messenger

In the spring of 1982 I was the speaker at a morning prayer group which meets in a town near Springfield, Illinois. Before I spoke, a neighboring pastor shared about his recent trip to Mexico.

He, along with several others, had gone there on a preaching mission. While they were returning, their van developed mechanical problems. After jacking up the van, the pastor crawled underneath to check out the problem. The jack collapsed, and he suddenly felt the crushing weight of the van on his chest. His companions quickly grabbed the bumper to lift the van. They weren't able to budge it. He cried out, "Jesus! Jesus!" Within a few seconds a youthful-looking man came running toward them. He was thin and small in stature. He was smiling. As he reached them, he grabbed the van and lifted it. The others joined in, and the van lifted like a feather.

As he was freed, the pastor felt his chest expand and the broken bones mend. The visitor then lowered the van, waved to them, and ran in the direction from which he had come until he disappeared on the horizon. No one knew who the mysterious visitor was or where he had come from![28]

Of all the personalities or supernatural beings talked about in the Bible, it's the angels who are most constantly depicted as being completely identified with heaven. As you read through the Bible and look up the angel stories, you will read such things as when the angel of the Lord called to Hagar in the wilderness "from heaven."

Then there is the time when Jacob saw angels at Bethel . . . there he saw a ladder reaching to heaven on which the angels of God were ascending and descending. In many other places the angels are named the "heavenly ones" or the "heavenly host."

When the angelic choir had finished their special song for the shepherds at the announcement of the birth of Jesus Christ, it says that they "went away into heaven." It was an angel "from heaven" who came and rolled away the stone from the tomb of Jesus. And it was our Lord himself who spoke often of "the angels in heaven." Angels make one of the most interesting biblical studies!

Then King Nebuchadnezzar leaped to his feet in amazement and asked his advisers, "Weren't there three men that we tied up and threw into the fire?" They replied, "Certainly, O king." He said, "Look! I see four men walking around in the fire, unbound and unharmed, and the fourth looks like a son of the gods" (Dan. 3:24-25).

༄

Deut. 17-19; Ps. 78:54-72; Prov. 2; Acts 13

April 3 — You Never Really Know

• Albert Einstein couldn't talk until he was four years old and couldn't read until he reached seven. He was described by his teacher as "mentally slow, unsociable, and adrift forever in his foolish dreams." He was later expelled from the Zurich Polytechnic School.

• When Peter J. Daniel was a fourth grader, Mrs. Phillips, who happened to be his teacher, told him often, "Peter, you're no good, you're a bad apple and you're never going to amount to anything." Peter never did learn to read or write until he was 26. What made a change? A friend stayed with him and read to him the book, *Think and Grow Rich* by Napoleon Hill. Today he owns many of the street corners that he used to fight on and authored his book, *Mrs. Phillips, You Were Wrong!*

• Beethoven was not very good on the violin because he preferred playing his own compositions rather than working to improve his techniques. His teacher said, "You are hopeless as a composer."

• Louis Pasteur was just a very mediocre student in his undergrad studies. Later he ranked 15th out of 22 students in his chemistry major.

• Babe Ruth is considered by many sports authorities and historians to be one of the greatest athletes of all time. Of course he is best known for hitting the most home runs in a season . . . but did you know he also holds the record for most strike-outs?

• Enrico Caruso had parents who wanted him to become an engineer. They were motivated by his voice teacher who said, "He has no voice and cannot sing."

• The noted sculptor Rodin had a father who said, "I have an idiot for a son." Rodin attempted three different times to gain admittance to an art school. He had been described by a teacher as "the worst pupil in this school." His uncle chimed in by calling him uneducable.

• Fred Astaire took a screen test from the testing director at MGM in 1933. The director wrote a memo: "Can't act! Slightly bald! Can dance a little!" Astaire had that memo framed and hung over the fireplace in his Beverly Hills home.

• Leo Tolstoy, who later wrote *War and Peace*, flunked out of college. They described him as "both unable and unwilling to learn."

Surprise, surprise . . . we just never really know about people. As teachers we must be very careful not to tag, categorize, finalize, or write some people off prematurely. It's easy to be wrong when with some encouragement we might be teaching a future president!

Jesus looked at them and said, "With man this is impossible, but not with God; all things are possible with God" (Mark 10:27).

◦◦◦

Deut. 20-21; Ps. 79; Prov. 3; Acts 14

April 4 — How to Become a Hall-of-Famer

When former Brave great Henry Aaron returned to Milwaukee's County Stadium on the opening day of the 1975 season to play for the Brewers, one of the first players to greet him was the team's young shortstop. "Hello, Mr. Aaron," said the 19 year old who was entering his second season as the youngest player in the majors. "I'm Robin Yount."

Mr. Yount and Mr. Aaron will undoubtedly be reunited in Cooperstown in the summer of 1998. That's when Yount, who announced his retirement at the age of 38, after 20 years with the Brewers, figures to be inducted into the Baseball Hall of Fame. But Yount, in typically laconic fashion, downplayed that prospect. "It's not my position to make that decision," he said. "I can only say I'm happy with the way my career went."

Only four men . . . Pete Rose, Aaron, Carl Yastrzemski, and Ty Cobb . . . have more big league at-bats than Yount's 11,008. He was the MVP (Most Valuable Player) at two positions, shortstop in 1982 and centerfield in 1989, and his 3,142 hits place him thirteenth on the all-time list. Once asked to name the game's three most dangerous hitters, Boston Red Sox pitcher Roger Clemens said, "Robin Yount in the first, Robin Yount in the fourth, and Robin Yount in the seventh."

At the retirement press conference, a tearful Bud Selig, the Brewers' owner, said, "I don't think many people understand how rare it is for a player to come to a franchise, play two decades, and never cause one iota of a problem. He played the game every single day the way it's supposed to be played."

Before Christmas, Yount found himself playing golf with future Chicago White Sox minor leaguer Michael Jordan. Yount, who won the match, said, "Michael told me how great retirement was, playing golf all the time. That didn't last long. In a week or two I might go to the Bucks (Milwaukee's NBA basketball team) and ask for a tryout."[29]

To become a Hall-of-Famer isn't easy . . . and we must also acknowledge that Yount is a gifted athelete. Yet there are life lessons for all of us. Commitment to his chosen lifestyle, consistency that lasted over two decades, people relationships that worked, a team player, a role model, and a man who made a difference in his community. It's not so important how you start or what you choose to do with your life. What is important is how you finish. Life is not a sprint . . . it's a marathon!

Trust in the Lord with all your heart and lean not on your own understanding; in all your ways acknowledge him, and he will make your paths straight (Prov. 3:5-6).

Deut. 22-23; Ps. 80; Prov. 4; James 1-2

April 5 — Real Love

Moses Mendelssohn, the grandfather of the well-known German composer, was not handsome. He had a grotesque hunchback.

One day he visited a merchant in Hamburg who had a lovely daughter named Frumtje. Moses fell hopelessly in love with her. But Frumtje was repulsed by his misshapen appearance.

When it came time for him to leave, Moses gathered his courage and climbed the stairs to her room to take one last opportunity to speak with her. She was a vision of heavenly beauty. After several attempts at conversation, Moses shyly asked, "Do you believe marriages are made in heaven?"

"Yes," she answered, looking at the floor. "And do you?"

"Yes, I do," he replied. "You see, in heaven at the birth of each boy, the Lord announces which girl he will marry. When I was born, my future bride was pointed out to me. Then the Lord added, 'But your wife will be humpbacked.'

"Right then and there I called out, 'Oh Lord, a humpbacked woman would be a tragedy. Please, Lord, give me the hump and let her be beautiful.' "

Then Frumtje looked up into his eyes and was stirred by some deep memory. She reached out and gave Mendelssohn her hand and later became his devoted wife.[30]

There's a wonderful line that describes this kind of love from the writings of the apostle Paul which says love "always protects, always trusts, always hopes, always perseveres."

Bennett Cerf relates this story about a bus that was bumping along a back road in the South. In one seat a wispy old man sat holding a bunch of fresh flowers. Across the aisle was a young girl whose eyes came back again and again to the man's flowers. The time came for the old man to get off. Impulsively he thrust the flowers into the girl's lap. "I can see you love the flowers," he explained, "and I think my wife would like for you to have them. I'll tell her I gave them to you." The girl accepted the flowers, then watched the old man get off the bus and walk through the gate of a small cemetery.

Love is a very special kind of gift . . . in order to be loved it is given without thought of a reward coming back. Let's always remember to love in action as well as in words.

And so we know and rely on the love God has for us. God is love. Whoever lives in love lives in God, and God in him (1 John 4:16).

⬠

Deut. 24-25; Ps. 81; Prov. 5; James 3-5

April 6 — Mary and Salome

Mary, the mother of Jesus, was referred to by the Jews as the daughter of Eli; but early Christian writers called her the daughter of Joakim and Anna. She was related by marriage to Elizabeth, the wife of Zacharias, the priest.

Salome, most biblical scholars agree, was the name of the beloved disciple's (John) mother . . . but further conjecture, on quite reliable grounds, states that she was the sister of Mary. Very little is written about her in the Gospel narratives. What is evident is that she, like her two sons John and James, was a very devoted follower of Jesus and was present at the Crucifixion and assisted at His entombment.

We can only speculate about the sister relationship between Mary and Salome. What did this sister do when Mary announced that she was pregnant by the Holy Spirit?

Perhaps no other mother in history has suffered so long or so intensely in long travail for her son as Mary did in deep concern for Jesus from His conception, His birth in Bethlehem, to the final tragic night on Golgotha. Mary, we can also assume, was marked by profound thoughtfulness and a maternal kind of love. This is indicated in the biblical passage which says that, "His mother kept all these things in her heart." I tend to picture Salome as being the more happy, the more out-going, the bubbly one of these two sisters. Do you think they laughed together? Can you imagine what some of their sister-to-sister talks would have covered? It's so hard for us to see the human side of such awesome biblical people, especially Mary. Have you wondered who would have been her support system? My premise is that her own sister, her own flesh and blood, Salome, was there to listen, to comfort, to pray with, and encourage. Even at the foot of the Cross when Jesus committed his mother to the care of John, His beloved disciple, by saying, "Mary, behold your son," and to John, "Behold your mother." The Bible indicates that Salome would have been there, too!

In the sixth month, God sent the angel Gabriel to Nazareth . . . to a virgin pledged to be married to a man named Joseph, a descendant of David. The virgin's name was Mary (Luke 1:26-27). Many women were there, watching from a distance. They had followed Jesus from Galilee to care for his needs. Among them were Mary Magdalene, Mary the mother of James and Joses, and the mother of Zebedee's sons (Matt. 27:55-56).

Deut. 26-27; Ps. 82; Prov. 6; Acts 15

April 7 — The Guardian Angel

A young couple, let's call them Paul and Mary, had struggled with life and as most young couples do, attempted everything they could to scrape together enough money to purchase their first house. Both worked and both were diligent so they could reach their goal. After some years of married life they had enough to purchase a small house on the edge of a modest development. It had one drawback . . . but which also put the purchase price of the house within their reach. The railroad tracks ran across the back of their property. They hesitated, but purchased the house and put up a fence across the back.

Children were soon born. First a son, then a daughter, nearly two years apart in age. The backyard was the favorite outdoors play area . . . sand box, swing set, and a little treehouse. The children were always warned, "Don't leave the backyard and don't go on the railroad tracks!"

Mary was standing at the kitchen sink washing the dishes one glorious spring morning. Just cleaning up after breakfast, Paul had left for work and the two kids were in the back yard. The garden was alive with flowers, rows of carefully planted veggies were peaking up through the soil. The smell of clover filled the air. What a gorgeous day to be alive after the long Minnesota winter had finally passed.

As she looked out, she was suddenly aware that the backyard gate was ajar, open! How? She didn't know. She searched the backyard with her eyes and didn't see the kids! Then she spotted four-year-old Jason . . . sitting casually on the railroad tracks playing with the stones. Two-year-old Melissa was toddling after her big brother and was just starting the climb up to the railway bed. Mary's heart stopped! Panic! Then at almost the same moment . . . she saw the train coming around the bend with whistle blaring. She raced from the house screaming, "Jason! Melissa!" She knew from the nearness of the approaching train and the distance she still had to cover that she would never be able to reach her kids. She shouted a prayer, "Jesus! Jesus! Jesus!"

As she ran shouting, she saw a figure, pure white, striking, and heavenly, lift Jason off the tracks and reach down to grab Melissa. While the train roared past . . . this being, whatever it was, stood by the track with an arm around each child as they watched the train go by.

When the mother reached the tracks, Jason and Melissa were standing alone!

See that you do not look down on one of these little ones. For I tell you that their angels in heaven always see the face of my Father in heaven (Matt. 18:10).

⌒⌒

Deut. 28; Ps. 83; Prov. 7; Gal. 1-2

April 8 — Portrait of a Thief

Elmer Kelen turned to leave the studio of a young Hungarian artist named Arpad Sebesy. He was angry and his parting words were, "That's a rotten portrait and I refuse to pay for it!" The artist was crushed. He had spent weeks on this painting, and now the 500 pengos that he was going to lose on the deal flashed through his mind. Bitterly he recalled that the millionaire had only posed three times so that the painting had to be done virtually from memory. Still, he didn't think it was such a bad likeness.

Before the millionaire left his studio the artist called out, "One minute. Will you give me a letter saying you refused the portrait because it didn't resemble you?" Glad to get off the hook so easily, Kelen agreed.

A few months later the Society of Hungarian Artists opened its exhibition at the Gallery of Fine Arts in Budapest. Soon afterwards Kelen's phone began to ring. Within half an hour he appeared at the art gallery and headed for the wing where a Sebesy painting was on display. It was the one he had rejected.

He glanced at the title and his face turned purple. Storming into the office of the gallery manager, he demanded that the portrait be removed at one. The manager explained quietly that all of the paintings were under contract to remain in the gallery the full six weeks of the exhibit.

Kelen raged, "But it will make me the laughingstock of Budapest. It's libelous! I'll sue!"

The manager turned to his desk, drew out the letter Kelen had written at Sebesy's request, and said, "Just a moment. Since you yourself admit that the painting does not resemble you, you have no jurisdiction over its fate."

In desperation Kelen offered to buy the painting, only to find the price was now ten times that of the original figure. With his reputation at stake, Kelen immediately wrote out a check for 5,000 pengos.

Not only did the artist sell the rejected portrait to the man who had originally commissioned it, he also received ten times the first price and achieved his revenge by exhibiting it with the title: "Portrait of a Thief."

Revenge is a tricky kind of a thing. How many put-downs will equal one insult? How many wrongs will make a right? When is enough revenge enough? The Lord tells us that we are to leave such things to Him. In an honest act of forgiveness we can cut the endless act of a wrong, followed by an act of revenge, followed by. . . .

Do not take revenge, my friends, but leave room for God's wrath
for it is written: "It is mine to avenge; I will repay,"
says the Lord (Rom. 12:19;NIV).

⁓

Deut. 29-30; Ps. 84; Prov. 8; Gal. 3-4

April 9 — The Human Presence

Dr. Paul Brand, in his book *Fearfully and Wonderfully Made,* tells this story:

> As an intern on night duty in a London hospital, I called on 81-year-old Mrs. Twigg. This spry, courageous lady had been battling cancer of the throat . . . but even with a raspy hoarse voice she remained witty and happy. Surgeons had removed her larynx and malignant tissue around it.
>
> She seemed to be making a good recovery until 2:00 a.m. one morning, when I was urgently summoned. She was sitting on the bed, leaning forward, blood spilling from her mouth. Immediately I guessed that an artery had eroded. I knew no way to stop the bleeding other than to thrust my finger into her mouth and press on the pulsing spot. I explored with my finger until I found the artery and pressed it shut.
>
> Nurses cleaned up around her face while Mrs. Twigg recovered her breath. Fear slowly drained from her as she began to trust. After 10 minutes had passed and she was breathing normally again, with her head tilted back, I tried to remove my finger to replace it with an instrument. Each time I removed my finger, blood spurted afresh and Mrs. Twigg panicked. Her jaw trembled, her eyes bulged, and she forcefully gripped my arm
>
> We settled into position. My right arm crooked behind her head, supporting her. I could see in her intense blue eyes a resolution to maintain that position for days if necessary, I could sense her mortal fear. She knew, as I did, if we relaxed our awkard posture, she would bleed to death.
>
> We sat like that for nearly two hours . . . I, an intern in my twenties, and this 81-year-old woman clung to each other because we had no other choice.
>
> The surgeon came and Mrs. Twigg and I, still entwined together in this strange embrace, were wheeled into the operating room. With everyone poised, I eased my finger out of her mouth . . . the blood clot held . . . her hand continued to clutch my shoulder and her eyes stayed on my face. In those two hours we had become almost one person.[31]

When pain or need or emergency strikes . . . it's the PRESENCE of another human being that really counts!

A despairing man should have the devotion of his friends (Job 6:14).

❧

Deut. 31-32; Ps. 85; Prov. 9; Gal. 5-6

April 10 — Starting All Over Again

Why is it that some people seem to radiate joy and enthusiasm in spite of adversity or trouble? How can it be that some people are excited all the time? These are some of the choice people that we all should be able to count as friends. Let's get into the story. The late Governor Charles Edison of New Jersey told this story about his father, a man of a resilient, undefeatable spirit — yes, the famous inventor, Thomas A. Edison.

On the night of December 9, 1914, the great Edison Industries of West Orange was virtually destroyed by fire. Thomas Edison lost two million dollars that night and much of his life's work went up in flames. He was insured for only $238,000, because the buildings had been made of concrete, at that time thought to be fireproof.

"My heart ached for him," Charles said. "He was 67 . . . not a young man . . . and everything was going up in flames. He spotted me. 'Charles,' he shouted, 'where's your mother?' 'I don't know, Dad,' I said. 'Find her,' he told me. 'Bring her here. She will never see anything like this again as long as she lives.' "

The next morning, walking about the charred embers of all his hopes and dreams, Thomas Edison said, "There is great value in disaster. All our mistakes are burned up. Thank God we can start anew."

And three weeks after the fire, his firm delivered the first phonograph! Now that's the story of a man who had learned how to face the adversities and disasters of this human existence. He also knew that 67 years were in the past . . . that the loss of money was nothing really, because there was that inner strength that would allow him to build again.

So what if life has collapsed around you, relationships have fallen apart, friendships are gone? There is always the possibility of starting all over again! Take heart, my friend. Today can be a new day! You can make a new start! The problems that have come into your life are an opportunity to give it another go. Build that friendship once more! There is always hope and help for you when you build on God's Word!

I have told you these things, so that in Me you may have peace. In this world you will have trouble. But take heart! I have overcome the world (John 16:33).

Deut. 33-34; Ps. 86; Prov. 10; Acts 16

April 11 — Killing the Rat

Some years ago, during the pioneer days of aviation, when things were new and flight was in its infancy, things were pretty crude. The sophistication and technology of our day was unheard of. There were problems and dangers which present no problem to us today. With that background in mind this story makes sense.

A brave pilot was making a flight around the world in one of those earlier, crudely built airplanes. It was built with a wooden frame and fabric covered the frame. Very fragile. On this particular leg of his journey, he had been in the air about two hours since his last landing, when he heard a noise in the plane. He looked all around, curious, then was alarmed when he recognized it as the gnawing of a rat! He realized that while his plane had been on the ground a rat had gotten in the plane, somehow. The danger of the rat was that it could easily gnaw through a vital cable or control line or even one of the important wooden struts. It was a very serious problem.

What to do? He was anxious and concerned. He was about two hours from his next landing strip. Perhaps we can appreciate his dilemma. He tried to think of a solution as he flew . . . then it dawned on him — the rat was a rodent. It was not made for heights, it was made for the ground and under the ground living. That presented the solution . . . therefore the pilot began to climb until he was flying at an altitude of more than 20,000 feet. Soon the gnawing ceased. The rat was dead! The rat couldn't survive in the atmosphere at that height. More than two hours later the pilot brought the plane safely to the next landing field and looked through the plane until he found the dead rat!

I can think of many kinds of rats that can kill a friendship . . . worry, fear, dishonesty, gossip, anger, and lying, to name a few, and you perhaps have more to add to this list. How do we rid ourselves of such rats which can gnaw and destroy relationships? The solution is really quite simple. Such things cannot live or breathe in the atmosphere of the secret places of the Most High. Such things die when we ascend to the Lord through prayer, reading His Word, and a commitment to follow Him. Here is one of the major keys to being a friend and making friends. The things which seek to destroy your friendships can be put aside into perspective in the presence of the Most High God.

We ought always to thank God for you, brothers, and rightly so, because your faith is growing more and more, and the love every one of you has for each other is increasing (2 Thess. 1:3).

❧

Josh. 1-3; Ps. 87; Prov. 11; Phil. 1-2

April 12 — The Scarred Stranger

A small orphaned boy lived with his grandmother. One night their house caught on fire, and the grandmother, attempting to rescue the boy who was asleep upstairs, perished in the flames. A crowd gathered around the burning house, and the boy's cries for help were heard above the crackling of the blaze. No one seemed to know what to do, for by this time the front of the house was a mass of flames.

Suddenly a stranger rushed from the crowd and circled to the back where he spotted an iron pipe that reached upstairs. He disappeared for a minute and then reappeared with the boy in his arms. Amid cheers, he climbed down the hot pipe as the boy hung around his neck.

Weeks later, a public hearing was held in the town hall to determine in whose custody the boy would be placed. Each person wanting the boy was allowed to speak briefly.

The first man said, "We have a big farm. Everybody needs the out-of-doors."

The second man told of the advantages he and his wife could provide. "I'm a teacher. I have a large library, and he would have an excellent education."

Others spoke, then finally the richest man in the small community said, "I am wealthy. I could give the boy everything already mentioned tonight — farm, education, and more, including money and travel. I'd like to take him home."

The judge asked, "Would anyone else like to say a word?"

From the back seat rose a stranger who had slipped into the hearing unnoticed. As he walked toward the front, deep suffering showed in his face. Reaching the front of the room, he stood directly in front of the little boy who sat with his head down. Slowly the stranger removed his hands from his pockets. A gasp went up from the crowd. The man's hands were terribly scarred.

Suddenly the boy let out a cry of recognition. Here was the man who had saved his life. His hands were scarred from climbing up and down the hot pipe. With a leap of joy, he threw himself around the stranger's neck and held on for dear life.

The farmer rose to leave, the teacher, too, and then the richest man also left. Everyone else had also departed, leaving the boy and his rescuer to face the judge alone. The scarred stranger had won without a word!

It is impossible for the blood of bulls and goats to take away sins
(Heb. 10:4).

✒

Josh. 4-5; Ps. 88; Prov. 12; Phil. 3-4

April 13 — The Empty Chair

Leslie Weatherhead tells the story of an old Scotsman who was quite ill. The family called for their "Domini," or minister. As the minister entered the sick room and sat down, he noticed that another chair on the opposite side of the bed had also been drawn up close.

The pastor said, "Well, Donald, I see I'm not your first visitor for the day."

The old man looked up, was puzzled for a moment, then recognized from the nod of the head that the pastor had noticed the empty chair. "Well, Pastor, I'll tell you about that chair. Many years ago I found it quite difficult to pray, so one day I shared this problem with my pastor. He told me not to worry about kneeling or about placing myself in some pious position. Instead he said, 'Just sit down, put a chair opposite you, and imagine Jesus sitting in it; then talk with Him as you would a friend.' " The aged old Scotsman then added, "I've been doing that ever since."

A short time later the daughter of the Scot called the minister once again. When he answered, she informed him that her father had died very suddenly. She was quite shaken for she had no idea death was so near. Then she continued, "I had just gone to lie down for an hour or two because he seemed to be sleeping so comfortably. When I went back, he was dead." Then she added thoughtfully, "Except now his hand was on the empty chair at the side of the bed. Isn't that strange?"

The minister said, "No, it's not so strange. I understand."

For all of us, prayer and the presence of Jesus must be as near and real as it was with this old Scot. In our mind we understand that, yes, Jesus Christ is near and real and that He hears us when we pray. But too often we act like He is such a great distance removed from us that we cannot reach Him in our times of need.

One of these days, all of us will have to face the reality of death. In that moment, you must move forward whether you want to or not. What a comfort it will be to reach out and place your hand into His and pass into eternity with Jesus!

For what is your life? It is even a vapor, that appeareth for a little time, and then vanisheth away (James 4:14;KJV).

࿇

Josh. 6-7; Ps. 89:1-18; Prov. 13; Acts 17

April 14 — Only One Plan

A legend recounts an incident that could have happened when Jesus Christ returned to heaven after His time on earth. Even in glory, He still carried the marks of His earthly journey with its cruel Cross and the shameful death He suffered.

The angel Gabriel approached Him and said, "Master, you must have suffered terribly for mankind down there."

Jesus replied that He had.

Gabriel continued, "And do they know and appreciate all about how You loved them and what You did for them?"

Jesus replied, "Oh, no! Not yet! Right now only a handful of people in Palestine know."

Gabriel was perplexed. He asked, "Then, what have You done to let everyone know about Your love for them?"

Jesus said, "I've asked Peter, James, John, and the other disciples, and a few more of their friends to tell others about Me. Those who are told will tell others in turn, and My story will be spread to the farthest reaches of the globe. Ultimately, all of mankind will have heard about My life and what I have done for them."

Gabriel frowned and looked rather skeptical. He knew what poor stuff men were made of. He said, "Yes, but what if Peter, James, John, and the others grow weary and give up? What if the people who come after them forget? What if way down in the twentieth century people just don't tell others about You? What if the plan breaks down?"

And Jesus answered, "I haven't made any other plans. I'm counting on them and the others who will follow!"

Twenty centuries have just about passed since this simple plan was set into motion. Jesus still has no alternative plan that any of us know about. It's still the same. The gospel of Jesus Christ, which is also called the "Good News," is still dependent upon telling others.

The first church and the early disciples simply adopted His priorities and devoted themselves to reaching their world with this message. In those days, they had no sophisticated communication systems. All they did was tell others about Jesus Christ.

Christ counted on them, and they delivered. Now, it's our turn. Have we done as well? Can you be counted on?

But you will receive power when the Holy Spirit comes on you; and
you will be my witnesses in Jerusalem, and in all Judea and
Samaria, and to the ends of the earth (Acts 1:8).

ॐ

Josh. 8-9; Ps. 89:19-37; Prov. 14; 1 Thess. 1-3

April 15 — Sisters of Fortune

It is said that tragedy brings siblings together like nothing else ever could. Such was the case with the three Fortune sisters — Ethel, Alice, and Mabel — who survived the sinking of the *Titanic* on the night of April 14-15, 1912.

Although the girls were young, the horror of the event remained in their memories.

As ship's officers and crew scrambled frantically to fill lifeboats, Mrs. Mark Fortune stood on the deck with her husband. Their son, Charles, stood nearby. Mark Fortune assured his wife that he and the boy would find passage on another ship or lifeboat. However, the word had passed rather quickly that any rescue would probably come too late. Most of the men knew this and urged their wives to scramble aboard boats. Many women refused.

As the Fortune family huddled on the slanting decks, one of the girls called out to Charles to "take care of Father." Finally, the ladies entered the creaking lifeboat and were dropped into the inky darkness below, settled in for a four-hour journey on the choppy waves of the North Atlantic. Toward dawn, the rescue ship *Carpathia* steamed into view and fired rockets.

Upon stepping onto the deck of *Carpathia*, the girls and their mother discovered that Mark and Charles were not among the survivors. The grief on that chilly morning was horrible to see.

History tells us little of the rest of these girls' lives, but you can count on the fact that arguments were few and far between. Tragedy has a way of drawing close those who love each other. Especially sisters. They are better able than most to convey feelings and fears and joy.

Have you and your sister (or sisters) walked through a valley together? Has the experience strengthened you because you didn't have to walk alone? Perhaps your lives together have been richer than they would have been otherwise . . . because of the healing only a sister can bring.

It might be good to remember that the next time you are mad at your sister — or vice versa — that she once dried your tears over a broken romance, or reassured you after the death of a parent. Remembering the bad makes it all good. Tough times make us grateful for each other.[32]

Where you go I will go, and where you stay I will stay. Your people will be my people and your God my God. Where you die I will die, there I will be buried (Ruth 1:16-17).

╰∾╯

Josh. 10-11; Ps. 89:38-52; Prov. 15; 1 Thess. 4-5

April 16 — The Gentle Touch

Terror tightened the native's throat as he clutched his dying son and ran through the hot dust two miles to Africa's Baragwanath Hospital. Instinctively he knew it was too late and upon arrival had to sadly turn homeward with the baby cold in his arms. The child had died of gastric enteritis and tears dropped in the dirt as the sobbing father carried the lifeless form.

Vusamazulu Mutwa built the crude coffin and prepared his tiny son's body for burial. To a Bantu, proper burial is of vital importance. To be buried in an unknown grave or a pauper's grave is the deepest disgrace that can befall a Bantu anywhere in Africa. But the Bantu has no access to any cemetery unless he belongs to a recognized church and the funeral is presided over by a minister. A well-known authority has said, "Determination to have a proper burial is a strong reason why natives turn to Christianity."

The grief-stricken parents went to their "Christian" pastor, whose church the wife had attended many years; the father had never accepted the faith. When they asked for a funeral the pastor flatly refused, giving no reason for that denial. Later Mutwa acidly wrote, "Strangely, the priest knew exactly what he was doing to me when he refused to bury my son, for over the years I had explained to him all the laws and customs of the Bantu. He refused simply because I was not, with the rest of my family, a member of his church."

From this tragic experience Vusamazulu Mutwa wrote a scorching essay on "Why Christianity Has Failed in Africa." It is part of his bitter book, *Africa Is My Witness*.[33]

Most of us and most of the people we lead in some small or large way have been hurt by rigid and pharisaical leaders who in the name of Christ or religion have demanded a legalism, a hard rigid code of action devoid of human compassion and love. Jess Moody said, "God never called us to be dour judges, standing in robes of prudery. We are in the business of redemptive involvement . . . not hyper-righteous investigation. We must not be a terror for sinners, but a haven for them."

There's a distinct danger that we can become like the "whited sepulchers" which Jesus denounced in holy anger. Paul the Apostle wrote that "the fruit of the Spirit is GENTLENESS!"

The fruit of the Spirit is love, joy, peace, patience, kindness, good-ness, faithfulness, gentleness, self-control; against such there is no law . . . if we live by the Spirit, let us also walk by the Spirit (Gal. 5:22-25).

༜

Josh. 12-14; Ps. 90; Prov. 16; 2 Thess. 1-3

April 17 — Earthquakes and Questions

Terror struck that April morning in 1906 when the San Andreas Fault settled, shaking San Francisco to the ground! While thousands of panic-stricken refugees struggled to get out of the burning city, a man with rumpled hair, keen eyes, and a hawk-like nose rode into the city on the only train to reach it that day.

He was William James, the famous psychologist who was then in his sixty-fourth year and suffering from a severe heart condition. For the next 12 hours James scrambled amid roaring flames, falling buildings, and piled rubble. He had a notebook in hand, all the while eagerly asking the fleeing inhabitants, "How did you feel when the shaking began?" He then proceeded to ask, "What thoughts flashed through your mind?" and concluded with, "Did your heart beat faster?"

This was the passion and drive that made Will James one of the foremost scientists of his generation. His thirst for truth caused him to explore, experiment, change, and grow. He had an insatiable curiosity to learn about every facet of the human personality and all he could about the secrets of life and living.

Tragically, the difference between scientists like William James and some religionists is, the scientist openly admits he does not possess all of truth and passionately seeks it. On the other hand, too many religionists sit smugly claiming they have the answer to all of life's problems. Because of this attitude, some thinking people have looked upon religion as arrogant ignorance and there is very little about it which seems appealing. It really doesn't take much of a genius to know there are many unanswerable problems to life, and even Paul, the great Apostle, freely admitted, "We see through a glass darkly."

Life and Christianity have great areas of questions that have not been answered at this point. What an adventure awaits us as we continue to explore the new areas yet unexplored. The Bible tells us that we are to "seek to excel." This is in the use of the gifts of the Holy Spirit, but the application can also be made for other areas.

Explore the Word of God, devour it for life's answers. Become a sharp student and develop your powers of observation. Ask questions. Look for answers. There are new truths for you to discover from the Bible.

Do your best to present yourself to God as one approved, a workman who does not need to be ashamed and who correctly handles the word of truth (2 Tim. 2:15).

❧

Josh. 15-16; Ps. 91; Prov. 17; Acts 18

April 18 — Who Did You Say?

A teacher of English Literature began her class session by challenging her students to identify this poem and the author:

Listen my children and you shall hear
Of the midnight ride of Paul Revere,
On the 18th of April in '75;
Hardly a man is now alive
Who remembers that famous day and year.

The first hand that went up got it right, "Teacher, that is the first verse of Henry Wadsworth Longfellow's poem, "Paul Revere's Ride." Then she read the last four lines of the poem, not quite as familiar as the first verse:

In the hour of darkness and peril and need,
The people will waken and listen to hear
The hurrying hoofbeats of that steed,
And the midnight message of Paul Revere.

The teacher's question this time was, "What was the name of Paul Revere's horse?" The students were then assigned to read all 13 verses to see if anyone could come up with the name of his trusty horse. The horse is mentioned a number of times but the name is never given.

What's the point this teacher was attempting to get across? That while Paul Revere got all the mention and glory, some unknown horse made a most significant contribution in order to make the famous ride possible. Now I'm also aware that many historians feel that this poem gives Revere more credit than should have been due to him, but that's another issue.

While Emmit Smith of the Dallas Cowboys gets the credit for another record-setting year of carrying the football, very few can name the players in front of him who do the blocking to open up the holes through which he makes his spectacular runs.

No one who experiences any kind of success in life does it completely alone. We have all received support from some behind-the-scenes person, be it a friend, parents, teacher, or mentor. Let's learn to share the credit where credit is also due.

Tychicus, the dear brother and faithful servant in the Lord, will tell you everything, so that you also may know how I am and what I am doing. I am sending him to you for this very purpose (Eph. 6:21-22).

⌥

Josh. 17-18; Ps. 92; Prov. 18; 1 Cor. 1-2

April 19 — Sisters

We had the usual fights and bickering as children, but once we reached our teenage years my sister and I left all that behind. I can't remember a quarrel between us after we were grown. Everyone agreed we were almost clones of each other, with mutual passions for cooking, sewing, and singing. I always wanted to have the red hair and green eyes Sharon was born with; she envied the blond hair and blue eyes I inherited.

She always said I had the "brains," but after her children were grown she attended college and became an accomplished bookkeeper. I admired her flair for nourishing and loving not only her own, but also a number of foster children, and also the strength to relinquish her place in their lives when the time came. We always celebrated each other's accomplishments and steps forward with a total lack of jealousy or envy, and we bore each other's hurts as though they were our own.

But our sisterhood was cut short by her early death due to many medical problems. She had cancer and conquered it — remaining free of it 12 years after the surgery that removed it. But she was also diabetic, and that disease followed her with a vengeance beyond its usual limits. The far-reaching effects of it finally caused kidney failure, near-blindness, and eventually, death at the age of 45. However, even that could not obliterate the intertwining of our lives. The memories live on; they even continue to be made.

This sister thing even transcends generations. I revel in the accomplishments of her children, and the joy of the arrival of each of her grandchildren. Many times her children and mine blend to celebrate a holiday. It's a normal "family" thing to do, but there is an underlying grasp at continuity that makes it more. It's as though a part of her "motherhood" has been passed on to me. Her children know it, and I know it, but it's a gentle, subliminal thing of which we never speak.

Ten years after her death I still cannot eat a patty melt (Sharon's favorite) without a lump forming in my throat — in fact, I have even stopped trying. Sometimes when I'm flipping through my recipe cards and I come to one in her own handwriting, my heart does a double thump. When something remarkable (or unremarkable) happens in my life, I even yet occasionally think, *I must call Sharon.*

Yes, my sister was my soulmate and filled a part of my heart that no one else ever could. But there is no void — she is still there.

In my Father's house are many rooms; if it were not so, I would have told you. I am going there to prepare a place for you (John 14:2).

༄

Josh. 19-20; Ps. 93; Prov. 19; 1 Cor. 3-4

April 20 — The Twenty-six Million Dollar Snub

It was 1884 and a young man and his parents were visiting in Europe. The young man died and his grieving parents returned sorrowfully with his body back home to America.

When the funeral was over the parents began to discuss what might be a fitting memorial to his memory. They eliminated tombstones, ornate graves, or a statue and decided that it should be a living memorial, something that would benefit other young people.

After looking at many possibilities they finally decided that something in the field of education would be most fitting.

An appointment was set to meet with Charles Eliot, then-president of Harvard University. He asked what he could do for them.

Together, they explained about the untimely death of their beloved son and expressed their desire to create or establish a memorial to his memory. Something that would live on to help others like their son to be educated.

Eliot looked at this couple with aristocratic disdain. "Perhaps you have in mind a scholarship," he said crisply and curtly.

"No," said the lady, "we were thinking of something more substantial than that."

Eliot interrupted, "I must explain to you," with a patronizing air, "that what you suggest costs a great deal of money. Buildings are expensive."

There was a pause, the lady got up from her chair slowly and asked, "Mr. Eliot, what has this entire university cost?"

Eliot muttered something about several million dollars.

"Oh, we can do much better than that," replied the lady who seemed to have made up her sharp mind. "Come, dear," she motioned to her husband, "I have an idea." And together they left.

The following year, President Charles Eliot of Harvard heard about the unpretentious couple, who had given $26 MILLION for the memorial to their son.

The memorial was to be built in California and would be named "Leland Stanford Jr. University."

It can be very costly to mis-judge or pre-judge anyone we meet in life.

Do not consider his appearance or his height for I have rejected him. The Lord does not look at the things man looks at. Man looks at the outward appearance, but the Lord looks at the heart (1 Sam. 16:7).

Josh. 21-22; Ps. 94:1-11; Prov. 20; 1 Cor. 5-6

❦

*Today one has to pass more tests to
get into college than Dad had to pass
to get out.*

❦

April 21 — Everybody Should Have a Friend Like . . .

Just about everybody knows the Jim Brady story . . . how the big, bluff, quick-witted "Bear," only two months after becoming White House press secretary, was shot in the head during the attempted assassination of President Reagan and how he has fought his way back from brain surgery and the enduring damage from the stray bullet.

Not many people know, however, about the ceaseless single-minded devotion of Bob Dahlgren, a man who loved Brady like himself.

A few months ago, Bob Dahlgren died in his sleep, at 52 years of age. It didn't even make the morning news. But during the long months following the shooting, it was Dahlgren who took the vigil with Brady's wife, Sarah, through the long series of brain operations. It was Dahlgren and his wife Suzie who took the Bradys' young son Scott into their home through the early days of the ordeal.

It was Dahlgren who helped recovery by arranging convivial "happy hours" with Brady's friends by his hospital bedside.

As Brady recovered and was able, in a wheelchair, to return to a semi-normal life, it was Dahlgren, always Dahlgren, who scouted out the advance arrangements, who helped load and unload his friend from the specially equipped van in which Brady did most of his traveling.

It was Dahlgren who helped Sarah field the interminable questions about Brady's health and who spent countless hours keeping Brady's friends posted on his condition, who dealt with the doctors, lawyers, exploiters, bandwagon-climbers. It was Dahlgren who helped organize a foundation to assure financial support for the family.

For more than four and one-half years after Brady was shot, Bob Dahlgren devoted virtually all his time to the man he loved. And he did so with little recognition, and no hint of seeing anything in return. Never, ever did Dahlgren complain or hesitate when needed.

As Dr. Arthur Kobrine, the surgeon who lived through Brady's long ordeal with him, once said, "Everyone should have a friend like Bob Dahlgren!"[34]

And it has been said, "It's the thought that counts." Do you know what? It's not really the thought that counts. What really counts in friendship is action! We need more than words to make friendships happen and last!

Dear children, let us not love with words or tongue but with actions and in truth (1 John 3:18).

❧

Josh. 23-24; Ps. 94:12-23; Prov. 21; 1 Cor. 7-8

April 22 — Relative Importance

George had a friend with a very inflated opinion of himself. George decided to help his friend lose this quirk. Subtly, George mentioned that he knew Jay Leno. The friend said, "Oh yeah . . . prove it!" So in a few minutes of driving they were in front of this huge house overlooking the beach at Malibu. It was most impressive.

After knocking, out came Jay who immediately said, "Come on in, George, and bring your friend!"

On the way home, this friend grudgingly said, "Okay, so you know Jay Leno."

Obviously this was not enough, so George let it slip, offhandedly, "Yes, Jay and I and the president are quite well acquainted."

The friend tossed his head and shouted, "Now, that's too much . . . I'll pay the airfare . . . let's go to DC and we'll see about that!"

At the White House, they had just arrived and out came President Clinton to greet them saying, "Hi George. Come on in, George, old buddy, and bring your friend."

Later, George's friend looked around sheepishly and admitted, "Well, yeah, you do know the president."

George sensed his friend needed further deflation, so he casually remarked, "Yes, but you know the pope has an even nicer office than the president has."

"What?!" yelled his wide-eyed friend. "You know the pope? I'll put up $10,000 that you can't even get in to see the pope!"

In a few days they were in Rome, with George knocking on a door to the Vatican. A cardinal came out, extending his hand to George, saying, "Your friend will have to stay outside, but come on in, George, what a delight to have you again."

About an hour went by, when out came the pope onto the balcony, waving to the crowd, and with one arm around George, he made his speech to the gathered crowd in St. Peter's Square.

Later, outside, George looked around for his friend and found him out cold in the courtyard. George rushed over and helped his friend up and apologized for shocking him so much. But his friend simply shook his head and mumbled, "It's not that you knew the pope. It was the crowd! They kept asking each other, 'Who's that guy with George?' "

Do not exalt yourself in the king's presence, and do not claim a place among great men; it is better for him to say to you, "Come up here," than for him to humiliate you before a nobleman (Prov. 25:6-7).

Judg. 1-2; Ps. 95; Prov. 22; 1 Cor. 9-10

April 23 — The Restroom Angel

He was overdressed for the assignment and out of character for his immediate job! He was whistling while he toiled, smiling and greeting me as I ambled to my place.

This man was removing cigarette butts from the bathroom urinals, utilizing small scissors to retrieve the soggy and offensive stubs.

"That's not an envious job you're doing," I said.

"No Sir! No Sir! It's not! But it must be done. Looks bad when customers come into the bathroom. Makes people think we don't care or that we are not clean. So, I clean them up."

"Do men throw their cigarette butts in the urinals very often?" I inquired, as this well-dressed man checked the bathroom stalls.

"Often?! Every morning I pick several just out of one urinal."

"Why do people throw them in there?" I asked.

"Lazy, just lazy; or they don't care! Maybe they never were raised any better; maybe they have never grown up, perhaps they do it for meanness," he whispered determinedly under his breath. "And maybe they never had to clean up after themselves."

Upon leaving, I inquired, "You been working here long?"

I was startled out of idle chitchat when he replied, "I don't work here! I come here almost everyday. I have an office across the street."

"YOU WHAT??? You don't work here, and you clean up the bathroom? Why?"

"Because of the next man who comes in here and uses this place; I want him to notice the area is clean and that someone cares."

"Even if he throws a butt into your cleaned urinal?"

"Doesn't matter," said the stranger. "What counts is that this facility is clean for an hour, maybe two. And if the next man comes in here and notices this bathroom is clean, maybe he will comprehend the cleanness and leave the bathroom a better place when he walks out."

I washed my hands, tore paper from the towel dispenser, and found myself wiping up the extra water around the sink and cleaning the water droplets from the mirror. While throwing the paper towel into the garbage I picked up a piece of wet, used towel and placed it in the can.

Once outside I saw him walking and whistling his way out of the building, straightening his tie, sauntering across the street to his office.[35]

If I speak in the tongues of men and of angels, but have not love, I am only a resounding gong or a clanging cymbal (1 Cor. 13:1).

Judg. 3-4; Ps. 96; Prov. 23; 1 Cor. 11-12

April 24 — Driven to the Edge

The enemy of our soul is wise in waging warfare. We are prepared for the major battles . . . but the drip, drip, erosion of the never-ending attacks behind the scenes get to us. Here's a poem that seems to sum this struggle up. The author is unknown.

> I thought, if defeat came at all,
> It would be in a big, bold
> Definite joust
> With a cause or a name.
> And it came.
>
> I had not thought the daily skirmish
> With a few details, worthwhile;
> And so I turned my back upon them
> Year on year; until one day
> A million minutia blanketed together
> Rose up and overwhelmed me.

A pastor from Texas, who shall remain unnamed, was scheduled to speak at a minister's conference. He was running late because the alarm hadn't gone off. In his hurrying he cut himself while shaving — lots of blood. Then his shirt wasn't properly ironed from the dry-cleaners. And when he left the hotel, running to his car, he noticed a flat tire!

Really disgusted and harried by this time, quickly changing the tire, running back to his room to wash his hands, he finally got underway with a squeal of tires and a burst of speed. Racing through town he ran a stop sign. As fate or whatever would have it, a police squad was checking that intersection and he immediately heard the scream of a siren and saw the flashing of red lights!

Really agitated now, the minister jumped out of his car, nearly ran back to the patrol man, almost shouting, "Well, go ahead and give the ticket. Everything else has gone wrong today!" The policeman quietly got out of his car and walked to meet the minister saying quietly, "Sir, I used to have days like that before I became a Christian."

Needless to say, the quiet rebuke from this stranger did its work. The pastor apologized, asked forgiveness, and went on his way . . . this time praying for strength and discipline to correct a faulty attitude.

Not only so, but we also rejoice in our sufferings, because we know that suffering produces perseverance; perseverance, character; and character, hope (Rom. 5:3-4).

∽

Judg. 5-6; Ps. 97; Prov. 24; 1 Cor. 13-14

April 25 — Who You Are Makes a Difference!

A teacher in New York decided to honor each of her seniors in high school by telling them the difference they each made. Using a process developed by Helice Bridges of Del Mar, California, she called each student to the front of the class, one at a time. First she told them how the student made a difference to her and the class. Then she presented each of them with a blue ribbon imprinted with gold letters which read: "WHO I AM MAKES A DIFFERENCE."

Afterwards the teacher decided to do a class project to see what kind of impact recognition would have on a community. She gave each of the students three more ribbons and instructed them to go out and spread this acknowledgment ceremony. Then they were to follow up on the results and report back to the class in about a week.

One of the boys went to a junior executive in a nearby company and honored him for helping him with his career planning. He gave him the blue ribbon, two extra ribbons, and said, "We're doing a class project on recognition, and we'd like you to go out, find somebody to honor, and give them a blue ribbon, then give them the extra ribbon so they can acknowledge a third person to keep this acknowledgment ceremony going. Then please report back to me and tell me what happened."

Later that day the junior executive went to his boss, a grouchy fellow. He told him he deeply admired him for being creative, and then asked him to acknowledge someone else with the remaining ribbon.

The boss was greatly surprised to receive the honor. That night he came home and said to his 14-year-old son, "The most incredible thing happened to me today. One of the junior executives came in and told me he admired me and gave me a blue ribbon for being a creative genius. Imagine! I started thinking about whom I would honor and I thought about you. I want to honor you. My days are hectic and when I come home I don't pay a lot of attention to you. Sometimes I scream at you for not getting good grades or leaving your room in a mess . . . but somehow, tonight, I just wanted to let you know that you do make a difference. Besides your mother, you are the most important person in my life. You're a great kid and I love you!"

The startled boy started to sob and sob and couldn't stop crying. His whole body shook. He looked up through his tears and said, "I was planning on committing suicide tomorrow, Dad, because I didn't think you loved me. Now I don't need to."[36]

Do not withhold good from those who deserve it, when it is in your power to act (Prov. 3:27).

❦

Judg. 7-8; Ps. 98; Prov. 25; 1 Cor. 15

April 26 — The Kiss

Dr. Richard Selzer who is a surgeon, has written some very interesting human interest stories in one or more of his books, based on his life experiences as a doctor. One of my favorites is the following:

> I stand by the bed where a young woman lies, her face post-operative, her mouth twisted in palsy, clownish. A tiny twig of the facial nerve, the one to the muscles of her mouth has been severed. She will be thus from now on. The surgeon had followed with religious fervor the curve of her flesh; I promise you that. Nevertheless, to remove the tumor from her cheek, I had cut the little nerve. Her young husband is in the room. He stands on the opposite side of the bed, and together they seem to dwell in the evening lamplight, isolated from me, private. *Who are they,* I ask myself, *he and this wry-mouth I have made, who gaze at and touch each other so generously, greedily?*
> "Will my mouth always be like this?" she asks.
> "Yes," I say, "it will be. It is because the nerve was cut."
> She nods and is silent. But the young man smiles. "I like it," he says. "It is kind of cute."
> All at once I know who he is. I understand, and I lower my gaze. One is not bold in an encounter with a god. Unmindful, he bends to kiss her crooked mouth, and I am so close I can see how he twists his own lips to accommodate hers, to show her that their kiss still works.[37]

Love that is love is considerate. It's putting others at ease. It's a time to lift the spirits of another. It's to help put aside any fears of the future. What a way to open the inside doors of the spirit of another.

In our story we see a special kind of loving, doing all that is possible to avoid what may prove to be a point of concern. It's also given at what may be a great sacrifice, going the second mile, doing the very nice thing, accommodating actions so that somebody precious may be spared more pain. One of the things being discovered about relationships and marriages is that when a handicapped child is born into a home, in about 80 percent of the cases, that home will eventually come to divorce because of the extra pain, problems, and hurts to overcome. Let's make the accommodations necessary . . . even with a kiss, if necessary!

> *So I will very gladly spend for you everything I have and expend myself as well. If I love you more, will you love me less?* (2 Cor. 12:15).

❧

Judg. 9; Ps. 99; Prov. 26; 1 Cor. 16

April 27 — What Is Vitally Important?

A story is making the rounds about a recently widowed lady who was encouraged by her family to get a parrot to keep her company. "It will be some live creature that can talk to you and help you with your loneliness."

She went to a local pet store where the owner showed her a bird and enthusiastically sold this bird as having a 500-word vocabulary. She returned the next day to the pet store owner to report: "That parrot hasn't said one word yet!" A bit angry I might add.

"Does it have a mirror?" asked the storekeeper. "Parrots like to be able to look at themselves in the mirror. They think it's another bird to talk to."

The next day she was back, even a bit more angry, announcing that the parrot still didn't say a word!

"What about a ladder?" the storekeeper replied. "Parrots enjoy walking up and down a ladder and get so excited that they talk." So she bought the ladder and put it in the cage.

Sure enough, the next day she is back, the parrot will not talk! Not one word! "Does the parrot have a swing? Birds enjoy swinging so much that it induces them to talk." She bought the swing.

Two days later the lady returns to the store, obviously upset, to announce that the parrot had died! "I'm so terribly sorry to hear that, ma'am," said the saddened store keeper. "By the way, did the bird ever say anything, anything at all, before it died?"

"Yes," replied the lady. "It said, 'Don't they sell any bird food down there at that store?' "

Aren't we funny people? We are into readily buying mirrors by which to primp the outward looks; ladders so that we and others can climb higher; swings so that we have the latest and best in entertainment. But where is the sustenance for soul and spirit? And it still holds true that nobody can live on bread alone. Teacher, ma'am, sir, what are you feeding into the minds and spirits of your charges? Think of the implications of molding the life and character and soul and spirit of a human being that will live forever!!

These are the commands, decrees and laws the Lord your God directed me to teach you to observe in the land that you are crossing the Jordan to possess, so that you, your children and their children after them may fear the Lord your God as long as you live by keeping all his decrees and commands that I give you, and so that you may enjoy long life" (Deut. 6:1-2).

Judg. 10-11; Ps. 100; Prov. 27; 2 Cor. 1-2

April 28 — Acres of Diamonds

This classic story, "Acres of Diamonds" was told by Rev. Russell Conwell more than 5,000 times! The proceeds from this provided the funds to found Temple University. The story:

Is about a wealthy farmer who was probably one of the richest men in Africa. Hafid owned a large farm with fertile soil, herds of camels and goats, orchards of dates and figs. One day a wandering holy man visited his farm and mentioned that huge fortunes were being made discovering and mining diamonds — fortunes greater than even Hafid's.

This news captured Hafid's attention. He inquired of the holy man what diamonds were and where they could be found. The holy man said he wasn't sure of all the details but he had heard that diamonds were usually found in the white sands of rivers that flowed out from valleys formed by V-shaped mountains.

Hafid, eager to increase his fortune, sold his farm, herds, and orchards. He placed his family in the care of someone else and set out to find his fortune. Hafid's travels took him all over Africa. Finally, in deep despair he threw himself off a mountain and died a frustrated, broken, poor man.

The farmer that bought his farm was watering his camels one day and noticed a pretty rock in the river, because it sparkled. He took it home and put it on a shelf where the sun would strike it and splash rainbows of color across the room.

The same holy man came back to this same farm. He was immediately startled by the rainbow of light from the rock. Had Hafid returned? Well, no he hadn't, and he was no longer the owner of this farm.

Then taking the rock from the shelf, the holy man became animated. "That's a diamond!" he excitedly told the farmer. "Where did you find it?" The farmer, somewhat confused in the flurry of excitement explained that it came from down by the river.

"Show me," insisted the holy man.

The two of them went out to the river, which flowed out from a valley formed by a V-shaped mountain. And there they found a larger diamond, then another, and many more diamonds, large and small.

Actually the land, which Hafid sold to pursue his fortune elsewhere, turned out to be acres and acres of diamonds. In fact, it became the Kimberly, the richest diamond mine in all of South Africa![38]

The worries of this life, the deceitfulness of wealth and the desires
for other things come in and choke the word, making it unfruitful
(Mark 4:19).

☙

Judg. 12-14; Ps. 101; Prov. 28; 2 Cor. 3-5

April 29 — Does It Pay?

Max Jukes lived in the state of New York. He was not a Christian and did not believe in any sort of Christian training. His was the life of a reprobate. The girl he married was of the same opinion and had the same sort of questionable character. These were not nice people by any stretch of the imagination. Their personal lives and their home life was a mess.

Out of this union they have 1,026 descendants. Each of these descendants were followed through their lifetime with these results:

Three hundred of them died prematurely. One hundred of these descendants were sentenced to spend an average of 13 years each in prisons. One hundred-ninety of the girls were public prostitutes. There were more than 100 drunkards.

The results are that this family of descendants ended up costing the state and federal government millions of dollars — dollars that were spent to care for them on the welfare rolls, as well as making room for them in the prisons — and let alone what they cost in their immoral influence. Not a one of these descendants made any kind of a positive contribution to society that could be found.

But . . .

Jonathan Edwards lived in the same state at about the same time. He believed in Christian training. He was a well-known preacher in his day. The girl he married also was a committed Christian and set about to raise their family in these same concepts.

From this union they had 729 descendants that were studied. Out of this family have come 300 preachers. Further, 65 went on to become college professors and 13 became college presidents. Sixty of these family members became authors of what would be considered good books with a positive influence. Three were elected to become United States congressmen, and one was elected vice-president of the United States.

And except for Aaron Burr, a grandson of Edwards who married a lady of questionable character, the family has not cost the state or federal government a single dollar to care for. The Edwards family was a family who impacted our nation in a very positive way.

What's the major difference? Christian commitment and training against the absence of such. We must also add that the vast majority of the Edwards family became Christians at an early age.

Train a child in the way he should go, and when he is old
he will not turn from it (Prov. 22:6;NIV).

꙳

Judg. 15-16; Ps. 102:1-17; Prov. 29; 2 Cor. 6-7

April 30 — The Ugly Pet

A young boy and his family moved from a small southern town to a large metropolitan area in the northeastern United States. The young boy was very unhappy with the move for he had to leave behind all his friends. Beside, he knew he was going to hate big-city life. The one bright spot for the boy was that he had been allowed to bring his pet.

After moving into their new home, the boy and his pet went for a walk to see the neighborhood. As they strolled across a school yard, they were suddenly face to face with a local gang. The leader looked at the boy and said, "So you're the new kid in town. If you plan to live here, you have to join a gang and it better be mine!"

The boy told him, "We didn't have gangs where I came from, and I don't think it'd be right for me to join."

The bully responded, "You don't have a choice." Just then he noticed for the first time the boy's pet and began to laugh. "Look at that ugly dog. That is the ugliest thing I ever saw! Yellow, beady-eyed, short-tailed, long-nosed, short-legged ugly dog! What kind of a dog is it? Never mind, I tell you what I'm going to do. If you don't join my gang by tomorrow evening, I'm going to have my dog Killer rip up that ugly yellow, beady-eyed, short-tailed, long-nosed, stumpy-legged dog of yours to shreds. You be here tomorrow night or else!"

The boy said, "I'll be here, but I don't think I'll join your gang."

The next evening the boy and his pet were there at the school yard. Sure enough here came the gang, and one of them was holding onto a chain hooked to Killer, a German Shepherd about three feet high at the shoulders. With his enormous, slavering mouth full of large teeth, Killer was straining to get at that ugly yellow dog. The gang leader released Killer, "Get 'em, Killer!"

Killer circled a couple of times, then jumped in on that ugly creature. In the middle of its jump, the boy's pet opened the largest mouth the gang had ever seen and in one bite killed Killer! The gang was shocked!

Finally, the gang leader asked the boy, "What kind of dog is that ugly yellow, short-tailed, long-nosed, beady-eyed, stumpy-legged thing anyway?"

"Well," the boy replied, "before we cut his tail off and painted him yellow, he was an alligator!"

Yes, my friend, appearances can be deceiving. Watch out, today!

Be sober, be vigilant; because your adversary the
devil, as a roaring lion, walketh about, seeking
whom ever he may devour (1 Pet. 5:8;KJV).

Judg. 17; Ps. 102:18-28; Prov. 30-31; 2 Cor. 8-9

May 1 — Unselfish Giving

One afternoon three children entered a flower shop, two boys and a girl. They were about nine or ten years old, raggedly dressed, but at this moment well-scrubbed. One of the boys took off his cap, then came up to the person who owned the store and said, "Sir, we'd like something in yellow flowers."

There was something in their tense nervous manner that made the man think that this was a very special occasion. He showed them some inexpensive yellow spring flowers. The boy who was the spokesman for the group shook his head no. "I think we'd like something better than that."

The man asked, "Do they have to be yellow?"

The boy answered, "Yes, sir. You see, mister, Mickey would like 'em better if they were yellow. He had a yellow sweater. I guess he liked yellow better than any other color."

The man asked, "Are they for his funeral?"

The boy nodded, suddenly choking up. The little girl was desperately struggling to keep back the tears. "She's his sister," the boy said. "He was a swell kid. A truck hit him while he was playing in the street." His lips were trembling now.

The other boy entered the conversation. "Us kids in his block took up a collection and we got 18 cents. Would roses cost an awful lot, sir . . . yellow roses, I mean?"

The man smiled. "It just happens that I have some nice yellow roses here that I'm offering on special today for 18 cents a dozen." The man pointed to the flower case.

"Those sure would be swell! Yes, Mickey'd sure like those."

The florist said, "I'll make up a nice spray with ferns and ribbons. Where do you want me to send them?"

One of the boys responded, "Would it be all right, mister, if we took them with us? We'd kind of like to . . . you know . . . give 'em to Mickey ourselves. He'd like it better that way."

The florist fixed the spray of flowers and accepted the 18 cents gravely and watched the youngsters trudge out of the store. What kind of a feeling do you imagine that florist had at this moment? I believe he and all who give unselfishly will feel a heart warm with the glow of God's presence!

The flower fadeth; but the word of our God
shall stand for ever (Isa. 40:8).

⁓

Judg. 18-19; Ps. 103; Prov. 1; 2 Cor. 10-11

May 2 — Was Everybody Rescued?

On the New England coastline a number of years ago, a ship was wrecked in one of the many storms that lash that area. A large crowd gathered on shore to help with the rescue. Lifeboats were launched into the raging surf, and soon they began coming back to shore with survivors.

One of the rescuers shouted over the noise of the storm to the captain of the wrecked vessel, "Was everybody rescued?"

The captain replied, "Everybody but one! There was one man out there that we just couldn't wait for. He had fallen off the ship, and it was ready to go down. The last time we saw him he was holding on to some of the wreckage."

John Holden said to the captain, "Let's go back and find him!"

But standing next to John Holden was his mother, and she said, "John, have you forgotten that your father went down four years ago and was drowned? And that your brother Will went out to sea months ago, and we haven't seen him since? John, you are all that I have left. I beg of you not to go out there to look for that other man!"

John replied, "Mother, I must. There is a man out there who needs saving!"

He and the captain got into the flimsy rowboat. It didn't look good; the storm was still raging. As the mother watched her son John and the captain make their way out into the ocean, she turned aside to weep with a broken heart convinced that her last loved one would also be lost.

Several hours passed with the anxious crowd still assembled in the rain and wind. They huddled together in quietness, knowing the gravity of the moment. The mother still wept, and others attempted to comfort her. Some stood as curiosity seekers. Finally someone spotted that little lifeboat making its way back to shore, "Did you find the man?"

John Holden stood up and shouted back from the little boat bobbing on the waves, "Yes, we found the man — tell my mother the man is Will!"

Her other son was found on the sea that day, and what a reunion was had by all. What if John had not gone back for the lost man?

Aren't you glad that, like John Holden, Jesus Christ is still seeking after the lost! And aren't you glad that, like John's mother, His Father let Him come to rescue the perishing?

"I am the gate; whoever enters through me will be saved. He will come in and go out, and find pasture (John 10:9).

❧

Judg. 20-21; Ps. 104:1-17; Prov. 2; 2 Cor. 12-13

May 3 — Light for Another

Some years ago Alexander Woolcott described a scene in a New York City hospital where a grief-stricken mother was sitting in the hospital lounge in stunned silence, tears streaming down her cheeks. She had just lost her only child to disease and was gazing blindly into the future while the head nurse talked to her. It is the duty of the head nurse to try to bring comfort in such circumstances.

"Mrs. Norris, did you notice the poorly dressed little boy waiting around in the hall just next to your daughter's room?" the nurse asked.

"No," Mrs. Norris had not noticed him.

"There," continued the head nurse, "there is a case. That little boy's mother is a young French woman who was brought in a week ago by ambulance from her shabby, one-room apartment. She and her son came alone to this country scarcely three months ago. They lost all their people in the old country, and they know nobody here. The two only had each other. Every day that lad has come and sat there from sunup to sundown in the vain hope that his mother would awaken and speak to him. Now he has no home at all!"

Mrs. Norris was listening now. So the nurse went on, "Fifteen minutes ago that little mother died, dropped off like a pebble in the boundless ocean. Now it is my duty to go out and tell that little fellow that, at the age of seven, he is all alone in the world."

The head nurse paused, then turned plaintively to Mrs. Norris. "I don't suppose," she said hesitantly, "I don't suppose that you would go out and tell him for me?"

What happened in the next few moments is something that the nurse would remember forever. Mrs. Norris stood up, dried her tears, went out, and put her arms around that lad. She led the homeless youngster off to her childless home, and in the darkness they both knew, they became a light to each other!

Dark days and much tragedy have encompassed this world, and the future may become darker before the dawning. The Bible strongly urges that all of us who have the light are to "shine forth as a light in the world, holding forth the word of life." You can be the light to light the way for someone who walks in the darkness.

In the same way, let your light shine before men, that they may see your good deeds and praise your Father in heaven (Matt. 5:16).

❧

Ruth 1-2; Ps. 104:18-35; Prov. 3; Acts 19

May 4 — The Unlocked Door

In Glasgow, Scotland, a young lady, like a lot of teens today, got tired of home and the restraints of godly parents. The daughter rejected them and said, "I don't want your God. I give up, I'm leaving!"

She left home, deciding to become a woman of the world. Before long, however, she became dejected with being unable to find a job, so took to the streets to sell her body as a prostitute. The years passed by, her father died, her mother grew older, and the daughter became more and more entrenched in her wretched manner of living.

No contact was made between mother and daughter in the intervening years. The mother, having heard of her daughter's whereabouts, made her way to the skid row section of the city in search of her daughter. She began by stopping at each of the rescue missions with a simple request, "Would you allow me to put up this picture?" It was a picture of the smiling, gray-haired mother with a hand-written message at the bottom: "I love you still . . . come home!"

Some more months went by, and nothing happened. Then one day that wayward girl wandered into a rescue mission for a needed meal. She sat absentmindedly listening to the service, all the while letting her eyes wander over to the bulletin board. There she saw the picture and thought, *Could that be my mother?*

She couldn't wait until the service was over and went to look. It was her mother, and there were those words, "I love you still . . . come home!" As she stood in front of the picture, she began to weep. It was too good to be true.

By this time, it was night, but she was so touched by the message that she started walking for home. By the time she arrived it was early in the morning. The wayward daughter was afraid and made her way timidly, not really knowing what to do. As she began to knock, the door flew open on its own. She thought someone must have broken into the house. Concerned for her mother's safety, the young woman ran to the bedroom and found her still sleeping. She shook her mother awake and said, "It's me! It's me! I'm home!"

The mother couldn't believe her eyes. She wiped her tears and they fell into each other's arms. The daughter said, "I thought someone had broken open the door."

The mother replied gently, "From the day you left, that door has not been locked."

This is love: not that we loved God, but that he loved us and sent his Son as an atoning sacrifice for our sins (1 John 4:10).

❦

Ruth 3-4; Ps. 105:1-15; Prov. 4; Acts 20

May 5 — Keeping Mom Running Smoothly

What is needed to keep "moms" running smoothly? Just maybe . . . mothers should come with a maintenance agreement or service schedule much like a new car or washer or dryer. Think . . . this agreement could provide for a complete overhaul every five years, every three kids, or 100,000 miles, whichever comes first.

Now, if such a manual existed, in my opinion, it should include these items:

FUEL: While it seems that too many mothers will run indefinitely on hot coffee, pizza, hamburgers, and cold leftovers, think what an occasional gourmet meal for two in elegant surroundings would do to add increased efficiency!?!

DRIVE TRAIN: A mother's motor and drive train is probably one of the most dependable you can ever find. A mother can start quickly and reach top speed from a prone position in a single cry from a sleeping child. To keep that drive train working at peak efficiency, regular breaks are recommended. How about a leisurely bath and nap every 1,000 miles or so, a baby sitter every 5,000 miles, and a two-week live-in sitter every 50,000 to do wonders in lubricating the motor and drive train.

BATTERY: Batteries need regular charging and re-charging for peak performance, especially if you need to have a start on cold mornings. Roses, candy, notes, cards, and thoughtful and unexpected gifts help here.

CHASSIS: Mothers, like cars, operate best when the chassis is regularly greased and serviced. Her wardrobe needs changing every spring and fall. Regular exercise should be encouraged. The complete new hairdo and make-up should not be overlooked. When the chassis sags some possible remedies are Weight Watchers, jogging, aerobics, or health club membership.

TUNE-UPS: These are needed regularly, and honest compliments are the cheapest and most appreciated.

By following these simple and regular instructions the average mother will last a lifetime to provide love and care for those who need her most![39]

Be strong and take heart, all you who hope in the Lord (Ps. 31:24).

☙

1 Sam. 1-2; Ps. 105:16-45; Prov. 5; Eph. 1-2

❧

Countless times each day a mother does what
no one else can do quite as well.
She wipes away a tear, whispers a word of hope,
erases a child's fears. She teaches, ministers, loves,
and nurtures the next generation of citizens.
And she challenges and cajoles her kids
to do their best and be the best.

James C. Dobson and Gary L. Bauer

❧

May 6 — The Train at Modane

Modane is a little town in Southern France near the Italian border. It was there that the tragedy began. On December 12, 1917, 1,200 soldiers of France, fresh from the battlefront and anxious to get home for Christmas, boarded this passenger train. It was a festive time. There was much good-natured shouting back and forth as they jammed the train and yelled for the engineer to get on the way.

But the engineer was not about to start this train. He refused to even climb into the cab. Instead he stood on the platform shaking his head. He would not move the train one inch, he said. It was much too heavily loaded. There were mountains ahead of them with sharp curves and steep grades. It would be suicidal to take the train in these conditions.

Someone went for the highest official of the railroad and for the local military commander. "What is the meaning of this?" these officials shouted. "What? You will not move this train? Listen, you are going to climb into that cab and get these men on their way home. If you do not get this train started, you will be shot! Is that clear?"

Crestfallen and worried, the engineer shrugged his shoulders and obeyed against his will. A train so heavily loaded would strain the brakes.

Carefully he eased the train into the main line, keeping his speed down and conserving his brakes. In less than 30 miles the trouble began. The brakes began to smoke. On the next downgrade they would not hold. The train picked up speed, deadly speed, killing speed. In terror, the engineer shut off the steam and applied the brakes. There were no brakes!

From beneath the railway cars, smoke began to pour and then flames could be seen. The soldiers in the coaches knew that something was wrong. Some prayed, some broke out windows to jump to a death. In minutes the train was hurtling at speeds in excess of 80 miles per hour. The end was here.

The runaway train plunged through a village station, its whistle screaming. Just beyond that station, the engineer knew, was the sharpest curve on their way down. There they would die.

They hit the curve, the engine rocked, then plunged to the canyon floor below, the cars piling like matchsticks. Five hundred forty-three men died, including the brave engineer, and 243 were injured. What a tragic score to tally. All because a warning was ignored!

Yet, if you warn the wicked, and he does not turn from his wicked-ness, nor from his wicked way, he shall die in his iniquity; but you have delivered your soul (Ezek. 3:19;NKJ).

~❧~

1 Sam. 3-5; Ps. 106:1-15; Prov. 6; Eph. 3-4

May 7 — A Happy Soul

Born Frances Jane Crosby in 1820, this extraordinary woman was to become known as "Aunt Fanny," the world's greatest and most prolific hymn writer. If you were in church this past Sunday, you may well have sung one of her hymns.

Brought up in an area that straddled the Connecticut-New York border, Fanny as an infant caught a slight cold that inflamed her eyes and eventually resulted in blindness. Because her mother insisted that Fanny be raised as a normal child, the girl could be found climbing trees and playing with the other children despite the inherent dangers.

Even in those early years, Fanny wrote poetry and showed the greatness of her talent. Here's a sample of one of her very first poems:

> Oh, what a happy soul I am, although I cannot see.
> I am resolved that in this world, contented I will be.
> How many blessings I enjoy that other people don't.
> To weep and sigh because I'm blind, I cannot nor I won't.

What a beautiful outlook on life.

When, in 1834, Fanny's mother learned about the work being accomplished at the New York Institute for the Blind, she enrolled Fanny the next year — just a few weeks before the girl's fifteenth birthday. Within five years, Fanny's poems were appearing in the *Saturday Evening Post*.

In 1843 Fanny addressed a joint session of Congress when a group of students were invited to Washington, and in 1844 her first book, *The Blind Girl and Other Poems*, was published.

In 1851 a chance conversation started Fanny on the career she would pursue. George F. Roat, a music instructor at the Institute played an original composition, and Fanny asked why he didn't publish it. He explained that he had no words for it, so Fanny wrote "Fare Thee Well, Kitty Dear," the first of more than 50 songs she would write with him.

Fanny left the Institute in 1858 and married Alexander Van Alstyne who had also been a student there. He was an accomplished musician and composed the music to several of Fanny's hymns during their more than 40 years of married life. Through the years, Fanny composed more than five thousand hymns. She died in 1915, but her name and accomplishments live on. Fanny never allowed her disability to dictate her life or to slow her contributions to others!

Sing joyfully to the Lord, you righteous; it is fitting for the upright to praise him (Ps. 33:1).

෴

1 Sam. 6-7; Ps. 106:16-33; Prov. 7; Eph. 5-6

May 8 — Eyes of Forgiveness

A man came back to work in a place from which he had been fired several months previously. After he was re-hired, the man turned in superior work. The boss asked, "What happened to make such a difference in you?" The man told the following story:

When I was in college, I was part of a fraternity initiation committee. We placed the new members in the middle of a long stretch of country road. I was to drive my car at as great a speed as possible straight at them. The challenge was for them to stand firm until a signal was given to jump out of the way. It was a dark night. I had reached 100 miles an hour and saw their looks of terror in the headlights. The signal was given and everyone jumped clear . . . except one boy.

I left college after that. I later married and have two children. The look on that boy's face as I passed over him at a hundred miles an hour stayed in my mind. I became hopelessly inconsistent, moody, and finally became a problem drinker. My wife had to work to bring in the only income we had.

I was drinking at home one morning when someone rang the doorbell. I opened it to find myself facing a woman who seemed strangely familiar. She told me she was the mother of the boy I had killed years before. She said that she had hated me and spent agonizing nights rehearsing ways to get revenge. I then listened as she told me of the love and forgiveness that had come when she gave her heart to Christ.

She said, "I have come to let you know that I forgive you and I want you to forgive me." I looked deep into her eyes that morning, and there I saw the permission to be the kind of man I might have been had I never killed that boy. That forgiveness changed my whole life.

Living with guilt is a torturous existence.

I've often wondered how the woman caught in the act of adultery felt as she was unceremoniously brought in front of Jesus Christ. The way He looked at her must have been the turning point in her life.

There is still forgiveness for whatever action has brought you guilt!

When Jesus had lifted up himself, and saw none but the woman, he said unto her, Woman, where are those thine accusers? hath no man condemned thee? She said, No man, Lord. And Jesus said unto her, Neither do I condemn thee: go, and sin no more (John 8:10-11;KJV).

❧

1 Sam. 8-9; Ps. 106:34-48; Prov. 8; Rom. 1

May 9 — Oops!

Once upon a time there was this man who could not give a very convincing explanation about his broken arm. He kept muttering about trying to stick his arm through his car window and getting it hit on a street sign.

That was the public version. In private, to a few good friends, when pressed, he confesses that it happened when his wife brought some potted plants inside that had been out on the patio all day. They had to be brought in because it looked like a storm was brewing. A garter snake that had hidden in one of the pots, when inside had slithered out from the plant and across the floor where the wife had spotted it.

"I was in the bathtub when I heard her scream," he related. "It sounded as though she was being murdered, so I jumped out of the tub, soaking wet, dripping water and soap, and didn't even grab a towel.

"When I ran into the living room she was on top of a chair and yelling that a snake had crawled under the couch. She was screaming all the time. I got down on my hands and knees to look for it and our dog came up behind me and cold-nosed me. I guess I thought it was the snake and I fainted.

"My wife thought I'd had a heart attack and called 911 for the medics and an ambulance. I was still groggy when they arrived, so the medics rolled me onto the stretcher. When they were carrying me out, the snake slithered out from under the couch and scared one of the medics. He was so frightened that he forgot where he was and dropped his end of the stretcher, and as I fell I broke my arm!"

Well, what more can be said? Other than it's okay to live to see the humor in life. Mothers need the lubricating flow of laughter to keep them going! People who learn to laugh in life are the people who last in life.

Say, Mother, have you had your quota of laughs today?

A cheerful heart is good medicine, but a crushed spirit dries up the bones (Prov. 17:22).

❧

1 Sam. 10-11; Ps. 107:1-22; Prov. 9; Rom. 2-3

May 10 — A Mother Is Waiting

John Todd was born in Rutledge, Vermont, into a family of several children. At a very early age, both of John's parents died.

One dear and loving aunt said she would take little John. The aunt sent a horse and a slave, Caesar, to get John who was only six at this time. On the way back, this endearing conversation took place.

John: Will she be there?

Caesar: Oh, yes, she'll be there waiting up for you.

John: Will I like living with her?

Caesar: My son, you fall into good hands.

John: Will she love me?

Caesar: Ah, she has a big heart.

John: Will I have my own room? Will she let me have a puppy?

Caesar: She's got everything all set, Son. I think she has some surprises, John.

John: Do you think she'll go to bed before we get there?

Caesar: Oh, no! She'll be sure to wait up for you. You'll see when we get out of these woods. You'll see her candle in the window.

Sure enough, as they neared the house, John saw a candle in the window and his aunt standing in the doorway. As he shyly approached the porch, she reached down, kissed him, and said, "Welcome home!"

John Todd grew up in his aunt's home and later became a great minister. She was mother to him. She gave him a second home.

Years later his aunt wrote to tell John of her own impending death because of failing health. She wondered what would become of her.

This is what John Todd wrote in reply:

My Dear Aunt,

Years ago I left a house of death, not knowing where I was to go, whether anyone cared, whether it was the end of me. The ride was long, but the servant encouraged me. Finally I arrived to your embrace and a new home. I was expected; I felt safe. You did it all for me.

Now it's your turn to go. I'm writing to let you know, someone is waiting up, your room is all ready, the light is on, the door is open, and you're expected! I know. I once saw God standing in your doorway . . . long ago!

Her children arise and call her blessed; her husband also, and he praises her. . . . Give her the reward she has earned, and let her works bring her praise at the city gate (Prov. 31:28,31).

❧

1 Sam. 12-13; Ps. 107:23-43; Prov. 10; Rom. 4-5

May 11 —Overcoming Obstacles

Life is not always easy! In fact, for most of us life has not been fair and certainly there have been difficulties, trials, and tests. Many of the world's great people have been saddled with disabilities and adversities, but have managed to overcome them. The question is: Were they great people, or did their overcoming the difficulties make them great? Consider. . . .

Cripple him and you have a Sir Walter Scott.

Lock him in a prison cell, take away his freedom, take him out of circulation, and you have a John Bunyan.

Bury him in the snows of Valley Forge, facing an enemy which far outnumbered his troops, and you have a George Washington.

Raise him in abject poverty, make him struggle through political defeat after defeat, let him lose the love of his life, and you have an Abraham Lincoln.

Subject him to a difficult upbringing, expose him to bitter religious prejudice, and you have a Disraeli.

Strike him down with infantile paralysis, take away his legs, make him dependent utterly on others, and he becomes a Franklin D. Roosevelt.

Have him or her born black into a society which is filled with racial discrimination, and you have a Booker T. Washington, a Harriet Tubman, a Marian Anderson, a George Washington Carver, a Martin Luther King Jr., or a Nelson Mandela.

Make him the first child in an Italian family of 18 children, subject him to abject poverty, gift him musically, and you have an Enrico Caruso.

Have him born of parents who survived a Nazi concentration camp, paralyze him from the waist down when he is four years old, and you have an incomparable concert violinist, Itzhak Perlman.

Call him a slow learner, tab him as being retarded, write him off as being uneducable, and you have an Albert Einstein.

Deafen a musical genius composer and you have made a Ludwig van Beethoven.

Ban him to an island prison, give him visions, and you have a John the Beloved.

I can do everything through him who gives me strength (Phil. 4:13).

◦✐

1 Sam. 14; Ps. 108; Prov. 11; Rom. 6-7

May 12 — Choices

This is a story about a man named Joe who inherited a million dollars. The will, however, provided that he had to accept it either in Chile or Brazil. He chose Brazil. Unhappily it turned out that in Chile he would have received his inheritance in land on which uranium, gold, and silver had just been discovered.

Once in Brazil, he had to choose between receiving his inheritance in coffee or nuts. He chose nuts. Too bad! The bottom fell out of the nut market, and coffee went up to $1.50 per pound, wholesale. Poor Joe lost everything he had to his name.

He went out and sold his gold watch for the money he needed to fly back home. It seems that he had enough for a ticket to either New York or Boston. He chose Boston. When the plane for New York taxied up, he noticed it was a brand-new 747 super-jet with all the latest technology. The plane for Boston arrived, and it was a 1928 old Ford tri-motor with a sway back. It was filled with crying children and tethered goats and sheep. It seemed like it took all day to get off the runway.

Over the Andes, one of the engines fell off. Our man Joe made his way to the captain and said, "I'm a jinx on this plane. Let me out if you want to save your lives. Give me a parachute."

The pilot agreed, but added, "On this plane, anybody who bails out must wear two parachutes."

So Joe jumped out of the plane. As he fell through the air, he tried to make up his mind which ripcord to pull. Finally, he chose the one on the left. It was rusty, and the wire pulled loose. So he pulled the other handle. This chute opened, but its shroud line snapped. In desperation, Joe cried out, "St. Francis, save me!"

A hand reached out of heaven and grabbed the poor man by the wrist and let him dangle in mid-air. Then a gentle but inquisitive voice asked, "St. Francis Xavier or St. Francis of Assisi?"

Choices! Choices! I had a person tell me one day, "Life would be just great if I weren't confronted with so many choices."

My friend, life is nothing more or less than a series of choices. It's a fantastic power that has been given to each human being. Use this power well. It's called choice!

And if it seem evil unto you to serve the Lord, choose you this day whom ye will serve; whether the gods which your fathers served that were on the other side of the flood, or the gods of the Amorites, in whose land ye dwell: but as for me and my house, we will serve the Lord (Josh. 24:15;KJV).

⌇

1 Sam. 15-16; Ps. 109:1-13; Prov. 12; Rom. 8

May 13 — A Position of Love

About six o'clock on a Wednesday morning, James Lawson of Running Springs, California, in the San Bernardino Mountains, left home to apply for a job. About an hour later, his 36-year-old wife, Patsy, left for her fifth-grade teaching job down the mountain in Riverside. She was accompanied by their two children, Susan, age five, and Gerald, age two. They were to be dropped off at the babysitter's.

Unfortunately, they never got that far.

The alarm was spread that Patsy and her two little ones had not arrived at the babysitter's, nor at her school post. Eight and one-half hours later, James Lawson found his wife and daughter dead in their wrecked car, upside down in a cold mountain stream. His two-year-old son was just barely alive in the cold 48-degree water.

As the father scrambled down the cliff to what he was sure were the cries of his dying wife, he found something else. She was dead. But she was locked in a position that was holding her little boy's head just above the water in the submerged car.

What had happened could be pieced together from the scene. The five-year-old daughter had evidently been killed in the accident. Patsy had attempted to get out, but the position of the car had her trapped. Little Gerald had survived the crash along with his mother. There was nothing else for Patsy to do but hold little Gerald's head above the water in the little pocket of air that remained in the car.

For the long eight and one-half hours, she had held that painful position until her body had almost frozen in the pose of self-giving love. Then she had finally succumbed to hypothermia and died.

Patsy Lawson, though dead, was still holding her baby up so he could breathe. He survived the ordeal. She died that another might live. That's the essence of a mother's sacrificial love.

This tragic yet heart-rending story brings to mind another kind of love. God sent His only beloved Son into the hostile environment of this world so that He could take up a position of love, with outstretched arms, to die so that we might live. We marvel at such love.

Do you think little Gerald really knows what it cost his mother so that he might live? Have you ever considered what it cost God to give His Son so you could have eternal life?

For God did not send His Son into the world to condemn the world, but to save the world through him (John 3:17).

❧

1 Sam. 17; Ps. 109:14-31; Prov. 13; Rom. 9-10

May 14 — Like Mother, Like Daughter

"When are you coming?"
"On Sunday, why?"
"Because I want to get some things, make the bed. . . ."
"Oh, Mom," she said.
I felt an echo in me:
I had made the beds just the week before
on a visit to my mother's,
because of her back.
Always before she had,
but now I did, knowing where everything was:
I had moved her there.

Looking for recipes of dishes my daughter likes,
I found the ones for meals I had made my mother,
in her new kitchen,
and put them away
like an echo in a drawer.
Reviewing their ways, looking for similarities
in their rhythms (there were none);
I weighed them against my need to be alone.

I am related to neither now
(their blue eyes are so dissimilar)
and yet I am their link.
There are echoes back and forth through me:
I live alone, as do my mother and my daughter,
none of us in the house
where we were raised
or spent our marriages.
Each of us is careful of the others,
unyielding in small significant ways.

I now mother my mother
when I can no longer mother my daughter
who is older than I have ever felt myself to be.
(Susan S. Jacobson)

Do not say, "Why were the old days better than these?" For it is not wise to ask such questions (Eccles. 7:10).

1 Sam. 18-19; Ps. 110; Prov. 14; Rom. 11-12

May 15 — But I Am Only . . .

Have you been guilty of hiding behind the excuse, "I am only a senior citizen," or "I am only one person," or "I am only a one-talent person." It's a human tendency to excuse our inactivity or lack of action.

A couple of years ago the *Wall Street Journal* carried the interesting story about Harry Lipsig, 88 years young, who at that age decided to begin a new law firm. He had worked for over 60 years in a New York law firm helping build their clientele, now he was going to start a whole new firm by himself. The first case accepted was unusual . . . here it is:

A lady was bringing suit against the city of New York because a police officer was driving while drunk in a squad car which struck and killed her 71-year-old husband. Her argument was that the city had deprived her of her husband's future earnings potential. The city countered back with their argument that at age 71, he had little or no earnings potential. They thought they had a clever defense . . . UNTIL it dawned on them that this lady's argument about her husband's future potential was being advanced by a vigorous 88-year-old attorney! The city of New York settled out of court for $1.25 million!

Even our attitudes are the result of choices we make.

Talking about choice. . . . Back when the Romans were the top world power, there was one Roman general who had a unique way in which he dealt with condemned spies who had been caught and brought to trial. Once condemned by trial, he offered the prisoner a choice: The execution squad, or the "Black Door."

It happened again, the spy had been caught, tried in his courtroom and stood before the general as a condemned spy. The general asked, "What will you choose, the execution squad or the black door?" The man's choice was the execution squad.

He was led away and the sounds of the judgment carried back into the room where the general and his aide are sitting. "General," the aide asked, "what is behind the black door?"

"Freedom," the general replied, "but few men have the courage to choose the unknown, even over death."

Let's make our attitudinal choice. No longer will we say, "I am only. . . ." Instead we will choose freedom, choose to be involved, choose to make a difference. The bottom line is that an attitude of "I am only" is not pleasing to God. Please note our verse for today!

The Lord said to me, "Do not say, 'I am only a child.' You must go to everyone I send you to and say whatever I command you. Do not be afraid of them, for I am with you and will rescue you" (Jer. 1:7-8).

❦

1 Sam. 20-21; Ps. 111; Prov. 15; Rom. 13-14

May 16 — The Power of a Wasted Day

None of us will ever know, this side of eternity, what kind of influence we have on others. And for all of you who have been discouraged because the day seemed so wasted, take heart as you read the following.

During World War II a woman received a letter from a soldier she didn't know. His name was Murray and he wrote from the battlefield.

Murray wrote that he had once been in her Sunday school class and she had spoken about Jesus Christ as a hero for boys. He mentioned the date when this woman's words had altered his whole perspective on life.

This lady had kept a diary all of her life, so she quickly turned to the date that Murray had mentioned. She learned that she had come home from that Sunday school session very discouraged and even thought about giving up teaching.

The entry for that day read "Had an awful time. The boys were so restless. I am not cut out for this kind of thing. I had to take two classes together. No one listened, except at the end, a boy named Murray from the other class seemed to be taking it in. He grew very quiet and subdued, but I expect he was just tired of playing."[40]

Just as the shadow of that nameless woman had fallen across that boy's life to make a lasting impression, none of us will ever know how our lives and faith and talk will influence others around us.

Mother, you have no idea how those seeds of love and caring will impact a young life! The Bible reminds us that we should not grow weary in our well-doing, because sometime down the road, "in due season," we will be reaping a harvest! No day is wasted when it is spent with your children! Don't give up! Don't be discouraged — today may impact a life forever!

And how good is a timely word! (Prov. 15:23).

❧

1 Sam. 22-23; Ps. 112; Prov. 16; Rom. 15

A pastor received a call from a new father, which was not unusual. The father, however, went on to explain that he wanted the pastor to be present when the mother came out from under the anesthetic and would be told she had given birth to a beautiful baby boy — healthy in every way — but the newborn had no ears.

When the pastor arrived, the nervous father and the doctor went into the room where the mother lay on her bed, now recovered after a hard birth. The doctor explained that the baby had auditory openings and all the inner ear parts necessary to receive sounds, but no fleshy part outside that we commonly call the ear. The doctor assured the parents that the problem would be corrected when the child's growth was completed and a matching donor was found.

School was a tough experience for this little guy. Many times he would come home crying, "I'm a freak! I'm nothing but a freak!" He was too well-aware of the stares, whispers, taunts, and nicknames given to him by the other kids. Junior High was the worst of his growing-up experiences, but the young man began to adapt, and learned to live with his disfigurement. He became an excellent student and entered college on a scholarship with plans to study geology.

One spring day his father phoned him and said, "Well, Son, we've finally found an ear donor for you. Plan to come home because the operation will take place this summer."

The day of the operation came and went as a rousing success. This young man was so happy as he returned to college in the fall. His new ears were beautiful, and life took on new meaning for him.

He graduated with honors and his parents were so proud of him as he left to take a job in the Midwest. Life was great. Then a call came from his father who said, "Son, your mother has had a heart attack. Please come right home.

The young man arrived on the next flight, only to learn his mother had died before his arrival. The next day at the funeral home his father walked with him to the casket where she lay and pushed back his mother's hair to show the son . . . the mother didn't have any ears!

She gave a part of herself to meet her son's need.

The love of God is greater even than this mother's love. God gave us more than ears . . . He gave His Son!

For God so loved the world that he gave his one and only Son, that whoever believes in him shall not perish but have eternal life (John 3:16).

᧞

1 Sam. 24-25; Ps. 113; Prov. 17; Rom. 16

May 18 — False Prophets

Tragedy spilled over this world because two people were believers in a false prophet. The tsar and empress of Russia were misled by a miracle, and this in turn caused the downfall of their empire.

After many years of anxiously waiting for an heir to the Russian throne, Tsar Nicholas II and his German wife, Federovna, were blessed with a son. Their hopes for the future were cruelly crushed six weeks later when doctors discovered the infant had hemophilia, an incurable blood disease that could kill at any moment. All of his short life was to be lived in the shadow of terror, with death stalking every footstep. This tragedy introduced the royal family to one of the most evil men who ever lived.

Several times the young tsarevish slipped close to death. Seeing him writhing in pain, his tormented parents would beg doctors to do something, but all were helpless in the face of this disease. In those moments of grief they turned to Gregory Rasputin, a religious mystic of very questionable credentials. He was to be known later as the "Mad Monk of Russia."

He would pray for the boy and there would be improvement. Even doctors today are at a loss to explain how those healings took place, but history testifies to them. After praying for their son, Rasputin would warn the parents that the boy would live only as long as they listened to him.

Rasputin's power over this royal family became so great that he could, with a word, obtain the appointment or dismissal of any government official. He had men appointed or dismissed on the basis of their attitudes toward himself rather than on their abilities. Consequently the whole Russian government reeled under the unwise counsel of this evil man. Seeds of revolution were planted and watered with discontent. It finally erupted into the murder of the royal family, internal civil war, and the communistic takeover.

Alexander Kerensky, a key government official during those trying times, later said, "Without Rasputin, there could have been no Lenin!"

Jesus told us to check out people who will be leading us by the fruits of their lifestyle. In following a leader there is more than miracles to be considered. Jesus really lived among mankind to show to us a style of living that was dramatically different from that of the world. People, and that includes all of us, are to be judged by what they are, not what they do!

Thus, by their fruit you will recognize them (Matt. 7:20;NIV).

෴

1 Sam. 26-27; Ps. 114; Prov. 18; Acts 21

May 19 — Experience Counts

Hank, a landscape contractor, had landed his first, full-fledged job. Of course he didn't want to appear to be the rank amateur he knew he was, so he pretended a casual kind of nonchalance and expertise.

One of the first tasks he had to tackle was blasting out a farmer's tree stumps with dynamite. Since the farmer was watching, Hank went to some length to measure out the fuse and set the dynamite. So far so good, and he continued to go about the task as if he really knew what he was doing. There was one problem. He didn't know how much dynamite would be just right to do the job. It was an estimate, a guesstimate.

When Hank was all set up, he breathed a prayer that he had enough dynamite packed under the stump and yet not so much it would blow it to kingdom come. The moment of truth came.

Hank glanced at the farmer with a knowing look of what he hoped came across as confidence and pushed down the plunger. The stump rose high in the air with a resounding boom and arched magnificently over toward his pickup truck and landed right on the roof of the cab.

The farmer turned to Hank and said, "Son, you didn't miss it by much — just a couple of feet. With a bit more practice you'll be able to land those suckers in the truck bed every time!"

Well, so much for experience and the old theme that practice makes perfect. There are lots of things in life for which we don't have the time to practice, and there are some moments when it is best just to act. Try this next story on for application.

A young man was busy at his job of sacking and carrying groceries out into the parking lot for the local supermarket. He had been in and out of the store on his helpful errands a number of times that morning. Something drew his attention to a woman in the parking lot who was struggling with her groceries. Her cart was filled, as were her arms.

His path back to the store took him in her direction. She put one of her packages on the roof of the car while she hunted for her keys. Then she began to load her packages from the cart to the car. But as she got in, started her car, and began to drive away, the young man saw her forgotten package on the roof. Now he was closer and began to run after the lady. When she made a turn to exit the parking lot, the package on the roof rolled off. Fortunately, the young man caught the package, a baby, before it hit the pavement!

Remain in me, and I will remain in you. No branch can bear fruit by itself; it must remain in the vine. Neither can you bear fruit unless you remain in me (John 15:4).

❧

1 Sam. 28-29; Ps. 115; Prov. 19; Acts 22

May 20 — The Soapmaker

Years ago a young man of 16 left home to seek his fortune. All of his earthly possessions were tied up in a bundle. As he walked down the path, he met an old neighbor, the captain of a canal boat, and the following conversation took place.

"Well, William, where are you going?" the captain asked.

"I don't know," he answered. "My father is too poor to keep me at home any longer and says I must now make a living for myself."

"There's no trouble with that," said the captain. "Be sure you start right, and you'll get along fine."

William told his friend that the only trade he knew anything about was soap and candlemaking, at which he'd helped his father.

"Well," said the old man, "let me pray with you once more and give you a little advice, and then I'll let you go."

They both kneeled down on the tow path along which the horses walked as they pulled the boat in the canal. The man prayed and then gave his advice: "Someone will soon be the leading soapmaker in New York. It can be you as well as anyone. Be a good man, give your life totally to Christ, pay the Lord all that belongs to Him beginning with your tithe of every dollar you earn, make an honest soap, give a full pound, and I'm certain you will yet be a prosperous and rich man."

When young William arrived in the city, he found it hard to get work. Now lonesome and far from home, he remembered his mother's words and the last words of the canal boat captain. He was led to "seek first the kingdom of God and His righteousness," and became part of a growing church. He remembered his promise, and out of the first dollar he earned, he gave God His portion. He began with ten cents on the dollar. Finding regular employment, he soon became a partner in the business, and in a few years he became the sole owner.

He now resolved to keep his promise to the captain. He made an honest soap, gave a full pound, and instructed his bookkeeper to open an account with the Lord and place one-tenth of all company and personal earnings to that account.

He prospered, his business prospered, his family was blessed, his soap sold. Soon he was giving it all to the Lord's work. Who was this soapmaker? William Colgate, today a household name.

Command those who are rich in this present world not to be arrogant nor to put their hope in wealth, which is so uncertain, but to put their hope in God, who richly provides us with everything for our enjoyment (1 Tim. 6:17).

❧

1 Sam. 30-31; Ps. 116; Prov. 20; Acts 23

May 21 — Genius

There is nothing in his background to suggest that he might have been extraordinary. He was a bit less than an average student in school, and at times was a problem pupil. An incident occurred when he was 15 years old and in high school. The teacher called Victor Seribriarkoff a "dunce!" That's not all — this teacher gave him the advice that it would be better if he dropped out of school and learned a trade.

Victor took that advice and acted upon it. He dropped out of school and for the next 17 years went from job to job and became a wanderer, living life without a purpose and acting out the fact that he was a dunce.

At the age of 32, however, something amazing took place! It was a moment that would change his life forever. Somehow, somewhere, somebody gave him an IQ test. The results? They revealed that he was a genius with an IQ of 161! Most of us are average with an IQ between 90 and 110.

From that moment, Victor Seribriarkoff began acting like the genius the IQ test indicated he was! Today he is quite a remarkable fellow. No longer is he a vagabond — he is a very successful business-man. He is the author of several books and has invented some new discoveries for which he holds the patents.

His name is not exactly a household word, but those who have heard of Victor know that he was elected to be the chairperson of the International Mensa Society. To belong to Mensa a person must have an IQ of 140 or above.

Once Victor realized who he really was, his entire life changed.

The way we see ourselves often determines what we become. Our self-image often develops from what other important people say about us. We listen to what they tell us, and then begin to act upon it. If we believe that we are a failure, then we act like a failure. If someone calls us a dunce and we believe that, we act like a dunce.

Today, my friend, do you really know who you are?

Think with me a moment or two about who you are. The Bible says you are God's greatest miracle! You are the salt of this earth and the light of this dark world. You have been given the secret of moving mountains. You are more precious than all this world's material things. You are rich, you are an overcomer, you are a child of the King of all kings! Act like who you are!

For you created my inmost being; you knit me together in my mother's womb. I praise you because I am fearfully and wonderfully made (Ps. 139:13-14).

❧

2 Sam. 1-2; Ps. 117; Prov. 21; Acts 24

May 22 — Life and Accountability

Grand Admiral Karl Doenitz — Adolf Hitler's personally appointed successor who presided over Nazi Germany's unconditional surrender in World War II — died in 1980 in Hamburg at the age of 89. A West German Defense Ministry spokesman said that Doenitz, who commanded Germany's U-boat campaign against Allied shipping, was buried without military honors. Why? The ministry, fearing pro-Nazi demonstrations, had also banned any soldiers from attending the funeral in uniform.

Doenitz, a brilliant submarine strategist, was appointed by Hitler as his successor on April 30, 1945. In that role he presided over Germany's surrender after a futile attempt to surrender in the West, and Doenitz continued to fight on against the Russians in the East.

After Hitler notified Doenitz that he was to succeed him as head of state, the Nazi leader committed suicide the same day. In fact, Doenitz had been exercising supreme authority for some days since Hitler had become so overwrought he had been unable to make decisions. Doenitz was arrested by the British on May 22, 1945.

Karl Doenitz, slightly built and taciturn, was imprisoned for ten years after his conviction for war crimes at the Nuremberg trials in 1947. His was the lightest sentence given to any of the major war criminals convicted at the Nuremberg trials. After completing his sentence, he was released from Berlin's Spandau Prison on October 1, 1956.

The admiral's memoirs, published in 1959, attempted to refute the Nuremberg verdict in his case, maintaining, as did many other Nazis, that he was following military orders. He said he was shocked when, at the war's end, he learned of the atrocities committed by Hitler.

What does a story like this say to us today? One of the first lessons is that every one of us is responsible for our life actions, and we will be held accountable for them. This applies to all people, whether you have been a world leader, a decorated war hero, or just an average Joe. We all must face the inevitability of death, which in turn will be followed by a judgment.

How can we prepare for such an event? One thing is positively certain — you can make no further preparations after you have died. This fact calls forth from all of us a consciousness of an eternity for which we must prepare!

And as it is appointed unto men once to die, but after this the judgment: So Christ was once offered to bear the sins of many (Heb. 9:27-28;KJV).

⌒⌒

2 Sam. 3-4; Ps. 118:1-14; Prov. 22; Acts 25-26

May 23 — Taking the Initiative

He was born in Columbus, Ohio, in 1890, the third of eight children. At age 11 he quit school to help with the family expenses and got his first, full-time job at $3.50 per week for a 60-hour week.

At 15 he became interested in automobiles and went to work in a garage at $4.50 per week. Knowing he would never get anywhere without more schooling, the teenager subscribed to a correspondence home study course on automobiles. Night after night, following long days at the garage, he worked at the kitchen table by the light of a kerosene lamp.

His next step was already planned in his mind. It was a job with the Frayer-Miller Automobile Company of Columbus. One day, when he felt he was ready and had prepared himself, he walked into the plant. Lee Frayer was bent over the hood of a car. The boy waited. Finally, Frayer noticed him. "Well," he said, "what do you want?"

"I just thought I'd tell you I'm coming to work here tomorrow," the boy replied with an air of confidence about him.

"Oh! Who hired you?" asked Frayer.

"Nobody yet, but I'll be on the job in the morning. If I'm not worth anything, you can fire me!"

Early the next morning, the young man returned to the garage. Frayer was not there yet. Noticing that the floor was thick with metal shavings and accumulated dirt and grease, the boy got a broom and shovel and set to work cleaning up the place.

The rest of this young man's future was predictable. He went on to a national reputation as a race car driver and automotive expert. During World War I, he was America's leading flying ace. Later he was the founder of Eastern Airlines. His name is, and you may well have guessed — Eddie Rickenbacker.

Initiative is defined in Random House Dictionary as "an introductory act or step; leading action; to take the initiative." It's an attitude that is sorely missing on the horizon of human endeavors. We live in a society that wants everything in life handed to them on a silver platter.

The same thinking holds true in Christian living. We want it all done for us so all we have to do is enjoy the final result. How about beginning a revival of good old fashioned initiative in our living? Long live initiative!

For even when we were with you, we gave you this rule: "If a man will not work, he shall not eat." We hear that some among you are idle. They are not busy; they are busybodies (2 Thess. 3:10-11).

⤲

2 Sam. 5-6; Ps. 118:15-29; Prov. 23; Acts 27

May 24 — A Loser?

When he was a little boy, the other children called him "Sparky" after a comic-strip horse named Sparkplug. Sparky never shook that nickname.

School was all but impossible for Sparky. He failed every subject in the eighth grade. Every subject! In high school, he flunked physics by receiving a flat zero in the course. Sparky distinguished himself as the worst physics student in his school's history.

He also flunked Latin. And algebra. And English. He didn't do much better in sports. Although he managed to make the school golf team, he promptly lost the only important match of the year. There was a consolation match, but Sparky lost that, too.

Throughout his youth, Sparky was awkward socially. He was not actually disliked by the other youngsters, it's just that no one cared that much. If a classmate ever said hello to him outside of school hours, Sparky was astonished. There was no way to tell how he might have done at dating since, in high school, Sparky never once asked a girl out. He was too afraid of being turned down.

Sparky was a loser. He, his classmates, everyone knew it to be true. So he rolled with it. He would be content with the inevitable mediocrity.

But, there's more to Sparky: drawing. He was proud of his own artwork. Of course, no one else appreciated it. In his senior year of high school, he submitted some cartoons to the editors of the class yearbook. Almost predictably, Sparky's drawings were rejected.

He decided to become a professional artist. After graduation he wrote to Walt Disney Studios telling of his qualifications to become a cartoonist for Disney. He received a form letter requesting some samples of his work. Sparky waited for the reply, but deep down he knew that, too, would be rejected, which it was.

So what did Sparky do? He wrote his autobiography in cartoons. He described his childhood self — the little-boy loser, the chronic under-achiever — in a cartoon the whole world now knows.

The boy who failed the eighth grade, the young artist whose work was rejected by Walt Disney and his own yearbook staff is known to us today as "Sparky" Charles Monroe Schulz. He created the "Peanuts" comic strip and the cartoon character whose kite would never fly — CHARLIE BROWN!

All men will hate you because of me, but he who stands firm to the end will be saved (Matt. 10:22).

2 Sam. 7-9; Ps. 119:1-16; Prov. 24; Acts 28

May 25 — What Is a "Real" Saint?

Once upon a time many, many years ago, a young man decided to become a saint. He left home and family, sold all he owned, gave the money to the poor, and walked off into the desert to find God.

He walked through the desert sands until he found a cave. *Here*, he thought, *I will be alone with God. Here nothing can distract me from God.* He prayed day and night in his cave. Temptations came . . . he imagined all the good things of life and wanted them desperately. He was determined to give it all up to have God alone. After many months of struggle the temptations stopped. St. Anthony of Egypt was at peace, having nothing but God.

Then, according to this story, God said, "Leave your cave for a few days and go off to a distant town. Look for the town shoemaker. Knock on his door and stay with him for a while."

The holy hermit was puzzled by God's command but left the next morning. By nightfall he came to the village and found the home of the shoemaker and knocked on the door. A smiling man opened it.

"Are you the town shoemaker?" the holy hermit asked.

"Yes, I am," the shoemaker answered. "Come in," he said. "You need something to eat and a place to rest." The shoemaker called his wife. They prepared a fine meal to eat and a bed for him to sleep on.

The hermit stayed for three days. He asked many questions about their lives but he didn't tell them much about himself even though they were curious about his life in the desert. They became friends.

The hermit left on the morning of the fourth day. After saying goodbye he walked back to his cave wondering why God had sent him to visit the shoemaker and his wife.

"What was the shoemaker like?" God asked the hermit after he had settled down in his dark cave.

"He is a simple man," the hermit began. "He has a wife who is going to have a baby. They seem to love each other very much. He has a small shop where he makes shoes. He works hard. They have a simple house. They give money and food to those who have less than they have. He and his wife believe very strongly in You and pray at least once a day. They have many friends. And the shoemaker enjoys telling jokes."

God listened carefully. "You are a great saint, Anthony," God said, "and the shoemaker and his wife are great saints, too."

Greet all the saints in Christ Jesus. The brothers who are with me send greetings. All the saints send you greetings, especially those who belong to Caesar's household (Phil. 4:21-22).

❦

2 Sam. 10-11; Ps. 119:17-32; Prov. 25; Col. 1-2

Accidents can happen to any one of us at almost any time, in some of the most unusual of circumstances. Accidents happen. They are not planned, they are always unexpected, and that's why they are accidents. But in spite of all that can happen to the human being, humor can also play a part in the re-telling of an accident.

Some of the people who had automobile accidents while being policyholders with a particular insurance company were asked to summarize exactly what happened on their insurance report forms. The following quotes were taken from these actual forms and were published in the *Toronto Sun* on July 20, 1977:

"Coming home, I drove into the wrong house and collided with a tree that I don't have."

"I collided with a stationary truck coming the other way."

"The guy was all over the road; I had to swerve a number of times before I hit him."

"I had been driving my car for 40 years when I fell asleep at the wheel and had an accident."

"My car was legally parked as it backed into the other vehicle."

"An invisible car came out of nowhere, struck my vehicle, and vanished."

"I told the police that I was not injured, but on removing my hat, I found that I had a skull fracture."

"The pedestrian had no idea of which way to go, so I ran over him."

"The indirect cause of this accident was a little guy in a small car with a big mouth."

"The telephone pole was approaching fast. I was attempting to swerve out of its path when it struck my front."

Well, there you have it. People and accident reports. How do you go about preparing for an accident to happen? Possibly among us there are some who are known as being "accident-prone." These are people who just naturally are the accidents-waiting-to-happen folks. The worst thing about accidents is that they can hurt, maim, and be fatal. Most of us do all that we can to avoid accidents. But if an accident happens with the suddenness of a moment, it pays to be prepared ahead of time. I refer mostly to the spiritual preparation of being ready at all times to meet your Maker. It's being in a constant state of readiness and being aware that life is fragile.

Therefore you also be ready, for the Son of Man is coming at an hour when you do not expect Him (Matt. 24:44;NKJV).

❧

2 Sam. 12-13; Ps. 119:33-48: Prov. 26; Col. 3-4

May 27 — The Vanishing Hitchhiker

One recurring story about angels pops up everywhere with all kinds of variations or adaptations. Practically every publication about angels will have a version and most people you ask can tell you about somebody they know who has had such an experience. Perhaps it could be called the "classic" automobile angel legend/story. It usually goes something like this.

A girl and her father were driving along a country road on their way home from their cabin when they saw a young lady hitchhiking. They stopped and picked her up and she got in the back seat. She told the girl and her father that she lived in a house about five miles up the road. She didn't say anything, but sat and watched out the window. When the father saw the house, he drove up to it and turned around to tell the girl they had arrived . . . but she wasn't there!

Both he and his daughter were mystified and knocked on the door to tell the people what had happened. They in turn told them that they once had a daughter who answered the description of the girl they supposedly had picked up, but she had disappeared some years ago and had last been seen hitchhiking on this very road.

Or it can be heard much like this: Pastor Hernandez was on his way to make a call on a sick member of his church. It was a 15-mile desolate stretch of barren land when he stopped to pick up a young hitchhiker. As they drove along, the pastor began to share with the young man about the love of Jesus Christ.

Pastor Hernandez specifically said in the course of conversation, "I believe the Lord's return is getting very close."

The young man softly, yet forcefully, replied, "Well, that will be sooner than you think." Which was a surprise to the pastor.

They continued to drive further and the young man continues, "Please make sure you are ready and all of your congregation also gets this warning."

The pastor now contemplates this message, feeling some kind of special occurrence is happening. He keeps his eyes on the road.

But when the pastor turns to look at his passenger, the young man is gone! He stops the car, gets out, and looks up and down the lonely road but is unable to see anyone in any direction!

Do you think the frequency of this story is a message to us who are living in what may be called "the last days"?

Whether you turn to the right or to the left, your ears will hear a voice behind you, saying, "This is the way; walk in it" (Isa. 30:21).

୶

2 Sam. 14-15; Ps. 119:49-64; Prov. 27; Heb. 1-2

The curious angel asked, "Whatcha doin', God . . . working a puzzle?"

"No," God answered, smiling, "I'm making a family."

The idea was most interesting, and the curious angel began asking questions. "A family . . . sure are a lot of parts. What are the big pieces?"

"Those are the fathers."

"Aren't they too large?"

"No, they have to be strong. They work hard and bear a lot of burdens. They're the image of the Heavenly Father and the security for their families. The big shoulders are for carrying kids and for mothers to cry on. The large feet symbolize the solid foundation. But they can also kill snakes, be a rocking horse, and they make good footprints for children to follow," said God.

"And the pretty pieces," the angel asked, "what are they?"

"They're the mothers," God answered.

"They sure are pretty, but fragile, too, huh, God?"

God replied, "Don't let their looks deceive. They are small and pretty, but most of them are stronger than men. You see, fathers look tough — it makes everyone feel secure. Mothers need to look pretty, but they are strong inside. Their greatest strength is their love. They love ugly men and runny-nose babies — and even stray puppies."

"What are the little pieces?"

"They're the children," God answered. "They make the families complete. Fathers and mothers conceive the little children, but I give them a soul. We work together to bring a new life into the world. Mom and Dad are the parents, and they then teach their children how to be good parents."

"This puzzle over here has a missing piece," the angel said.

"Yes, not all families have all the pieces, but they're still a family. When a father is missing, the mother does both parts. And fathers can take mothers' places, too, if they have to."

God continued, "Some families have just one member, but they're families, too. When they get lonely, then members of the family of God help them. Families are held together by love — Mine and theirs."

"I hope it works," the angel sighed.

"It has to," God said. "Families hold the world together."[41]

Be imitators of God, therefore, as dearly loved children and live a life of love, just as Christ loved us and gave himself up for us as a fragrant offering and sacrifice to God (Eph. 5:1).

⟨∽⟩

2 Sam. 16-17; Ps. 119:65-80; Prov. 28; Heb. 3-5

*Before we can feel the deepest
tenderness for others,
we must feel the deepest
tenderness for God.*

Emily Morgan

May 29 —Sifting

A "house-church" in a city of the USSR had managed to receive a single copy of the Gospel according to Luke. This was the only written copy of the Scripture that many of these Christians had ever seen. They tore it into small sections and distributed them among this body of believers. Their plan was to memorize the portion they had been given, then on the next Sunday they would meet and redistribute the scriptural sections to memorize more.

On Sunday, these believers arrived inconspicuously in small groups or as singles throughout the day so as not to arouse the suspicion of KGB informers. By dark they were all safely inside and doors were locked. They began by singing a hymn quietly but with deep emotion.

Suddenly, the door was forced open and in walked two soldiers with loaded automatic weapons. One shouted, "All right, everyone line up against the wall. If you wish to renounce your commitment to Jesus Christ, leave now!"

Two or three quickly left. After a few moments, two more.

"This is your last chance. Either turn against your faith in Christ," he ordered, "or stay and suffer the consequences."

Another left. Finally, two more in embarrassed silence with their faces covered, slipped out into the night. No one else moved. Parents with small children trembling beside them, looked down reassuringly. They fully expected to be gunned down or at best, to be imprisoned.

After a few more moments of complete silence, the other soldier closed the door, looked back at those who stood against the wall and said, "Keep your hands up . . . but this time in praise to our Lord Jesus Christ. Brothers and sisters, we, too, are Christians! We were sent to another house church several weeks ago to arrest a group of believers."

The other soldier interrupted, "But, instead, we were converted! We have learned by experience, however, that unless people are willing to die for their faith, they cannot be fully trusted."

Stories like this from the underground church in Russia have a way of jolting us! Immediately, this question comes to my mind: Would I be willing to die for my faith in Jesus Christ? Talk about a commitment. Yet, it was exactly this kind of total giving that brought our modern day church into being. Pioneers have gone before who were willing to give everything, including life to preserve and spread this gospel! Can we do less?

Commit thy way unto the Lord; trust also in Him; and He shall bring it to pass (Ps. 37:5;KJV).

∽

2 Sam. 18; Ps. 119:81-96; Prov. 29; Heb. 6-7

May 30 — It's Good to Remember

It is good to remember and some of our loveliest memories are a special gift to ourselves. Memorial Day is this kind of a day.

It was so in the experience of O'oka, a Japanese soldier. He had been fighting against our troops in the Philippines and after that bloody struggle was over, he wrote a letter home. In this letter he described how a young Yank had carelessly stood up in his foxhole to present a perfect target. O'oka took aim with his rifle, but he did not, could not pull the trigger. He watched this young American soldier through his gunsights, all the time wondering about him.

Then he wrote: "I, a father, smiled to myself afterwards, thinking of the mother in America whose son's life I had spared."

War is bitter and a cruel exercise but on occasion shining through the hurt of it is the memory of a generous impulse. This particular Japanese father found a beautiful comfort and satisfaction in the memory of his own compassion. But on thousands of other situations there was no compassion, but more killing, which is what war is all about.

So once more we are thinking about Memorial Day, a day to remember. For most of us we are asking, "What is there to remember?"

This is a special day that has been set aside to remember the war dead of battles and wars past. It was declared by Congress to do so. Today it is nothing more than another vacation day, a day to picnic, to fish, or to play ball . . . but not to remember, because our generation has been so far removed from the actual happenings of World Wars I and II.

We are to remember with thankful hearts the men and women who were willing to turn their backs on ease or comfort and give the ultimate sacrifice. We are to remember their readiness to risk, to take a chance to keep us free as a nation. We are to remember the blood they shed, the lives they gave, the weary hours they spent, and the courage they displayed. We are to remember the deadly combats they fought, the pain and anguish suffered, the loneliness that was theirs, and for this we thank them. We are to remember that it was a noble cause of freedom for which they died. We are to remember the cherished freedom, the honor they secured.

Memorial Day is still to treasure, to remember, to recall, to cherish, and we are now to preserve what has been won at great cost . . . our freedoms enjoyed as Americans.

Glory to God in the highest, and on earth peace to men on whom His favor rests (Luke 2:14).

⌒

2 Sam. 19-20; Ps. 119:97-112; Prov. 30; Heb. 8-9

May 31 — Hall of Famers Have Done It, Too

In the sports world, it's been easy to see the errors committed by some of the biggest names — even "Hall of Famers" have messed up. Here follows some of the biggest names in baseball, record holders all, but did you know about these other records they set? For example:

BABE RUTH — an absolutely awesome home run hitter with 714 in a career, a record which he held for 39 years. But he also held the strike-out record of 1,330 times until broken by another hall of famer.

TY COBB — fantastic competitor, batting champ, and the holder of most base steals in a season and a career until 1982. Cobb also held the record for being thrown out the most times attempting to steal in a season, 38 times in 1915.

CY YOUNG — terrific pitcher and still holds the most career victories, 511, in a lifetime. However, he also holds the record for most life-time losses, 313! He once posted a 13-win, 21-loss season.

HANK AARON — the home run slugger who bested Babe Ruth's career home run record with 755 homers. But Aaron holds the career mark for hitting into the most double plays, ever.

WALTER JOHNSON — one of the greatest pitchers, who, until recently bested, had posted the most strikeouts — 3,508. Johnson also holds the record for hitting the most batters — 204.

JIMMY FOXX — perhaps the greatest righthanded batter to ever play the game. He once hit 58 home runs in a season. And he holds the record for leading the league in strikeouts for the most consecutive seasons — seven!

ROBERTO CLEMENTE — famous Pittsburgh Pirate star struck out four times in one All-Star game — still a record.

SANDY KOUFAX — pitching sensation for the Dodgers, pitched four no-hitters in his career, but was a lousy batter. He still holds the record for striking out the most consecutive times at bat — 12!

REGGIE JACKSON — home run hitter for the Angels. On May 13, 1983, against the Twins, he became the first major leaguer to strike out 2,000 times. When asked what this kind of record meant to him, this slugging California Angel outfielder said, "It means I did nothing but miss the ball for four full seasons!"

So my pastor friend, take heart! In a few years after you've decided to hang it up, maybe history and people will be kind enough to remember our wins and forget the losses!

But we have this treasure in jars of clay to show that this all-surpassing power is from God and not from us (2 Cor. 4:7).

❧

2 Sam. 21-22; Ps. 119:113-128; Prov. 31; Heb. 10

June 1 — Changing Tags

When war is in progress, there is a medical practice and policy by which assistance to the wounded is given. Known as "triage," this practice involves "sorting" the wounded into categories. It is up to the judgment of the doctors or medical people on duty to "color tag" the wounded according to their condition.

One color of tag means the case is hopeless — there is nothing that can be done medically to save the soldier's life. Another color means that this person will recover with or without medical help. The third color indicates a doubtful prognosis — these might have a chance only if medical assistance is given. When medical supplies and personnel are in short supply, assistance is to be given only to this third category — people who might make it if given medical help. Nothing is done for the other two categories.

Lou, who served with the U.S. armed forces in Korea, was hit by a grenade. His body was blown apart and one leg was severely damaged. The first doctor who examined him made the decision that Lou was a hopeless case and beyond medical assistance, and tagged him as such. In this act, the doctor in actuality left Lou to die.

One of the nurses noticed Lou was conscious and began talking with him. In the course of conversation, they discovered they were both from the same state back home, Ohio. Since getting to know Lou in this short period of time as a person and not just another soldier, his nurse felt she couldn't just let him die. So she disobeyed orders and broke all the rules. She changed his color tag to the category that indicated he might make it if given medical help and assistance.

Lou was placed in an ambulance that took two days to transport him to the nearest field hospital where he spent months in recovery.

Lou made it! He recovered. While in the hospital he met a nurse who later became his wife. Even without one leg, which was amputated, Lou has led a full and happy life. All this was possible because a field nurse broke all the rules of triage and changed a tag! Just maybe, the job of the Church is to go around and change tags! That's what Jesus did when He touched the lepers. Nobody is hopeless.

A man with leprosy came to him and begged on his knees, "If you are willing, you can make me clean." Filled with compassion, Jesus reached out his hand and touched the man. "I am willing," he said. "Be clean!" (Mark 1:40-41).

❧

2 Sam. 23-24; Ps. 119:129-144; Prov. 1; Heb. 11

June 2 — Miss Thompson

Teddy Stallard certainly qualified as "one of the least" . . . disinterested in school, musty, wrinkled clothes, hair never combed, one of those kids with a deadpan face, unfocused stare. Unattractive, unmotivated, and distant, he was just plain hard to like.

Even though his teacher said she loved all in her class the same, she wasn't completely truthful. She should have known better, she had Teddy's records and she knew more about him than she wanted to. The records showed that while Teddy was a good boy, he had little help from home. His mother was dead, and his father was disinterested.

Christmas came and the boys and girls in Miss Thompson's class brought Christmas presents. Among the presents was one from Teddy Stallard, wrapped in brown paper and Scotch tape. When the teacher opened it, out fell a gaudy rhinestone bracelet with half the stones missing and a bottle of cheap perfume.

The other children began to giggle . . . but Miss Thompson put on the bracelet and some of the perfume on her wrist. Holding up her wrist for the children to smell, she said, "Doesn't it smell lovely?" The children ooohed and aaahed, taking the cue from their teacher.

When school was over that day, Teddy lingered behind. He slowly came over to her desk and said softly, "Miss Thompson . . . Miss Thompson, you smell just like my mother . . . and her bracelet looks real pretty on you, too."

The next day the children had a new teacher; Miss Thompson had become a different person, no longer just a teacher, but now an agent of God. She truly loved them all . . . but especially the slow ones and particularly Teddy. Soon Teddy showed dramatic improvement!

She didn't hear from Teddy for a long time. Then this note: *Dear Miss Thompson: They just told me I will be graduating first in my class. I wanted you to be the first to know. Love, Teddy Stallard.*

And four years later: *Dear Miss Thompson: As of today, I am Theodore Stallard, M.D. How about that? I wanted you to be the first to know I am getting married next month on the 27th. I want you to come and sit where my mother would sit if she were alive. You are the only family I have now; Dad died last year. Love, Teddy Stallard*

Miss Thompson went to that wedding and she sat where Teddy's mother would have sat!

Oh, that their hearts would be inclined to fear me and keep all my commands always, so that it might go well with them and their children for ever! (Deut. 5:29).

∽

1 Chron. 1-2; Ps. 119:145-160; Prov. 2; Heb. 12-13

June 3 — Little Things Matter

At age 21, Jacques Lafitte, a son of a very poor carpenter of Bayonne, set out to seek his fortune and future life's work. He had no references from influential people, no brilliant academic career behind him, but he was young and full of hope.

Jacques arrived in Paris and with his usual thoroughness began looking for a job. Days became weeks, and still he had no job or income. But he kept at it. Nobody in Paris noticed this determined young man.

One morning Jacques applied at the office of a famous Swiss banker, Monsieur Perregaux. The banker asked him a few questions about himself. Then he slowly shook his head and said there would be no job offered at the moment.

Sadly, and more discouraged than ever, Jacques left the bank and walked slowly across the courtyard. As he did so, he paused, stooped, and picked something up. Then he continued into the busy street, wondering if perhaps it wasn't time to return home to Bayonne.

At about that moment, he was overtaken by a man who tapped him on the shoulder. "Excuse me, sir," he said. "I'm an employee at the bank. Monsieur Perregaux wishes to see you again."

For the second time that morning Jacques faced the famous banker. "Pardon me," said Monsieur Perregaux, "but I happened to be watching you as you crossed the courtyard of the bank. You stooped and picked something up. Would you mind telling me what it was?"

"Only this," replied Jacques, wonderingly, as he took a bright new straight pin from the underside of the lapel of his coat.

"Aaah," exclaimed the banker, "THAT changes everything. We always have room here for anyone who is careful about little things. You may start at once."

Thus Jacques Lafitte began his long and amazingly successful association with the bank, ultimately assuming complete control of what became "Perregaux, Lafitte, and Company," one of the largest banks of Europe.

How many futures have hinged on such insignificant things? Little things are important in life and to God. Learn to pay attention to the little details of life, and you'll be amazed what this can lead to.

There be four things which are little upon the earth, but they are exceeding wise: the ants . . . the conies . . . the locusts . . . the spider
(Prov. 30:24-28;KJV).

❧

1 Chron. 3-5; Ps. 119:161-176; Prov. 3; Titus

June 4 — The Fruit of Kindness

It was a very nasty, stormy night at a small hotel in Philadelphia. An elderly man and woman approached the registration desk. Their question was, "Do you have room for us tonight?" Then, with a slight pause, the woman briefly explained, "We have been to some of the larger hotels, and they are all full."

The clerk explained that there were several conventions in town at the time, and indeed no rooms were available anywhere in Philadelphia that particular night. He also pointed out to them that all of the rooms in his hotel were full as well. But the clerk went on, "I wouldn't feel right about turning you out on such a nasty night. Would you be willing to sleep in my personal room?"

The couple was taken back at the generous offer and didn't know how to respond. The young man insisted that he would be able to get along just fine if only they would use his room.

The next day as the elderly couple was checking out, the man told the young clerk, "You are the kind of man who should be the boss of the best hotel in the country. Maybe someday I'll build one for you." They all smiled at the little joke, and then the clerk helped them carry their bags out to the street to load into their car.

Two years later, the clerk received a letter from the old man. He had almost forgotten the incident, but the letter recalled that night and his kindness. The letter also included a round trip ticket to New York City with the request that he come to be their guest for a visit.

When the young clerk reached New York City, there to meet him was the elderly couple. The old man drove him to the corner of Fifth Avenue and Thirty-fourth Street and pointed to a beautiful new building. It was like a palace of reddish stone with turrets and watchtowers like a castle. The older man said, "That is the hotel I have built for you to manage!"

"You must be joking," the young man said. He couldn't believe what he heard.

The old man said, "I'm not joking." And simply stood there and smiled.

The young man asked, "Who . . . who are you that you can do this?"

"My name is William Waldorf Astor." And the hotel was the original Waldorf-Astoria of New York City. The young clerk's name is George C. Boldt, and he did become the first manager of this historic hotel!

Love is patient, love is kind (1 Cor. 13:4).

෴

1 Chron. 6; Ps. 120; Prov. 4; Philemon

June 5 — What to Do?

The controversial Evelle Younger, California's former attorney general, was slated to be the featured speaker at the annual "Law Day Activities" which was held in Oakland. Just before he was to speak, the Alameda Bar Association presented a large cash award for a winning essay about law which had been written by a graduating senior from law school. The winner was then asked to read her speech, which turned out to be a bitter and biting attack on the American system. As she continued reading, tension began to mount in the crowd. There were several hundred people present and they seemed to cringe under the scathing attack on injustices which had been committed. Finally she finished, to sit down amid a thundering silence.

Evelle Younger was then introduced as the featured speaker. When he rose to speak he told the press to ignore his prepared remarks, and that he would now answer the bitter charges made by this law student. He began his rebuttal by recounting heathenistic practices of exorcising evil by beating one's body. He told of pagans who beat their backs bloody with reeds, cut their faces, crawled on their knees for miles, and maimed and disfigured themselves in an attempt to make themselves free from evil.

Then to bring the point home Younger said, "In the past few years we in America have been doing the same thing. We have been beating ourselves because of evils within our land and it is just as senseless as the heathenistic practices." He went on to admit that there are many inequities and problems within our system. But he also said that the way to work out these problems is by constructive, concerned change, not destructive criticism. Criticism may sound good, and is so easy to say, but it does nothing to change the wrongs about us.

What has happened politically in America has also happened in our churches. It's become quite popular to criticize organized religion by saying it is too irrelevant and wants too much money. Admittedly, there are many wrongs, but the answer doesn't lie in beating ourselves and self-destruction. In regards to the church, let me ask: What would you put in place of the church in today's world?

We tend to do the same criticizing on an individual level. It's easy for us to pick out the hypocrites in a room at the drop of a hat. The church is charged with being full of hypocrites, but what better place for them?

For God sent not his Son into the world to condemn the world; but that the world through him might be saved (John 3:17;KJV).

᪤

1 Chron. 7-8; Ps. 121; Prov. 5; 1 Tim. 1-3

June 6 — Fifty-seven Pennies

She was just a little girl, one of those non-persons. Nothing to make her stand out from other little girls. She was not from a wealthy family in fact she was from a poor family. Fifty-seven pennies were found under her pillow the night she died and this simple act made an indelible mark on the city of Philadelphia, Pennsylvania.

This little girl had made an attempt to become part of a Sunday school in Philadelphia years ago and was told she could not come because there was no room for her. She began saving her pennies in order to "help the Sunday school have more room."

Two years later she became sick and in a couple of weeks, died. Beneath her pillow they found a small, tattered book with the 57 pennies and a piece of paper on which she had printed neatly: "To help build the Little Temple bigger, so more children can go to Sunday school."

This little story and the purse with the 57 pennies were brought to the pastor, and if I have my memory on correctly, this was the Rev. Russell H. Conwell, and he told this humble story to his congregation. Then, the newspapers picked up the story and took it across the country. This triggered a spontaneous wave of gifts and giving. Soon the pennies grew and grew and today the final outcome of the humble 57 pennies offering can still be seen in Philadelphia today.

The "Little Temple" church had been replaced by a church which seats 3,300 people with lots of room for Sunday school. There is also a "Temple University" which accommodates and educates thousands of students. And there is also a "Temple Hospital" dedicated to humanity. And it all began with a nameless little girl who set out to do something about a need. Her beautiful, unselfish, dedicated attitude is what started this project. All it really takes in life to begin making a difference is one person with concern and dedication followed by an action. Let's add one more ingredient to this mix and call it love. Little people, in fact, all people are important to the future of the kingdom of God. Don't be discouraged with your little contribution. God can take your action and turn it into something big for His kingdom. Don't give up! I think of the little boy and his simple lunch . . . but in the Master's hands it was about to feed thousands and there was some left over. God needs a willing person first and watch it happen, again!

But Jesus called the children to him, and said, "Let the children come to me, and do not stop them, because the Kingdom of God belongs to such as these (Luke 18:16;TEV).

꩜

1 Chron. 9-10; Ps. 122; Prov. 6; 1 Tim. 4-6

June 7 — Love and a New York Cabbie

I was in New York the other day and rode with a friend in a taxi. When we got out, my friend said to the driver, "Thank you for the ride. You did a superb job of driving."

The taxi driver was stunned for a second. Then he said, "Are you a wise guy?"

"No, my dear man, I'm not putting you on. I admire the way you keep cool in traffic."

"What was that all about?" I asked.

"I am trying to bring love back to New York," he said. "I believe I have made that taxi driver's day. Suppose he has 20 fares. He's going to be nice to those 20 fares because someone was nice to him. Those fares in turn will be kinder to their employees or shopkeepers or waiters, or even their own families. Eventually the goodwill could spread to at least 1,000 people. Now that isn't bad, is it?"

"But you're depending on that taxi driver to pass your goodwill to others."

"I'm not depending on it," my friend said. "I'm aware that the system isn't foolproof so I might deal with 10 different people today. If out of 10 I can make 3 happy, then eventually I can indirectly influence the attitudes of 3,000 more."

"It sounds good on paper," I admitted, "but I'm not sure it works in practice."

"Nothing is lost if it doesn't. It didn't take any of my time to tell that man he was doing a good job. If it fell on deaf ears, so what? Tomorrow there will be another taxi driver I can try to make happy."

"You're some kind of a nut," I said.

"That shows how cynical you have become. I have made a study of this. The thing that seems to be lacking, is that no one tells people what a good job they're doing."

"But you can't do this all alone!" I protested.

"The most important thing is not to get discouraged. Making people in the city become kind again is not an easy job, but if I can enlist other people in my campaign. . . ."

"You just winked at a very plain-looking woman," I said.

"Yes, I know," he replied. "And if she's a school teacher, her class will be in for a fantastic day.[42]

Therefore, as God's chosen people, holy and dearly loved, clothe yourselves with compassion, kindness, humility, gentleness and patience (Col. 3:12;NIV).

❧

1 Chron. 11-12; Ps. 123-124; Prov. 7; 2 Tim. 1-2

Nurse Edie Murphy worked at a state psychiatric hospital in Massachusetts. Such a job is challenging, and one of the hardest parts is admitting new patients being brought in by ambulance. "You're never sure what state they're in, if they're violent, for instance," she says. Ambulances discharged patients in a deserted basement area. Procedure involved *two* people meeting the ambulance, an admitting nurse and a male mental-health technician.

One night Edie was helping out in a ward other than her own, when she learned that a patient was on his way by ambulance. Because everyone else was busy, Edie volunteered to meet him. "I was uneasy because I rarely did admissions, and the technician who accompanied me was new and very hesitant," she says. However, as the two came down the quiet corridor, Edie saw Dan waiting for them. This was a relief, since Dan was a strong and reliable tech with whom she had often worked. What a nice coincidence! The ambulance drove up, deposited the patient, and left.

"Hi, I'm Edie Murphy." Edie smiled at the young man who she later learned was psychotic. "I'll be doing your admission." She watched as his expression began to change. This could be a dangerous point, when a patient realized he was going to be hospitalized.

Without warning, the young man lunged at Edie, grabbing for her throat. Dan, instantly alert, caught the patient in a basket-hold and subdued him while Edie summoned additional help.

Her heart was still racing an hour later when she and Dan discussed the close call. "I'm so glad you were there," Edie told him.

"It was lucky you phoned," Dan agreed. "But how did you know I was working overtime, and five buildings away from you?"

Edie frowned. "What do you mean? I didn't call you."

"But. . . " Dan stared at her. "Some woman phoned our medical-room nurse. She said, 'Send Dan to Admissions. Edie needs help.' "

Some woman . . . but who? The busy nurses on Edie's floor hadn't phoned. They had already sent an escort with Edie and were not aware Dan was still on duty. The nurses on Dan's ward didn't know Edie or anything about a new admission. When the phone rang, that nurse was in the usually vacant cubbyhole, pouring a medication.

Who summoned Dan before Edie had even arrived?[43]

In speaking of the angels He says, "He makes His angels winds, His servants flames of fire" (Heb. 1:7).

❧

1 Chron. 13-15; Ps. 125-126; Prov. 8; 2 Tim. 3-4

Storm clouds and strong gusts of wind had come up suddenly over Columbus, Ohio. The Alpine Elementary School radio blared tornado warnings. It was too dangerous to send the children home. Instead, they were taken to the basement, where the children huddled together in fear.

We teachers were worried, too. To help ease tension, the principal suggested a sing-along. But the voices were weak and unenthusiastic. Child after child began to cry — we could not calm them.

Then a teacher whose faith seemed equal to any emergency, whispered to the child closest to her, "Aren't you forgetting something, Kathie? There is a power greater than the storm that will protect us. Just say to yourself, 'God is with me now.' Then pass the words on to the child next to you."

As the verse was whispered from child to child, a sense of peace settled over the group. I could hear the wind outside still blowing with the same ferocity of the moment before, but it didn't seem to matter now. Inside, fear subsided and tears faded away. When the all-clear signal came over the radio sometime later, students and staff returned to their classrooms without their usual jostling and talking.

Through the years I have remembered those calming words. In times of stress and trouble, I have again been able to find release from fear or tension by repeating, "He's with me now."[44]

Life has storms and will continue to have storms. There is no way to escape entirely the storms, tests, and trials of life. It's part of the human condition. There is no way to have any guarantee that life from this moment on will never be filled with storms. But there are plenty of promises that God has given to us from His Word that He will be with us no matter what may come our way. We do everything humanly possible to avoid these storms and attempt to protect our loved ones from their storms, unsuccessfully. The promises are not that we will have a storm-free life, but that in every storm which comes our way, He will be there to comfort, guide, and protect. The promises are for good days and bad days, and every kind in between. He hasn't promised cloud free days, but He has promised strength. Whatever the day or test, He has promised to be there with you. And the bottom line is that there is no positive security in this life but there is a positive promise of strength for each day!

For God did not give us a spirit of timidity, but a spirit of power, of love and of self-discipline (2 Tim. 1:7).

৵৶

1 Chron. 16-17; Ps. 127; Prov. 9; 1 Pet. 1-2

June 10 — The Animal School

Once upon a time, the animals decided to do something special to meet the problems of a "new world." So they organized a school.

They adopted an activity curriculum consisting of running, climbing, swimming, and flying. To make it easier to administer the curriculum, all the animals took all the subjects.

The duck was excellent in swimming, in fact better than his instructor, but he made only passing grades in flying and was very poor in running.

The rabbit started at the top of the class in running, but had a nervous breakdown because of so much make-up work in swimming.

The squirrel was excellent in climbing until he developed frustration in the flying class where his teacher made him start from the ground up instead of from the treetop down. He developed a "charlie horse" and then got a C in climbing and a D in running.

The eagle was a problem child and was disciplined severely. In the climbing class he beat all the others to the top of the tree, but insisted on using his own way to get there.

At the end of the year, an abnormal eel who could swim exceedingly well, and also run, climb, and fly a little, was valedictorian.

The prairie dogs stayed out of school and fought the tax levy because the administration would not add burrowing to the curriculum. They apprenticed their children to the badger and later joined the groundhogs and gophers to start a successful private school.[45]

Does this fable have a moral?

And does the moral have an application? Yes, lots of applications. Probably the most important is the process of attempting to fit every one into the same mold. The lives we are touching are impressionable, printable, moldable — but how are we pressing and forming and guiding? Do we insist that all must look alike when their education is completed? When they graduate are they still as excited about learning as when they began? God created each individual with uniqueness that is not shared by anyone else — different fingerprints, personal DNAs. There are no copies. Why is a bronze by Degas or a violin by Stradivarius or a painting by Rembrandt so valuable? They each had a unique creator and are so rare in number. Think a moment about what makes people so valuable — who created them?

I will praise You, for I am fearfully and wonderfully made;
Marvelous are Your works, And that my soul knows
very well (Ps. 139:14;NKJV).

❧

1 Chron. 18-20; Ps. 128; Prov. 10; 1 Pet. 3-5

June 11 — The Emergency Angel

It was a cold early December night in 1990 when Edwin Craig, just newly trained and graduated from the police academy was on duty. He had been assigned to work a patrol at the Denver Airport. As he was making his rounds, he started down a very long deserted walkway/hallway. Quite a ways ahead of him he watched as an older man slowed, stopped, then collapsed and slumped against the wall.

Ed ran quickly to attempt to help the man. He was trying to remember his training as he reached to check a pulse . . . and found none. The man also stopped breathing!

Here it was, his first emergency and he was alone, no backup. He immediately called for medical help on his police radio. The sterile classroom training seemed so long ago. He sensed that if he didn't do something the man would die before help arrived . . . but what to do? What could he do? He breathed a prayer, "Jesus, please help me. Help me to know what to do."

Just then, coming from behind he heard this woman's voice telling him, "I'm an emergency room nurse. I'll do the chest compression if you will do the CPR breathing." Ed was thinking, *Where did she come from, I didn't hear any steps in the hallway.* Steps could have been heard from a long way off echoing . . . but nothing. She was just there.

Edwin began the mouth-to-mouth CPR while she did the chest compressions. When the paramedics arrived and took over, the man began reviving.

"Then," Edwin says, "the most peculiar thing happened. I stood up and looked around for the nurse so I could thank her but she was gone! No one was there! The hallway was long and no exits were handy. She should have been seen easily. She had just appeared out of nowhere when I needed help desperately and when the crisis was over she was gone, vanished!"

Do angels know how to perform CPR? Would an angel have to resort to CPR to revive someone? Well, to this day Edwin Craig believes that angels know CPR! At least one who appeared out of nowhere when needed in Denver. And as a policeman, to this day, he is one cop who now makes his patrols with a sense that there can be divine help in times of need.

Jesus did many other miraculous signs in the presence of his disciples, which are not recorded in this book. But these are written that you may believe that Jesus is the Christ, the Son of God, and that by believing you may have life in His name (John 20:30-31).

❧

1 Chron. 21-22; Ps. 129; Prov. 11; 2 Pet. 1-3

June 12 — Keeper of the Springs

There was a quiet forest dweller who lived high above an Austrian village along the eastern slope of the Alps. The old gentleman had been hired many years ago by an earlier town council to clear away the debris of leaves and branches from the pristine springs up in the mountain ravines. These springs served the town.

With consistency, the old man removed dead leaves and branches, and cleared away the dirt, dead animals, and silt that otherwise would clog and contaminate the fresh supply of water. In time, the village prospered and became a popular vacation spot for tourists. The mill wheels ran day and night, farmlands were irrigated, the water was unpolluted, the village healthy, and it was picture-postcard beautiful.

Years passed. At one town council meeting to review the budget, one member noticed the salary figure paid to the obscure "keeper-of-the-springs." The treasurer questioned the expense and asked, "Who is this old man? Who hired him? Is he productive?" The treasurer paused, then went on, "For all we know, this stranger up in the hills might be dead. He isn't needed any longer." So by a unanimous voice vote the council did away with the old man's services.

For several weeks nothing happened. Then came autumn, leaves were dropping, small branches snapped off, silt began to fall into the springs, and the flow began to slow. One householder noticed a slight yellowish-brown tint in the water. In a few days the gathering pool showed more dark color. In another week, a slime began covering some sections of the canal banks . . . then an odor was detected. The mill wheels ground to a halt, tourists disappeared, children began to get sick.

Quickly, the embarrassed town council called a special meeting. They realized their error. They voted to re-hire the old keeper of the springs and within several weeks the sparkling river of life cleared up . . . mill wheels turned again, tourists came back, children stopped being sick, and a renewed life returned to this Alpine village!

And what was the name of the old "Keeper-of-the-Springs"? Well, according to this story which has been told and retold in many versions, you will find his name possibly recorded as: Integrity, love, character, sound doctrine, prayer, Jesus, Joshua, perseverance, solid homes — well, you get the idea. And now that you know, you can put most anything foundational in as the keeper of your springs. We, as well as the people we lead, all are in need of the KEEPER OF THE SPRINGS!

Above all else, guard your heart, for it is the
wellspring of life (Prov. 4:23).

༄

1 Chron. 23-25; Ps. 130-131; Prov. 12; 1 John 1-2

June 13 — Greed Separates a Son from His Father

"Dear Abby" is a phenomena of our day. She seems to have an answer for all kinds of human needs and problems. The following is not from Abby, but a reader who wrote the following to Abigail Van Buren.

Dear Abby:

The letter concerning the minister who, on receiving a pair of leather gloves for services rendered, was disappointed, until he discovered a $10 bill stuffed into each finger, reminded me of this story:

A young man from a wealthy family was about to graduate from high school. It was the custom in that affluent neighborhood for the parents to give the graduate an automobile. "Bill" and his father had spent months looking at cars, and the week before graduation they found the perfect car.

Imagine his disappointment when, on the eve of his graduation, Bill's father handed him a gift-wrapped Bible! Bill was so angry, he threw the Bible down and stormed out of the house. He and his father never saw each other again. Years later, it was the news of his father's death that brought Bill home again.

As he sat one night, going through his father's possessions that he was to inherit, he came across the Bible his father had given him. He brushed away the dust and opened it to find a cashier's check, dated the day of his graduation . . . in the exact amount of the car they had chosen together.

Beckah Fink, Texas

And here is the response from Abby:

Dear Beckah: I hope Bill read the Bible cover to cover, for it contained much he needed to learn: "A foolish son is a grief to his father, and bitterness to her who bore him" (Prov. 17:25).[46]

There is not a whole lot to be added to this story . . . it says it all. Would it be fair to say that sometimes youth is wasted on the young? We get smart too late. We wake up to the lessons of life after the lesson has been experienced. Too often, it's painful. Greed is one of those passions which must be conquered early on, or it will haunt you the rest of your life. After all, how much of this world's toys can you take with you when you die? Remember that there are no U-Haul trailers behind hearses.

Such is the end of all who go after ill-gotten gain; it takes away the lives of those who get it (Prov. 1:19).

⟨∾⟩

1 Chron. 26-27; Ps. 132; Prov. 13; 1 John 3-5

June 14 — Flag Day

Hopefully, everyone knows that the American flag is honored not for what it is . . . a bit of bunting . . . but for what it represents. To the veteran of the old Rainbow Division is symbolizes glory on the battlefield, but to the immigrant it is more apt to symbolize the security of freedom. To the skeptic and cynic it represents the right to dissent, but to many others it represents the power of a democratic society. To the entrepreneur it may represent free enterprise, but to the investor it means protection against unbridled capitalism.

If there were such a thing as the "American way of life," that is what the flag would represent to everybody . . . but there is no such a thing. What we may refer to as this American way is really the sum of all the different ways in which Americans live and think and work and worship, not always compatibly, but always under the same flag. There is really only one thing we have in common and that is our diversity.

There is nothing holy about the flag or about our soil or the institutions and ideals it represents. We are "a nation under God" but so is every other country also a nation under God. Patriotism is not religion.

Patriotism is not nationalism, either, although a great many of us seem to think it is. Love of one's own country does not mean hatred to the rest of the world. The true patriot will honor the flag today and every day in many constructive ways.

How? Simply by honoring and defending those great, broad principles which this scrap of bunting represents. The flag is honored when justice has been done . . . when a patriot restores reason . . . when others are treated fairly . . . when there is freedom to worship God as we know we should . . . when our government works as it should.

There is no easy way in which to honor our American flag . . . red, white, and blue . . . stars and stripes, and there never has been. That is why it needs honoring on Flag Day as well as on every other day of the year.

During the entire history of America our flag has been the flag of a country, not the personal standard of a king or an emperor. It stands and it has stood for us as the symbol of an abstract idea, not the sign of the power of any ruler. It is and it has been a national flag, not a personal standard. Our flag is a symbol that stands for a people and a nation just like the cross stands for Christianity. The freedoms which have been won are now ours to keep! Today is another reminder of that challenge.

Then He said to them: "Give to Caesar what is Caesar's, and to God what is God's" (Matt. 22:21).

෴

1 Chron. 28-29; Ps. 133-134; Prov. 14; 2, 3 John

June 15 — The Gift of the Rabbi

There was a famous monastery which had fallen on hard times. Formerly its many buildings had been filled with young monks and its big church resounded with singing but now was nearly deserted. A handful of old monks shuffled through the cloisters and praised and prayed with heavy hearts.

At the edge of the monastery woods, an old rabbi had built a little hut. He went there from time to time to pray and fast. No one ever spoke with him, but the word would be passed when he appeared, "The rabbi walks in the woods." And as long as he was there the monks felt sustained by his prayerful presence.

One day the abbot decided to visit the rabbi and to open his heart to him. As he approached the hut, the rabbi was standing in the doorway with outstretched arms in welcome. It was as though he had been waiting a long time. They embraced like long-lost brothers.

The rabbi motioned the abbot to enter. In the middle of the room was a plain wooden table with the Scripture open on it. They sat in the presence of the Book — then the rabbi began to cry, and as the abbot could not contain himself, he also began to cry.

After the tears had ceased and all was quiet, the rabbi said, "You and your brothers are serving God with heavy hearts. You have come to ask a teaching of me. I will give you this teaching but you can only repeat it once. After that, no one must say it aloud again."

Then the rabbi looked at the abbot and said, "The Messiah is among you." The abbot left without a word and without looking back.

The next morning he called his monks together and told them he had received a teaching from "the rabbi who walks in the woods." Then he looked at each of his brothers and said, "The rabbi said that one of us is the messiah." They were startled, but no one ever mentioned it again.

As time went by, the monks began to treat each other with a very special reverence. Visitors were deeply touched by their lives. People came from far and wide to be nourished by the prayer life of the monks, and young men asked about becoming part of this community. The rabbi no longer walked in the woods, but the monks who had taken his teaching to heart were still sustained by a prayerful presence.

Behold, how good and how pleasant it is For brethren to dwell together in unity! It is like the precious oil upon the head, Running down on the beard, The beard of Aaron, Running down on the edge of his garments. It is like the dew of Hermon. . . . For there the Lord commanded the blessing . . . Life forever (Ps. 133:1-3;NKJV).

⌒☙

1 Kings 1; Ps. 135; Prov. 15; Jude

June 16 — Thy Father Seeketh Thee

A Quaker family lived in Pennsylvania. Against the father's wishes, his son Jonathan ran off and enlisted in the cause of the North during the Civil War. Time passed, and no word came from Jonathan. One night the father had a dream that his son had been wounded in action, was in distress, and needed the care of his father.

The father left the farm and attempted to discover where the troops might be camped. Making his way by horse-drawn buggy, he came to the scene of action. He inquired until he found the commander and asked about his son. The commander replied that there had been heavy action earlier in the day, and many had fallen wounded. Some had been cared for; others were still out in the trenches. Pointing in the direction of where the fighting had taken place, he gave permission to the father to go and try to find his son.

It was now dusk, and the father lit a lantern. While searching for his son, he came across many wounded young men. Some were calling for help, and others were too seriously wounded to cry for assistance.

The task seemed impossible. How could he find his son among all those wounded and dying? He devised a little plan. Methodically, he would comb the scene of action with his lantern. But that wasn't fruitful as he stumbled over body after body.

Then he began calling loudly as he walked, "Jonathan Smythe, thy father seeketh after thee!" He would walk a little ways and call again, "Jonathan Smythe, thy father seeketh thee. . . ." A groan and response could be heard here and there, "I wish that were my father."

He kept diligently at his search. Then, he heard a very faint, barely audible reply, "Father, over here." And as the father approached closer — "I knew you would come."

The father knelt down, took his son into his arms, comforted him with his presence, gave him some water to drink, dressed the wound, carried him to the buggy, and took him to a place of seclusion to nurse him back to health.

It reminds me of another father with a wayward son whose story Jesus told us in the Bible (Luke 15). This in turn reminds me of our loving kind Heavenly Father who is constantly on the lookout for His hurting, wounded, lost children.

My friend, if as you read this, you are one of those lost ones, I assure you that the Heavenly Father is only an invitation away!

Cast all your anxiety on him because he cares for you (1 Pet. 5:7).

᭡

1 Kings 2; Ps. 136; Prov. 16; Rev. 1

A small boy at a summer camp received a large package of cookies in the mail from his mother. He ate a few, then placed the remainder under his bed. The next day, after lunch, he went to his tent to get a cookie, but the box was gone.

That afternoon a camp counselor, who had been told of the theft, saw another boy sitting behind a tree eating the stolen cookies.

He returned to the group and sought out the boy whose cookies had been stolen. He said, "Billy, I know who stole your cookies. Will you help me teach him a lesson?"

The puzzled boy replied, "Well . . . yes, but aren't you going to punish him?"

The counselor explained, "No, that would make him resent me and hate you. No, I want you to call your mother and ask her to send you another box of cookies."

Billy did as the counselor asked, and a few days later received another box of delicious homemade cookies in the mail.

The counselor said, "Now, the boy who stole your cookies is down by the lake. Go down there and share your cookies with him."

The boy protested, "But, he's the thief."

"I know. But try it, and see what happens," replied the counselor.

About half an hour later, the camp counselor saw the two come up the hill, arm in arm. The boy who had stolen the cookies was earnestly trying to get the other to accept his jackknife in payment for the stolen cookies, and the victim was just as earnestly refusing the gift from his new friend, saying that a few cookies weren't important anyway.

We all have a great hunger for forgiveness as this next story indicates. It happened in Spain that a father and teenage son had a broken relationship. The son ran away, but the father searched for his rebellious son. Finally, in Madrid, in a last desperate attempt to find him, the father put an ad in the newspaper. The ad read: "Dear Paco, Meet me in front of the newspaper office at noon. All is forgiven. I love you. Your father."

The next day at noon, in front of the newspaper office, eight hundred "Pacos" showed up! It seems that all these young men with the name Paco were seeking forgiveness and love from their fathers.

Does a child of yours need your forgiveness today? Or maybe, you need to seek your father's forgiveness. Remember, God, the Father, still forgives! And so should we.

The Lord is gracious and righteous; our God is full of compassion
(Ps. 116:5).

༄

1 Kings 3-4; Ps. 137; Prov. 17; Rev. 2

❦

Father made me learn so many Bible verses
every day that by the time I was eleven years
of age, I had learned about three-fourths of
the Old Testament and all of the New by heart.

John Muir

❦

June 18 — Just "Dad"

Father's Day, which is observed the third Sunday of each June, was not the brainchild of a group of disgruntled fathers who resented the attention given to mothers. According to the National Father's Day Committee — a volunteer organization of notables from every walk of life united to promote better father-child relationships — it was initiated on June 19, 1910, three years *before* the first official Mother's Day.

This commemoration was the idea of Mrs. John Bruce Dodd of Spokane, Washington. She had suggested the idea to honor her own father, William Smart, a veteran of the Civil War, who had reared his six motherless children on an eastern Washington farm. Smart was a widower left with these children after the birth of their sixth child. His daughter thought he had done such an outstanding job as both father and mother that she had wanted to do something to perpetuate his memory. The occasion was soon expanded to include all American fathers.

William Jennings Bryan was one of the first to give his endorsement to Mrs. Dodd's plan. Then James Whitcomb Riley wrote, "My heart is with you in this great work."

In 1924 President Calvin Coolidge was the first president to recommend the national observance of Father's Day. The original intent of this day was a dedication to the building of good citizenship at home, in the nation, and in the church. That should be a challenge to all us fathers.

When is a father just "Dad"? H.C. Chatfield answers: "If he's wealthy and prominent and you stand in awe of him, call him 'Father.' If he sits in his shirt sleeves and suspenders at ball games and picnics, call him 'Pop.' If he tills the land or labors in overalls, call him 'Pa.' If he wheels the baby carriage, call him 'Papa' with the accent on the first syllable. If, however, he makes a pal of you when you're good, and is too wise to let you pull the wool over his loving eyes when you're not; if you're sure no one else has quite so fine a father, you may call him 'Dad.' "

"Honor your father and mother" — which is the first commandment with a promise — "that it may go well with you and that you may enjoy long life on the earth" (Eph. 6:2-3).

⟨~⟩

1 Kings 5-6; Ps. 138; Prov. 18; Rev. 3

June 19 — The Fog Lifted

One of the most famous battles in history took place on June 18, 1815, and is known as the Battle of Waterloo. As we look back from our viewpoint in history, it's one of those on which destinies of nations rested.

The French army was fighting under the command of Napoleon. The armies of the "Allies," which were made up of the British, Dutch, and Germans, were fighting under the command of Lord Wellington.

Communications were not the sophisticated instant science they are today, and so the people of England were dependent upon a system of semaphore signals to find out how the battle was going. It was primitive and not too reliable, being subject to human error. One of these signal stations was located on the tower of the Winchester Cathedral in London.

Quite late in the day, while still light, this signal was flashed from the tower to the people who were waiting for news: "W-E-L-L-I-N-G-T-O-N—D-E-F-E-A-T-E-D—." Just at that moment, one of those sudden and thick London fogs made it impossible to read the rest of the message. The news of the defeat quickly spread through London. Then from London, it spread to the surrounding countryside. The whole country was sad and gloomy when they heard the news that their country had lost this crucial war.

In the morning, the fog lifted and the complete message could be read. The message had four words . . . not just two. The complete message was this: "W-E-L-L-I-N-G-T-O-N—D-E-F-E-A-T-E-D—T-H-E—E-N-E-M-Y!"

It took a few minutes for the good news to sink in and to spread as far as the bad news. Sorrow was turned into joy! Defeat was turned into victory!

And defeat became victory when Christ rose from the grave, giving us the ultimate gift through His love for us.

The true spirit of the holiday season began that day, and the challenge to Christians is to keep on giving love in the midst of any and all circumstances.

Then the angel spoke to the women, "Don't be frightened!" he said. "I know you are looking for Jesus, who was crucified, but He isn't here! For He has come back to life again (Matt. 28:5-6;LB).

❧

1 King 7; Ps. 139; Prov. 19; Rev. 4-5

June 20 — Foolish Heroics?

The young farmer sat happily on the wagon seat as his spirited team made their way into the little Kansas town. After hitching the team to a rack near the corner of the main street, he walked down to the general store to buy the week's supply of groceries and goods.

He had hardly entered the store when a bunch of boys came walking down the street lighting and flipping firecrackers. One of the boys flipped one directly in front of the team of horses. When the firecracker burst, the team reared and lunged against the lines holding them. The lines snapped. When the team came down, the scared animals laid back their ears and thundered down the main street.

At that moment the young farmer looked out of the store to take in the scene. Without a bit of hesitation, he threw himself into the street just as the frightened horses came by with manes flying. With a jump he managed to grab the bridle of the horse nearest to him.

The running team jerked him off his feet and dragged him down the street with them. But with an iron grip he held on, and the team began to slow down a bit. In about one hundred yards he was able to get around in front to reach for the other bridle. But the horses wouldn't give in quite so easy and reared again. With front hooves flying, down they came. One of those deadly, flying hooves caught the farmer full in his face. Slowly that iron grip began to relax on the bridle as he slumped into the dust of the street. Other men by this time were able to get the team under control.

They carried the dead young farmer to the plank sidewalk and laid him down. One of the men spoke out of his frustration and said, "The fool! The crazy fool! Why didn't he just let them go? They would have run themselves out on the prairie. He didn't have to die like this! The crazy fool!" The rest of the men and the gathering crowd nodded in agreement. It had been a foolish kind of heroics.

Just about then they heard a sound coming from the inside of the wagon box. Every person looked in that direction. Above the sideboards came the blond head of a scared little boy crying for his daddy.[47]

The world may look back on the sacrifice of Jesus Christ on the cross of Calvary and think it unnecessary. There is no greater demonstration of love than the giving of one's own life for another. He did it for you and me.

For God so loved the world that he gave his one
and only Son, that whoever believes in him
shall not perish but have eternal life (John 3:16).

❧

1 Kings 8; Ps. 140; Prov. 20; Rev. 6-7

June 21 — Some Fathers Do

A soldier returning home from the Vietnam War got off the train with a limp and an arm in a sling. A small gray-haired woman ran to him, followed by a big man who kept up with her by simply walking faster. She embraced the boy and shed some tears. The father moved closer and stated, "I'm glad to see you, Son." Not much more was said until they reached home and the boy was in the kitchen with his mother.

"You know, Mom, I get a kick out of Pa," he said. "Did you notice him at the station? No dramatics. No frog in his throat like a lot of men would have. Of course, you understand, I know he likes me . . . I mean, he probably loves me . . . but what I mean is you'll never catch Pop losing his head. Boy, he's got ice water in his veins. What a general he would have made!"

"Son," his mother said, "he loves you very much. I know."

"Sure, I know, too. Say, where is Pop?"

"He's outside. You better run in and see how we've fixed your room."

The young man left, and she went out the back door, knowing exactly where to find her husband. She looked through the crack of the garage door and saw him on his knees. The step stool was his altar.

"I want to thank You, God," the big man was saying. "I asked You, God, to give me a break and let him come out all right, though I knew then I didn't have any more right to ask than anybody else. But now he's back safe. So I want to thank You, God. I want to thank You very much. Amen." He rose slowly.

The woman returned to her kitchen. The young man came back saying, "The room looks swell. Say, where did Pop go?"

"He'll be right in," his mother said. "There was just something he had to do."

Many times fathers attempt to hide their real feelings. Why? Probably because in our society, men are still taught to be macho, silent, and tough.

Sir, it's okay to express how you feel. Allow yourself to be human, to show an expression, to be loving and caring.

Being a father in today's world requires the best from every man who is a father. And what about your father? Have you prayed for him lately? Have you taken the time to express thanks to him for what he has done in your life?

As a father has compassion on his children, so the Lord has compassion on those who fear him (Ps. 103:13).

1 Kings 9-10; Ps. 141; Prov. 21; Rev. 8-9

June 22 — Forgiven

A certain seminary professor always introduces his class on the New Testament with a story from his own life. As a young man he told a lie to his father and hurt him deeply. For years the matter went unresolved, but the guilt and remorse kept gnawing away at him until, finally, he wrote his father a letter.

Because he was not even sure that his father would remember, the professor reviewed the entire episode and asked his father to forgive him. A few days later he received a reply in which the father said, "Of course I remember, and of course I forgive you."

The son said it was like a great weight had fallen from his shoulders, and it made all the difference in his life. But the real payoff came several years later when both his mother and father died within a short time of each other.

As the oldest son, he went to their house and was going through their things. Up in the attic he found a box containing little treasures his parents had kept through the years from their marriage and from his childhood. As he looked through the box, his eyes welled up with tears because he felt so close to his parents and the things that had been most important to them.

Then he found the letter that he had written, asking for forgiveness. He opened it and began to read, and with tears running down his cheeks, he turned it over. And there, in his father's handwriting, was one word: "FORGIVEN!" And it was underlined.

In that moment he realized that his father had really let go of the issue that had come between them. He had written "forgiven" on the letter, then put it aside in the box of treasures because it was over. There was no unfinished business.

What a great gift it was for that son to discover that his father had relinquished all traces of the hurt and the resentment and the bitterness!

What a fantastic gift it is when we are able to forgive and let go — to forgive and forget. This is exactly the way in which God, our Heavenly Father, deals with us. When we are forgiven by God, it is as if we had never done that which caused our estrangement from Him.

Where are you in regard to forgiveness today? Do you need to forgive another, or are you in need of forgiveness yourself? God will help in both situations.

For if you forgive men when they sin against you, your heavenly Father will also forgive you. But if you do not forgive men their sins, your Father will not forgive your sins (Matt. 6:14-15).

❧

1 Kings 11; Ps. 142; Prov. 22; Rev. 10-11

June 23 — Who Is Handicapped?

Arnold Palmer was once invited to speak to a convention of blind golfers. (This story has many versions, so the truth cannot be absolutely guaranteed.) He asked them how they were able to know what direction to hit the ball. One blind golfer explained that the caddie went on ahead of him with a little bell, which he would ring as he stood near the hole. The blind golfer would then hit the ball toward the sound of the bell.

Arnold asked how well it worked, and the blind golfer said that it worked so well he was willing to take on Palmer for a round of golf! Just to make it interesting, he was willing to bet Palmer $10,000 he could beat him. That just blew Palmer's mind! Ten thousand dollars!

Palmer was a bit hesitant, so this blind golfer pushed him by saying, "What's the matter, are you afraid to play a blind golfer?"

So the deal was struck. Palmer said, "When do we tee off?"

And the blind golfer said, "Tonight at 11:30!"

Under this set of circumstances, I don't know if I'd call that a handicap. But handicaps come in all sizes, and they can be mental just as well.

In the country church of a small village, an altar boy serving the priest at Sunday mass accidentally dropped the cruet of wine. The village priest struck the altar boy sharply on the cheek and in a gruff voice shouted, "Leave the altar and don't come back!"

The altar boy grew up — his name was Tito, the Communist leader!

In the cathedral of a large city, an altar boy at Sunday mass accidentally dropped the cruet of wine. With a warm twinkle in his eyes, the bishop gently whispered, "Some day you will be a priest."

That boy grew up to become the late Archbishop Fulton J. Sheen.

Think of the fantastic power of words. This is not to say that the entire life pattern for these men was set by the incident at the altar. Much more goes into making a life. But it is true that life can turn on a hinge of words spoken.

With the words we speak, we can add to the burden of life or lift the cares from the shoulders of another. Handicapping often occurs because we have allowed others to dictate our future or, by our own words, have hindered those to whom we speak. The blind golfer had worked to overcome his handicap and, in fact, turned it to an advantage.

How about lifting someone's burden today with a kind, encouraging word? Who knows whom you may be talking to!

The thief comes only to steal and kill and destroy; I have come that
they may have life, and have it to the full (John 10:10).

❧

1 Kings 12-13; Ps. 143; Prov. 23; Rev. 12-13

June 24 — Black Pebble? White Pebble?

Many years ago, when people who owed money could be thrown into jail, a merchant in Rome had the misfortune to owe a huge sum of money to a mean moneylender. The moneylender, who was quite old and ugly, took a fancy to the merchant's beautiful young granddaughter, whom they had been raising because her parents had died. The money-lender proposed a bargain. He would cancel the merchant's debt if he could have the granddaughter instead and make her his wife.

Both the merchant and the granddaughter were horrified at the bargain, so the cunning moneylender schemed that they would let "Providence" decide the matter. He told them that he would put a black pebble and a white pebble into an empty bag and the granddaughter would pick out one of the pebbles. If she picked the black one, she would become his wife, and her grandfather's debt would be canceled. If she refused to pick a pebble, her grandfather would be thrown into jail and eventually she would starve with no one to care for her.

Reluctantly, the grandfather agreed. They were standing on a pebble strewn path in the merchant's garden as they talked. The moneylender stooped down to pick up the two pebbles. As he did, the girl, senses heightened by fright, sharp-eyed, noticed that he picked up two black pebbles and put them into the bag. He then asked the girl to pick out the pebble that would decide her fate and that of her grandfather.

What would you have done if you were the girl? If you had to advise her, what would you have advised her to do?

1) The girl should refuse to pick a pebble?

2) The girl should show that there are two black pebbles in the bag and expose the moneylender as a cheat?

3) The girl should pick the black pebble and sacrifice herself in order to spare her grandfather from prison?

The girl put her hand into the bag and drew out a pebble. But, without looking at it, she fumbled it and let the pebble fall onto the path where it was immediately mixed in among all the other pebbles. "Oh, how clumsy of me," she said. "Never mind, however. If you look into the bag, you'll be able to tell which pebble I dropped by the color of the one that remains."

Since the remaining pebble, was, of course, black, it had to be assumed that she had picked the white pebble. Then, for sure, the moneylender dared not admit his own dishonesty!

I am sending you out like sheep among wolves. Therefore be as shrewd as snakes and as innocent as doves (Matt. 10:16).

❧

1 Kings 14-15; Ps. 144; Prov. 24; Rev. 14-15

Robert today owns an over-the-road transport company, but before he got into the trucking business he had purchased a sporting goods store. He was the lone employee to start with. The store happened to be in an out-of-the-way part of town, sort of isolated, by itself.

One day while expressing his concerns to his pastor, the idea struck him to ask the pastor and some of the elders to come over and pray for the protection of Robert and his store. They also prayed that anyone who came to buy a gun for the wrong purposes would not be able to.

One afternoon a very tough, rough-looking character entered the store to buy a gun. Through the store-front window Robert saw that this man was accompanied by six or seven other equally tough-looking men on motorcycles now parked in front. Immediately Robert had the sense that this man did not have good intentions for purchasing a gun. So he refused to sell any guns or ammunition to this customer. The man left in an angry huff, jumped on his bike, motioned for the others to follow, made an obscene gesture through the window at Robert, and pealed out of the parking lot with tires squealing and pipes roaring.

The next morning this same man returned with his gang but didn't enter the store . . . they simply began circling the store on their bikes, no doubt, with the intent of intimidating Robert. They kept up this harassment most of the day. They would drive out of the lot and return again in a few minutes to circle the store again. All the while they would stare through the front window. Robert, alone in the store, began to pray: "Lord, help me. Please send your angels to protect me and keep the store safe from any harm."

After several hours of this harassment the leather-jacketed gang drove out of the lot . . . and never returned again!

Later, one of Robert's regular customers dropped by the store to visit. He mentioned that he'd been by earlier in the day but didn't bother to come in. Robert asked him why he hadn't.

"Well, because the inside of your store was packed full of customers. I knew you'd be so busy you wouldn't have time to visit with me," he replied.

Yet . . . NO ONE was in the store at any time that day!

Daniel answered, "O king, live forever! My God sent His angel, and he shut the mouths of the lions. They have not hurt me, because I was found innocent in his sight. Nor have I ever done any wrong before you, O king" (Dan. 6:21-22).

〰️

1 Kings 16-17; Ps. 145; Prov. 25; Rev. 16-17

June 26 — Schwarzkopf's Leadership Principles

General H. Norman Schwarzkopf gained prominence as the commander of the U.S. forces in the Persian Gulf War. In a recent interview with *INC.* magazine, the general shared his leadership principles:

1) You must have clear goals and you must be able to articulate them clearly to others.

2) Give yourself a clear agenda. Every morning, write down the five most important things to accomplish that day, and get those five done.

3) Let people know where they stand.

4) What's broken, fix now. Don't put it off. Problems that aren't dealt with lead to other problems.

5) No repainting the flagpole. Make sure all the work your people are doing is essential to the organization.

6) Set high standards. People won't generally perform above your expectations, so it's important to expect a lot.

7) Lay the concept out, but let your people execute it.

8) People come to work to succeed. So don't operate on the principle that if they aren't watched and supervised, they'll bungle the job.

9) Never lie. Ever.

10) When in charge, take command. Some leaders who feel they don't have adequate information put off deciding to do anything at all. The best policy is to decide, monitor the results, and change course if it is necessary.

11) Do what is right. The truth of the matter is that you always know the right thing to do. The hard part is doing it.[48]

When I read these "Schwarzkopf Principles" my first thought is *Where did they come from? Who was the major influence in his life? How did he come to believe what he believes? How young was he when he began to formulate life principles?*

Most of us tend to put off such thinking about life. We're waiting for all the conditions to be just right before we begin living. You know, the bottom line is that life is what happens to you while you are waiting for life to begin. Formulate your own life philosophy and then live by it. By not thinking through these issues, you are creating a lifestyle for yourself.

Do not let this Book of the Law depart from your mouth; meditate on it day and night, so that you may be careful to do everything written in it. Then you will be prosperous and successful (Josh. 1:8).

❧

1 Kings 18-19; Ps. 146; Prov. 26; Rev. 18

June 27 — Sisterhood

Of all the many relationships that are part of a woman's life, the bonds between sisters are unique. Sisterhood is stretching, bending, whether close at hand or from a distance, but very rarely breaking. The ties that bind sisters together seem to be plagued by less relational knots than mothers and daughters. Sisters at one and the same time can be girlfriends, listening ears, best friends, shopping collaborators, just plain buddies, confidantes, rivals, and much, much more.

Some research studies show that older women who have strong sister relationships are less likely to become depressed than the women who don't have a sister. One of these studies uncovered the fact that many women felt the world was a safer place because their sisters would be there in times of crisis. Sisters, whatever you may say or think, function as one of the best support-systems/safety-nets in a world churned by the chaos of change all around us. Just the fact that a sister will be there is great comfort.

Now take brothers, they share the same biological links with each other . . . but they are so different. Brothers don't seem to have that same kind of emotional glue holding them together as sisters. Sisters are different from brothers in that sisters have something very intimate . . . a sharing of a soul, something that brothers are not usually open enough to obtain.

The memories for sisters are better than brothers . . . sharing a bathtub together, goodnight kisses and snuggles, watching each other's bodies grow, who had the first period, the one who never gains weight, who is aging better, who has more wrinkles, and so on. The memories extend beyond the same roof to social milestones . . . always boyfriends, competition, clothes wars, shopping sprees, dance lessons, cheerleading, pompoms, first solo, music contests, marching bands, and family picnics. Then there are the emotional memories . . . advice whispered, loyalty that cannot be broken, phone calls that are endless in length, going to church together, being Daddy's little girl, who is getting the most attention, who might be Mom's favorite, and always, who is rejected.

Sisterhood is the interweaving of life lessons that are funny, happy, angry, and hurtful, and such memories build the foundation on which the very special, unique, and wonderful relationship of sisterhood rests and is built.

Jesus loved Martha and her sister (John 11:5).

෴

1 Kings 20; Ps. 147; Prov. 27; Rev. 19

Rachael recently had a nightmarish experience and lived to tell the story. As she was returning to her car which was parked at the mall she was accosted by two men, who at gunpoint forced her into their car. They blindfolded her and hurriedly drove out to a deserted woods where she was raped. Before her attackers left, one of them drew out the gun and shot her three times and fled.

Several hours had passed, she had no recollection of how many . . . but somehow she started to revive and managed to struggle to her feet. She futilely searched for her shoes and couldn't find them. In her bare feet she fell, stumbled, walked, crawled out to the country road. She knew that if she were to get some help, she'd have to walk the miles to town. With her goal in focus . . . she began to make her way on the harsh gravel of the roadway, stopping frequently to rest. She would walk and fall, then sit for a while to gather some strength and get up to go again. She feared she would die before she found help.

She began to pray and asked God to please send someone to help her. In her weakened state, and near delirious with pain and loss of blood, she all of a sudden felt like she was being helped along — almost like being carried and she didn't stumble and fall anymore. Finally she reached the first house on the edge of town and at that moment it seemed as if she were placed gently back on the ground.

There was a light on in the house . . . so she managed to walk up the three steps onto the porch and knocked on the door. A young woman answered . . . took one long look at Rachael and crumpled to the floor in a dead faint. Her husband stepped over his wife to help Rachael inside to a couch on which to lie down. He quickly phoned 911 for an ambulance then went back to help his wife who was beginning to revive. When she was back functioning and seated in a chair across from the couch, Rachael somehow managed a wan smile said, "I'm sorry that I frightened you like this. I know I must look terrible."

The wife replied, "No, that's not why I fainted. I saw this great shining angel holding you up as you stood in the doorway!"

Later at the emergency room of the hospital where the ER doctor examined her he noted that even though she had gunshot wounds and bruises from the rape . . . and had covered several miles on the rough gravel road, there was not even a scratch or bruise on her bare feet!

The Egyptians mistreats us and our fathers, but when we cried out to the Lord, He heard our cry and sent an angel and brought us out of Egypt" (Num. 20:15-16).

❧

1 Kings 21-22; Ps. 148; Prov. 28; Rev. 20

June 29 — Statistical Nonsense

There really is good news for the American family! You have heard all about the glum statistics that say one out of two marriages will end in divorce. You've read that half of all marriages end in divorce! Not! Wrong! According to pollster Louis Harris, only one in eight marriages will end in divorce!

Americans have been led to believe for the last decade that the institution of marriage is decaying, since the government's National Center for Health Statistics revealed that there had been 2.4 million new marriages and 1.2 million divorces in 1981. Overlooked in calculating the divorce statistics was the number of already existing marriages.

"What was left out is that there are 54 million other marriages that are going on very nicely, thank you," Harris said. Each year ONLY 2 PERCENT of existing marriages will actually end in divorce, according to calculations by Harris which combine ongoing and new marriages. A statistician with the U.S. Census Bureau agreed that the divorce statistics presented for the last few years have been deceiving because the number of ongoing marriages were not calculated.

"A number of academics made a sensational splash out of the statistics released in 1981," Harris said, "and the media got a lot of mileage out of it. Ever since then, an indelible message has been chorused in church pulpits, academic broadsides, and political prophecies of doom for the American family. In reality, the American family is surviving under enormous pressure."

Harris questioned the much-touted divorce statistics after polling 3,001 persons for a family survey. The study showed a "glowing picture of the American family."

Among the findings of the poll:

85 percent of American families have happy marriages!

94 percent are highly satisfied with family relationships!

86 percent said they are happy with the support they receive from family members during a crisis!

Twenty percent, ONLY 20 PERCENT, said they are not happy with their family life!

Harris called the one-out-of-two divorce-marriage ratio "one of the most specious pieces of statistical nonsense ever perpetrated in modern times!"[49] THEREFORE . . . never again tell anyone that one of two marriages ends in divorce! And decide that yours will not be one of the few that eventually does!

Submit to one another out of reverence for Christ (Eph. 5:21).

⌒♪

2 Chron. 1-2; Ps. 149; Prov. 29; Rev. 21

What a child is taught on Sunday,
he will remember on Monday.

Welsh Proverb

It was a night at home, quiet, a time for some reading in front of the fireplace. I picked up the current issue of *Sports Illustrated* and as is my custom turned to the tidbit section, I believe it used to be called the "Scorecard" section. It's where short, interesting little stories of sports people from all around the globe are reported.

My attention was focused on the tragic story of Rico Leroy Marshall, an 18-year-old senior at Forestville High School in Glenarden, Maryland. Rico was a basketball star with everything going his way . . . a promised athletic scholarship to the University of South Carolina, first place winner in his school's talent contest, and he was one of the most popular kids in school.

That's background, here's the story . . . Rico was driving home from a high school basketball game on a Friday night when he was stopped by a county sheriff in a patrol car. On the seat of the car beside Rico was a plastic bag with several chunks of crack, the highly-concentrated and addictive form of cocaine. So that he wouldn't be arrested for illegal possession, he swallowed the drugs as the sheriff made his way to the stopped car. Later that night he went into convulsions. His parents rushed him to the hospital, but early on Saturday morning Rico Leroy Marshall died of a drug overdose.

One more element appears in this story . . . on the wall of Rico's bedroom, was a huge poster of his hero . . . basketball star Len Bias. Bias was the star of the University of Maryland basketball team and for that year was the #1 draft pick for the NBA (National Basketball Association). He was chosen by the Boston Celtics. But on the night he was drafted #1 . . . Len Bias died of an overdose of cocaine!

A very sad story? Yes! Are you surprised? Maybe not. But consider . . . Rico's role model was Len Bias. I can only imagine that one of the first things he saw in the morning and the last thing at night before closing his eyes was Len. Len was the hero, dream, goal of Rico.

Now my question to you: Who is your role model? Who is on the poster in your bedroom? Who would you like to follow? When you are dreaming of your future, who is the one person that comes to your mind, who do you see? Who do you have pasted on the inside of your locker door? Who is on the dash of your car? Who do you want to be like? Choose well! Heroes are important . . . but even more important is the hero you choose to follow.

> *Let us fix our eyes on Jesus, the author*
> *and perfecter of our faith . . . (Heb. 12:2).*

꒢

2 Chron. 3-4; Ps. 150; Prov. 30-31; Rev. 22

A church gave its pastor a citizen's band radio for a birthday present. A month or two later he received this letter from his church board:

"Dear Pastor: We might suggest that you are getting a little carried away with your CB hobby. Last Sunday your prayer started: 'Do you read me, Big Daddy?' You then went on to describe our crowd as 'wall-to-wall and treetop-tall.'

"It was a bit much when you kept referring to Moses the Lawgiver as the 'Sinai Bear.' We believe our congregation would have better understood your sermon on the hereafter without constant reference to 'negatory purgatory.' And last, we prefer a reverential 'Amen' to 'From Holy Roller to Big Daddy . . . ten-four!' Signed, Your Church Board."

Funny, isn't it, how our language took a turn with the coming of the ever-present CB? All of us had to have a CB in our car or pickup so we could keep up with the 18 wheelers. For a time it even affected country music. It really has turned out to be another passing fad.

Our nation moves from one fad to another. If you are old enough, you can remember the Davy Crockett craze, or the hula hoop, which was really a lot of hoop-ala over nothing. Today it's designer jeans at a very inflated price.

One of the newer problems facing doctors is the "electronic wrist" which is a severe pain in the wrist from playing too many video games non-stop. It's sort of like having "tennis elbow" or a "football knee."

Where will it all stop? When will the next new wave of mania flow over us? What will be the next craze and who is the instant millionaire?

In such a changing world, does anything stay the same? Do we have anything on which to anchor a life? The songwriter gives us a clue:

"On Christ the solid rock I stand,
All other ground is sinking sand."

There is something that never changes! The methods by which the message of Jesus Christ is communicated have changed but the message and the Man are still the same yesterday, today, and forever! There is a foundation upon which you can build a life! This is not a fad that will be here today only to be discarded tomorrow. That foundation is Jesus Christ and He has an invitation for days like today: "Come to me, all you who are weary and burdened, and I will give you rest" (Matt. 11:28). Put something functional into your life.

Heaven and earth shall pass away: but my words shall not pass away (Luke 21:33;KJV).

❧

2 Chron. 5-6; Ps. 1; Prov. 1; Matt. 1-2

July 2 — The Rules for Being Human

1. You will receive a body.

You may like it or hate it, but it will be yours.

2. You will learn lessons.

You are enrolled in a full-time informal school called Life. Each day in this school you will have the opportunity to learn lessons. You may like the lessons or think them irrelevant and stupid.

3. There are no mistakes, only lessons.

Growth is a process of trial and error: Experimentation. The "failed" experiments are as much a part of the process as the experiment that ultimately works.

4. A lesson is repeated until learned.

A lesson will be presented to you in various forms until you have learned it.

When you have learned it, you can then go on to the next lesson.

5. Learning lessons does not end.

There is no part of life that does not contain its lessons. If you are alive there are lessons to be learned.

6. "There" is no better than "here."

When your "there" has become a "here," you will simply obtain another "there" that will again look better than "here."

7. Others are merely mirrors of you.

You cannot love or hate something about another person unless it reflects something you love or hate about yourself.

8. What you make of your life is up to you.

You have all the tools and resources you need. What you do with them is up to you. The choice is yours.

9. Your answers lie inside you.

The answers to life's questions lie inside you. All you need to do is look, listen, trust, and choose rightly.

10. You will forget all this.

11. You will need help with your life.

No one can make it alone in life. All need help. That help is in a relationship with God, Creator of this universe. You choose to invite Him into your life.

12. You can remember it whenever you want.

*Keep your heart with all diligence, For out of it spring
the issues of life* (Prov. 4:23;NKJV).

❧

2 Chron. 7-8; Ps. 2; Prov. 2; Matt. 3-4

July 4, 1776, is a day which all Americans can point to as a day of beginning for our country. It's a day to remember and still celebrate. Many are the names we have connected with this day. Let's take a look at just two of them — two who shared a unique friendship.

Are you aware that both John Quincy Adams and Thomas Jefferson died on the very same day, 50 years to the day after their Declaration of Independence had been adopted by Congress? Both Adams and Jefferson, having lived through so much together as patriots, statesmen, and debaters, died on July 4, 1826. They were friends for many years before bitter political disagreements divided them for decades.

Jefferson's death and Adams' was in itself a kind of curious coincidence. Jefferson died first, and legend has it that he asked for Adams. A few hours later, Adams' last words were, "Thomas Jefferson still lives." And in part it was true.

The part that remains has been left us in the writings of these two men. I doubt that the contemporaries of these men had bestowed greatness upon them, nor anything that they have said has taken greatness from them. But because of the momentous times in which they lived, their friendship is often left to gather dust. After all, Jefferson was our country's third president; Adams was the sixth. Both were diplomats, statesmen, and intellectuals.

History tells us that these were paradoxical men — sometimes troubled men. They both failed in their humanness, alienating each other over squabbles, but shared their remarkable gifts with a new nation. They are to be remembered for their greatness and not their weakness. It's good that we remember.

Jefferson designed his own gravemarker, which did not mention his presidency! In the twilight of his life, perhaps he realized that simpler things were most important.

One thing I would call to your mind is: No matter the disagreement, eternal things are what count. One day, on your deathbed, you might wish for laughter with an old friend.

I have done what is righteous and just; Do not leave me to my oppressors (Ps. 119:121).

෴

2 Chron. 9-10; Ps. 3; Prov. 3; Matt. 5

July 4, Independence Day — What Price Freedom?

Have you ever wondered what happened to those brave men who signed the document we call the "Declaration of Independence"?

Five signers were captured by the British as traitors and tortured before they were executed. Twelve had their homes ransacked and burned. Two lost their sons in the Revolutionary War; another had two sons captured. Nine of the 56 fought and died from wounds or the hardships of the Revolution.

What kind of men were they? Twenty-four were lawyers, 11 were merchants, 9 were farmers or plantation owners. Most were men of means and well-educated. Yet they signed this document knowing full well that the penalty would be death or worse if captured.

They pledged: "For the support of this declaration, with a firm reliance on the protection of the Divine Providence, we mutually pledge to each other our lives, our fortunes, and our sacred honor."

Carter Baxton of Virginia, a wealthy trader, saw his ships swept from the seas by the British navy. He sold his home and properties to pay his debts and died in rags.

Thomas McKeam was so hounded by the British that he was forced to move his family constantly. He served in the Congress without pay, and his family was kept in hiding. Eventually, his possessions were taken from him, and poverty overtook him.

Vandals or soldiers or both looted the properties of Ellery, Clymer, Hall, Walton, Gwinnett, Heyward, Ruttledge, and Middleton.

At the Battle of Yorktown, Thomas Nelson Jr. noted that British General Cornwallis had taken over the Nelson home for his headquarters. The owner quietly urged General George Washington to open fire, which was done. The home was destroyed and Nelson died bankrupt.

Francis Lewis had his home and properties destroyed. The enemy jailed his wife and she died in a few short months.

John Hart was driven from his wife's bedside as she was dying; their children fled for their lives. Hart's fields and mill were laid waste. He died from exhaustion and a broken heart.

Norris and Livingston suffered the same fates.

And such are the stories of the American Revolution. These were not wild-eyed, rabble-rousing ruffians; these were men of means. They had security, but they valued liberty more. They may have lost their lives and fortunes, but their sacred honor is preserved today in the hearts and minds of all freedom loving people throughout the world.

Blessed is the nation whose God is the Lord (Ps. 33:12).

༄

2 Chron. 11-13; Ps. 4; Prov. 4; Matt. 6

July 5 — Silk Pajamas

Harry Emerson Fosdick is credited with the observation that history is filled with the sound of wooden shoes climbing up the stairs and velvet slippers walking down. The famous jockey Eddie Arcaro made the same point when he confessed that he found it really tough to get up at 5 a.m. to ride and exercise horses once he started wearing silk pajamas. Humanly speaking, the prize tends to go to those who want it most and work the hardest for it.

Comfort takes over creativity. Security becomes a stronger passion than challenge. Velvet slippers and silk pajamas don't bring to mind such people as Daniel Boone, Lewis and Clark, or Thomas Edison. Some historians have claimed that the Roman Empire fell because its people took too many baths!

The sound of wooden shoes on the stairs can still be heard all over the world. Tragically, there is somewhat of a haunting feeling in the United States and perhaps in Canada, that we have peaked. It's nothing for a 19 year old, upon applying for a first job, to inquire about vacation benefits and the company's retirement plan. A senior pastor tells of a recent seminary graduate whom he was interviewing for a ministry staff position making it clear that he would only work a five-day, 40-hour week. And any evening work would have to be compensated for by time off during the day.

A variety of conclusions could be drawn from our present subject. This much is for sure: NOTHING STAYS WON! It's always easier for people and nations to struggle than it is for them to arrive. Out of the depths we cry to God . . . but from the heights, it's hard to see the need for prayer. When life makes it easy to believe in God, it's hard to believe in God. Part of it comes from our having to deal with people and our own attitudes that velvet slippers and silk pajamas are a sign that God is pleased with us and wants us to enjoy a time of ease.[50]

Life does not always yield secrets to the most gifted or the most talented or the best looking, but will to those who are persistent, committed, and willing to work and not give up too soon. Work is a therapy, struggle can be the vehicle through which lifestyle changes can come about. When life is a challenge, reaching a goal is much more appreciated. There is never a time when we have arrived. It's a marathon, not a sprint. So . . . welcome the struggle! Go after the prize! Increase your desire! Go for it!

Woe to you who are complacent in Zion, and to you who feel secure on Mount Samaria . . . (Amos 6:1).

༄

2 Chron. 14-17; Ps. 5; Prov. 5; Matt. 7-8

July 6 — A Trio of Angel Stories

• DURING WW II Wayne was the navigator on a B-24 bomber and stationed in Italy. On one particular bombing run over central Europe, as they were approaching the target area, he felt a strong hand on his shoulder and a voice which said, "Get up and go to the back of the plane!" He immediately got up and in that brief time of walking to the back and returning they had taken some limited anti-aircraft fire. When Wayne took his place back in the cockpit, he noticed a shell had blown a hole in the ceiling of the plane and right through his navigator's seat!

• IN CHINA, a 70-year-old mother was the only one who had knowledge of most of the daily operations of the family as well as how the operations of their house church were carried out. She alone knew where the Bibles were hidden, who the messengers were, who could be trusted. Then, suddenly she died of a heart attack. Her family felt the loss. She had not been able to pass on to them the vital information that was so needed. So they began to pray, "Lord, restore our mother back to life!"

After being dead for two days she came back to life! She scolded her family for calling her back. They reasoned with her. They said they would pray that in two more days she could return to the Lord as it would take that much time to set all these matters straight. After two days, the family and friends began to worship the Lord and prayed that the Lord would take her back home. The mother's final words were, "They're coming! Two angels are coming!" And this incident caused an entire village to become Christian!

• SIX SOVIET COSMONAUTS said they witnessed a most awe-inspiring spectacle in space. They saw a band of glowing angels! According to *Weekly World News,* cosmonauts Vladimir Solovev, Oleg Atkov, and Leonid Kizim said they first saw the celestial beings during their 155th day aboard the orbiting "Salyat 7" space station. "What we saw," they said, "were seven giant figures in the form of humans, but with wings and mist-like halos, as in the classic depiction of angels." Twelve days later the figures returned and were seen by three other Soviet scientists, including woman cosmonaut Svetlann Savitskaya who said, "They were smiling, as though they shared in a glorious secret."

He then added, "I tell you the truth, you shall see heaven open, and the angels of God ascending and descending on the Son of Man"
(John 1:51).

෴

2 Chron. 18-19; Ps. 6; Prov. 6; Matt. 9

July 7 — The Ultimate Sacrifice

Linda Birtish literally gave herself away. Linda was an outstanding teacher who felt that if she had the time, she would like to create great art and poetry. When she was 28, however, her doctors discovered she had an enormous brain tumor. They told her that her chances of surviving an operation were about 2 percent . . . they chose to wait six months.

She knew she had great artistry in her. So during those six months she wrote and drew feverishly. All of her poetry, except one piece, was published . . . all of her art, except one piece, was shown and sold.

At the end of six months, she had the operation. The night before the operation, in case of her death, she wrote a "will" in which she donated all of her body parts to those in need.

Her operation was fatal. Her eyes went to an eye bank in Bethesda, Maryland, and to a recipient in South Carolina. A young man, age 28, went from darkness to sight. He wrote to the eye bank thanking them for existing. It was only the second "thank you" the eye bank had received after giving out in excess of 30,000 eyes!

Furthermore, he wanted to thank the parents of the donor. He was given the name of the Birtish family and flew to see them on Staten Island. He arrived unannounced. After making his introduction, Mrs. Birtish embraced him. She said, "Young man, if you've got nowhere to go, my husband and I would love for you to spend your weekend with us."

He stayed, and as he was looking around Linda's room, he saw that she'd read Plato. He'd read Plato in Braille. She'd read Hegel. He'd read Hegel in Braille.

The next morning Mrs. Birtish was looking at him and said, "You know, I'm sure I've seen you somewhere before, but I don't know where." All of a sudden she remembered. She ran upstairs and pulled out the last picture Linda had drawn. It was a portrait of her ideal man.

The picture was virtually identical to this young man who had received Linda's eyes.

Then her mother read the last poem Linda had written on her deathbed. It read:

Two hearts passing in the night, falling in love, never able to gain each other's sight.[51]

Once you spoke in a vision, to your faithful people you said: "I have bestowed strength on a warrior; I have exalted a young man from among the people" (Ps. 89:19).

⌒

2 Chron. 20-21; Ps. 7; Prov. 7; Matt. 10

July 8 — You're Fired!

Have you heard the true story about a teen who went to work in a grocery store after his high-school graduation? A couple of weeks had passed and one evening his dad said, "Son, now let's talk about college."

"Oh, Dad, I didn't tell you. . . . I'm not going to go to college."

"You're not going to college? Why?"

"I'm not going to college because I have found my life's work!"

"What do you mean . . . you found your life's work?"

"You know," he said, "I'm driving the truck there and I love delivering groceries. The boss is happy and I just got a raise! It's really wonderful work."

"Well, son," his dad replied, "you can do something more challenging than this."

"Wait," the son returned, "didn't you tell me life is to be happy?"

"Yes."

"Well," the son said, "I'm really happy and that's what I'm going to do. I'm not going to college!" So the dad was the victim of his own myopia. He knew he'd have to use another approach.

The father went to the store and told the manager, "John, you're going to fire my son."

"What do you mean, fire your son? I've never had a young employee like him. I just gave him a raise. He shines the truck, even . . . keeps people very happy. He's a great employee!"

"Well, he's not going on to college," said the father, "and if you don't fire him you're going to ruin his life."

The grocer had to do something. On Friday when the teen came to get his check the grocer said, "Just a minute . . . you're fired!"

"What'd I do?"

"You're fired!"

"What's wrong?"

"You're fired!"

"Wha . . .?"

"You're fired!"

This teen got the idea . . . he was fired! He came home all dejected. He met his dad and said, "All right, Dad, I'll go to college this fall." Some 30 years later, after this teen had gone on to become the president of one of the leading universities, he told his aging father, "Dad, I want to thank you for the time you got me fired!"

Listen, my son, to your father's instruction and do not forsake your mother's teaching (Prov. 1:8).

❧

2 Chron. 22-23; Ps. 8; Prov. 8; Matt. 11

One day the woodcutter took his grandson into the forest to select and cut oak trees, which they would later sell to boat builders. The woodcutter explained that the purpose of each tree is contained in its natural shape: some are straight for planks, some have the proper curves for the ribs, and some are tall for masts. The woodcutter told his grandson that by paying attention to the details, and with experience, someday he might become the woodcutter of the forest.

A little way into the forest the grandson saw an old oak tree that had never been cut. The boy asked his grandfather if he could cut it down because it was useless for boat building . . . there were no straight limbs, the trunk was short and gnarled, and the curves were going the wrong way. "We could cut it down for firewood," the grandson said, "at least then it will be of some use to us."

The woodcutter replied that for now they should be about their work cutting the proper trees for the boat builders; maybe later they could return to the old oak tree.

After a few hours of cutting the huge trees the grandson grew tired and asked if they could stop for a rest in some cool shade. The woodcutter took his grandson over to the old oak tree, where they rested in the cool shade beneath its twisted limbs. After they had rested a while, the woodcutter explained to his grandson the necessity of attentive awareness and recognition of everything in the forest and in the world. Some things are readily apparent, like the tall, straight trees; other things are less apparent, requiring closer attention, like recognition of the proper curves in the limbs. And some things might initially appear to have no purpose at all, like the gnarled old oak tree.

The woodcutter stated, "You must learn to pay careful attention every day so you can recognize and discover the purpose God has for everything in creation. For it is this old oak tree, which you so quickly deemed useless except for firewood, that now allows us to rest against its trunk amidst the coolness of its shade."

"Remember, my grandson, not everything is as it first appears. Be patient, pay attention, recognize, and discover."[52]

What great life lessons are in this simple story. But who will have the patience and time to teach these to the young? To the grandchildren? To the next generation? Grandparents who might have the time, patience, attention, recognition, and have already made the discovery?

No good tree bears bad fruit, nor does a bad tree bear good fruit.
Each tree is recognized by its own fruit (Luke 6:43-44).

⁕

2 Chron. 24-25; Ps. 9; Prov. 9; Matt. 12

July 10 — My Mother's Sisters

In the early part of my childhood I did not know any of my relatives because they lived in Nova Scotia, 2,000 miles away. My parents had left Nova Scotia during the Depression because there were no jobs there; by the time I was born, the Second World War had begun, and nobody traveled great distances without official reasons and gas coupons. But although my two aunts were not present in the flesh, they were very much present in the spirit. The three sisters wrote one another every week, and my mother read these letters out loud to my father, but by extension to myself and my brother, after dinner. They were called "letters from home."

But it was not my invisible aunts in their present-day incarnation who made the most impression on me. It was my aunts in the past. There they were as children, in the impossible starched and frilled dresses and the floppy satin hair bows of the first decades of the century, or as shingle-haired teenagers, in black and white in the photograph album, wearing strange clothing . . . cloche hats, flapper coats up over the knee . . . standing beside antique motor cars, or posed in front of rocks or the sea in striped bathing suits that came halfway down their legs. Sometimes their arms would be around one another. They have been given captions, by my mother, in white pencil on the black album pages: "We Three," "Bathing Belles." Aunt J. was thin as a child, dark-eyed, intense. Aunt K., the middle sister, looked tailored and brisk, in a Dutch cut. My mother, with huge pre-Raphaelite eyes and wavy hair and models' cheekbones, was the beauty, an assessment she made light of — but all three sisters had the same high-bridged noses; Roman noses, my mother said. I pored over these pictures, intrigued by the idea of the triplicate, identical noses. I did not have a sister myself, then, and the mystique of sisterhood was potent for me.[53]

If you were to spend time around sisters, likely you would discover the ones who are the closest shared several things in common . . . parents had been committed to making sure that their daughters would be friends, a high regard for each other, respect for the other, felt as though they were equals regardless of other factors, and when a sister was in need the other became the caregiver. Just knowing that a sister is there at all times is a great comfort. The continual sharing, the can't-wait-to-tell-my-sister, is part of the bonding between sisters. It's a relationship that is not to be taken lightly.

She had a sister called Mary, who sat at the Lord's feet listening to what he said (Luke 10:39).

༐

2 Chron. 26-28; Ps. 10; Prov. 10; Matt. 13

July 11 — A Courageous Woman

In 1921 Lewis Lawes became the warden at Sing Sing Prison. No prison was tougher than Sing Sing during that time. But when Warden Lawes retired some 20 years later, that prison had become a humanitarian institution. Those who studied the system said credit for the change belong to Lawes. But he said: "I owe it all to my wonderful wife, Catherine, who is buried outside the prison walls."

Catherine Lawes was a young mother with three small children when her husband became the warden. Everybody warned her from the beginning that she should never set foot inside the prison walls, but that didn't stop Catherine! When the first prison basketball game was held, she went . . . and sat in the stands with the inmates.

Her attitude was: "My husband and I are going to take care of these men and I believe they will take care of me! I don't have to worry!"

She insisted on getting acquainted with them and their records. She discovered one convicted murderer was blind so she paid him a visit. Holding his hand in hers she said, "Do you read Braille?"

"What's Braille?" he asked. Then she taught him how to read. Years later he would weep in love for her.

Later, Catherine found a deaf-mute in prison. She went to school to learn how to use sign language. Many said that Catherine Lawes was the body of Jesus that came alive again in Sing Sing from 1921 to 1937.

Then, she was killed in a car accident. The next morning Lewis Lawes didn't come to work, so the acting warden took his place. It seemed almost instantly that the prison knew something was wrong.

The following day her body was resting in a casket in her home, three-quarters of a mile from the prison. As the acting warden took his early morning walk he was shocked to see a large crowd of the toughest, hardest-looking criminals gathered like a herd of animals at the main gate. He came closer and noted tears of grief and sadness. He knew how much they loved Catherine. He turned and faced the men, "All right, men, you can go. Just be sure and check in tonight!" Then he opened the gate and a parade of criminals walked, without a guard, the three-quarters of a mile to stand in line to pay their final respects to Catherine Lawes. And every one of them checked back in. Every one!

The power of love never ceases to amaze me, especially when we see it in a person like Catherine. It's amazing what one life can accomplish when that person believes in others!

But God demonstrates His own love for us in this: While we were still sinners, Christ died for us (Rom. 5:8).

⌒◞

2 Chron. 29-30; Ps. 11; Prov. 11; Matt. 14

July 12 — The Dramatic Change

Larry and Jo Ann were an ordinary couple. They struggled to make ends meet and to do the right things for their children. They were ordinary in yet another way . . . they had their squabbles. Much of their conversation concerned what was wrong in their marriage and who was to blame. Until one day when a most extraordinary event took place.

"You know, Jo Ann, I've got a magic chest of drawers. Every time I open them, they're full of socks and underwear," Larry said. "I want to thank you for filling them all these years."

Jo Ann stared at her husband over the top of her glasses. "What do you want, Larry?"

"I just want you to know I appreciate those magic drawers."

Jo Ann pushed the incident out of her mind until a few days later.

"Jo Ann, thank you for recording so many correct check numbers in the ledger this month. You put down the right numbers 15 out of 16 times. That's a record."

Disbelieving what she had heard, Jo Ann looked up from her mending. "Larry, you're always complaining about my recording the wrong check numbers. Why stop now?"

"No reason. I just wanted you to know I appreciate the effort."

Jo Ann shook her head and went back to her mending. *What's got into him?* she thought.

She tried to disregard it, but Larry's strange behavior intensified.

"Jo Ann, that was a great dinner," he said one evening. "I appreciate all your effort. Why, in the past 15 years I'll bet you've fixed over 14,000 meals for me and the kids."

Then, "Jo Ann, the house looks spiffy." And even, "Thanks, Jo Ann, for just being you. I really enjoy your company."

Jo Ann was growing worried. *Where's the sarcasm, the criticism?*

But Jo Ann's step was now a little lighter.

That would be the end of the story except one day another extraordinary event took place. This time it was Jo Ann who spoke.

"Larry," she said, "I want to thank you for going to work and providing for us all these years. I don't think I've ever told you how much I appreciate it."

Larry never revealed the reason for his dramatic change of behavior . . . but it's one I'm thankful to live with.

You see, I am Jo Ann.[54]

A word aptly spoken is like apples of gold
in settings of silver (Prov. 25:11).

❧

2 Chron. 31-32; Ps. 12; Prov. 12; Matt. 15

July 13 — First Desire

John Jasper was a former slave, and following the Civil War, pastored the Sixth Mt. Zion Baptist Church in Richmond, Virginia. This was a great church.

He was preaching one Sunday morning about heaven and joys which will await us on the other side. He made an attempt to describe those beauties and the joys of heaven. His avid imagination and emotions were caught up and as he opened his mouth to speak he couldn't say a word. He tried several times and the great congregation sat in anticipation. He tried again but no sound. He was overcome with emotion.

Then the tears began to roll down his black cheeks. Still, as he would attempt to articulate, no sound would come out. Finally, he just shook his head and waved the crowd to the doors but they continued to sit. Then he walked to the side of the pulpit, with his hand on the door to his study and again waved the crowd toward home. Again no one moved.

Then, he moved to the pulpit and with great effort composed himself and leaned over it and said: "Brothers and Sisters, when I think of the glory which shall be revealed in us, I can visualize that day when old John Jasper's last battle has been fought and the last burden has been borne. I can visualize that day when this tired servant of God shall lay down his burdens and walk up to the battlements of the City of God. I can almost hear the Mighty Angel on guard say 'John Jasper, you want your shoes?' And I'se gonna say, 'Course I wants ma shoes, ma golden slippers to walk the gold-paved streets of the City of God, but not now.

"Then I can hear the Mighty Angel as he says, 'John Jasper, don't you want your robe?'

"I'se gonna say, 'Course I wants ma robe, that robe of linen clean and white which am the righteousness of the saints, but not now.'

"Then the Angel would say, 'John Jasper, you want your crown?'

"I shall say, 'Course, Mighty Angel. I wants all the reward that's comin' to me, this poor black servant of the Lamb, but not now.'

"Then the Angel would say, 'John Jasper, wouldn't you like to see Elijah, John the Beloved, and Paul?'

"I'll say, 'Course Mighty Angel. I wants to know and to shake hands and yes, I have loved ones over here, but not now. Fust, I wants to see Massa Jesus . . . I wants to see Him fust of all!' "[55]

Then I saw a new heaven and a new earth, for the first heaven and the first earth had passed away, and there was no longer any sea. I saw the Holy City, the new Jerusalem (Rev. 21:1-2).

༼ ༽

2 Chron. 33-34; Ps. 13; Prov. 13; Matt. 16-17

July 14 — The High Cost of Caring

At the 1980 International Youth Triennium in Bloomington, Indiana, Professor Bruce Riggins of McCormick Theological Seminary was speaking before 3,800 young attendees. In his message he shared the story of a lady who had impressed him in an amazing way with her dedicated Christian ministry to the underprivileged people in London, England. He was so taken with her lifestyle and ministry that he asked her what had inspired her Christian faith and the actions of her life.

She told him that it was because she had experienced and seen the life and actions of another lady's Christian faith. And here's the story.

She was a Jew running from the German Gestapo, which was invading France during World War II. She knew she was very close to being caught and had become so tired of the chase and efforts to elude her enemies that she wanted to give up. By chance she came to the home of a French Huguenot.

While there, a widow lady came to that home to say that it was time to flee to another safer hiding place. This Jewish lady said, "It's no use, they will find me anyway. They are so close behind."

The Christian widow said, "Yes, they will find someone here, but it's time for you to leave. Go with these people to safety. I will take your identification and wait here."

The Jewish lady then understood the plan . . . the Gestapo would come and instead of finding her they would find this Christian widow with her identification papers and think she was the fleeing Jew.

As Professor Riggins listened to this story, the Christian lady of Jewish descent looked him in the eye and said, "I asked her why she was doing that and the widow responded, 'It's the least I can do; Christ has already done that and more for me.' "

The widow was caught and imprisoned in the Jewish lady's place, allowing time for her to make her escape. Within six months of being placed in the concentration camp she was dead.

This Jewish lady never forgot the selfless act of friendship she was shown. Shortly after, she, too, became a follower of Jesus Christ and from that moment on lived her life in serving others in the slums and inner city of London. She met God through the greatest gift of friendship anyone can give . . . personal self-sacrifice. In reality, an authentic Christian lives her/his life in serving others.

He died for us so that, whether we are awake or asleep, we may live together with Him. Therefore encourage one another and build each other up, just as in fact you are doing (1 Thess. 5:10-11).

❦

2 Chron. 35-36; Ps. 14; Prov. 14; Matt. 18

July 15 — How to Make a Difference

Charles Colson told the following story in a commencement speech at Reformed Theological Seminary in Jackson, Mississippi,

I love the illustration about a man named Jack Eckerd. A few years ago I was on the Bill Buckley television program, talking about "restitution" and criminal justice. A few days later I got a call from Jack Eckerd, a businessman from Florida who was the founder of the Eckerd Drug Chain, the second largest in America. He saw me on television and asked me to come to Florida. He agreed Florida had a criminal justice crisis and asked if I would I come down and do something about it.

And we did. We went around the state of Florida advocating criminal justice reforms, and everywhere we would go, Jack Eckerd would introduce me to the crowds and say, "This is Chuck Colson, my friend. I met him on the Bill Buckley television program. He's born again, I'm not. I wish I were." And then he'd sit down.

We'd get on the airplane and I'd tell him about Jesus. We'd get off at the next stop, he'd repeat it, we'd do the same thing again. About a year later he called me up to tell me he believed that Jesus was God and had been raised from the dead. When he got through, I said, "You're born again!"

He said, "No, I'm not, I haven't felt anything."

I said, "Yes, you are! Pray with me right now."

The first thing he did was to go to one of his drugstores. There he saw *Playboy* and *Penthouse* magazines. He'd seen them many times before, but it had never bothered him.

He went back to his office, called in his president and said, "Take *Playboy* and *Penthouse* out of my stores."

The president said, "You can't mean that, Mr. Eckerd. We make three million dollars a year on these magazines."

Eckerd said, "Take 'em out of my stores." And in 1,700 stores across America those magazines were removed from the bookshelves because a man had given his life to Christ.[56]

By being his friend, Colson led this man to Christ *and* removed a terrible blight from 1,700 stores!

What good is it, my brothers, if a man claims to have faith but has no deeds? Can such faith save him? (James 2:14).

⌒⌣

Song of Sol. 1-4; Ps. 15; Prov. 15; Matt. 19-20

It was almost one in the morning when the phone rang in the Winter's home. Dr. Leo Winters, the highly acclaimed Chicago surgeon, was awakened with a start.

Tonight it was a young boy, they said, tragically mangled in a late-night accident. Could not someone else handle it? Not this time. This time his hands were possibly the only ones in the city, or maybe even in the whole region, which were skilled enough to save a life.

The quickest route happened to be through a rather tough area, but with time being a critical factor, it was worth the risk. Then, at a stop light, his door was jerked open by a man in a gray hat and a dirty flannel shirt. "I've got to have your car!" the man screamed, pulling the doctor from his seat. Winters tried explaining the gravity of his situation, but the man was not listening.

The doctor wandered for over 45 minutes looking for a phone. When the taxi finally got him to the hospital, over an hour had passed. He burst through the doors and into the nurses' station but the nurse on duty only shook her head. Too late. The boy had died about 30 minutes earlier. "His dad got here just before he died," the nurse told him. "He is in the chapel. Go see him. He is awfully confused. He could not understand why you never came."

Without explaining, Dr. Winters walked hurriedly down the hall and entered the chapel. At the front knelt the huddled form of a weeping father, in a gray hat and dirty flannel shirt. Tragically, he had pushed from his life the only one who could have saved the life of his son![57]

As I have written down this story, I also have the strangest feeling that somewhere in the past I have known that same father. With a marriage coming apart, he just could not find time for his wife or to spend cultivating a relationship with the Lord of life. With a business rapidly sliding downhill, he will further put off a decision about Jesus Christ.

Tragically, there is a tendency to push away some of the only sources of help we have access to in our desperate time of need. It's best to be prepared for the worst — with relationships in order, on a steady walk with God, working on marital harmony on an on-going basis, keeping things clear between ourselves and our kids. Hindsight is always 20/20, but the problem with that is life is not lived in reverse . . . it's in forward, and to most of us it's fast-forward. Therefore, let's keep short accounts!

The righteous man is rescued from trouble, and it comes on the wicked instead (Prov. 11:8).

෴

Song of Sol. 5-8; Ps. 16; Prov. 16; Matt. 21

July 17 — The Power of Perseverance

He was born on a Kansas farm and educated in a simple one-room schoolhouse. The country schoolhouse that he and his siblings attended was heated by an old-fashioned, pot-bellied stove, and it was Glenn and his older brother's responsibility to keep the school's fire going in cold weather. This they had to do before the students and teacher arrived.

One morning, Glenn and his brother poured kerosene on some live coals still in the stove and it blew up! Glenn could have escaped but his brother would have been left behind. The brother had been knocked out by the explosion. Instead of escaping, Glenn struggled with the rescue of his brother. Both boys suffered horrible burns. The brother died and Glenn, with severe burns over the lower half of his body, was taken to the nearby hospital. The doctor told his mother that this son would almost surely die, hinting at the fact that it might be for the best. If he should live, this son would likely never walk again.

This brave boy didn't want to die, and to the amazement of the attending doctor he survived. But with all the damage to his legs, the doctor reminded his mother again that he would be a lifetime invalid.

Once more this boy made up his mind — he would NOT be a cripple, not be an invalid, he would walk and run! It looked hopeless — the legs dangled uselessly. He was released from the hospital and his mother massaged those legs after the burns had healed. When he was taken outside in his wheelchair he threw himself from the chair on wheels and pulled himself across the grass, dragging those useless legs to the picket fence, where, with great effort, he managed to raise himself to a standing position. He would then walk around the yard, pulling himself along beside the pickets. Soon he wore a path.

With more struggle, daily massages by his mother, an iron will, and determined perseverance he began to stand alone, walk with help, then walk alone. Soon he was running! His goal was to become the fastest human in the mile distance. Soon the sheer joy of running became his life. In college he made the track team and one day in Madison Square Garden, this young man with perseverance ran the mile faster than any human being before him. And who was the burned little boy who refused to give up? Dr. Glenn Cunningham, in his day the fastest human miler!

As you know, we consider blessed those who have persevered. You have heard of Job's perseverance and have seen what the Lord finally brought about. The Lord is full of compassion and mercy
(James 5:11).

᠁

Eccles. 1-2; Ps. 17; Prov. 17; Matt. 22

Knit your hearts
with an unslipping knot.

William Shakespeare

July 18 — Record-Breaking Love

Robert Ripley of "Believe-It-or-Not" declared that the longest, and maybe the simplest, love letter ever written was the work of a very romantic French artist named Marcel de Leclure. In 1875 he undertook the task of sending Magdelene de Villalore this communiqué which expressed his deep feelings for her. It was quite simple in content. How effective it was is anybody's guess.

What Leclure's letter contained was the phrase "Jevous Aime" — in English, "I love you." This phrase was written 1,875,000 times! That's all! 1,875,000 "I love you's"! His plan was to write this message 1,000 times for each year of the calendar to date. So we have the year 1875 times 1,000 to arrive at his romantic love letter!

Leclure did not write this letter in his own hand. No . . . he hired a secretary, a scribe, in that day. But this prodigious lover must have been entranced by the words. Therefore he dictated the letter to the scribe word for word, verbatim for the entire letter!

Then he had the scribe repeat the letter back to him word for word each time he wrote the phrase! By our calculations, this phrase was uttered by mouth and in written form 5,625,000 times before it was sent! What a monumental task! And I wonder how much this letter weighed when finished, or how many pages it filled up!?

What did the lady, Magdelene de Villalore, say when this was delivered to her? How long did it take? Did they ever marry?

There are spouses who never utter these words.

This Frenchman must have been something else, and his effort must be appreciated. But I happen to think that Mr. Ripley was wrong in his statement.

Something else comes to mind. Did he do anything else except write out and speak out his love for Magdelene? Love, to be love, must be much more than mere words, no matter how many million times you may say or write it. Actions better express love than words. I'm not downplaying the words, but the two must go together, words and actions. Actions and words. Love is to be expressed as well as acted out. Really, you can never tell someone "I love you" too often. Let's make it a habit of our relationship. One of the saddest emotions felt is love that is never expressed. So, what are you waiting for? Tell that one you love, "I LOVE YOU!" NOW!

Forsake her not, and she shall preserve thee: love her, and she shall keep thee (Prov. 4:6).

❧

Eccles. 3-5; Ps. 18:1-15; Prov. 18; Matt. 23

July 19 — Entertaining the Stranger

Eugene and Judy had eight kids ranging in age from 5 to 15. They were a church-going, loving family. Gene had worked at a lumber mill for years and when it folded he was left with doing odd jobs for a living. One day he had a small job in town working on a car. Judy on this day was doing the laundry when some church ladies dropped over for a visit.

Their conversation was broken when Judy's oldest came into the house, "Mom, there's a black man coming around to the back door. Says he's got to talk to you."

Immediately these church ladies warned, "Be careful. Don't have anything to do with a man who's comin' begging! Now hear!"

At the back door stood the elderly black man with greying hair and soft, warm eyes. "Ma'am, sorry to bother you, but my truck broke down and I'm walking to town. I would appreciate it if you could give me some water and just a bit of food if you could spare it."

Judy was stunned . . . she found herself hesitant to do the right thing. She had been influenced by the ladies. Instead of getting the water and food she stood there. Eyes met and the old man waited a few seconds and then silently he turned away. Judy felt ashamed as she went back to the table, but worse was the condemning look from her oldest son.

Quickly she grabbed a pitcher of lemonade, some cookies, and ran out the front door to find the old man on his knees with the children around him listening as he was telling them a Bible story. She offered the cookies and lemonade and told him to wait as she went back to prepare a sack lunch. She returned, "I'm sorry about the way I acted."

"That's all right . . . too many people are influenced by others. But unlike some, you have overcome it and this speaks well for you."

That night Gene had wonderful news! The car he had repaired belonged to a man whose brother ran a repair garage and was looking for a mechanic. He hired Gene on the spot!

Later, Judy told Gene about the events of the afternoon. When finished, he asked, "Did you say this was an elderly black man? Kind-looking eyes and gray hair?" He jumped out of bed and went through his pockets until he found a piece of folded paper which he handed to Judy and said, "I met that man walking down the road when I came from town. He waved me over and gave this to me. When I finished reading it, I looked up and he was gone, just disappeared!"

Judy began to cry as she read the note, our verse for today.

Do not forget to entertain strangers, for by so doing some people have entertained angels without knowing it (Heb. 13:2).

❧

Eccles. 6-7; Ps. 18:16-36; Prov. 19; Matt. 24

July 20 — Send Us the Money!

Shortly after the Dallas Theological Seminary was founded in 1924 it nearly went under. In fact, the school came to the very point of bankruptcy and teetered on the edge. The creditors were planning to foreclose at noon on this particular day, in spite of the fact that everything humanly possible had been tried to raise the needed money.

On this morning of doomsday, many of the faculty and board members met in the president's office with Dr. Chafer to pray that God would somehow provide the miracle of finance. As is the custom in Baptist circles, a prayer circle was formed, and each man prayed in turn.

Among those present was Dr. Harry Ironside. When it was his turn, he prayed in his characteristic to-the-point manner: "Lord, we know that the cattle on a thousand hills are Thine. Please sell some of them and send us the money." When completed, the next person prayed, and they continued on around this very concerned group of men.

While they were in their prayer meeting, a tall Texan with boots, jeans, and an open collared shirt walked into the business office and said to the receptionist, "I just sold two carloads of cattle in Fort Worth. I've been trying to make a business deal go through, and it won't work. Now I feel compelled to give the money to the seminary. I don't know if you need it or not, but here's the check!"

The little secretary reached for the check and looked at the amount. Aware of the critical nature of the situation, she immediately got up and headed in the direction of the prayer meeting. Knocking timidly, she did not want to disturb the prayers but needed to get somebody's attention. She kept on tapping until finally, the president, Dr. Chafer, went to the door.

With great excitement, she explained what had happened and handed him the check. Dr. Chafer took the check from her hand and noticed it was made out in exactly the amount for which they had been praying. He then examined the name on the check and recognized it as the cattleman from Forth Worth. Turning around, he re-entered the circle and interrupted one of the men in mid-prayer. Turing to Dr. Harry Ironside, he almost shouted in his excitement, "Harry, God sold the cattle!"

Today, you may be hurting in a financial way. You may be questioning God and His provision. Keep on praying. God still cares and He still provides!

And my God will meet all your needs according to his glorious riches in Christ Jesus (Phil. 4:19).

❧

Eccles. 8-9; Ps. 18:37-50; Prov. 20; Matt. 25

July 21 — The Power of Conviction

"Why are you bothering yourselves with a knitting machine?" asked Ari Davis of Boston, a manufacturer of instruments. "Why don't you make a sewing machine?" That particular question was overheard by a young man of 20, Elias Howe.

No one took that question seriously, except the young Howe. It haunted him day and night until he resolved to produce one. He had an almost insane conviction that it could be done. Although he nearly starved in the process, some friends helped him to survive financially. Finally, in July of 1845, the machine was completed and proved its practicality by sewing the seams of two suits of woolen cloth! It could sew nearly three hundred stitches a minute. The mechanism was nearly perfect in this first attempt, and the sewing machine remains today, almost unchanged in design and mechanics — and all because of one man's conviction that it could be done!

Take the automobile. One man, Henry Ford, had the conviction that millions of cars could solve our transportation problems. He created the first assembly line for production, and the rest is history!

Samuel Morse had the conviction that electricity would carry a message over a wire! He was laughed at. Although Congress refused to appropriate the money to try the experiment, Morse held on to his conviction. He erected a wire between a hotel in Baltimore and a hotel in Washington, DC, and a United States senator heard the first message: "Behold what God hath wrought!"

What one thing can change your life around? What single obstacle stands behind the reality of progress? Truth becomes effective in your life by becoming a *conviction!*

Religious conviction is essential to spiritual success! The apostle Paul was invincible because he could say, "I know whom I have believed!"

The weakness of many a church pulpit today is due to the fact that the preacher has no strong convictions of the truth! Your life will remain weak and useless until you come to a place of conviction. Paul said, "I am persuaded . . ." which is another way of saying, "I have the conviction!"

For I am persuaded, that neither death, nor life, nor angels, nor principalities, nor powers, nor things present, nor things to come, Nor height, nor depth, nor any other creature, shall be able to separate us from the love of God, which is in Christ Jesus our Lord (Rom. 8:38-39;KJV).

༄

Eccles. 10-12; Ps. 19; Prov. 21; Matt. 26

July 22 — One Huge Hamburger

Maybe you have already heard about the world's largest hamburger. If not, or even if you have, I'm going to tell you about it anyway. It weighed in at 3,591 pounds. It was created by the people of Rutland, North Dakota, and was cooked on a Saturday afternoon barbecue back in July of 1982.

Yes, it was a single hunk of meat that measured 2-1/2 inches thick and 16 feet across. The meat was provided by local farmers. It was cooked on one of the largest griddles you can imagine. The griddle was made of a 201-square-foot steel plate that was heated by 1.5 million BTUs of propane. It must have been quite some contraption.

The hamburger patty was brought from a processing plant via refrigerated truck. On the way to the barbecue, the patty was weighed at the local grain elevator, beating the former world record (set by the people in Perth, Australia) by a total of 332 pounds. The new record now stands in the Guinness Book of World Records. I suppose under the "foods" category.

The mayor of Rutland, Ronald Narum, said it was the biggest thing to hit his little town since the town burned down three years previously. The big cookout was part of the centennial festivities for the small town nestled in the southeastern part of North Dakota.

It took two hours of cooking to get the huge hamburger ready to eat. They then cut it into sixty-five hundred patties and served it to approximately six thousand people. I suppose they could all brag about having had a bite of the world's largest sandwich.

I can tell you, though, that each of those six thousand people got hungry again the next day! Even a good-sized bite from the world's largest hamburger can't keep a person from getting hungry again.

Everybody has a hunger, but it's a hunger for something more than the world's biggest or best. It's a hunger to know God. Every person has been created with a "God-shaped vacuum" inside, which only He can satisfy. We live in a world that strives to satisfy its hunger for God with all kinds of bogus meals, none of which does the trick. The answer is not in pleasure, food, possessions, money, power, fame, or self-satisfaction. It's in a personal relationship with an eternal loving God.

Jesus talked about food and the satisfaction that there is only in Him. Taste and see that the Lord is good!

Then Jesus declared, "I am the bread of life. He who comes to me will never go hungry, and he who believes in me will never be thirsty" (John 6:35).

〜

Joel; Ps. 20; Prov. 22; Matt. 27

July 23 — Angel in the Pool

It was a hot, humid summer day in the Midwest. Jamie went to one of his friend's homes to spend the early afternoon in the pool. It was great to spend time with the old gang and the swimming and diving and horse-play was fun. Reluctantly he left to do his summer job.

Later that night, he had a date with Jennifer in a neighboring town. As Jamie drove home he noticed the night, it was special . . . stars and moon had disappeared. The hot summer's day seemed to have permeated the night and almost cast a spell of darkness and humidity over the countryside. It was still hot and muggy, just perfect for a late night swim to cool off. On his way home, he passed his friend's home and decided to take a midnight swim. It was late, the house was dark. He was welcome to use the pool, but didn't want to awaken anybody in the house . . . as he quietly made his way through the back yard, he imagined how good the cool water would feel on a hot, muggy night that only other midwesterners can identify with.

Jamie quickly changed into his swimsuit in the pool cabana and climbed the diving board, paused, then was poised to make his dive head first into the pool. As he looked down into the pool, shrouded in darkness . . . he looked again. There beneath him, in the pool was something he'd never seen before. There was something that glowed with brilliance, sort of in the shape of a cross. He saw what looked like something glimmering in the darkness below. He thought, *Maybe it looks like an angel.*

Never taking his eyes off the silvery, shimmering, brilliant form, he slowly climbed back down the ladder of the diving board and walked to the edge of the pool for a closer look. When he knelt down to look closer . . . this thing was gone! Just disappeared! Gone! He was positive it could have been an angel. Then Jamie realized that he was looking into a swimming pool with no water in it!

When he stopped back by the next day he learned that his friend's parents had drained the pool after the guys had finished swimming in it the previous day so that cleaning and repairs could be done to it. It's with fond memories that Jamie recalls that special summer night when an angel saved his life . . . or at the least from a life-changing, crippling, head, back, or neck injury. It could have been fatal.

Even though I walk through the valley of the shadow of death, I will fear no evil, for You are with me; Your rod and Your staff, they comfort me (Ps. 23:4).

∽

Obad.; Ps. 21; Prov. 23; Matt. 28

Several years ago a public school teacher was hired and assigned to visit children who were patients in a large city hospital. Her job was to tutor them with their school work so they wouldn't be too far behind when well enough to return to school.

One day this teacher received a routine call requesting that she visit a particular child. She took the boy's name, hospital, and room number and was told by the teacher on the other end of the line, "We're studying nouns and adverbs in class now. I'd be grateful if you could help him with his homework so he doesn't fall behind the others."

It wasn't until the visiting teacher got outside the boy's room that she realized it was located in the hospital's burn unit. No one had prepared her for what she was about to discover. She had to put on a sterile hospital gown and cap because of the possibility of infection. She was told not to touch the boy or his bed. She could stand near but must speak through the mask she had to wear.

When she had finally completed all the preliminary washings and was dressed in the prescribed coverings, she took a deep breath and walked into the room. The young boy, horribly burned, was obviously in great pain. The teacher felt awkward and didn't know what to say, but she had gone too far to turn around and walk out. Finally she was able to stammer out, "I'm the special visiting hospital teacher, and your teacher sent me to help you with your nouns and adverbs." Afterward, she thought it was *not* one of her more successful tutoring sessions.

The next morning as she returned, one of the nurses on the burn unit asked her, "What did you do to that boy?"

Before she could finish a profusion of apologies, the nurse interrupted her by saying, "You don't understand. We've been worried about him, but ever since you were here yesterday his whole attitude has changed. He's fighting back, responding to treatment . . . it's as though he's decided to live."

The boy himself later explained that he had completely given up hope and felt he was going to die, until he saw that special teacher. Everything had changed with an insight gained by a simple realization. With happy tears in his eyes, the little boy who had been burned so badly that he had given up hope, expressed it like this: "They wouldn't send a special teacher to work on nouns and adverbs with a dying boy, now, would they?"

Lay hold upon the hope set before us: Which hope we have as an anchor of the soul, both sure and stedfast (Heb. 6:18-19;KJV).

⸙

2 Kings 1-2; Ps. 22:1-21; Prov. 24; Mark 1

July 25 — I Need You

A country doctor told of a patient whose husband was one of those strong, quiet, taciturn men, not given to expressing his feelings. The woman was tiny and quite frail, had suffered a ruptured appendix and was rushed to the county hospital. Despite all that medicine could do she continually grew weaker. The doctor attempted to challenge her will to live by saying, "I thought you would like to try to be strong like John."

She replied, "John is so strong that he doesn't need anyone."

That night the doctor told the farmer he didn't think his wife wanted to get well. John said, "She's got to get well! Would another transfusion be of help?"

The rancher's blood proved to be the same type, so a direct transfusion was arranged. As John lay there beside his wife, his blood flowing into her veins, he said, "I'm going to make you well."

"Why?" she asked, eyes closed.

"Because I need you," he answered.

There was a pause, then her pulse quickened a bit, her eyes opened, and she slowly turned her head in his direction. "You never told me that before," she said with feeling.

The doctor, telling of this incident said, "It wasn't the transfusion, but what went with it that made the difference between life and death! Yes, the patient recovered very nicely."

Love, in order to really work, is a two-way street. We give and receive. Some of the most memorable moments of life can be the instant when someone who means much to you will whisper, "I need you."

To hear those beautiful words, as well as to say them, can make a difference in a life. The same concept holds true in the spiritual realm as well as the human. Think about this: NOT ONLY DO WE NEED GOD, BUT GOD NEEDS US! There is a constant reaching into the human realm by God. He created human beings with the ability of choice — to respond or not respond to God. That was quite a venture, quite a chance. What if man does not respond? God sent His only Son so that fallen mankind would understand about this thing called love.

Have you told someone near to you today, "I need you!" Further, have you told God today that you need Him? In order for love to be real it requires that it be reciprocal. Say it with me, "I NEED YOU!"

For God so loved the world that he gave his only begotten Son, that whosoever believeth in him should not perish, but have everlasting life (John 3:16;KJV).

༺༻

2 Kings 3-4; Ps. 22:22-31; Prov. 25; Mark 2

July 26 — Another Man's Wife?

The frustrated associate pastor approaches the much more experienced senior pastor and tells him that he is ready to give up, resign, move some place else, do another kind of a job. The veteran pastor patiently inquires as to the reason.

The young assistant says, "Whenever I lead worship, as you have hired me to do, nobody pays any attention . . . they talk, they read bulletins, they read handout papers, anything but give me attention!"

The senior pastor, after contemplation, replies, "Now, let's think about this. . . . First, you must stride with vigor to the pulpit, act as if you're completely in charge, and this will help get their attention."

And the young associate nods and responds, "Okay, that gives me some help. I'll practice until I get it down good."

Then the senior pastor comes back with, "In a few weeks we'll be having Mother's Day to celebrate. Next Sunday, why not start off with something like this, 'Some of the most wonderful moments of my life have been spent in the arms of another man's wife.' Now . . . that will get their attention! Then pause as they will all be looking at you, then tell them, 'This other man's wife was my mother.' Then, I'll immediately step to the pulpit with an announcement about our upcoming special Mother's Day service. This will be dramatic and attention-grabbing."

Well, the next Sunday rolled around as usual but this time it was to be different. The young associate had been practicing all week and was pleased with his progress. Exactly at the starting moment he strode to the pulpit with purpose and vigor and in his best voice, dramatically said: "Some of the most wonderful moments of my life have been spent in the arms of another man's wife!" He paused, looked out at the crowd. HE HAD THEIR ATTENTION . . . USHERS STOPPED MOVING . . . the silence was pregnant . . . people looked at each other, expectantly, shocked. It was his moment and how he was enjoying it.

However, what he hadn't done was to tell his little red-headed wife about this new approach! She slammed down her hymnbook, threw her bulletin and purse on the seat of the pew with a flourish of red-hot anger, and started for him, climbing over the pews.

Hurriedly, flustered, quickly, he stammered, "For the life of me I can't remember who she was!"

Though the fig tree does not bud and there are no grapes on the vines, though the olive crop fails and the field produce no food, though there are no sheep in the pen and no cattle in the stalls, yet I will rejoice in the Lord, I will be joyful in God my Savior (Hab. 3:17-18).

❧

2 Kings 5-6; Ps. 23; Prov. 26; Mark 3

*One of the marks of true
greatness is the ability to
develop greatness in others.*

J.C. Macaulay

July 27 — A Goal for Life

One of the most fascinating stories of goal setting comes out of the sports world. An eight-year-old boy told his mother and everyone who would listen, "I am going to be the greatest baseball catcher that ever lived!"

People would laugh at him and say, "Dream, you silly boy."

His mother patiently told him, "You are only eight years old, that's not the time to be talking about impossible dreams." He refused to listen to those who would attempt to talk him out of his goal.

When he finished his high school career and walked across the platform to get his diploma, the superintendent of schools stopped him and said, "Johnny, tell these people what you want to be."

The young man smiled, squared his shoulders, and said, "I am going to be the greatest baseball catcher that ever lived!" And you could hear the snickers across that graduation crowd.

The rest is history. On one occasion, the former great manager of the New York Yankees, Casey Stengel, was asked about this young man. Casey replied to the question like this: "Johnny Bench is already the greatest baseball catcher that ever played the game!"

What makes this story so amazing? Already, at age eight, Johnny Bench had set his goal in life. During his playing career, he was twice voted the most outstanding player in baseball. It began as a dream, then became a goal that was translated into reality.

Statistics tell me that if I were to poll each of you, less than 5 percent could say what their life goal is! Ninety-five out of every one hundred people are simply floating along on the tides of life.

Where are you planning to go with your life? Setting a goal for your life may well be the most important thing you will ever do! The starting point in any achievement begins with a goal! The apostle Paul knew the power of a life-goal when he said, "This one thing I do . . . ."

People with goals push ahead in the roughest, toughest, and most impossible kinds of situations and accomplish what they have set out to do.

Many of life's greatest achievements have yet to be met! Will you be one of those who sets a goal and discovers that your life can be changed and productive for the good of mankind? What is stopping you?

This one thing I do, forgetting those things which are behind, and reaching forth unto those things which are before, I press toward the mark for the prize of the high calling of God in Christ Jesus (Phil. 3:13-14;KJV).

෴

2 Kings 7-8; Ps. 24; Prov. 27; Mark 4

July 28 — Lying

Dear Ann Landers:

I was a compulsive liar who started young. Although my parents did all they could to stop it, I kept lying. My problem was trying to impress people. My life never seemed glamorous enough. Here is a short history of what happens to a liar:

I went through school lying to my friends, trying to be a big shot. When I graduated I had no friends, so I started to look for new ones. By then lying was a way of life.

In order to support the lies I needed more money than I had, so I wrote checks I couldn't cover. I also impersonated a naval officer and later a successful businessman.

My wife found out that I had totally misrepresented myself and invented friends and businesses I never had. She left me. The same thing happened with my second wife. I decided I had to change. Shortly after I married my third wife, I went to prison for passing bad checks. She divorced me while I was in prison.

This advice is for the kid who lies. Please think about the future. A lie not only hurts you, but it poisons all your relationships.

I'll get out of prison some day, and when I do I vow to tell the truth. I will probably still be called a liar, but after a while people will find out that they can trust me. I'm now 26, and by the time I'm 50, I will have built a good reputation. A kind teacher once told me that a person's word is worth more than gold. It's too bad that it took me so long to wake up.

If you are a liar, stop while you still have friends. I hope my letter will help somebody who is where I was about 15 years ago.

Steve M. in Oregon, Wisconsin

Pretty sobering when we can see a whole lifestyle condensed down to a tragic letter like this one. If you are not a liar . . . don't become a liar. If you are a liar . . . stop. If you have told a lie or lived a lie . . . is it possible to have that erased from your record? Yes! Ever hear of the word, "forgiveness"? Only God can forgive sin and lying because, ultimately, all sin is against God. Ask Him for forgiveness — it is His to give . . . His grace and mercy removes the sin . . . but it's our responsibility to humble ourselves, admit the problem, and ask for forgiveness.

You shall not give false testimony
against your neighbor (Exod. 20:16).

෧

2 Kings 9-10; Ps. 25; Prov. 28; Mark 5

July 29 — The Sickness Is Swallowed

A medical missionary serving in Egypt was very distressed that the people he was serving continued to suffer and die from a very strange kind of anemia. He and his wife had grown to love these humble, trusting people, as they ministered to their physical and spiritual needs. All of his medical efforts to relieve the suffering and find a cure for the disease had made no difference. In his research, he learned that the disease came from a liver fluke (a parasitic flatworm like a bloodsucker) which was found to live in the soil in and around the people's water supply in their villages.

Having isolated the culprit, he wrote to John Hopkins Medical Research Center and made arrangements so that on his return to America research could be performed in the hopes of developing a cure. However, immigration authorities stopped him at the airport as he returned to the USA. They examined his luggage and asked for an explanation about the container of flukes. He explained the need for research, but their reply was, "No way! Under no circumstances are you going to bring diseased liver flukes into our country."

He begged, pleaded, and explained again, to no avail. He was faced with a decision — either destroy the flukes or not enter the country. He was allowed to go into the men's rest room to destroy, then flush the flukes down the drain. He took the top off of the container and prepared to destroy and then empty them down the sewer. . . .

Then he thought again of his many friends and patients and the intense suffering and sorrow they were facing because of this rare disease. He lifted the container to his lips and swallowed the diseased liver flukes. He then successfully made his way through customs.

Over the next five years he, too, struggled for life while he and researchers at Johns Hopkins searched for a cure. After much trial and error a cure was eventually found. Five years after coming back home he was able to return to his mission field with a cure for the dreaded disease among the beloved people of his mission.

The principle is quite simple: He was not alone in his struggle with this disease — he identified with and became one with his friends!

The major elements of friendship are empathy, compassion, caring, loving, and identification. A great friend will not ask anyone else to do what he's not willing to do himself.

When he saw the crowds, he had compassion on
them, because they were harassed and helpless, like
sheep without a shepherd (Matt. 9:36).

ᔆᕱᓫ

2 Kings 11-12; Ps. 26; Prov. 29; Mark 6

July 30 — Because of Trouble

About the turn of the century, young Clarence took his girlfriend for a picnic at a nearby lake. He was typically dressed in a suit with a tight, high collar. She wore a long dress with about a dozen petticoats and carried a parasol. As Clarence rowed laboriously in the hot sun, his young lady friend relaxed beneath the shade of her parasol, looking sweet and feminine. As he rowed, he drank in the aroma of her perfume.

Despite the hot sun and the sweat on his face, Clarence became hypnotized by his girlfriend's beauty as he watched her smile. They finally reached their destination, a small island in the center of the lake. Clarence dragged the boat onto the shore and then helped his girlfriend out of the boat.

After he placed their picnic beneath a shade tree, she began speaking to him in soft whispers. He loved her voice and listened intently.

She whispered, "Clarence, honey, you forgot the ice cream."

"Ice cream," muttered Clarence, finally remembering that they'd planned on ice cream for the dessert. He got back into the boat and rowed to shore. He found a grocery store, bought the ice cream, and made his way back across the lake. He got out of the boat and trudged up to the shade of the tree.

She looked at the ice cream, batted long eyelashes over her deep blue eyes and purred, "Honey, you forgot the chocolate syrup."

Love makes people do strange things. So, Clarence got into the boat, rowed across the lake, went to the same grocery store, bought the chocolate syrup, returned to the boat, and began to row in the steaming, afternoon sun. He rowed about halfway across and stopped. He sat there for the rest of the afternoon thinking that there must be a much better way. By the end of that hot, summer afternoon, Clarence Evinrude had invented the outboard motor!

Before you come to the conclusion that this is fiction, just check the history of the Evinrude outboard motor. In the first four months of their advertising campaign for the new outboard motor, this story was told as the origin of the idea. Oh, yes, Clarence later married the girl he had left stranded on the island for an afternoon.

Most of this world's discoveries and inventions have come out of times of trouble and need. Why? Because people look for opportunity in the worst of situations. When you cultivate the attitude of looking for opportunity out of adversity, you, too, will find success in life.

Answer me when I call to you, O my righteous God. Give me relief from my distress; be merciful to me and hear my prayer (Ps. 4:1).

༺ঌ

2 Kings 13-14; Ps. 27; Prov. 30; Mark 7

July 31 — Arthur and Walter

Arthur and Walter were good friends, but it's Arthur who really missed out on a wonderful opportunity . . . a once-in-a-lifetime kind of opportunity. One day, Walter took his good friend Arthur for a ride out into the country. They drove off the main highway and down a small graveled road through groves of fruit trees to a large, uninhabited expanse of land. A few horses were grazing here and there as well as a few head of cattle. They could see the falling-down remains of a couple of old shacks. A tumbleweed blew across the road and dust swirled up behind the tires of the car.

Walter stopped the car, got out followed by Arthur, and began to describe with great enthusiasm and vividness the wonderful things he was going to build. He went on at great length and in extreme detail, painting word pictures. He was excited! He was enthused!

He then turned to Arthur and invited him to buy some land surrounding his proposed project in order to get in on the ground floor.

But Arthur was thinking to himself: *Who in the world is going to drive 25 miles for this crazy project? The logistics of the venture are staggering!*

Walter went on explaining to his friend, Arthur, "I can handle the main project myself, but it will take all my money. In just a couple of years the land bordering it, where we're standing now, will be jammed with hotels and restaurants and convention halls to accommodate the people who will come to spend their entire vacation here at my park." He continued, "I want you to have the first chance at this surrounding acreage, because in the next five years it will increase in value several hundred times."

"What could I say? I knew he was wrong," Arthur tells the story later. "I knew that he had let this dream get the best of his common sense, so I mumbled something about a tight money situation, and promised that I would look into the whole thing a little later on."

"Later on will be too late," Walter cautioned Arthur as they walked back to the car. "You'd better move on it right now."

And so Art Linkletter turned down the opportunity to buy up all the land that surrounded what was to become Disneyland! His friend, Walt Disney, tried to convince him . . . but Art thought him crazy! So now, you, too, know the rest of that story of friendship! Incredible! Talk about a lost opportunity!

So, as the Holy Spirit says: "Today, if you hear his voice, do not harden your hearts" (Heb. 3:7-8).

❦

2 Kings 15-16; Ps. 28; Prov. 31; Mark 8

August 1 — Belief

A world famous bird watcher had seen every bird in the United States except one that lived in the mountains of Colorado, so he traveled to find this rare bird. After a couple of days of searching, he finally spotted it and immediately became fixed on the size and beauty of the creature. He started to walk in the direction of the rare beauty, forgetting he was near the edge of a cliff. Sure enough, he walked off the edge, but as he was tumbling down he hit a small tree and was able to grab on. He was dangling 100 feet from the top and 1,000 feet from the bottom.

He cried for help and heard a reassuring voice say, "I'm here."

The man was thrilled that someone had heard him, and he asked, "Who are you?"

The voice replied, "I am the Lord."

The man said, "I am *sooo* glad You came along. I can't hold on much longer."

The voice said, "Before I help you, I want to know if you believe in Me."

The man answered, "Lord, I certainly believe in You. I go to church every Sunday, sometimes even on Wednesday. I read my Bible at least once a week, even though I don't understand it. I pray at least every other day, and I even put a few dollars in the offering plate."

The voice replied, "But do you really believe in Me?"

The man was getting more desperate. "Lord, You can't believe how much I believe in You. I am 100 percent committed to You. I believe totally in what You say. I BELIEVE!"

The Lord said, "Good. Now let go of the branch!"

The man stammered, "But Lord. . . ."

The voice of the Lord came back, "If you believe in Me, let go of the branch."

The man was silent for a minute, and then he yells, "Is anybody else up there?"

Belief is not belief until it is translated into action! Whoever said that an exercise of faith would be easy? Head games are not belief.

Faith is a substance. It becomes a reality when it is put into action. The other Apostles said they believed in Jesus Christ, but it was only the apostle Peter who walked on water. Yes, I know he got wet in the process, but his action translated into a peerless walk!

But without faith it is impossible to please him: for he that cometh to God must believe that he is, and that he is a rewarder of them that diligently seek him (Heb. 11:6;KJV).

❧

2 Kings 17; Ps. 29; Prov. 1; Mark 9

August 2 — Protection in Israel

The Reverend Frankie Walker, a traveling evangelist, related the following story.

I was released from a Bible school in Virginia in August of 1990 to go to my next assignment in Israel. The Gulf War was threatening to go full-scale and Saddam Hussein was a great threat to Israel at this time. President Bush had encouraged the American people to stay away from Israel. It was not uncommon to have two or three tourist cars blown up each week and many senseless killings, especially of the blue-eyed, blonde-hair people . . . Americans or those who looked like Americans. The importance of missionaries to be led and guided by the Holy Spirit was a major factor in their protection.

I was not afraid the whole three and one-half months I was there, but I was always in tune with the leading of the Holy Spirit and sensed the presence of angels with me at all times.

This experience, only one of many, was to do with Jerusalem. I traveled there from Rehovot, where I lived while there. It was approximately an hour's bus ride. I had gone to Jerusalem many times and stayed there, sometimes for days at a time.

I had not been able to go the Upper Room, where all Christians want to go, because of the danger. I was determined to make a visit there, nevertheless. One Sunday after church I headed for the Damascus Gate and just before the street I was to turn down to go there, I had a strong impression not to go and to go instead to the YMCA for tea. I had learned to rely on such promptings so I immediately proceeded to the YMCA. I ordered tea and had sat there for a short time when some people from Europe came and sat at the table next to me. In a loud and clear voice I overheard one man say, "I'm glad we were not inside the Damascus Gate when the riots broke out." Then another added, "They had all those homemade bombs and the knives and rocks were flying and they destroyed the police booth and locked out the police that came to reinforce the soldiers who were inside."

Praise welled up inside of me. If I had not been in tune with the Spirit, I could have been injured or killed, because many were hurt and several killed that day.

Obedience is a must for all of God's children who might travel to dangerous places, because your very life may depend upon it.

The Son of Man will send out His angels, and they will
weed out of His kingdom everything that causes sin and
all who do evil (Matt. 13:41).

⌁

2 Kings 18-19; Ps. 30; Prov. 2; Mark 10

August 3 — Incarnation

In 1873 a Belgian Catholic priest named Joseph Damien de Veuster was sent to minister to lepers on the Hawaiian Island of Molokai. When he arrived he immediately began to meet each of the lepers in the colony in hopes of building a friendship and a ministry. Wherever he turned, people shunned him. It seemed as though every door to ministry was closed. He poured his life into his work, erecting a chapel and beginning worship services and pouring out his heart to the lepers. But it was to no avail! No one responded to his ministry. After 12 years of rejection and failure Father Damien decided to leave.

Dejected, he made his way to the docks to board a ship to take him back home to Belgium. As he stood on the dock he wrung his hands nervously as he recounted his futile ministry among lepers. As he did he looked down at his hands . . . he noticed some mysterious white spots and felt some numbness. Almost immediately he knew what was happening to his body. He had contacted leprosy! He was now a leper!

It was at that moment he knew what he had to do. He returned to the leper colony and to his work. Quickly the word spread about his disease through the colony. Within a matter of hours everyone knew. Hundreds of them gathered outside his hut. They understood his pain, fear, and uncertainty about the future.

But the biggest surprise was the following Sunday as Father Damien arrived at the chapel to conduct the morning service. He found hundreds of worshippers already there. By the time the service began there was standing room only — the place was packed with people and many more were gathered outside the chapel!

The rest is history! Father Damien had a ministry that became enormously successful. If you have traveled to Hawaii lately, it's not long before you are reminded about that ministry. What was the reason? It's a simple concept of working with human beings . . . he was now one of them, he understood them, he hurt with them, and was able to empathize with them. There was now an identity. There was no question if he cared or not.

And this is the essence of why Christ came. There's a big word that describes this action, it's called "incarnation." It's when God became a man, a human being just like all of us.

The Word became flesh and made his dwelling among us. We have seen the glory, the glory of the One and Only, who came from the Father, full of grace and truth (John 1:14).

◞◟

2 Kings 20-21; Ps. 31; Prov. 3; Mark 11

August 4 — Going Home to Roost

John L. Smith was a loyal and hard working carpenter who had worked for the same very successful contractor for many years. John was the kind of man whom any employer would be pleased to employ.

One day the contractor called John into his office and said, "John, I'm putting you completely in charge of the next house we build. I want you to order all the materials and oversee the entire job!"

John accepted the assignment with great enthusiasm and excitement. Here was his big break! For ten days John studied the blueprints. He checked every measurement, every cut, every specification. Suddenly he had a thought: "If I am really in charge, why couldn't I cut a few corners, use less expensive materials and put the extra money into my pocket? Who would know the difference? Once the house is finished and painted, it will look just great."

So John carefully laid out his scheme. He ordered second-grade lumber, but his reports indicated that it was top-grade. He ordered inexpensive concrete for the foundation and used the very cheapest subcontractors on the job. All the while, he reported higher figures than were quoted. He had the least expensive wiring put in that would pass the inspector's close watch. Cutting corners in materials as well as in construction, John continued to report the purchase of the best materials. Soon the home was finished, landscaped, and painted. He asked the contractor to come by and see the finished product.

The contractor walked through the house, stopped in the kitchen, turned to John L. Smith, loyal employee, and said, "John, what a magnificent job you have done! You have been such a good and faithful employee all these years in my firm that I have decided it's time to show my gratitude to you and your family. I am giving you this house you have built, as my gift!"

There are no easy short-cuts in life! There is no way that you can just barely get by, especially when it comes to laying foundational truths into your own personal life. If the foundation is strong and built with the best of materials, it allows the structure erected upon it to also stand the test of time. Cutting corners, using shoddy materials, taking the easy way out always, eventually, leads to disaster. At some point in life, all of us must pay our dues.

We, who are followers of the Carpenter of Nazareth, are called upon to live in obedience — this is a life well constructed.

For we are taking pains to do what is right, not only in the eyes of the Lord but also in the eyes of men (2 Cor. 8:21).

❦

2 Kings 22-23; Ps. 32; Prov. 4; Mark 12

August 5 — Staying in Touch

Back in the days when New Bedford, Massachusetts, was a major seaport, scores of ships involved in the whaling industry went out from it each year. They covered all the seas and often spent many years away from their home base. Of all the captains made famous for their seamanship, none was more highly regarded than Elieazar Hall. He went further, stayed out longer, brought back more whale oil, and lost fewer men than anyone else.

Captain Hall had little formal education and had learned all that he knew by sailing. When asked about his almost uncanny gift in navigation, his ability to know just where he was and how to get where he wanted to go, Captain Hall would answer in this way: "Oh, I just go up on the deck; I listen to the wind in the rigging; I get the drift of the sea; I take a long look at the stars; and then I set my course."

Well, times changed, and the owners of Captain Hall's vessel were informed that the insurance underwriters would no longer agree to cover a vessel that did not carry a formally trained and certified navigator. They were then confronted with the problem of how to break the news to Captain Hall. He must either sign on some youngster or go to navigation school himself. The directors of the company drew straws, and finally one was assigned the dreadful task of breaking the news to the salty sea captain. But to everyone's astonishment, Captain Hall greeted the announcement with no particular emotion. Since he had always been curious about this new business of scientific navigation, he was glad for the opportunity to study it.

At the expense of the company, he went to navigation school and graduated near the top of his class. Then he shipped out for two years on the high seas. The day Captain Hall returned to port after his first voyage, half of the marine population of New Bedford was on the docks to greet him. And, of course, the first question asked was how he enjoyed the experience of navigation by scientific means.

He said, "It was wonderful. I don't know how I have gotten on without it all these years. Whenever I wanted to know my location, I would go into my cabin, get out my charts and tables, work the proper equations, and set my course with scientific precision. I would then go up on the deck, and I would listen to the wind in the rigging. I'd get the drift of the sea, and I would take a long look at the stars. Then I would go back and correct my errors in computation."

In all your ways acknowledge him, and he will make your paths straight (Prov. 3:6).

෴

2 Kings 24-25; Ps. 33; Prov. 5; Mark 13

August 6 — Remember the Duck?

While a little boy was visiting with his grandparents, his grandfather helped him make his first slingshot. He had great fun playing with it. He would take aim and let the stone fly, but he never hit a thing.

Then, on his way home for lunch, the little boy cut through the backyard and saw one of Grandmother's pet ducks. He took aim at the moving target and let the stone fly. Lo and behold, it went straight to the mark and hit the duck in the head, instantly killing it! Talk about a lucky shot, a one in a million!

The boy panicked. In frightened desperation he picked up the dead duck and hid it in the nearby woodpile. At that instant, he saw his sister Sally standing over by the corner of the house. She had seen the whole thing. They went into eat, but Sally said nothing.

After lunch was over, Grandmother said, "Okay, Sally, let's clear the table and wash the dishes."

Sally said, "Oh, Grandmother, Johnny said he wanted to help you in the kitchen today. Didn't you, Johnny?" And then she whispered to him, "Remember the duck!"

So Johnny helped with the dishes. Later in the day, Grandfather called the children to go fishing. Grandmother said, "I'm sorry, but Sally can't go. She has to stay here and help me."

Sally smiled and said, "Johnny said he wanted to help today, didn't you Johnny?" And then she whispered, "Remember the duck!"

Now this went on for several days. Johnny did all the chores — his and those assigned to Sally. Finally, he could stand it no longer, so he went to his grandmother and confessed it all.

His grandmother took him in her arms and said, "I know, Johnny. I was standing at the kitchen window, and I saw the whole thing. And because I love you, I forgave you. I wondered just how long you would let Sally make a slave of you by using your guilt against you. Didn't you know that I love you and would always forgive you?"

That night Sally again tried her tactic. She volunteered Johnny with her whispered threat, "Remember the duck!"

This time Johnny almost shouted it out loud, "That won't work on me anymore. Grandma knows all about it, and I'm free!"

Jesus Christ came to set us free from our guilt and shame. With one simple confession of our sin, we can receive God's forgiveness.

But if we walk in the light, as he is in the light,
we have fellowship with one another, and the blood of Jesus,
his Son, purifies us from all sin (1 John 1:7).

❧

Jonah; Ps. 34; Prov. 6; Mark 14

Life seems to hold at least two kinds of people — negativists and positivists. But we find that the pessimists are more vocal in their expressions of why something cannot be done. It's a whole lot wiser and healthier to listen and become one of those persons who say it can be done! So the next time you are confronted with negatives and negative people, take the time to read again what one very creative, positive thinker has written.

IT COULDN'T BE DONE
Somebody said that it couldn't be done,
But he with a chuckle replied
That "maybe it couldn't," but would be one
Who wouldn't say so till he'd tried.
So he buckled right in with the trace of a grin
On his face. If he worried he hid it.
He started to sing as he tackled the thing
That couldn't be done, and he did it.

Somebody scoffed: "Oh, you'll never do that;
At least no one ever has done it;"
But he took off his coat and he took off his hat,
And the first thing we knew he'd begun it.
With a lift of his chin and a bit of a grin,
Without any doubting or quiddit,
He started to sing as he tackled the thing
That couldn't be done, and he did it.

There are thousands to tell you it cannot be done,
There are thousands to prophesy failure;
There are thousands to point out to you, one by one,
The dangers that wait to assail you.
But just buckle in with a bit of a grin,
Just take off your coat and go to it;
Just start to sing as you tackle the thing
That "cannot be done," and you'll do it.
    — Edgar A. Guest

Whoever would love life and see good days must keep his tongue from evil and his lips from deceitful speech. He must turn from evil and do good; he must seek peace and pursue it (1 Pet. 3:10-11).

Amos 1-3; Ps. 35:1-16; Prov. 7; Mark 15

August 8 — The Bullfighters' Resolve

In Costa Rica, the traditional Spanish/Mexican bullfight has undergone some important changes that distinguish it from what a tourist would be able to see in Spain or Mexico. The Costa Ricans no longer allow the toreador to kill the bull during the classic fight.

As a result, there has been a plunge in the quality of bullfighters.

No longer do any of the good or great bullfighters stop in to fight in Costa Rica. And further, no native bullfighters are really being developed. Therefore, the Costa Ricans have altered their fights to allow anyone who is 18 or older and sober to fight the bull.

It's quite a spectacle, even comedic. Many of the bullfights begin with as many as 100 to 150 young men dressed in bullfighting clothes, holding the cape, standing proudly in the ring, waving to the crowd, enjoying the attention. At the sound of the trumpet . . . all turn, waiting for the bull to break wildly through the gate of the chute.

When the bull enters, snorting, pawing, looking for something to charge . . . immediately, most of the would-be bullfighters scramble wildly over the sides of the ring to safety. The bull makes the first charge . . . and more scramble over the side.

From that beginning mob of so-called "toreadors," just a few are really ready to challenge the bull. All want the name of "BULL-FIGHTER," but only a few will receive it. Many want the glory of the moment . . . but few are willing to go through the preparation that it takes to become a bullfighter. They are nothing but pretenders.

In life you will come across lots of people who can talk the talk . . . but can't walk the walk. Here's where the rubber meets the road and the boys are separated from the men and the girls are separated from the ladies. It's about maturity and coming through when the chips are down. It's being there time and time again.

Teddy Roosevelt said it better than I can: "The credit belongs to those who are actually in the arena, who strive valiantly; who know the great enthusiasms, the great devotions, and spend themselves in a worthy cause; who at the best, know the triumph of high achievement; and who, at the worst, if they fail, fail while daring greatly, so that their place shall never be with those cold and timid souls who know neither victory or defeat."

Let's be the real thing!

So do not throw away your confidence; it will be richly rewarded. You need to persevere so that when you have done the will of God, you will receive what he has promised (Heb. 10:35-36).

❧

Amos 4-6; Ps. 35:17-28; Prov. 8: Mark 16

What do you do when your sister comes to you out of great sorrow, or from dealing with feelings of loneliness, hurting from the fall-out of grief, fighting depression, or just deep into a funk? How about sharing one or all of these "blue-mood-beaters." Perhaps you'll discover they will work for you as well as a sister:

1) It's maybe too simple . . . but start with asking God for strength to overcome this mood you find yourself stuck in.

2) Follow that by saying to yourself, "Self, I've been here before, felt this way before. It did not come to stay, it came to pass." The hurt or pain may not leave permanently . . . but the present mood often lifts.

3) Deliberately switch your thinking. Shift from unhappiness to one of those pleasant memories of growing up, put something pleasant into the thought mill. Change your mind from the negative to the positive.

4) Take a long walk. Weed the garden. Shovel the walks. Rake the leaves. Bathe the dog. Wash the car. Do something outside. If that's impossible, do something active indoors.

5) Count your present blessings. Even get out a sheet of paper and begin to list all of your present blessings, your past blessings, and what you anticipate as blessings in the future.

6) Help someone else who might be in worse condition than you are. Find a neighbor, a friend, a sister, a relative. Go to a nursing home . . . read to someone. Get out of your shell of self-pity and place yourself in a positive way in somebody else's.

7) Check to be sure this particular mood is not caused by a physical reason. Do something brave that sisters will do, go see your doctor for help.

8) Have the confidence that if you have really placed yourself in God's care — that someone or something will come along to help you through your mood or test or trial. Believe that God will help you deal with the unthinkable, bear the unbearable.

9) It helps to remember that every other person you meet has also had to deal with some of the tough problems of life, been depressed, been hurt, been lonely, been grieving. And some of these have not had the many tools available to you to cope with their needs. Take heart!

10) Believe that tomorrow will be a better day! Have faith in the future! Have faith in God! Have faith in relationships! Believe it!

God has said, "Never will I leave you; never will I forsake you." So we say with confidence, "The Lord is my helper; I will not be afraid"
(Heb. 13:5-6).

෴

Amos 7-9; Ps. 36; Prov. 9; Luke 1

August 10 — The Spice of Wife

With the world spinning so fast and friendships being so few, a marriage may be the only stable and secure commitment a couple will know throughout their hurried life. It must be put on a higher priority if a person wants to enjoy rest over the long haul. John Fischer, a Christian musician, offers some sound advice along these lines. It seems that John had rented a room from an elderly couple who had been married longer than most people get a chance to live.

But even though time had wrinkled their hands, stooped their postures, and slowed them down, it hadn't diminished the excitement and love they felt toward each other. John could tell that their love had not stopped growing since the day of their wedding . . . over a half century before.

Intrigued, the singer finally had an opportunity to ask the old man the secret to his success as a husband.

"Oh," said the old gentleman with a twinkle in his eye, "that's simple. Just bring her roses on Wednesday . . . she never expects them then."

The conversation inspired a song:

Give her roses on Wednesday, when everything is blue,
Roses are red and your love must be new.
Give her roses on Wednesday, keep it shining through,
Love her when love's the hardest thing to do.
Love isn't something you wait for,
Like some feeling creeping up from behind.
Love's a decision to give more,
And keep giving all of the time.
Give her roses on Wednesday.

It's easy to love when it's easy,
When you're in a Friday frame of mind.
But loving when living gets busy,
Is what love was waiting for all the time.
Give her roses on Wednesday.[58]

*Husbands, love your wives and do not be harsh
with them* (Col. 3:19).

❧

Hos. 1-4; Ps. 37:1-22; Prov. 10; Luke 2

August 11 — Your Own Mike

What does it mean to have a best friend? What is really the meaning and purpose of a true friend? Let me share this short story with you and let's see if we can answer those questions.

Mike and Tim had been friends for 20 years. They had reached the prime of their lives. Both were married, had children, owned their own businesses — life had been good to them. For over 20 years hardly a week went by without the two of them, and then their families, getting together. Tim had told many people just how lucky he was to have a friend like Mike. He truly loved Mike. Why? Because Mike was the most selfless person he had ever met. He had seen Mike's selfless lifestyle in action for the last 20 years.

Then one day tragedy struck Tim's life. His father died in his sleep, totally unexpectedly. Within an hour of his father's death Tim called Mike, and asked if he would come over. Mike said "I'm on my way."

Tim was on the front lawn of his parent's house continuing to greet people as they came to comfort the family. All things considered, Tim seemed to be doing very well. He had barely shed a tear. Suddenly, he noticed Mike's pickup coming up the long lane of his parent's farm. Tim's eyes began to tear, his heart began to pound. As Mike started to walk toward the house Tim left the crowd and started to walk toward him. When Tim reached Mike he was sobbing uncontrollably. They embraced and Mike said words of comfort to him. The people in the yard stood in silence as they witnessed what true friendship was all about — one being there for the other.

Why would Tim cry when Mike came up? What was going on? There is something about that bond of a friend where you can just be yourself, and all the walls of life come down. It was just two souls comforting one another. It is one of the most powerful unions in this world. Mike and Tim's relationship is very simple. They think of the other person first, they share with each other their thoughts, dreams, and fears, and they truly love each other.

They are lucky to have each other. How many of us can say we have a friend like this? Unfortunately, not very many. In the hustle and bustle of today's life we seem to have very little time for friends and relationships. Loyalty is not a priority, but it should be. Slow down, reach out, and start a friendship. Maybe you'll meet your own Mike.

You, then, why do you judge your brother? Or why do you look down on your brother? For we will all stand before God's judgment seat
(Rom. 14:10).

❧

Hos. 5-7; Ps. 37:23-40; Prov. 11; Luke 3

Old friends, old scenes
Will lovelier be
As more of heav'n
In each we see.

John Keble

August 12 — The Friendly Favor

A friend of mine recently took a business problem to a friend of his in a different business and asked for his help in solving the situation. Then, to further add insult or whatever, he told him that he was doing him a great favor and that later he would be more than happy to have the favor returned by helping this friend with any business problems he may encounter in the future of his business.

Strange . . . you may be thinking, just like I did, How can I be doing a friend a favor by giving him one of my problems? But the more you think about this the more logical it becomes. After all, when we think about it there are several good reasons for sharing problems:

1) IF that person is really a friend, he/she will be glad to help you with your problems. If a real friend, they will welcome the opportunity to help.

2) BY giving another friend your problems, you are forcing them to think, and most likely to think in a whole new field of discipline. To creatively think is one of the highest functions of the human being.

3) YOU asking the friend to take a break from their own work changes the factors of another conundrum.

4) YOU make that friend realize that you value his/her opinions, thoughts, and answers. You are giving value and worth to that friend.

5) BY helping you solve a problem, you may have given the opportunity to come up with some excellent, creative ideas regarding their own business or living.

There is a story about Benjamin Franklin, who had a powerful enemy in Philadelphia. For some reason this person hated Franklin and made no bones about it. In attempting to come up with a creative solution to turn this enemy into a friend, Dr. Ben hit on the idea of asking to borrow a book he knew the man had in his possession. When asked, this enemy was happy to share the book and the cold war was broken between the two. It wasn't long before they became friends. We all need to work on our friendships.

A man named Hall (that's all I know about his name) wrote: "A friend should be one in whose understanding and virtue we can equally confide, and whose opinion we can value at once for its justness and its sincerity. He who has made the acquisition of a judicious and sympathizing friend may be said to have doubled his mental resources."

Like a madman shooting firebrands or deadly arrows
is a man who deceives his neighbor and says,
"I was only joking!" (Prov. 26:18-19)

⤮

Hos. 8-10; Ps. 38; Prov. 12; Luke 4

August 13 — A True Sportsman

The Olympic Games of 1936 were hosted in Hitler's Germany. The American entry in the running broad jump was Jesse Owens, a black athlete. Luz Long, a blond, blue-eyed athlete who had trained all his life for this event, represented Germany. Hitler desperately wanted Long to win to support his propaganda for the "master" race.

In the trails, Jesse Owens did badly. He had to jump a qualifying distance of 24'-6" but failed in his first attempt. Luz Long qualified easily. Then Owens, being extra cautious on his second attempt, fell three inches short of the qualifying distance.

Owens was now extremely nervous. Before his third and final try, he rested on one knee attempting to pray.

Then someone called his name and put a calm, reassuring hand on his shoulder. It was Luz Long! "I think I know what is wrong with you," said Luz. "You give everything when you jump. I, the same. You cannot do halfway, but you are afraid you will foul again."

"That's right," said Jesse.

"I have the answer," said Luz. "The same thing happened to me last year in Cologne." Luz told Owens to jump half a foot behind the takeoff board, using full power. That way it was possible not to foul and yet not hold back. Luz then put his towel down at the exact spot from which Jesse should jump.

It worked. Jesse qualified, setting an unofficial world record. Thanks to Luz, America's black man was still in the running.

The day of the finals, Luz jumped first, and Jesse jumped a bit further. Luz's second jump outdid Jesse's first; Jesse then jumped a half inch farther. Luz outdid himself on his third try, setting a new world record.

Now it was Jesse Owens' final turn. Before he took off, he caught Luz Long's eye. He said later he felt that his opponent was "wordlessly urging me to do my best, to do better than I'd ever done."

And Jesse did. Luz had set a new world record, and Jesse jumped further! "You did it!" said Luz. Then he held Jesse's arm up in the air. "Jazze Owenz! Jazze Owenz!" he shouted to the crowd, and soon one hundred thousand Germans were chanting with him, "Jazze Owenz!"

Luz failed to prove Hitler's theory of the master race and instead proved himself to be one of the finest sportsman of all time.

I do not run like a man running aimlessly;
I do not fight like a man beating the air. No, I beat my body
and make it my slave (1 Cor. 9:26-27).

～

Hos. 11-14; Ps. 39; Prov. 13; Luke 5

To My Sister

My sister! ('tis a wish of mine)
Now that our morning meal is done,
Make haste, your morning task resign;
Come forth and feel the sun.

One moment now may give us more
Than years of toiling reason;
Our minds shall drink at every pore
The spirit of the season.

Then come, my Sister! Come I pray,
With speed put on your woodland dress;
And bring no book: for this one day
We'll give to idleness.
— William Wordsworth

There is a very special kind of freedom that sisters enjoy. In fact, this sister-to-sister relationship may be the envy of all other kinds of human relationships. Sisters seem to have discovered the freedom to share their innermost thoughts without fear. There is a freedom to ask personal favors, favors which may greatly inconvenience the other sister, but nevertheless, it's this freedom which allows the question to be asked, the favor to be expected. Sisters have no problems in sharing their true feelings, feelings which are intimate and personal, revealing hidden inner thoughts which could be revealed to no one else, but it seems right and true that they should be shared with a sister who in turn will guard those feelings as Fort Knox guards our gold. But, perhaps most special about the sister relationship is the freedom to totally and completely be themselves — no put on, no pretense, no cover-up, no fear of being put down. This luxury of being able to simply be yourself is a fantastic benefit.

Sisterhood is more than just being a sister. It's wonderful to have each other as sisters, but the joy goes beyond to becoming and continuing to be the very best of friends. Many sisters will freely confess the blessings of being and having a sister but the real celebration is that here, too, is the very best of all best friends.

Pointing to his disciples, he said, "Here are my mother and my brothers. For whoever does the will of my Father in heaven is my brother and sister and mother" (Matt. 12:49-50).

༄

Isa. 1-2; Ps. 40; Prov. 14; Luke 6

This is how a military officer loved his wife out of a mental hospital. The psychiatrist had prescribed that his wife be admitted to the local mental hospital. He was stunned and challenged, but had no idea how to help her. He sought counsel from the chaplain and learned he should allow his wife to sit in his lap and share her true feelings about him.

He followed this advice with great difficulty because it hurt to hear the things she said he was doing to weaken their marriage. As she was talking, the telephone rang and he felt "saved by the bell." She was angry because she thought he would probably not return. But she overheard one statement he made that not only kept her from a breakdown, but prompted her to slip into a nightgown and actually desire to arouse him (something she had not done in years). After the call, she calmly snuggled back into his lap.

What had he said to his commanding officer?

He simply said, "Sir, could someone else take that assignment tonight? I'm in the middle of a very important time with my wife. It's serious and I really don't want to leave at this point."

That military officer had begun to prove to his wife that she was of high value to him. As a result, her mental condition stabilized . . . and she never had to go to the hospital![59]

Intimacy and attention . . . are they really that powerful in a relationship? Here's another interesting tidbit about a woman's capacity for intimacy . . . and therefore, her potential for a successful male relationship. This is directly linked to her father. A study of 7,000 women who worked in strip joints or topless bars revealed that most of the women came from "absent-father" homes. The researcher, Christopher P. Anderson, commented, "Most of these women conceded that they were probably looking for the male attention that they had never gotten during their childhood. Lacking that foundation, many of these women also admitted that they did not rely on men for intimacy."[60]

"Intimacy" is closeness, familiarity, caring, tenderness, fondness, dearness, affection, warmth, endearment, camaraderie, and lovemaking. It's something to be worked at because it just doesn't simply happen. It seems to come easier for women to do but is something that must be a real goal in relationships which men need to work on. It's powerful, it's therapeutic, it's bonding, it's a part of real love in action.

I am my lover's and my lover is mine (Song of Sol. 6:3).

❧

Isa. 3-5; Ps. 41; Prov. 15; Luke 7

August 16 — I Wish I Had Known

A man of mature years was asked to speak before a group of young people. He was to provide the reflection of years, which is an impossible experience for the younger folks. Here is the message that was given:

Having passed the first twoscore and ten years of my life, and realizing that the more sand that has escaped from the hourglass of life, the clearer we should see through it, I find myself more prone to meditate and philosophize.

My life has been rich. But there have been regrets, regrets which you, too, will experience in time. These can largely be grouped as "Things I wish I had known before I was 21."

I wish I had known that my health after 30 was largely dependent on what I had put into my stomach before I was 21.

I wish I had known how to take care of my money.

I wish I had known that a man's habits are mighty hard to change after the age of 21.

I wish I had known the world would give me just about what I deserved.

I wish I had known the folly of not taking the advice of older and much wiser people.

I wish I had known what it meant to Mother and Father to raise a son.

I wish I had known more of the helpful and inspiring parts of the Bible.

I wish I had known that there is no better exercise for the heart than reaching down and helping people up.

I wish I had known that the "sweat of my brow" would earn my bread.

I wish I had known that a thorough education brings the best of everything.

I wish I had known that honesty is the only policy, in dealing with my neighbors, and also in dealing with myself and with God.

And today I wish I knew the formula for impressing you and other young people that life is a mirror which will reflect back to you what you think into it.

I returned, and saw under the sun, that the race is not to the swift, nor the battle to the strong, neither yet bread to the wise, nor yet riches to men of understanding, nor yet favour to men of skill; but time and chance happeneth to them all (Eccles. 9:11;KJV).

❧

Isa. 6-8; Ps. 42; Prov. 16; Luke 8

August 17 — No Angels

You think there are no angels any more . . .
No angels come to tell us in the night
Of joy or sorrow, love or death.
No breath of wings, no touch of palm to say
Divinity is near.
Today
Our revelations come
By telephone, or postman at the door.
You say . . .
Oh no, the hour when fate is near,
Not these the voices that can make us hear.
Not these
Have power to pierce below the stricken mind,
Deep down into perception's quivering core.
Blows fall unheeded on the bolted door;
Deafly we listen; blindly look; and still
Our fingers fumbling with the lock are numb,
Until
The Angels come.
Oh, do you not recall
It was a tree,
Springing from earth so passionately straight
And tall,
That made you see, at last, what giant force
Lay pushing in your heart?
And was it not that spray
Of dogwood blossoms, white across your road,
That all at once made grief too great a load to bear?
No angels any more, you say,
No towering sword, no angry seas divide . . .
No angels . . .
But a single bud of quince,
Flowering out of season on the day
She died,
Cracked suddenly across a porcelain world!

(Anne Morrow Lindbergh)

*See, I am sending an angel ahead of you to guard you along the way
and to bring you to the place I have prepared* (Exod. 23:20).

∽

Isa. 9-10; Ps. 43; Prov. 17; Luke 9

August 18 — Say That Again?

Since trade and commerce crosses international borders, the business world is susceptible to the many errors that are made in translations and between cultures. One major foul-up in this regard happened to General Motors. With much ballyhoo, the giant company introduced its compact car, the Nova (Chevrolet) to a Latin American country only to discover too late that in Spanish the car's name means: "It doesn't go!"

Even when companies have taken pains to translate a product or directions, errors occur. Sylvia Porter, nationally syndicated business writer, offered some examples in a column:

> A company had to translate into Italian its English instructions on the use of a dentist's drill operated with a foot pedal. The translation later had to be corrected because it came out: "The dentist takes off his shoe and sock and presses the drill with his toe."
>
> But then, nobody holds a monopoly on error. "Monopoly," the very popular board game that is still selling briskly decades after being introduced in 1935, was actually turned down unanimously by executives at the Parker Company. Although they eventually did market Monopoly, the initial Parker reaction was that it contained "52 fundamental errors" which would prevent it from ever being successful!
>
> Even the heavyweights have problems. In 1982 a Coca-Cola bottler uncorked a new contest in which players had to acquire letter-embossed bottle caps spelling out "Home Run." To make certain there was not a flood of winners, the R-lettered caps were supposed to be few . . . the odds were 1 million to 1. But as a result of a mistake by the printer, the R-lettered caps popped up 18,000 times more than planned! Scores of people were turning up with winning entries . . . and collecting $100,000 in awards before the bottler, citing contest rules allowing it to back out in case of an error, apologized and ended the contest.
>
> One of the many angry contestants, however, voiced his discontent. Quoted in a *Newsweek* magazine story on the mistake, he said he was going to "let everybody know that Coke is not the real thing!"[61]

> *Do you see a man who excels in his work?*
> *He will stand before kings* (Prov. 22:29).

❧

Isa. 11-13; Ps. 44:1-8; Prov. 18; Luke 10

August 19 — Inseparable

Grace looked forward to the birth of the baby. Although her mother and father cautioned her against hoping too hard, Grace just knew she would have a sister. They would have teas together, read books about faraway princes and princesses, and do a thousand other things in the years ahead. They would be inseparable.

The months disappeared slowly for Grace. Finally, weeks from Christmas, the day came. But as her father hurried past her one morning, Grace became aware that people were in the house, and none of them looked happy. Didn't they realize her mother needed absolute quiet?

Hours later, the sad-faced doctor emerged from Mother's bedroom. He spoke in a low voice to Father, then left. Dread came upon Grace.

At the cemetery, Grace was aware of only a few things: steam from the horse's nostrils as the animals waited impatiently in the cold air; and Mother's forlorn expression as she sat stiffly in the carriage.

Years later, when Grace was having her own baby, she was naturally anxious. After the birth, she asked for the nurse who had held her hand and reassured her in the early morning hours when labor had started. *"We have no such woman here,"* said the director of nursing.

When Grace was 50, she received alarming news that her son was missing in action during the Allied invasion of Europe. Two agonizing months went by before word came — he was safe! Grace's son would have been added to the casualty list were it not for a courageous local who hid him in a cellar while enemy troops ransacked her farm. Later, Red Cross attempts to contact her turned up nothing.

Twenty years later, on the night of her husband's death, Grace held his hand in those last hours. Feeling so alone in the empty house, she finally drifted off to sleep. Oddly refreshed, she awoke to the sweet fragrance of her favorite tea, steaming in a cup by the bedside.

And two weeks past her 85th birthday, Grace felt her time drawing near. As she lay upstairs, a spring breeze fluttered the curtains. Grace closed her eyes, and an oddly-familiar hand grasped hers. Those who attended the funeral commented on her sweet smile.

Do you believe loved ones we've never known have no place in our hearts? Or do you believe that when the veil is finally lifted, we will enjoy reunions that only an omniscient Creator could provide? Make up your own mind, but I know what I believe!

See that you do not look down on one of these little ones.
For I tell you that their angels in heaven always see
the face of my Father in heaven (Matt. 18:10).

❦

Isa. 14-15; Ps. 44:9-26; Prov. 19; Luke 11

August 20 — What Is Really Important in Life?

GEORGE WASHINGTON CARVER was a man who lived with purpose, goodness, and balance. Born as a slave into a family of slaves, Carver struggled against tremendous odds to finally achieve a formal education. After years of abuse he did finish his master's degree and was invited to accept a position with Iowa University in Iowa City. It was a coveted position and no other black had ever been appointed to such a prestigious faculty in that university. Other members of the faculty learned to love him and students eagerly sought to be in his classes. Life was wonderful for Carver for the first time in his life.

Then . . . a letter arrived from Booker T. Washington asking the young scientist, Carver, to join together with him in a dream to educate the blacks of the South. After some soul-searching he resigned from the faculty of Iowa U. to give himself to the dream of Washington. Leaving the comforts of his prestigious position, Carver traveled to the parched cotton fields of the South to live and work and educate his starving people. People were not only starved for food but for learning and the opportunity to do better. Years of sacrifice and many insults followed . . . but surely and slowly this great soul began to make his mark. Education brought his people a dignity that would raise them forever from the slave class.

Whenever he was questioned about his brilliance as a scientist, Carver always said that the good Lord gave him everything. One unheard of characteristic was that he refused to accept money for any of his discoveries and would freely give those secrets to anyone who asked for them or their use! Three presidents would claim him as their friend and confidant. Industries would vie for his services. Would you believe that Thomas Edison offered him a beautiful new laboratory to be built to his specifications along with an unheard of salary in his day, $100,000 per year, if he would bring his services to the Edison laboratories?

When Carver turned down this very lucrative and enticing offer, some of his critics commented and questioned his motives. He was challenged: "If you had all this money you could help your people."

Carver simply replied, "If I had all that money I might forget my people."

The epitaph on his tomb sums up his life: "He could have added fame and fortune, but cared for neither, he found happiness and honor in being helpful to the world."

Greater love has no one than this, that he lay down his life for his friends (John 15:13).

Isa. 16-18; Ps. 45; Prov. 20; Luke 12

August 21 — "Nobody Loved Me Like Cliff Did"

Cliff had a heart for people. Driving down a busy street on the way to an important meeting, he'd routinely see someone down-and-out and forget all about the meeting and stop to help.

He knew what loyalty was, and how to show it to a world that had forgotten what it was. Reaching out to people — often impulsively — he asked for nothing in return. In short, he was one-of-a-kind.

Robert was lonely. His wife had passed away, he was being phased out of the business he had started, and his children were doing what children do when they move away from home. Careers, families, and vacations were ahead of old Dad on the priority list.

A man who had once meant something to a lot of people, Robert now found himself on the outside looking in. There just wasn't enough to fill the day. He felt as if he was trying in vain to get anyone's attention in a crowded room.

Robert and Cliff met in the winter of their lives, although the latter was much younger than the former. Joining forces in a particular enterprise, the two became like father and son. Cliff asked advice. Robert received validation. They benefited from each other's friendship. Bonds were forged.

For several years, Cliff gave Robert a reason to get up in the morning. Actually, he gave him several reasons; *Let's do this, let's do that. Tomorrow is important, can you be there?*

Sitting at his breakfast table early one spring day, Robert rose to answer the ringing phone. It was Cliff's wife. *Can you come? Cliff died this morning.*

As hundreds of mourners filed by the casket and extended their sympathies to the family, Robert stood patiently off to one side until most were gone, then he made his way to Cliff's widow. "Elaine," he began, taking her hand in his. "Nobody in my life loved me like Cliff did." With that, he walked away.

Wow . . . have you ever had a friend like that? One who would stick to you like glue? If you or I can find one person like that in a lifetime, we've been immeasurably blessed. That's what real friendship is: unyielding love. Hearts for each other.

What about you, friend? Do you know someone whose life is worth more than your own? Will someone say at your funeral, "Nobody loved me like _____ did"? What a jewel in your crown!

And Jonathan made a covenant with David because he loved him as himself (1 Sam. 18:3).

⮜⮞

Isa. 19-21; Ps. 46; Prov. 21; Luke 13

August 22 — 'Til Death Do Us Part

In John Hersey's novel, *The Wall,* there occurs a haunting scene. This is a novel about the Polish Jews and the Nazis. In this particular episode, John Hersey tells how the diabolical Nazis shipped Jews from the Warsaw ghetto to different concentration camps. A long column of men and women is passing in front of a Nazi officer.

> If a person looks fit, the officer sends him to another line, for work in a factory. If not, he goes to the death line. A man and wife, middle-aged, are in the column. They are quarreling venomously. Some irritation had become big as all life. Perhaps they are blaming each other for their plight. If their quarreling seems out of place, it is also understandable. In the face of danger confronting them, and their probable fate, all reserve and reticence have fled. Reason has left.

> Finally, the two arrive in front of the Nazi. He looks them over briefly and motions the man to the working line. The wife he sends to death. For a moment the man stands alone. Then, with a sob, he leaves his haven and slowly walks over to his wife. They stand together, wordlessly, and then they go off to death . . . together.[62]

Most wedding ceremonies have at their core this promise, "For better, for worse, for richer, for poorer, in sickness and in health, to love, and to cherish . . . till death do us part." Then, we, the participants, are called upon to make it permanent! It sounds simple enough at the time of the promise, but the living it out in good and bad times, through thick and thin, can only be done in total commitment!

Have you ever given thought to the first miracle of Jesus in His ministry? It was a wedding! It was a miracle of turning the water into wine to prolong the wedding party. It was a miracle of joy! To me, this is a strong indication that Jesus Christ is also interested in your marriage and the life which follows. It was done to bring joy to the bride and groom, and their guests! God cares enough to have sent His Son to help people have fun and He cares enough about you and your home to also be a welcomed guest! It's not until we get tired of each other . . . it's until death parts us! That's the covenant, and the choice is yours. The grace to pull it off comes from Him, the most honored wedding guest.

> *My command is this: Love each other as I have loved you.*
> *Greater love has no one than this, that he lay down*
> *his life for his friends* (John 15:12-13).

⟨∾⟩

Isa. 22-23; Ps. 47; Prov. 22; Luke 14

Sir Thomas More was an Irish poet. He married, early in life, a beautiful Irish lass. Her beauty was such that no one looking at her could fail to take note of her flaming red hair and green eyes. She and Sir Thomas were very happy, experiencing the heights and probing the depths of their intimacy on every level.

The time came when Sir Thomas was called away from home for a time. During his absence his lovely wife contracted the dread disease smallpox. And you know what scars this disease leaves. What had once been the loveliest of faces now became an ugly desecration of that loveliness. And she was so fearful of Sir Thomas's rejection that she resolved in her heart that he would never again see her face by the light of day. She kept herself in her room and had heavy drapes fitted for the bedroom to block out all the rays of the sun.

Sir Thomas returned late one evening. He was informed by the household staff of what had happened to his once lovely wife. He went to their bedroom, came to the door, opened it, entered, and began to move in the direction of the bed. She recognized his footsteps and said, "No, Thomas, come no nearer. I have resolved that you will never see me again by the light of day." Sir Thomas stopped, hesitated, and without saying a word turned and left the room.

He descended and moved to the music room where he sat at the piano working on the words of a poem. Through the night he labored, until early in the morning he folded the piece of paper, placed it in his vest, and returned to the stairs. He came to the door of the bedroom, pushed it open, and there in the hallway he read the poem:

> Believe me, if all those endearing young charms,
> Which I look on so fondly today, were to pass in a moment,
> And flee from my arms like fairy dreams fading away,
> Thou would'st still be adored, as this moment thou art.
> Let thy loveliness fade as it will;
> And around that dear visage each throb of my heart
> Would entwine itself verdantly still.

He finished reading the poem and threw open the heavy drapes. As he did the first rays of the early morning's light flooded into the room. He turned just in time to receive her into his arms and there the two of them knew the embrace that only those who truly love can know.[63]

Many waters cannot quench love; rivers cannot wash it away. If one were to give all the wealth of his house for love, it would be utterly scorned (Song of Sol. 8:7).

❧

Isa. 24-26; Ps. 48; Prov. 23; Luke 15

August 24 — The Different Perspective

The story is told about a freshman who was trying out for a college football team but there was a problem . . . the coach wasn't too impressed with his intelligence. He told him quite frankly that he didn't think he was smart enough to play football. The young man pleaded to be given a chance to prove himself. So the coach finally relented and said, "I'll make you a deal. I'll give you a test. In fact, I'll let you take the test home and think about it and if you can pass it tomorrow morning, I'll let you try out for the team. There are three questions on the test. First, figure out how many seconds there are in a year. Second, tell me the name of the two days in the week that begin with 'T,' and third, tell me how many D's there are in the song, 'Rudolph the Red-Nosed Reindeer.' "

So the young man said he'd go home and think about it. Sure enough, he was back to see the coach bright and early the next morning.

The coach said, "Okay, here we go. First question, how many seconds are there in a year?"

The young man smiled and said, "Coach, I figured that one out. There's 12." The coach looked puzzled and asked how he figured that.

The hopeful player said, "There are 12 seconds in the year, Coach . . . January 2nd, February 2nd, March 2nd, April 2nd, May 2nd . . . "

The coach said, "Okay, that's not what I had in mind, but I'll accept that. How about question number two, what are the names of the days of the week that start with 'T'?"

He came back with, "Oh, that's easy . . . today and tomorrow."

The coach was again impressed even though that wasn't what he'd had in mind. He said, "Okay, here's the last one, how many 'D's' are there in the song, 'Rudolph the Red-Nosed Reindeer'?"

The young man brightened and replied, "Oh, I know that one . . . there's 138!"

The coach was now really puzzled and asked, "How in the world did you figure that?"

The prospective, eager, potential football player immediately started counting on his fingers and began chanting the familiar Christmas tune, 'De De, De De De, Dee Dee, De De De De De De De. De, De, De De De Dee Dee. . . ."

That's so bad I couldn't find anybody who wanted to claim to be the source. But, there are other ways of doing things that can bring a fresh perspective. It's called *staying out of the rut of normal thinking.*

See, the former things have taken place, and new things I declare; before they spring into being I announce them to you (Isa. 42:9).

❦

Isa. 27-28; Ps. 49; Prov. 24; Luke 16

August 25 — Birdcages in the Mind

Most creative people aren't happy unless they are challenged by a problem that needs to be solved. Such people can't look at anything without thinking about how it could be improved, bettered, adapted, modified, or changed for the better, of course.

One such person was Charles F. Kettering, inventor who did so much for the automobile industry, especially General Motors Corporation. He laid the foundation for much of what we see in the car industry today. He loved to compare his kind of thinking, mind exercising, to "hanging birdcages in the mind."

Kettering had a friend and colleague who made a bet with him. If he were given a birdcage and hung it in his house in a prominent place, sooner or later this friend would have to buy a bird for the cage. The friend jumped at the bet.

So Kettering, on his next visit to Europe, purchased this very beautiful and ornate birdcage for his friend. "I got him an attractive birdcage made in Switzerland," recounted Kettering, "and my friend hung it near his dining room table. Of course, you know what happened. People would come in and say, 'Joe, when did your bird die?' 'I never had a bird,' Joe would say. 'Well, what have you got a birdcage for?' people would ask. Finally, my friend Joe said it was simpler to buy a bird than to keep explaining why he had an empty birdcage."

Kettering, who loved to recount this little story, would conclude, with a grin on his face: "If you hang birdcages in your mind, eventually you get something to put into them."

Teachers should be hanging empty birdcages in the minds of all their students! What an opportunity! The next time you're asked, "What do you do for a living?" You can graciously say, with a grin: "My job is to hang empty birdcages in people's minds." You can be sure once again that this will be a great conversation starter. I love it.

A Gallup Poll survey indicated that in the people surveyed, success is equated with good health, jobs they like, and happy families. This same survey also pointed out that the traits most common in successful people are: purpose in life, the willingness to take risks, to be able to exercise control, to solve problems rather than place blame, they care about quality of life, and they have opportunity to share their expertise and knowledge. All life elements that make for excellent teachers and the hanging of birdcages!

Until now you have not asked for anything in my name. Ask and you will receive, and your joy will be complete (John 16:24).

࿘

Isa. 29-30; Ps. 50; Prov. 25; Luke 17

August 26 — One Tiny Voice

This is the story of a man whom perhaps you have never heard about. He was Telemachus, a fourth-century Christian monk.

He lived in a remote village in Italy, tending his garden, and spending much time in prayer. One day he thought that he had heard the voice of God, or at least a strong impression that he should go to the city of Rome. He made his preparations and set out on foot. Some weary weeks later he arrived in the city at the time of one of the great festivals. Telemachus, not knowing what to do, followed the ever-increasing crowd surging down the streets and converging at the Colosseum. He watched as the gladiators stood before the Emperor saying, "We who are about to die salute you." THEN he realized these men were about to fight to the death for the entertainment of the raucous crowd that day. Telemachus shouted, "In the name of Christ, STOP!"

Nobody heard, nor did the ones near him respond. The games began, the gladiators were locked in battle. The monk pushed his way through the shouting crowd, climbed over the wall, and dropped to the dusty floor of the arena. The crowd watched in fascination as this tiny figure ran toward the gladiators, shouting, "In the name of Christ, STOP!"

The little monk continued until he was right in the middle of the gladiators who had also stopped to watch this interruption. Suddenly the crowd realized it wasn't part of the show and their laughter turned to anger and shouting. As Telemachus was pleading with the gladiators to stop, he turned to the emperor to plead for this carnage to end. One of the gladiators plunged a sword into his body. He dropped to the sand. As he lay bleeding and dying, his last words were: "In the name of Christ, STOP!" The crowd was hushed, they all heard his dying plea.

Then a strange thing happened. As the gladiators looked down at the tiny, bleeding figure in the sand, the crowd was gripped by the drama. Way up in one of the upper rows, one man stood and slowly began to make his way toward the exit. Others followed his lead. And soon, in hushed, deathly silence, everyone left the Colosseum.

That year was A.D. 391 and that was the last battle to the death ever fought in the Roman Colosseum. It changed the thinking of society.

It happened because of one small voice . . . barely heard above the clamor and shouting. Only one voice . . . one unknown, a nobody . . . one life who was willing to speak the truth in the name of God!

Be strong and very courageous. Be careful to obey all the law my servant Moses gave you; do not turn from it to the right or to the left, that you may be successful wherever you go (Josh. 1:7).

Isa. 31-33; Ps. 51; Prov. 26; Luke 18

August 27 — The Sky-Cycle Flop

On a sultry Sunday afternoon the Snake River Canyon coiled up, rattled its tail and sank its fangs into a would-be conqueror, as it opened its 1,700 foot jaws to swallow a strange-tasting capsule. This unique and different capsule was prepared and built by Dr. Robert C. Truax, the scientist-designer of "Sky-Cycle X-2."

Starring in this show was a guy who looked like Captain Marvel, but maybe a bit more like Billy Batson who was unable to remember the magic word. But before you judge him too harshly, let's consider the outcome of this showdown. You'll recall it as I continue with the story.

The sky-cycle leap was a triple-A flop — a classic fizzle! The sky-cycle gave up about halfway across. Spectators watched as the rider floated to earth under his parachute. Don't feel sorry for this rider, and you will not find him hiding in a corner, either.

Most people send an ambulance and a wrecker to mop up their mistakes . . . this guy could have sent a Brink's armored truck. As bystanders were shouting "Rip-off!" he was thinking of write-offs! Anyone who could walk away from a failure with a smile, a bulging back pocket, and his pride still intact, has to have something going for him. It was quite a show and quite an ending. The real six million dollar man, if you can believe it, was a motorcyclist stunt man named Evel Knievel. We haven't heard much from him lately.

Nobody, but nobody, in the long history of sports, and I use that term quite loosely, ever came off a more dismal failure than he did. The remains of the sky-cycle littered the canyon, but the man who attempted to take off like a bird made out like a banker! However, when you stop to hink it over there is a truth in that Idaho extravaganza for all of us. It's something that goes beyond money. It's more than a mere attempt to jump a canyon. It's a philosophy about life.

Teddy Roosevelt expressed it like this: "Far better it is to dare mighty things, to win glorious triumphs, even though checkered by failure, than to take rank with those poor spirits who neither enjoy much nor suffer much because they live in the gray twilight that knows neither victory nor defeat!"

Well, what are you waiting for? If you venture nothing, you gain nothing. Just for today, how about doing something you've never done before!

The people who know their God shall be strong,
and carry out great exploits (Dan. 11:32;NKJV).

❧

Isa. 34-36; Ps. 52; Prov. 27; Luke 19

Charles Swindoll writes: People who live above their circumstances usually possess a well-developed sense of humor, because in the final analysis that's what gets them through. I met such a person at a conference several years ago. We shared a few laughs following a session at which I had spoken. Later she wrote to thank me for adding a little joy to an otherwise ultra-serious conference. Her note was a delightfully creative expression of one who had learned to balance the dark side of life with the bright glow of laughter. Among other things, she wrote:

Humor has done a lot to help me in my spiritual life. How could I have reared 12 children, starting at age 32, and not had a sense of humor?

After your talk last night I was enjoying some relaxed moments with friends I met here. I told them I got married at age 31. I didn't worry about getting married; I left my future in God's hands. But I must tell you, every night I hung a pair of men's pants on my bed and knelt down to pray this prayer:

> Father in heaven, hear my prayer,
> And grant it if you can;
> I've hung a pair of trousers here,
> Please fill them with a man.

The following Sunday I read that humorous letter to our congregation, and they enjoyed it immensely. I happened to notice the different reactions of a father and his teenage son. The dad laughed out loud, but the son seemed preoccupied. On that particular Sunday the mother of this family had stayed home with their sick daughter. Obviously neither father nor son mentioned the story, because a couple of weeks later I received a note from the mother:

Dear Chuck: I am wondering if I should be worried about something. It has to do with our son. For the last two weeks I have noticed that before our son turns the light out and goes to sleep at night, he hangs a woman's bikini over the foot of his bed. Should I be concerned about this?

I assured her there was nothing to worry about. And I am pleased to say the young man recently married, so maybe the swimsuit idea works.[64]

The ransomed of the Lord will return. They will enter Zion
with singing; everlasting joy will crown their heads.
Gladness and joy will overtake them, and sorrow and
sighing will flee away (Isa. 51:11).

∽

Isa. 37-38; Ps. 53; Prov. 28; Luke 20

With the presses all set to run three million copies of Theodore Roosevelt's 1912 convention speech, the publisher found permission had not been obtained to use photos of Roosevelt and his running mate, Governor Hiram Johnson of California. Copyright laws at that time put the penalty for such oversights at one dollar per copy! They were faced with a seemingly insurmountable problem! Time was at a premium.

The chairman of the campaign committee was equal to the situation. He dictated a telegram to the Chicago studio that had taken the pictures, and it read like this: "Planning to issue three million copies of Roosevelt speech with pictures of Roosevelt and Johnson on cover. Great publicity opportunity for photographers. What will you pay us to use your photographs?"

An hour later the reply was wired back: "Appreciate opportunity, but can pay only $250."

That particular chairman displayed various traits of exciting leadership. He showed himself to be cool under fire. He didn't let what might have boggled the mind of a lesser man affect his thinking process. And he made the best of a bad situation that had all the earmarks of a disaster in the making.

Often in life when something goes wrong and appears to bring with it devastating consequences, there is a very human tendency to be overwhelmed. This in turn can lead to a sort of mental paralysis that results in no action being taken. Imagine where this country would be if all our leadership became paralyzed when faced with a problem.

When things go sour, remember to keep your wits about you. If you do, you may be able to think your way out of trouble. Or at the very least be able to lessen the blow.

Instead of allowing yourself the luxury of over-reacting, consider calmly the crisis you face; then consider the alternatives. Ask for help from a person or persons whose trusted knowledge and character you respect. Sometimes the cold shower of truth will bail you out. If worse comes to worst, don't attempt to cover it up, but face the situation squarely.

When you really become accomplished at handling the disadvantages of life or the negatives, you may even graduate to the point where you'll be able to turn them into advantages or positives!

In all thy ways acknowledge him,
and he shall direct thy paths (Prov. 3:6;KJV).

᠁

Isa. 39-40; Ps. 54; Prov. 29; Luke 21

August 30 — I Am a Teacher

I am a TEACHER.

I was born the first moment that a question leaped from the mouth of a child.

I am Socrates, exciting the youth of Athens to discover new ideas through the use of questions.

I am Annie Sullivan, tapping out the secrets of the universe into the outstretched hand of Helen Keller.

I am Marva Collins, fighting for every child's right to an education.

I am Mary McCloud Bethune, building a great college for my people, using orange crates for desks.

I am Bel Kaufman, struggling to go "Up the Down Staircase."

The names of those who have practiced my profession ring like a hall of fame for humanity . . . Booker T. Washington, Ralph Waldo Emerson, Leo Buscaglia, and Moses.

I am also those whose names and faces have long been forgotten but whose lessons and character will always be remembered in the accomplishments of their students.

I have wept for joy at the weddings of former students, laughed with glee at the birth of their children, and stood with head bowed in grief and confusion by graves dug too soon for bodies far too young.

Throughout the course of a day I have been called upon to be an actor, friend, nurse and doctor, coach, finder of lost articles, money lender, taxi driver, psychologist, substitute parent, salesman, politician, and a keeper of the faith.

A doctor is allowed to usher life into the world in one magic moment. I am allowed to see that life is reborn each day with new questions, ideas, and friendships.

An architect knows that if he builds with care, his structure may stand for centuries. A teacher knows that if he builds with love and truth, what he builds will last forever.

I am a warrior, daily doing battle against peer pressure, negativity, fear, conformity, prejudice, ignorance, and apathy. But I have great allies: Intelligence, curiosity, individuality, creativity, faith, love, and laughter all rush to my banner with indomitable support.

I AM A TEACHER![65]

You, then, who teach others, do you not teach yourself? (Rom. 2:21).

꩜

Isa. 41-42; Ps. 55; Prov. 30; Luke 22

August 31 — Angel in the Snow

When you live in Colorado, especially in or near the mountains, or must cross them in the wintertime, you travel with precautions. What happens when you travel without precautions? Well, J.D. and his family are native to Colorado and live in Grand Junction on the western slope of the Rockies. They, in late August, had taken a trip and now were returning home and had to cross Red Mountain Pass from Durango to Grand Junction. It was still summertime and their car wasn't equipped for winter traveling as yet. They were making their climb over the pass which is 11,008 feet in elevation on the top. The highway is named the "Million Dollar Highway" because of the great cost per mile to build it originally. It's one of the most treacherous roads to travel because of the steep grades and hairpin turns. When weather is bad . . . wet or snowy or icy, the road is downright dangerous.

This family was traveling with three little kids. As they neared the top they noticed cloud cover and a storm brewing, but didn't think too much about it. But as they topped out at the summit and started down, immediately they found themselves in a late summer's snowstorm. Wind was blowing and snow was falling and freezing to an icy glaze on the roadway. There was no place to turn around or stop, no shelter, nothing to do but be as cautious as possible in attempting to navigate the now ice-covered, slick hairpin turns. I must also tell you that there are very few stretches where there are guardrails. Conditions worsened quickly. What to do? The first thing was to pray . . . as J.D. drove, his wife Agnes and the kids were praying.

In spite of all careful precautions and gearing down, the car began to slip and slide. The edge, with no guardrail, was too close. The car continued to skid towards the edge with its thousands of feet to the valley below! ALL of a sudden, there appeared two men running beside the car . . . one with his right hand on the front left fender and the other with his right hand on the left rear fender. The car straightened out of the skid and these two men continued to run alongside the car until it maneuvered the last treacherous, icy hairpin curve to enter the town of Ouray. They slowed and stopped so as to inquire and thank the men who had come to their rescue . . . but there was no one to be found! There was no place to go but up or down the mountain road which was laid out before them. Safe, they expressed their thanksgiving to the Lord for His protection and whoever those two men were.

The angel of the Lord encamps around those who fear Him,
and He delivers them (Ps. 34:7).

⁓

Isa. 43-44; Ps. 56; Prov. 31; Luke 23

September 1 — Lessons from Salesmen

The sales manager was complaining to his secretary about one of his men: "Harry has such a bad memory; it's a wonder he remembers to breathe. I asked him to pick up a newspaper on his way back from lunch, but I'm not even sure he'll remember his way back to the office."

Just then Harry burst in the door, brimming with excitement and exclaimed: "Guess what, boss! At lunch I ran into old man Jones who hasn't given us an order in seven years. Before he left, I talked him into a multi-million-dollar contract!"

The sales manager sighed and looked at his secretary, "What did I tell you? He forgot the newspaper!"

Now there's a man who has his priorities turned around.

Another story tells about a young salesman who asked the receptionist for an appointment to see the company's sales manager. Ushered into the office, the young salesman said, "I don't suppose you want to buy any life insurance, now, do you?"

"No," replied the sales manager curtly.

"I didn't think so," said the salesman dejectedly, gathering up his briefcase as he got up to leave.

"Wait a minute," said the sales manager. "I want to talk to you." The salesman sat down again, obviously nervous and confused.

"I train salesmen," said the sales manager, "and you're about the worst I've seen yet. You'll never sell anything until you show a little confidence and accentuate the positive. You just have to get with it and be sold on your product. Now, because you're obviously new at this, I'll help you out by signing up for a $50,000 policy."

After the sales manager had signed on the dotted line, he said helpfully, "You are going to have to develop a few standard organized sales talks."

"Oh, but I have," replied the salesman with a big smile. "This is my standard organized sales talk just for sales managers! It works every time!"

Jesus stated that many times the people of this world are wiser than are the children who make up the kingdom of God. Innovation, creativity, and a new approach are too many times foreign to the people who make up the Church. It's time for us to be creative in our witness and ministry to this world! Go for it!

I am sending you out like sheep among wolves. Therefore be as shrewd as snakes and as innocent as doves. Be on your guard against men (Matt. 10:16-17).

Isa. 45-46; Ps. 57; Prov. 1; Luke 24

September 2 — Are You?

Shortly after World War II came to a close, Europe began to pick up the pieces. Much of the continent had been ravaged by war and was in ruins. The saddest sight of all, however, was that of little orphaned children starving and roaming the streets of those war-torn cities.

Early one chilly morning, an American soldier was making his way back to the barracks in London. As he turned a corner with his jeep he spotted a little boy dressed in tattered clothes, standing with his nose pressed against the window of a bakery. Inside, the baker was kneading dough for a fresh batch of donuts. The hungry boy stared in silence, watching every move of the baker.

The soldier pulled his jeep to the curb, got out, and walked quietly over to where the little guy stood. He did this unnoticed by the child.

Through the steamed-up window, the orphan could see the mouth-watering morsels as they were being dipped out of the huge skillet in which they were being made. They were piping hot. The boy watched as the donuts were covered with powered sugar and others were glazed with frosting. Salivating with hunger, the child let out a slight groan as he watched the baker carefully place them into the glass enclosed counter for sale.

The soldier's heart went out to the little one who stood beside him.

"Son, would you like some of those?" the soldier broke into the silence.

Startled, the boy looked up at the soldier and with enthusiasm, said, "Oh, yes! I would!"

The American GI stepped inside and bought a dozen of those delicious donuts. Then, taking the sack from the baker, walked outside to where the lad was standing in the cold, foggy London morning. He smiled, held out the bag, and simply said, "Here you are."

As the soldier turned to walk back to his jeep, he felt an insistent tug on his coat. He stopped, turned around and looked at the little boy. The child asked quietly, "Mister, are you God?"

We are never more like God than when we give, when we are touched with compassion, and when we act on that compassion. The Bible, in it's most familiar verse says, "God so loved the world that He gave. . . ." All of us have something to give to someone, today.

Then Peter said, "Silver or gold I do not have, but what I have I give you. In the name of Jesus Christ of Nazareth, walk" (Acts 3:6).

ᕠᕬᕡ

Isa. 47-48; Ps. 58; Prov. 2; John 1

September 3 — Take Another Look

A shoe company in America sent two salesmen to an emerging foreign country that was developing and moving into the 20th century. The shoe manufacturer wanted to expand their market.

One of the salesmen returned home within two weeks. He was discouraged, giving up, and complaining, "You stupid guys sent me to a country where no one wears shoes!"

The other salesman stayed behind. He was not heard from for several weeks. Then a large package arrived crammed with orders for shoes of all sizes and types. Included in this box of bulging orders was a hastily scrawled note that said, "Send me more order blanks! All the people here are barefoot, and everyone is a prospective customer!"

Perception is a tricky matter. In fact, it can be most illusive at times. Look at a glass of water that is exactly level at the middle. Will you describe it as being half-empty or half-full? It doesn't change the level of the water in the glass, but it does have a lot to do with your perspective.

Pull into a strange town or city and stop someone to ask directions to a particular destination. Invariably they will tell you, "Go to the third stoplight and turn left . . ." or something of the sort. Why not say, "Proceed to the first *go* light and . . . ." Stoplights spend as much time giving us the green light as they do displaying the red light. Why not call them "go lights?"

Listen to the next weather report on radio or television. The announcer will say, "Today is partly cloudy with a 30 percent chance of rain." He could just as easily say, "Today is partly sunny with a 70 percent chance of no rain."

Too many of us have adopted a very pessimistic view of life. Do we see our communities as being so wicked that people are not interested in the message of the Church? Or do we see them as so needy they are waiting anxiously to be introduced to Jesus Christ?

Our perception of things can make or break us. Now this isn't a departure from reality that I am encouraging, but simply the idea that a correct perception and outlook will affect the way we approach life.

Jesus challenged the outlook of the disciples when He said, "Stop saying there are four months until harvest, look on the fields, they are white already for harvest." So take another look at your life situation. Does it still look impossible or can you see a breakthrough?

Why art thou cast down, O my soul? and why art thou disquieted within me? hope in God: for I shall yet praise him, who is the health of my countenance, and my God (Ps. 43:5;KJV).

❦

Isa. 49-50; Ps. 59; Prov. 3; John 2

September 4 — Say Goodbye

There was an old man on the isle of Crete and during his lifetime he loved many things. He loved his wife, his children, and his job, but most of all he loved the land. He loved the very ground he walked on, worked, and fought for. When it was time for him to die he had his sons bring him outside his stone cottage and lay him on the hard earth. He reached down, grabbed a handful of Crete's soil and was gone.

He arrived at the gates of heaven and the Lord came out dressed in the long robes of a judge and said to him, "Old man, come in."

As the old man moved towards the gates the Lord noticed something in his hand and said, "What are you clutching in your hand?"

He said, "It is Crete. I go nowhere without it."

The Lord said, "Leave it, or you will not be allowed in."

The old man held his clenched fist up and said, "Never!" And he went and sat beside the outside wall of the heavenly city.

After a week had passed, the gates opened again and the Lord appeared a second time, in the guise of a man wearing a hat, looking like some of the old man's buddies down in Crete. He sat down next to the old man, threw His arm around his shoulder and said, "My friend, dust belongs in the wind. Drop that piece of earth and come inside."

But the old man was still adamant. He said, "Never!"

During the third week the old man looked down at the earth he was clutching and saw that it had begun to cake and crumble. All of the moisture of the earth had gone out of it. Also, his fingers were arthritic and could not handle it. The earth began to trickle through his fingers.

Out came the Lord, this time as a small child. He came up to the old man and sat next to him and said, "Grandfather, the gates only open for those with open hands."

The old man thought about this, finally stood up, and did not even look as his hand opened and the crumbled dirt of Crete fell through the sky. The child took his hand and led him toward the glorious gates, and as the gates swung open he walked in. Inside was all of Crete.

Now don't build a theology on this story for that is what it is — a story that illustrates a point that many of us must be reminded of now and then. There is nothing here that is worth missing heaven in order to keep.

And God shall wipe away all tears from their eyes; and there shall be no more death, neither sorrow, nor crying, neither shall there be any more pain: for the former things are passed away (Rev. 21:4;KJV).

༄

Isa. 51-52; Ps. 60; Prov. 4; John 3

September 5 — The Warning

It was a typical school day morning. Ruthie Hoferman was making the regular drive with her two kids to Eugene Field Elementary School. The kids were doing their usual bickering and fighting on the short ride. This morning was different. Ruthie was attempting to cope with a migraine headache and so her patience was short.

Shouts kept coming from the backseat, "Mommie . . . he's grabbing my lunch box!" It was the scream of eight-year-old Lisa.

"Did not!" shouted back her nine-year-old son Robbie, with as much volume.

"Enough! Stop it!" Ruthie screamed into the back seat, "No more of it, both of you!"

It was like shouting to the wind.

"There, he did it again!" cried Lisa.

Now . . . Ruthie gripped the wheel tighter, knuckles turning white, anger rising, prayed: "Please, Lord, help me make it this last half mile."

Quietly, then building, "Lisa is a tattletale! Lisa is a tattletale!!"

"He's teasing me! Make, him stop, Mommie!" shouted Lisa.

At that . . . Ruthie turned her head and scolded both kids vehemently! THEN . . . Ruthie distinctly heard a voice she had never heard before command: "Ruthie! Stop! Quick! Now!"

Stunned at the forcefulness of this strange voice, Ruthie quickly turned back to the road. There was a stop sign dead ahead! It was a four-way stop intersection. Slamming on her brakes, the car skidded, squealing to a violent stop. The seatbelts were the only restraint that kept the kids from being pitched into the front seat or windshield.

In mere nano-seconds after her stop . . . an old pickup loaded with trash plowed through the stop sign on her left at a high rate of speed. Then the driver lost control and veered hard right, hit the curb, and overturned, spilling its contents all over the street!

Other motorists rushed to help the pickup driver. Ruthie, still with the steering wheel in her white-knuckle grasp just sat there, then began to shake! One other driver approached her car, she cranked down the window and asked, "Is he hurt?"

"A little, more shook up than anything. He'll be all right." He added, "Lady, it's a good thing that you stopped when you did . . . that guy could have nailed you broadside. The angels sure must have been riding with you today, lady, is all I can say."

Whether you turn to the right or to the left, your ears will hear a voice behind you, saying, "This is the way; walk in it" (Isa. 30:21).

❦

Isa. 53-55; Ps. 61; Prov. 5; John 4

September 6 — Persistence

He was only 18 and badly in need of a job when this young man read on an ad in a Boston newspaper: "Wanted, young man to learn stock-brokerage business. P.O. Box 1720, Boston, Massachusetts."

He carefully prepared a letter and answered the ad, emphasizing his interest in the job. But he received no reply. He wrote again . . . no reply. He wrote a third time, but still no reply.

His next plan of action was a trip to the main post office in Boston where the postal box was located. He asked for the name of the holder of Box 1720, but the clerk on duty refused to give out this information. The young man then asked to see the postmaster. No go — no name of the boxholder because it was against policy to divulge this information.

What to do now? Then a thought came to the young man. He set his alarm for 4:00 a.m., got his own breakfast, and took the early morning train to Boston. He arrived at the post office about 6:15 a.m. and staked out a watch near Box 1720.

It was a long wait, but finally a man appeared who went over to the box with key in hand and took out the contents. The young man followed at a discreet pace to the destination. It was a stock-brokerage firm. The young man entered and requested to see the manager of the firm.

The young man told the manager how he had made application for the advertised job three times, with no response. Then of his trip to the post office to attempt to find out the name of the boxholder.

Before he could finish his story the manager interrupted him by asking "But how did you find out that it was our firm with the advertisement?"

The persistent young man replied, "I stood in the lobby of the post office near Box 1720 for several hours. Then when your man came in to get the mail from the box, I simply followed him to your office."

The manager smiled as he said, "Young man, you are exactly the kind of persistent person that we are looking for. Innovative, too. Welcome to our firm, you are now an employee!"

Persistence is a quality that wins the prize. Anything of value in this life that is worth going after demands the quality of persistence. Persistence is nothing more or less than seeing your goal and then keeping on with the pursuit until that goal is reached. Be persistent!

But none of these things move me; nor do I count my life dear to myself, so that I may finish my race with joy, and the ministry which I received from the Lord Jesus, to testify to the gospel of the grace of God (Acts 20:24;NKJV).

∽๑)

Isa. 56-57; Ps. 62; Prov. 6; John 5

September 7 — Labor Day

Archie Gordon, former labor attaché of the British Embassy, tells a story about two scientists who were watching three construction workers wheeling loads of bricks. Two of the workers were pushing their wheelbarrows, the other was pulling his. Suspecting they had stumbled upon a discovery that could revolutionize the construction industry, the scientists called their staffs for a conference. No one could come up with an answer to the question of why one of the workers pulled his wheelbarrow while the others pushed. Consultants were called in. One suggested that the way to get the answer was to question the workers.

This was done and the puzzled worker was instructed to take his time in answering the question because what he had to say might be of great scientific importance.

"Well," said the worker. "I can tell you why I pull my wheelbarrow instead of pushing it. I just can't stand the sight of the blasted thing!"

Sometime during this first week in September, we as a nation set aside a day to honor "labor" among us. The majority of us will do nothing more than picnic, play ball, fish, or holiday. We really don't stop to give much thought to how this day came to be set aside. Let's take a few moments to do just that.

T. North Whitehead wrote: "The worker is not an abstraction, an 'economic man' but a whole man with his hopes and fears, his customs and his ideals. It is the same man who is at work and at play, and in our thinking we must avoid building an artificial barrier between the different parts of the worker's life."

America has seen child labor controlled, the sweatshop outlawed and starvation wages done away with to a large degree. We still have unemployment and other problems but we are better off today than a few years ago. But we have not always been able to answer satisfactorily the deeper questions of life: Why am I here? Of what use can my life and work be? How can I discover what God wants me to do with my life?

Young people with an entire life ahead of them aren't the only ones asking such questions. All kinds of motives for working present themselves . . . money, success, importance, power, or social position may all be hollow. Let's allow our work to be an expression of obedience to what God expects of us.

Make it your ambition to lead a quiet life, to mind your own business and to work with your hands, just as we told you, so that your daily life may win the respect of outsiders and so that you will not be dependent on anybody (1 Thess. 4:11-12).

᳍

Isa. 58-59; Ps. 63; Prov. 7; John 6

September 8 — Be Thankful

For a number of years, the Northwestern University, located in Evanston, Illinois, had maintained a volunteer life-saving crew, recruited from its student body. In actuality, this group became quite famous and well-known for their heroics on Lake Michigan.

The story goes that on September 8, 1860, the *Lady Elgin,* a crowded passenger steamer, foundered and ran aground. As it began breaking apart on the rocks off the shore of the lake just above Evanston, a crowd soon gathered.

One of the students, Edward W. Spencer, who was attending the Garrett Biblical Institute (a part of Northwestern), was a member of the volunteer life-saving crew. He spotted a woman hanging on to some of the wreckage and threw off his coat to swim out through the heavy waves to rescue her, which he was successful in doing.

Fifteen more times, on this day, the young and brave Spencer swam out into the treacherous water to save a total of 17 persons. Following his last rescue attempt, he collapsed in a heap on the shore. He was totally exhausted!

Recovery from the total giving of himself on that day was a slow process. Exposure and exertion had taken their toll. In fact, he never completely recovered. His health was broken so completely that he had to drop out of the Bible institute, and his dream of entering the ministry was over. He lived the rest of his life in isolated seclusion, hoarding his fragile health. His life, marked by his devotion to the Lord Jesus Christ, was a living example of what Christianity is all about. He moved to California for health reasons and lived there until he died at the age of 81.

In the simple notice of his death that appeared in the local paper, it was mentioned that not one of those 17 persons he had rescued ever came to thank him or wrote him or in any way expressed gratitude!

Samuel Liebowits, an attorney who has specialized in snatching killers from the death chambers, notes that — of the 78 men he has been able to save from the electric chair — not one ever sent him as much as a Christmas card or note of thanks.

Even Jesus bore the disservice of ingratitude from the people He healed. Let's give thanks, always!

But mark this: There will be terrible times in the last days.
People will be lovers of themselves, lovers of money,
boastful, proud, abusive, disobedient to their parents,
ungrateful, unholy (2 Tim. 3:1-2).

༄

Isa. 60-61; Ps. 64; Prov. 8; John 7

September 9 — The Impact of a Leader

In September of 1862, the Civil War tilted decisively in favor of the South. The morale of the Northern army had dipped to its lowest point of the war. Large numbers of Union troops were in full retreat in Virginia. Northern leaders began to fear the worst. They could see no answer to turning the beaten, exhausted troops into an army again.

There was only one general with this kind of leadership. General George McClellan had trained these troops for combat and they loved him. The War Department or the Cabinet could not see the connection. Only President Lincoln recognized his remarkable leadership skills.

Lincoln, ignoring the protests of his advisors, reinstated McClellan in command. He told the general to ride to Virginia and give the troops something no other man on earth could give them: enthusiasm! strength! resolve! and hope! McClellan accepted the command. He mounted his huge horse and cantered down the dusty Virginia roads.

What happened next is impossible to explain. Northern leaders couldn't explain it. Union soldiers couldn't explain it. Even McClellan couldn't later explain it. As the general met the retreating Union columns, he waved his hat over his head and shouted encouragement. When these bedraggled, worn-out troops saw their beloved leader/teacher they took heart!

Bruce Catton, the Civil War historian, describes the enthusiasm that grew when word spread through the ranks that General George McClellan was back in command: "Down mile after mile of Virginia roads the stumbling columns came alive. Men threw their caps and knapsacks into the air, and yelled until they could yell no more . . . because they saw this dapper little rider outlined against the purple starlight.

"And this, in a way, was the turning point of the war. No one could ever quite explain how it happened. But whatever it was, it gave President Lincoln and the North exactly what it needed. And history was forever changed because of it."

This story out of our history dramatically illustrates the impact one leader can have on the human being! General George McClellan inspired these burned-out troops to take another grip on life. That's why leaders are leaders! That's the challenge of the pastor/leader who points to the ultimate leader — Jesus Christ!

For you yourselves know how you ought to follow our example. We were not idle when we were with you. . . . We did this, not because we do not have the right to such help, but in order to make ourselves a model for you to follow (2 Thess. 3:7, 9).

❧

Isa. 62-64; Ps. 65; Prov. 9; John 8

September 10 — Some Retirement Definitions

Sixty-five is the age when one acquires sufficient experience to lose his/her job.

There are a lot of books telling you how to manage when you retire. Most people want one that'll tell them how to manage in the meantime.

Retirement can be a great joy if you can figure how to spend time without spending any money.

Forty years ago when a person said something about retiring, they were usually talking about going to bed.

Today, "retirement security" is making sure all the doors are locked before you go to bed.

One wife's definition of retirement: "Twice as much husband and only half as much income."

Mandatory retirement is another form of compulsory poverty.

Retirement has cured many a businessman's ulcers ... and given his wife one!

And now let's read a tidbit from the life of Carl Johnson of Kankakee, Illinois: My wife and I took our grandchildren to visit my parents in Missouri. When we were ready to leave, my dad gave me a picture of myself. I had sent it to my parents during the Second World War. I was dressed in my complete army uniform on which I had pinned my medals. As I walked out the door and into the yard, Amy, my five-year-old granddaughter, asked, "Who is that? Papa, is that you?"

I answered, "Yes, that is a picture of me."

Then she asked, "Did you you fight in the war?"

I replied, "Yes, I fought in the war."

When we arrived home, my daughter and son-in-law came to get the children. Amy was still excited, she could hardly wait to tell her parents about her war hero. She grabbed the picture and ran to her mother. Excitedly, she said, "Mother, I think I know something you don't know. Did you know that Papa fought in the Civil War?"[66]

What is the bottom line? Too many seniors have been taught to study, know, proclaim, and practice the Word of God. Yet there are still people who think seniors are only scarred, cracked, chipped, crumbled, and broken antiques of no value. Therefore they are set aside.

Don't let anyone put you down because you're a senior! You have great value . . . especially to grandkids and their parents.

The righteous will flourish like a palm tree. . . .they will still bear fruit in old age, they will stay fresh and green, proclaiming, "The Lord is upright; He is my Rock" (Ps. 92:12-15).

❧

Isa. 65; Ps. 66; Prov. 10; John 9

September 11 — Why Do You Do That?

Josh looked up from his super-hero action figure and watched his grandmother ease out of her chair. There she went — so slowly and unobtrusively that not a soul would notice.

Not a soul but Josh. He continued to watch her curiously as she picked up his shoes from the middle of the floor and put them where they belonged, near the back door.

"Grandma," he called out casually, "why do you do that?"

"Do what, dear?" his grandmother asked as she stepped gently away from the door.

"You know . . . make those noises. Grandma Jean doesn't make noises when she stands up or sits down, and she digs in the garden and helps Grandpa with his chores and everything. But you make noises all the time, Grandma."

This dignified lady who had just been told she "made noises" worked very hard not to betray the smile hidden behind her lips as she faced Observant Josh.

"Can you tell me what kind of noises I make?"

"Oh sure," the tyke said as he took her place in the comfortable chair. He placed his hands on each armrest, furrowed his brow, and with a theatrical flourish that would make an Academy Award-winner proud, began his best impersonation.

"Ohhhh . . . mmhh. Oh, my. . . ." The moaning and groaning became so exaggerated, Grandma was sure he was milking the performance for all it was worth. She stopped him and attempted to look stern.

"Now Joshua, surely it's not like that."

He thought for a minute. "No, Grandma . . . it's not. Usually, it's much worse!"

Oh, boy! Can our grandkids ever know how much truth they make us endure?

I'm not sure what life-changing lesson this little story serves us with, except, in everything we do, let's make sure we enjoy these wonderful gifts from God. Our Heavenly Father has entrusted these little charges to us and we never know when they're watching and observing us, so let's make sure our grandchildren see Christ in us.

Grandchildren.

They're totally unique!

Children's children are the crown of old men (Prov. 17:6).

෴

Isa. 66; Ps. 67; Prov. 11; John 10

September 12 — Age Discrimination

Warren Buffet of Omaha, Nebraska, made the cover story in *Fortune* magazine a few years ago. It's the story of one of our country's most successful billionaires. Warren Buffet has been an enormous success in investing in all kinds of companies. He's been called "The Wizard of Omaha" and looks for strong companies well-positioned in their markets. He is famous for taking over companies and leaving the current management in place rather than replacing them.

Now, here's our point of interest. One of his companies is the Nebraska Furniture Mart, founded by Rose Blumkin. Following is *Fortune's* description of Buffet's dealings with the Blumkins:

> With the family Buffet usually refers to as "the amazing Blumkins," who run the Nebraska Furniture Mart, the drill is dinner, held every few weeks at an Omaha restaurant. The Blumkins attending usually include Louis, 68, and his sons, Rom, 39; Irv, 35; and Steve, 33.
>
> The matriarch of the family and chairman of the Furniture Mart is Rose Blumkin, who emigrated from Russia as a young woman, started a tiny furniture store that offered rock bottom prices ... her motto is "Sell cheap and tell the truth" ... and built it into a business that last year did $140 million in sales. At age 94, she still works seven days a week in the carpet department. Buffet says in his new annual report that she is clearly gathering speed and "may well reach her full potential in another five or ten years. Therefore, I've persuaded the Board to scrap our mandatory-retirement-at-100 policy." It's about time, he adds: "With every passing year, this policy has seemed sillier to me."
>
> He jests, true, but Buffet simply does not regard age as having any bearing on how able a manager is. Perhaps because he has tended to buy good managements and stick with them, he has worked over the years with an unusually large number of older executives and treasured their abilities. . . . He says, "Good managers are so scarce I can't afford the luxury of letting them go just because they've added a year to their age."[67]

Now, I understand, that Rose Blumkin decided to retire . . . but that didn't work, so she has now started her own carpet company, separate from the Nebraska Furniture Mart, so she can manage it as she sees fit!

I was young and now I am old, yet I have never seen the righteous forsaken or their children begging bread (Ps. 37:25).

❧

Mic. 1-4; Ps. 68:1-18; Prov. 12; John 11

September 13 — What Do You See?

The following was written for her caregivers by a woman in a geriatric ward in an English hospital.

What do you see? Are you thinking when you look at me . . .
A crabbed old woman, not very wise, uncertain of habit with faraway
    eyes, who dribbles her food and makes no reply,
When you say in a loud voice . . . "I do wish you'd try."
Is that what you're thinking, is that what you see?
Then open your eyes, you're not looking at me.
I'll tell you who I am as I sit here so still, as I move at your bidding, eat
    at your will. I'm a small child of 10 with a father and mother,
        Brothers and sisters who love.
A young girl of 16 with wings on her feet, dreaming that soon a love she
    will meet. A bride at 20, my heart gives a leap, remembering vows
        I promised to keep.
At 25 now, I have young of my own who need me to build a happy home.
A woman of 30, my young now grown fast,
Bound together with ties that should last.
At 40, my young sons have grown up,
My man's beside me to see I don't mourn.
At 50 once more babies play around my knee.
Again we know children, my loved one and me.
Dark days are upon me, my husband is dead. I look at the future, I
    shudder with dread. For my young are all rearing young of their
        own, and I think of the years and the love that I've known.
I'm an old woman now and nature is cruel. 'Tis her jest to make old age
    look like a fool. The body it crumbles, grace and vigor depart.
        There is stone where I once had a heart.
But inside this old carcass a young girl still dwells, Now again my
    bittered heart swells. I remember the joys, I remember the pain
        And I'm loving and living life over again.
I think of the years, all too few, gone too fast, and accept the fact that
    nothing lasts. So open your eyes, open and see not a crabbed old
    woman, Look closer . . . see ME!

Cast all your anxiety on Him because He cares for you (1 Pet. 5:7).

❧

Mic. 5-7; Ps. 68:19-35; Prov. 13; John 12

September 14 — Enthusiastic Teaching

Howard Hendricks tells of an 83-year-old woman that he and some other conference leaders had lunch with during a Sunday school convention in Chicago. In the course of conversation it was learned that she was a teacher of 13 junior high boys in a church of 55 attendees. She was asked why she was attending the conference.

"I'm on a pension . . . my husband died years ago," she replied, "and, frankly, this is the first time a convention has come close enough to my home so I could afford to attend. I bought a bus ticket and rode all night to get here this morning and attend two workshops. I want to learn something that will make me a better teacher."

Three convention speakers slithered across the ground back to the convention after that encounter. I couldn't help thinking about all the frauds across America who would be breaking their arms patting themselves on the back if they had 13 boys in a Sunday school of 55 church-goers. "Who, me go to a Sunday school convention? Man, I can tell them how to do it!" Not this woman.

You know, she tipped her hand . . . she told us she had a passion to communicate! I heard a sequel to this story later. A doctor told me there are 84 young men in or moving toward the Christian ministry as a result of this woman's influence. We have some in our seminary.

I asked two of them, "What do you remember most about her?"

They said, "She is the most unforgettable person we've ever met. She's still going hard; fills her car with kids and brings them to church."[68]

Awesome! Yes, this kind of a life is a challenge to all of us. Too many Christians assume that they are in a red-light situation waiting for the light to turn green . . . let's assume, instead that we are at a green light waiting for the red light! It's a matter of perspective and how serious we are about making what we have left in our life count.

Let's combine that challenge with this: Look again at the name of God. Two-thirds of His name is "GO" and if that is turned around, by the same thinking, two-thirds of God's name is "DO"! Therefore the "gospel" is go and do it! Let's put the go and the do into our living. Words aren't enough. Praying isn't enough. It's a balance of doing and going with the message and lifestyle. And people are not very interested in what we say, anyway. People want to see this gospel message, if it's so good, put into an action that can be interpreted as living it out! Go and do . . . NOW!

He said to them, "Go into all the world and preach the good news to all creation" (Mark 16:15).

❦

Hab.; Ps. 69:1-15; Prov. 14; John 13

❧

*Motherhood is full of
frustrations and challenges . . . but,
eventually, they move out.*

❧

September 15 — What Is a Mother Worth?

Sylvia Porter, a noted financial analyst, states that 25 million full-time homemakers contribute BILLIONS to the economy every year, although their labor is not counted in the gross national product.

Porter says only the wealthiest families could afford to pay for the services a mother provides for love. She calculated how much the mother-at-home added to her family's economic well-being by assigning an hourly fee for nursemaid, housekeeper, cook, dishwasher, laundress, food buyer, chauffeur, gardener, maintenance person, seamstress, dietician, and practical nurse. She found that the labor performed by a mother at home would cost a family $23,580 in Greensboro, South Carolina, $26,962 in Los Angeles, and $28,735 in Chicago!

In a sense, even this analysis is demeaning to the mother at home because Porter only looked at the relatively menial duties. She did not consider the higher status jobs EVERY mother at home performs: coach, teacher, interior decorator, religious education instructor, and child psychologist, to name a few which come to mind.

"Your government should give you a medal for productivity," says Porter to the at-home mother. "Your family should appreciate and cherish you."[69]

Yes, indeed! The mother who stays at home is really one of the unsung heroines of today! Not only is she providing pricey, irreplaceable services for her family while she nurtures her children, but SHE is important to society at large!

Think of the BILLIONS of dollars which are part of our economy because the stay-at-home mother did her job well! Solid, stable homes produce solid, stable, productive citizens who make a difference in this world!

Mother, you have permission to salute yourself if no one else does it for you! YOU are valuable! YOU are providing services far beyond the call of duty! YOU are needed! YOU are important! Thank you!

She said to her husband, "I know that this man who often comes our way is a holy man of God. Let's make a small room on the roof. . . . Then he can stay there whenever he comes to us" (2 Kings 4:9-10).

༺❧༻

Zeph.; Ps. 69:16-36; Prov. 15; John 14-15

On the first day of class, as had been his custom, this particular college professor asked his Speech 101 students to introduce themselves. And in order to make the names stick with the faces they were to tell what they liked most and least about themselves. The students, in turn, would stand and give their names and what they liked most and least. There were some laughs, a bit of self-consciousness . . . but it was a great class-breaker.

Then . . . the class attention was focused on the next person, a young lady named Dorothy. She did not stand but kept her eyes glued to her desk top. She did not say a word. The professor thought that perhaps she had not heard or was shy and may have needed a bit more encouragement, "Dorothy, Dorothy, it's your turn." Still no response. Then he said it again, "Come on Dorothy. How about you?"

After a rather long pause, she stood but did not turn to face the class. She said, "My name is Dorothy Jackson." Then . . . she spun in the direction of the class and with a sweeping motion of her hand, she pulled her long hair away from her face. There for all to see was a large wine-colored birthmark covering nearly the entire left side of her face. She blurted it out, "Now you *all* know what I like least about myself."

Immediately, this sensitive, caring, professor moved to her side. He gently leaned over her shoulder and gave her a kiss on the birthmark and then followed that with a big hug. He straightened up and said, "That's okay. God and I think you're beautiful."

She began to cry and sobbed for a number of minutes. Other members of this class followed their professor's lead and gathered around her and took turns giving her hugs. After she had managed to gain her composure, she said, "Thank you. I have waited all my life for someone to hug me and say what you said." Dorothy paused, to regain her composure, then quietly, almost in a whisper, "Why couldn't my parents have done that? My mother has never even touched my face."[70]

Don't let anyone tell you that the human touch given in love is not powerful! Incredible! I wish I had the rest of the story to tell you but I would almost wager that Dorothy experienced a break-through. It was a liberating touch. When Jesus Christ came . . . He came to embrace us, to kiss us, even our ugliness, and to show us what the love of the Heavenly Father was all about. And . . . isn't this what we are all about, too?

How great is the love the Father has lavished on us, that we should
be called children of God! And that is what we are! (1 John 3:1).

❧

Jer. 1-2; Ps. 70; Prov. 16; John 16-17

September 17 — More Than Whoop-de-do

Dr. James Dobson (Focus on the Family) tells this story as it was told to him by his mother about the high school she attended.

Her high school was in a small Oklahoma town and it had fielded a series of very sorry, pathetic football teams. Losing was the norm for them, especially if it was a big game. Consequently, it affected not only the student body but the whole community . . . they were tired and depressed from this Friday night debacle of losing.

Finally a wealthy oil man could take it no longer. After another disastrous game, he asked the coach if he could make a locker room talk to the team. It had to be one of the most stirring speeches of all time. Certainly this team had never heard anything like that. This was the deal: to every boy on the team, to every coach . . . if they won, they would each be given a brand new Ford! All they had to do was win the next game — the game against their arch rivals. This was more than inspiring words . . . it was a hard offer! Think of it . . . a brand new Ford!

As you might expect, the team went nuts, slapping each other on the back, cheering, and otherwise carrying on. For seven days the team ate, drank, and breathed football. And when they slept, they dreamed of touchdowns and rumble seats. Of course the offer became public knowledge and the high school contracted a holiday-like fever. Each member of the team imagined himself in the driver's seat of a sharp little coupe with "girls in the front and girls in the back."

Finally it was time for the big game. The team assembled in the locker room; the atmosphere was electric. The remarks from the coach seemed anti-climactic. The team hurried out to face the enemy. They circled up at the sidelines, put out their hands, and shouted "Rah, rah, rah!" Then they went out onto the field . . . to be demolished, 38 to 0!

All the energy, the exuberance, the whoop-de-do, didn't amount to a single point on the scoreboard! A week of jumping and dreaming could not make up for a lack of discipline, coaching, talent, and character. Emotion, by itself, is not enough to prepare you for the battles of life. Feelings will let all of us down and leave us looking more than a bit foolish if that's all we depend on to accomplish life's tasks. Emotion, however, added to discipline, practice, knowledge, wisdom, character-building, a willingness to pay the price, and to delay gratification, can be the icing on the cake of life! Enthusiasm is great . . . but it takes more than just emotion to win big in life!

For all seek their own, not the things
which are Jesus Christ's (Phil. 2:21).

❧

Jer. 3; Ps. 71:1-16; Prov. 17; John 18

September 18 — Heaven Has a Face

Two young women, sisters for the hours they were to spend together in labor and childbirth, both prepared for the births of their first children. They were, after childbirth, placed in hospital rooms across the corridor from each other. The one mother-to-be had eagerly looked forward to and had planned for this blessed event. She and her husband had prepared a nursery, bought baby clothes, soft blankets, diapers, and everything else that the newborn could possibly need. But, regardless of this thought and anticipation . . . this baby girl was stillborn. The doctor expressed to these hurting, grieving parents his heart-felt sympathy.

This young mother-to-be was crushed, broken, and became bitter! "Why? Why?" she cried.

Across the hall, this sister in labor and childbirth didn't want her baby, had made no plans other than to give her baby away. Knowing this only embittered the mother whose baby had died. She went home, depressed, angry at the world, at the doctors, and angry at God.

"Why, oh why, did my baby have to die?" she cried.

Then in Sunday school one Sunday, she picked up a child's story paper and in it read the simple story of a shepherd and his sheep and the efforts to get them to cross a stream.

The frustrated shepherd attempted to drive them across, but it was fruitless. He tried to lead them across, but to no avail. The sheep were too fearful of the running water.

Finally, the shepherd picked up a tiny lamb in his arms and with the little lamb held tight, he waded across the stream. The mother ewe, hearing the bleating of her little lamb across the stream, walked into the water and on over to the other side, and all the other sheep followed.

This young mother, who had lost her child, who had grown so bitter, in that moment began to see some kind of a reason for her loss. It dawned on her that the Lord, the Good Shepherd, had taken her little lamb across to the other side. Her reasons and resolve to follow Him became greater than before. Her little lamb was in heaven . . . she knew it. From that moment on, heaven was no longer some strange, hazy place out there . . . no, her baby was over there! Heaven was not so far removed, now. Heaven now had meaning, substance, someone she knew and loved. Heaven now has the face of her baby over there.

As a shepherd looks after his scattered flock when he is with them, so will I look after my sheep. I will rescue them from all the places where they were scattered on a day of clouds and darkness (Ezek. 34:12).

꙰

Jer. 4-5; Ps. 71:17-24; Prov. 18; John 19

September 19 — Love from the Heart

Love affairs are not unusual for young teenagers today. It's not particularly surprising when such love affairs are broken for some reason or another. Normally, teens get over the hurt they feel for a broken relationship and discover that there are other "fish in the sea."

This very typical pattern of teen love began as Felipe Garza Jr. began dating Donna Ashlock. Felipe was 15 and Donna was 14. They dated until Donna cooled the romance and began dating other boys.

One day, Donna doubled over in pain. Doctors soon discovered that Donna was dying of degenerative heart disease and desperately needed a heart transplant. Felipe heard about Donna's condition and told his mother, "I'm going to die and I'm going to give my heart to my girlfriend." Boys say some irrational things like this from time to time. After all, Felipe appeared to his mom to be in perfect health.

Three weeks later, Felipe woke up and complained of pain on the left side of his head. He began losing his breath and couldn't walk. He was taken to a hospital where it was discovered that a blood vessel in his brain had burst and left him brain dead. Felipe's sudden death mystified his doctors! While he remained on a respirator, his family decided to let physicians remove his heart for Donna and his kidneys and eyes for others in need of those organs.

Donna received Felipe's heart! After the transplant, Donna's father told her that Felipe had evidently been sick for about three months before he had died. He said, "He donated his kidneys and eyes." There was a pause and Donna said, "And I have his heart."

Her father said, "Yes, that was what he and his parents wished." Her expression changed just a little. She then asked her father who knew. He told her, "Everybody." Nothing else was said.

Several days later, a funeral procession seemed to roll on forever through the orchards and fields of Patterson, California. The procession was so long it might have been that of a prince, but it was Felipe. His only claim to fame was his love and his heart. It's unforgettable when a person gives up his life so that someone he loves can live. It would be unforgettable if you had received a new and healthy heart from someone who loved you more than you could appreciate. Every moment you lived would be a tribute and testimony to the one who loved you so much that they gave their life for you.[71]

Think a moment . . . and make whatever life application comes to mind.

Blessed are the pure in heart: for they shall see God (Matt. 5:8).

❦

Jer. 6-7; Ps. 72; Prov. 19; John 20-21

September 20 — Eternal Gain

Russ Chandler, religion writer for the *Los Angeles Times,* wrote an excellent book a few years ago in which he tells the stories of 12 outstanding Christians who have dealt with significant problems in their lives. The book begins with Elisabeth Elliot, who first became prominent through her account of the martyrdom of the five young missionaries who were murdered by the Auca Indians in 1956, including her husband, Jim Elliot. She recalled some of the trying events of her life through which she learned important lessons.

Elisabeth, who first went to South America to do translation work in 1952, mentioned three experiences of loss in that first year working with a small tribe of Indians called the Colorados. The first calamity was the murder of the informant who was giving her information about the language and culture of the Colorados.

A second catastrophe was the loss of all the work Elisabeth did that year. All her files, tapes, notebooks, and vocabulary compilations were stolen and no copies or duplicates existed. The same year, Jim was reconstructing a small jungle mission station among the Quichua Indians. During a sudden flood one night, all of the buildings he had rebuilt, plus three new ones, were swept away down the Amazon River.

These three experiences of total earthly loss taught Elisabeth and Jim the deep lessons that Jesus taught His disciples: "Truly, I say unto you, unless a grain of wheat falls into the earth and dies, it remains alone; but if it dies, it bears much fruit" (John 12:24;RSV). The practical outcome of that lesson was this, according to Elisabeth: "I had to face up to the fact in those stunning losses that God was indeed sovereign; therefore, He was my Lord, my Master, the One in charge of my life, the One who deserved my worship and my service. The road to eternal gain leads inevitably through earthly loss. True faith is operative in the dark. True faith deals with the inexplicable things of life. If we have explanations . . . if things are clear and simple . . . there's not very much need for faith.

"Through these three experiences of loss we came to know Jesus Christ in a deeper way and began to enter into the lessons that Paul describes."[72]

Life is not fair. But there also is no gain without pain or loss.

But whatever was to my profit I now consider loss for the sake of Christ. What is more, I consider everything a loss compared to the surpassing greatness of knowing Christ Jesus my Lord, for whose sake I have lost all things (Phil. 3:7-8).

~❧~

Jer. 8-9; Ps. 73:1-14; Prov. 20; Acts 1

September 21 — Fellowship

Here's an old down-to-earth poem which I've always liked. The author is unknown, which is too bad . . . but it talks about the happiness for life which all can experience when a person lives in such a way as to care for others:

FELLOWSHIP
When a feller hasn't got a cent
And is feelin' kind of blue,
And the clouds hang thick and dark
And won't let the sunshine thro',
It's a great thing, oh my brethren,
For a feller just to lay
His hand upon your shoulder in a friendly sort o' way.

It makes a man feel queerish,
It makes the teardrops start.
And you kind o' feel a flutter
In the region of your heart.
You can't look up and meet his eye,
You don't know what to say
When a hand is on your shoulder in a friendly sort o' way.

Oh this world's a curious compound
With its honey and its gall;
Its cares and bitter crosses,
But a good world after all.
And a good God must have made it,
Leastwise that is what I say,
When a hand is on your shoulder in a friendly sort o' way.

Feeling towards others in the friendly way suggested by this poem goes a long way, too, toward giving another a greater sense of worth, something that helps all of us know that life can be meaningful!

For my yoke is easy and my burden is light (Matt. 11:30).

❧

Jer. 10-11; Ps. 73:15-28; Prov. 21; Acts 2

September 22 — Always Old

To all of us, Hannah and Aggie had always been "old." None of us remember a time when that were not "old." In retrospect, it seems that these two sisters have always been somewhere languishing in their senior years. It's now a mystery, but somehow they must have made the leap in time from girlhood to senior citizens without any kind of transition in between. They've always been old to the rest of us and just part of our little town, the Swenson sisters.

Another remarkable thing that comes to mind is that very rarely were they ever seen without the other. It seems to me that there might have been a short break when Hannah first married her husband Gus. And then Aggie married James. But that was a short period because Gus died of some mysterious sickness and Hannah moved back to the "home place." Quite shortly after that, they tell us, Aggie and James also moved into the same house. There were some children, it seems to me. I seem to recall that Hannah and Gus parented twin daughters, but that's kind of fuzzy. Then, James also died — cancer, they say. So Hannah and Aggie lived alone together in the same house.

Oh, yes, there was a housekeeper who happened to be the only person we knew about who had ever seen the inside of their house. It was a house of mystery. Nobody seemed to come calling, except a salesman or two who didn't know better.

Times did change, however, I'm told. Their house became the place where the quilting circle began to meet. But I've been told that no one was allowed to go upstairs.

There was talk of these Swenson sisters being placed in a nursing home in the later years . . . but it never happened. Hannah went first and the very next day Aggie died, too. The local funeral director and preacher were left to make the decisions as none of their children cared enough to come back home, not even to check the wills. There was nothing left except that old ramshackle, falling-down mysterious house. It sold on auction.

To the rest of us, their lives seemed to amount to nothing but speculation. What had they done to make our town a better place? What had they contributed in life? Nothing we could think of. Nothing . . . except having provided company for each other.

Behold, I am coming soon! My reward is with me, and I will to everyone according to what he has done (Rev. 22:12).

❧

Jer. 12-13; Ps. 74:1-11; Prov. 22; Acts 3

September 23 — Hope Beyond

At the age of 80, the poet Alfred Lord Tennyson was taken from his summer home at Aldworth, England, to his winter residence on the Isle of Wight. As the boat left the mainland and crossed the strait, Tennyson heard a moaning sound caused by the fierce beating of the waves against a large sandbar. He recognized this as a prelude to a coming storm.

A few days later, his health began to fail and a nurse was hired to stay with him. In conversing with him, she said quietly, "Sir, you've composed a great many poems, but few hymns. I wish you'd write one now on your sick bed. I'm sure it would help and comfort other poor sufferers."

The next morning, Tennyson handed her a scrap of paper, saying, "I followed your suggestion and wrote these verses during the night."

The poem/hymn proved to be a masterpiece filled with imagery about the sea, the emotions related to dying which the "moaning of the bar" brought to his mind and the glorious hope of seeing Jesus at the end of life's voyage. The selection reads in part:

Sunset and evening star, and one clear call for me!
And may there be no moaning of the bar, when I put out to sea.
Twilight and evening bell, and after that the dark!
And may there be no sadness of farewell, when I embark.
For though from out the bourne of time and place the flood may
bear me far,
I hope to see my Pilot face to face when I have crossed the bar!

There will come the time for all of us to cross the bar! It's a whole lot sooner today that it has been at any time in our past. When you become a grandparent, you begin to think about how this life is going to end. We have observed the cycles of life . . . birth and death . . . young and then old . . . in fact, we have lived through many of these life cycles. It's time to think about going home, running the last lap, finishing the race, putting the final AMEN to this life.

Will death be your enemy or your friend? The answer to that all depends upon how you have lived your life to this moment. If you, my friend, have never made a decision to make the Lord Jesus Christ your Saviour, this can be your moment. With your confession, you can invite Him to be your Guide, your "Pilot" as Tennyson put it, into and through all of eternity. It's a choice that only you can make.

For the wages of sin is death, but the gift of God is eternal life in Christ Jesus our Lord (Rom. 6:23).

Jer. 14-15; Ps. 74:12-23; Prov. 23; Acts 4

September 24 — The Last "I Love You"

Carol's husband was killed in an accident last year. Jim, only 52, was driving home from work. The other driver was a teenager with a very high blood-alcohol level. Jim died instantly. The teenager was in the emergency room less than two hours.

There were other ironic twists: It was Carol's fiftieth birthday, and Jim had two plane tickets to Hawaii in his pocket. He was going to surprise her. Instead, he was killed by a drunken driver.

"How have you survived this?" I finally asked Carol, a year later.

Her eyes welled up with tears. I thought I had said the wrong thing, but she gently took my hand and said, "It's all right, I want to tell you. The day I married Jim, I promised I would never let him leave the house in the morning without telling him I loved him. He made the same promise. It got to be a joke between us, and as babies came along it got to be a hard promise to keep. I remember running down the driveway, saying 'I love you' through clenched teeth when I was mad, or driving to the office to put a note in his car. It was a funny challenge.

"We made a lot of memories trying to say 'I love you' before noon every day of our married life.

"The morning Jim died, he left a birthday card in the kitchen and slipped out to the car. I heard the engine starting. *Oh, no, you don't buster,* I thought. I raced out and banged on the car window until he rolled it down. 'Here on my fiftieth birthday, Mr. James E. Garret, I, Carol Garret, want to go on record as saying I love you!'

"That's how I've survived. Knowing that the last words I said to Jim were 'I LOVE YOU!' "[73]

If you love somebody . . . tell them, NOW! Give them a call . . . drive to the office . . . send a special card . . . write a love note . . . rent a billboard . . . charter a sky-writing plane . . . buy a dozen roses . . . bring a box of candy . . . buy a book . . . do a back rub . . . plant a tree . . . make a favorite meal . . . buy the special dress . . . do the dishes . . . whisper it in the ear . . . pack a note in the lunch box . . . secure a coveted CD. Be imaginative, be creative, but do it NOW! If you love someone, tell them in ways that they will understand to be an expression of love!

Together, how about making this our daily prayer: "Lord, please remind me today and every day to say 'I LOVE YOU' out loud to the people whom I live with and whom I love! And, Lord, please help me to remember to put this love into actions which they will interpret as being acts of love!"

Love never fails (1 Cor. 13:8).

෨෧

Jer. 16-17; Ps. 75; Prov. 24; Acts 5

September 25 — Foundational Note

A shepherd living up in the hills of Idaho was a faithful listener to one of the finer musical programs that originated from a radio station in Los Angeles each Sunday night. One evening after listening to the concert of classical music, he wrote a letter to the radio station with a most unusual request.

The letter said in part, "I enjoy your program every week, and I'm writing to ask you a favor. It's rather lonely up here in the hills, and I haven't much to entertain me except listening to the radio. I have an old violin, which I once could play, but it has gotten badly out of tune. I wonder if you would take just a moment on your program next week to strike "A" on the piano so that I may tune my violin again."

At first they smiled about the letter, but then the station decided to honor the request. The following Sunday night when the program came on the air they interrupted it long enough to strike "A" on the studio piano in Los Angeles while the shepherd out in the hills of Idaho got the right pitch for his violin.

That's a great little story. Why? This world of ours is badly out of tune. We need a Higher Power to strike the right note, a foundational note, to give us the right pitch for our lives and living.

It was almost two thousand years ago, in a little-known corner of the world called Palestine, that God "in the fullness of time" sounded the master note upon the instruments of heaven.

Jesus Christ of Nazareth, the Son of Man and the Son of God, was that master note. He was the "Λ" sounded that men might tune their lives to Him and in doing so find the answer to life and the meaning of life.

Have you let Him strike "A" in your life? No matter what the discord — no matter how far off-key your life has gotten — He can turn your life into the symphony God intended it to be.

Life may prove to be harsh and difficult. Life may deny you your dreams and starve your precious hopes. Life may have taken from you that which you considered most precious. Life may have turned fickle and unpredictable. But in Jesus Christ there is an answer! He is the basic foundation on which you can build or rebuild your life. Let Him strike "A" in your life!

Then Peter said, "Silver and gold I do not have, but what I have I give you" (Acts 3:6).

෴

Jer. 18-20; Ps. 76; Prov. 25; Acts 6

September 26 — Inglisch Spocken Here

The following has been selected and collected for all English teachers who may have made it thus far in this book. These are a collection of notices in what may have been intended to be written in plain English. Upon reading this, our only hope is that somehow our language will survive.

From a hotel in Moscow: "If this is your first visit to the USSR, you are welcome to it."

Notice found in a travel agency in Barcelona: "Go away."

A Tokyo hotel has this notice on its elevator doors: "Do Not Open Door Until Door Opens First."

Another Tokyo hotel posted: "Is forbidden to steal towels, please. If you are not person to do such, please not to read notice."

A butcher in Nahariyya, Israel: "I slaughter myself twice daily."

This from a barber in Zanzibar: "Gentlemen's throats cut with nice sharp razors."

Hotel del Paseo, Mexico City: "We sorry to advise you that by a electric desperfect in the generator master of the elevator we have the necessity that don't give service at our distinguishable guests."

This notice was placed on every table in the dining room of a hotel in Columbo, Sri Lanka: "All vegetables in this establishment have been washed in water especially passed by the management."

A dentist in Hong Kong: "Teeth extracted by latest methodists."

Another elevator sign from Tokyo: "Keep your hands away from unnecessary buttons for you."

A hotel in Bucharest posted this notice: "The lift is being fixed for the next four days. During this time you will be unbearable."

Hotel Deutschland, Leipzig: "Do not enter the lift backwards and only when lit up."

From the bakery, Vale of Kashmir: "First-class English loafer."

From a little restaurant in Mexico City: "U.S. Hots Dog."

A barber in Tokyo: "All customers promptly executed."

The Restaurant des Artistes, Montmartre: "We serve five o'clock tea at all hours."

Don't you love this? What a delight! How about a hand for all those marvelous, wonderful people who have composed such signs and sentences! I only hope they never open any English dictionaries as long as they promise to keep on writing such notices.

He who answers before listening —
that is his folly and his shame (Prov. 18:13).

༄

Jer. 21-22; Ps. 77; Prov. 26; Acts 7

September 27 — To Catch a Hog

Many years ago, in the Smokey Mountains of Tennessee, some domesticated hogs escaped from a farmer's pen. Over a period of several generations of hogs, these pigs became wilder and wilder until they were a menace to anyone who crossed their path. A number of skilled hunters tried to locate and kill them, but the hogs proved to be too elusive.

One day an older man leading a small donkey pulling a cart came into the village closest to the habitat of these wild hogs. The cart was loaded with lumber and grain. The local citizens were curious about what he was going to do. He told them he had come "to catch them wild hogs." They laughed in disbelief that the old man could accomplish what the local hunters were unable to do.

Two months later the old man returned to the village and told the citizens that the hogs were trapped in a pen near the top of the mountain. The village people coaxed him into telling them how he had accomplished such a feat.

"First thing I done was find the spot where the hogs came to eat. Then I put a little grain right in the middle of the clearing. Them hogs was scared at first but curiosity finally got to them and the old boar started sniffing around. After he took the first bite the others joined in and I knew right then and there I had them."

"Next day I put some more grain out and laid one plank a few feet away. That plank kind of spooked them for awhile, but that free lunch was a powerful appeal. It wasn't long before they were back eating. All I had to do was add a couple of boards each day until I had everything I needed for my trap. Then I dug a hole and put up my first corner post. Every time I did something they'd stay away a spell. But they always came back to eat."

"Finally, the pen was built and the trapdoor was set. Next time they came to eat they walked right into the pen and I sprung the trap."[74]

The point is obvious . . . when you make any creature dependent upon something, it no longer has the need or will to make its own way. The same thing happens to young people. Sin's enticing pleasure pulls at us long enough to create the habit and we are caught! A government handout can do the same . . . taking away all incentive to work for our living. But with any handout also comes bondage and dependence and laziness and ultimately, entrapment . . . and then it's too late!

The thief comes only to steal and kill and destroy; I have come that they (you) may have life, and have it to the full (John 10:10).

〜

Jer. 23-24; Ps. 78:1-20; Prov. 27; Acts 8

Yvonne (name changed) was 17, pregnant, penniless, and afraid. She was at her wits' end not knowing what to do. As she sat, tearfully watching the sonogram of her baby, she saw the new life, alive and moving, and knew in that moment that an abortion would be out of the question for this helpless new life. Nightly, she cried herself to sleep.

Then, one night an angel appeared to her in a dream. It said, "Don't be afraid. Everything will be fine because you and your baby will be well taken care of."

The angel pulled back the curtain and gave her a look into the future. Yvonne watched as her baby, healthy, strong, and beautiful was placed by the angel into the arms of a wonderful, caring, loving couple. The next scene showed the baby as a grown woman, mature and happy. The angel told her God was concerned about the baby and would work it all out for good for her as-yet-unborn child. Then the angel turned to Yvonne and touched her with a light that seemed to give off a warm glow that stayed with Yvonne in her heart.

As Yvonne awoke the next morning she felt wonderful, loved, and that everything would be worked out for the best. On this same day she was introduced to a lady who told her about a support group/home for unwed mothers. The next day Yvonne found herself in attendance with this support group where she found healing for her emotions and help about the choices she could make as to her baby's future.

Her choice was to give birth and place the child with a Christian adoption agency. While she held her baby for the last time, Yvonne had her own dedication ceremony for her baby.

In Yvonne's story the angel appeared in a dream with a message. There is also a biblical story which parallels hers. About 2,000 years ago an angel appeared in a dream to a man named Joseph with instructions about another unborn child, even to giving him the child's name. Later, this same man, Joseph, had another dream in which an angel gave him the message that he was to take the young child to Egypt to escape the plans of King Herod, who intended to kill Jesus. The word "angel" in the Greek language originally means a "messenger."

But after he had considered this, an angel of the Lord appeared to him in a dream and said, "Joseph son of David, do not be afraid to take Mary home as your wife, because what is conceived in her is from the Holy Spirit. She will give birth to a son, and you are to give him the name Jesus, because he will save his people from their sins" (Matt. 1:20-21).

❧

Jer. 25; Ps. 78:21-33; Prov. 28; Acts 9

September 29 — A Horse Thief on Trial

A man in the Old West was being tried for stealing a horse. Just to refresh your memory, stealing a horse at that time was a very serious offense. A person could easily be shot or hanged if found guilty.

This gentleman was accused of stealing a horse from another man, but the man from whom he allegedly had stolen the horse was hated by every person in town. The horse owner had never done anything good for anybody other than himself, and he didn't have a single friend in town. However, the alleged thief was well-liked.

The case was presented to the jury. The evidence against the accused was pretty strong but not absolutely airtight. After about 30 minutes of deliberation, the jury returned to the court chambers. "Gentlemen and ladies of the jury, have you reached a verdict?"

"Yes, Your Honor, we have." There was a long dramatic pause, then the jury foreman continued, "We find the defendant not guilty if he will return the horse."

After the judge had silenced the laughter and cheering in the courtroom, he sternly addressed the jury, "I cannot accept this verdict. You will have to retire until you reach another verdict." The jury dutifully went back to their room to hammer out another verdict.

This time an hour had passed. I remind you that not a single person on the jury liked the man whose horse had allegedly been taken. They re-entered the courtroom and the place grew silent.

"Gentlemen and ladies of the jury," began the judge, "have you reached a verdict?"

The jury foreman stood up, "Yes, we have, Your Honor."

There was complete silence in the courtroom — you could have heard a pin drop. Everyone moved forward in their seats as they eagerly awaited the verdict.

"Well, what is your verdict?" asked the judge.

"The jury foreman pulled out his piece of paper, straightened it out, and read the decision rendered by these 12 jury members, "We find the defendant not guilty, and he can keep the horse!" Now the courtroom burst into wild cheering and laughing!

Is there a moral to the story? How about this? It pays to be interested in other people! If you spend your life only trying to take advantage of others, never caring for anybody else, you could end up a real loser — like the man who lost his horse!

Do not be deceived: God cannot be mocked.
A man reaps what he sows (Gal. 6:7).

✺

Jer. 26-27; Ps. 78:34-53; Prov. 29; Acts 10

September 30 — Comeback

Doug Williams, quarterback for the Washington Redskins lay in pain on the turf. This was the perfect excuse to give up, to quit. It was Super Bowl time, the 1988 match-up between the Denver Broncos and the Redskins and his team was behind 10-0. Keep in mind that no team in the Super Bowl had ever come back from such a deficit to win!

Doug Williams is a black quarterback who started that particular football season as a substitute school teacher. The prospects for him were not too bright. Ten years previous, Williams had led the Tampa Bay Buccaneers into their first appearance in the NFL (National Football League). His troubles really began when he jumped to the new rival USFL, an ill-fated league that didn't make it. Then, some months after giving birth to their baby daughter, his wife died from a brain tumor. And, the next disaster struck, the USFL folded. Now, no team in the NFL would allow him an opportunity to play, nobody touched him.

Then the fall of 1987 rolled around and the Washington Redskins needed an inexpensive backup in case something happened to their young star quarterback. He did play for the injured man. When the much younger player recovered, Williams knew his time and days were numbered, again.

His team moved through the season and then into the playoffs to determine who would play in football's biggest game for 1988. Well, it happened that Williams was to be the first black quarterback to ever start in a Super Bowl.

Back to our opening paragraph . . . after being taken out of the game, he gamely limped back to his team on the field and did something no team nor quarterback had ever done. In just one quarter of play, he threw four touchdowns, which tied a previous record and led his team to a 42-10 victory, a sweet come-from-behind-win that had not happened in this setting before. And yes, Doug Williams, the first black QB to start was named game's "most valuable player!"

To me, it's always great to watch somebody make a comeback from the brink of oblivion and defeat! There's an inspiration in watching this happen on such a scale. But this is a possibility for every person who has been subjected to the pounding of life. Life is not fair! Toughness is the mental attitude needed more than any other to make a comeback . . . this combined with faith are two elements that will allow you to come back!

Create in me a clean heart, O God, And renew a steadfast spirit within me (Ps. 51:12;NKJV).

❦

Jer. 28-29; Ps. 78:54-72; Acts 11

October 1 — It's Who You Know

During the Civil War, a young soldier walking over a battlefield came across a dear friend who was shot. His life was draining rapidly away. The soldier straightened out the shattered limb, washed the blood from his fallen comrade's face, and made him as comfortable as possible under difficult circumstances. He then said he would stay with his friend as long as life was still there. Then he asked if there was anything more he might do.

"Yes," replied the dying soldier, "if you have a piece of paper, I will dictate a note to my father, and I think I can still sign it. My father is a prominent judge in the North, and if you take him this message he will help you."

The note read, "Dear Father, I am dying on the battlefield; one of my best friends is helping me and has done his best for me. If he ever comes to you, be kind to him for your son Charlie's sake." Then with rapidly stiffening fingers, he signed his name.

After the war, the young soldier in ragged uniform sought out the prominent judge. The servants refused to admit him because he looked like the many other tramps coming by for handouts.

He made a ruckus and insisted he see the judge. Finally, hearing the commotion, the judge came out and read the note. He at first was convinced it was another beggar's appeal. But he studied the signature, and even in its scribbled state he recognized it as his own son's.

He embraced the soldier, led him into his home, and said, with tears coursing down his cheeks, "You can have anything that my money can buy, and everything that my influence can secure."

What brought about the sudden change in the judge's attitude? It was the signature of his son, Charlie, affixed to the bottom of that note. It was the father-son relationship that made the difference.

There is an old saying in our world: "It's not *what* you know, it's *who* you know, that counts!"

That same principle holds true in the spiritual realm. All the knowledge in the world will not help you as you approach your Heavenly Father, but your personal relationship with Jesus Christ, the Son, will open to you all kinds of possibilities! It's not too late to make right that relationship with the Son, who will in turn provide you an access to the throne room of heaven!

In that day you will no longer ask me anything. I tell you the truth, my Father will give you whatever you ask in my name (John 16:23).

Jer. 30-31; Ps. 79; Prov. 1; James 1-2

❧

The acid test of a father's leadership is not in
the realm of his social skills, his public
relations, his managerial abilities at the office,
or how well he handles himself before
the public. It is in the home.

Charles R. Swindoll

❧

October 2 — All I Had to Give

Many years ago, in Cornwall, New York, a new teacher came to the country school to teach the eighth grade. Miss Frances Irene Hungerford was a tiny mite of a woman but a warm and wonderful lady. This small community soon learned that she was a dedicated teacher and she also faithfully attended church.

On her first day of class, Miss Hungerford wrote this sentence on the blackboard: "Seest thou the man who is diligent in his business? he shall stand before kings" (Prov. 22:29). The pupils were all giggles as they read what she was writing. Who would ever stand before kings?

Steven Pigott, a tall, lanky student, was one who read the verse but didn't laugh at the suggestion. He was good at his studies. His father Pat, an Irish immigrant who could neither read nor write, couldn't understand why Steven was so interested in books.

Miss Hungerford asked him what he wanted to be, and Steven replied without a moment's hesitation, "A marine engineer!" She assured him that he could do just that and encouraged him to go on to college.

Entering Columbia University, he worked his way through and graduated in 1903 with honors. His former teacher sent him a telegram that simply said, "I told you so!"

Five years later he went to Scotland and was persuaded to remain. During the years ahead, he played a big part in building such ships as the Mauretania and the Lusitania.

Later he designed the machinery for British battleships, cruisers, and submarines. Because of his ability, he was knighted by the British government. "Sir Steven Pigott" became known the world over as a brilliant marine engineer. He was the father of Mrs. Estes Kefauver, wife of the former senator from Tennessee.

With all his honors, he never forgot the humble, little teacher who, when interviewed on her eighty-fifth birthday, was asked the secret in guiding boys and girls. She replied, "You see, all I had to give was love!"

Maybe it's time to take inventory again. What do you have to give to another person? Here is a gift we can all give: LOVE! And let that humble school teacher challenge you by her example.

Then Peter said, "Silver or gold I do not have,
but what I have I give you (Acts 3:6).

༄

Jer. 32; Ps. 80; Prov. 2; James 3-5

October 3 — Insurance Policy

During the middle of the "Great Depression" of the 1930s, we hear of the story of one poverty-stricken older woman. Life had become grim. Many widows were struggling for their meager meals.

One day this older woman, dressed very poorly, but neat and clean, timidly approached the front desk of an insurance office in Minneapolis, Minnesota. She asked if it would be possible for her to stop making payments on the yellowed policy clutched in her farm-weathered, work-worn fingers. Then she offered it to the clerk for a look.

The clerk gave it a quick, perfunctory glance, opened it, and studied it with intense amazement. "This is quite valuable," he said. "Yes, I would advise you to stop paying the premiums now, after all these years. Have you talked with your husband about this?"

"No," she said, looking down, "He's been dead three years, now."

"What!?" exclaimed the clerk. "But this is a policy on his life!"

She looked at him and said, "Please, I don't understand."

Carefully this time, he looked at her and replied, "Madam, this is a life insurance policy on his life in the amount of $300,000. This should have been paid to you upon his death."

Then he paused, "Please have a seat, I'll be right back." He took his leave with policy in hand and went for a supervisor. They both soon appeared, "Would you come with us?" They took her into one of the offices and explained to her again.

Soon, they had figured out the benefit of $300,000 which was to be paid to her plus the three years of overpaid premiums with the accumulated interest on those payments. She left that office with a very generous check in hand!

She was able to begin experiencing the financial security which had been hers all the time but had not been known to her! Can you imagine the sense of relief? Perhaps the impact of the money in her life was unknown until she stopped by her bank. What a happy day!

Is there a parallel in your life? When the decision has been made to become part of the kingdom of God, are you realizing all that you may have as benefits and blessings? Are you living beneath your privileges? We are all looking for security in life which can only be ours when we commit our living into God's hands. Security is not in the absence of danger or in having a large bank account, but in the presence of God!

Now all has been heard; here is the conclusion
of the matter: Fear God and keep His commandments,
for this is the whole duty of man (Eccles. 12:13).

❧

Jer. 33-34; Ps. 81; Prov. 3; Acts 12

October 4 — Life Cycles Go On

An old man and his grandson were spending time together one day. As often happened, the little boy was plying his grandad with questions. Suddenly, with a very serious tone the little boy asked, "Grandfather, what happens when you die?"

The old man explained to the best of his ability, but the boy only looked at him in wonder. "Does that mean you won't be here with me anymore?" the boy asked.

The old man shook his head and said, "Yes, that is true."

"Does that mean you won't be able to play catch with me anymore?" asked the boy.

"Yes," said the old man, "it is true."

"Does that mean you won't be able to fly a kite with me anymore?"

"Yes," said the old man, "it is true."

"Does it mean you won't be able to take me fishing anymore?" asked the boy.

"Yes," said the old man, "it is true."

"Well," said the boy, "who will do those things, if you are not?"

And the old man responded, "My son, when that time comes, it will be time for you to do those things for another little boy."[75]

Yes, the time will come for the next generation to pass it on. Which brings to mind another thought — what will they have from our generation to pass on to the next?

There is an old parable about a spider who decided one day to move, so he spun a long strand of web in a barn rafter. Then on the next level down he fastened himself to a two-by-four and spun a great web. By and by he died and left this estate to his son, who in turn left it to his son, who in turn left it to his son.

The carefully-built structure was a bit antique at this point and the great-grandson spider was walking along one day and tripped over a strand of old web. So he thought, *These are out of style right now and in the way.* He then reached over and nipped off what just happened to be the single strand upon which the whole web was hanging and he fell to his death on the barn floor below.

It's a challenge . . . but will our generation pass along life principles that are so important they will not be discarded by the next? Let's keep at it and not give up.

Train a child in the way he should go, and when he is old he will not turn from it (Prov. 22:6).

࿇

Jer. 35-36; Ps. 82; Prov. 4; Acts 13-14

October 5 — Angel in the Dorm

Evangelist Frankie Walker once told this story to the author.

For a "season" of time I was removed from my traveling ministry and taught in a Bible School, did some counseling, and was a dorm mother to some 20 girls.

One evening I had to leave the girls for about an hour and a half to pick up a lady who was coming from another state to be ordained through our church.

It was an extremely dark night as I drove from the parking lot. As I was a small distance from the dorm, I sensed a strong presence of fear and the thought came, *I cannot leave the girls alone.* I prayed, "Lord, what am I to do? I can't go back, someone has to go to the airport." The Lord impressed me to "charge the angels to guard about the dorm."

On arrival back at the dorm, Pastor Eula and I walked into what should have been a sleeping group of young women. Instead we found the whole group seated on the floor, singing. The girl whom I had put in charge met me at the top of the stairs. "I know we are supposed to be in bed, but allow me to tell you why we are not. After you left, we were visiting when another student came home from work. She said, ''Why is Sister Walker standing in her window, curtains open, looking out on the parking lot. She never does that . . . her curtains are always closed at night.' We laughed at her as we explained she must be seeing things because you had gone to the airport."

The girl in charge went on, "We continued talking, then the second carload came from work, three more girls who ride together every day. One of them asked, 'What is Sister Walker doing with her curtains open, watching the parking lot?' " At this, the girls freaked out, some of them frightened to the point of tears.

They decided to check into my room. They found the lights off and drapes closed, just as I had left them. Assured that everything was okay, still shaken, they began to sing and pray together. All of this had been related to me with eyes wide and some tears. Then I explained to them my experience on the road and my instructions to place the angels to guard about them in my absence. I explained the supernatural protection of angels and heard myself say, "That angel looked like me and was guarding you while I was absent."

> *So Peter was kept in prison, but the church was earnestly*
> *praying to God for him. . . . "You're out of your mind,"*
> *they told her. When she kept insisting that it was so, they*
> *said, "It must be his angel"* (Acts 12:5-15).

⁂

Jer. 37-38; Ps. 83; Prov. 5; Acts 15

October 6 — More Than One Way

Just before the morning service was about to begin on a beautiful fall day at Saint Bartholomew's Episcopalian Church on Fifth Avenue in New York City, a man wearing a very large hat was discovered to be sitting in the very front row! An usher hurried from the back, moved to this pew, leaned in toward the man with the large hat and discreetly asked him to please remove his hat. The man replied, "No, thank you."

The usher almost ran to the usher station in the back of the church and asked for the head usher. Who in turn, after being told about the situation, made his way to the front and made the same request of the man with the large hat and received the exact same answer.

About that time the president of the women of the parish arrived at the main entrance to overhear the conversation of the head usher in regards to the rude man with the large hat in the front row. She offered to be of assistance. She made her way to the front pew, leaned in and as graciously as she could, she asked him to please remove his hat. She had the same dismal response, "No!"

Finally, only two minutes remained before the opening hymn and the senior warden of the parish was summoned. He had the solution! He carefully tiptoed up beside the man and reached out to grab the hat, but the man saw him and his tactic in time, and was able to nimbly dodge and the hat remained firmly in place. There was no more time for any other kind of an attempt.

As the opening hymn began and the choir made their procession into the church, the man stood with the rest of the congregation, removed his hat and did not put it on again, until the service was concluded.

At the conclusion of the service, the four frustrated people waited for the man at the rear of the church. The senior warden approached him and said, "Sir, about the hat. Perhaps you don't understand, but in the Episcopal Church men do not wear hats at worship."

The man replied, "Oh, but I do understand. I've been an Episcopalian all my life. As a matter of fact, I've been coming to this church regularly for the past two years and I've never met a soul. But this morning I've met an usher, the head usher, the president of the church women, and the senior warden, thank you all."

Ouch! Another reminder to do what we know we should do in church!

Even my close friend, whom I trusted, he who shared my bread, has lifted up his heel against me (Ps. 41:9).

⤳

Jer. 39-40; Ps. 84; Prov. 6; Gal. 1-2

October 7— Liberal Arts Education

In 1942 the U.S. Navy was desperate for talent. Four young men stood shivering in their shorts while waiting in a small room. A grim-faced selection committee asked the first would-be-officer, "What can you do?"

The recruit replied, "I'm a buyer for Macy's, and I'm trained to judge quickly between markets and prices and trends."

The committee replied, "Can't you do anything practical?" And they shunted him off to one side.

When the committee asked the next man, a lawyer, if he could do anything practical, he said, "I can weigh evidence and organize information." He, too, was rejected.

The third man answered the same question, "I know language and a good deal about history," he replied. The committee groaned in unison and sent him off to the side.

Then the fourth man said boldly, "I'm a college-trained engineer, and I can overhaul diesel engines." The committee wanted to make him an officer on the spot.

By the time the war was over, the Macy's buyer was assistant to the Secretary of the Navy, with many complex responsibilities requiring instant good judgment. He became an expert by taking courses in naval management and government procedures.

The lawyer wound up as assistant to Admiral Halsey, and during a critical battle he deduced from intelligence reports where the enemy fleet was located. He left the military, bedecked with medals.

As for the third man, he got the job of naval secretary to several congressional committees and helped determine the future of American presence in the South Pacific.

And what was the fourth man, the college-trained engineer, doing at the end of the war? He was still overhauling diesel engines.[76]

Interesting how the fates of people can be intertwined about their gifts and talents and education. Who would have thought? This is not a knock against an education. There's a need to keep on learning after we have learned. All of life can be a school, if we will allow the lessons to become part of our personhood. Who knows what might happen in the future? Prepare now, build now, learn now — so that when opportunity comes knocking, you have an answer!

Do your best to present yourself to God as one approved, a workman who does not need to be ashamed and who correctly handles the word of truth (2 Tim. 2:15).

∽

Jer. 41-42; Ps. 85; Prov. 7; Gal. 3-4

The following story has been making its rounds through the upper Pacific Northwest area. Truth or not, I can't verify.

The story begins with this pathetic teenage boy sitting huddled by a beach fire on the chilled Pacific coast of the state of Washington. Lo and behold, a game warden appeared out of the nearby woods, approached the fire, and asked the youth what he was doing.

He said, "I am roasting a sea gull for my dinner. I haven't eaten in a couple of days."

The warden said, "What? A sea gull? Don't you know there is a law against killing sea gulls? They are a crucial part of our eco-system here. I'm going to cite you and it's a pretty stiff fine."

The young man pleaded, "Oh, come on, man, it's just one sea gull. And I'm hungry and I'm out of work. What's one lousy sea gull compared to one really hungry human? I had to leave my family and go look for work and I haven't been able to find anything. Please don't cite me. I don't have any money so they'll have to throw me in jail."

Well, the warden was touched by the story and began to weaken this one time. He said, "Okay, I'll let you go this time . . . but, be sure it doesn't happen again." At this the warden turned and started to walk off. Then, he turned back and asked, "By the way, I'm curious. What does a roasted sea gull taste like, anyhow? I've always kinda wondered."

The young man looked up from chewing on the bird's carcass to say, "Oh, it's a real different kind of taste, somewhere between the flavor of a Snowy White Owl and an American Bald Eagle."

Oh, well . . . what more need I say? As we scratch around in this story, the moral begins to take shape. It's straight out of God's Book. "Be sure your sins will find you out." That promise is about as intimidating and awesome as any from the Bible. More than that, it's frightening in its implications. Who wants to be found out? Not very many people who have done wrong. Why do people run away, go into hiding, change identities?

There really is only one answer to trying to cover up our sin problem. There is no way it can be covered . . . but it can be forgiven and removed and remembered against us no more! Who can do that? How can it be done? If your past is a problem, how about a few moments spent in asking God for His help to remove that sin? He hears and He forgives, and only He can remove the sin from your life.

He that covereth his sins shall not prosper: but whoso confesseth and forsaketh them shall have mercy (Prov. 28:13;KJV).

❧

Jer. 43-44; Ps. 86; Prov. 8; Gal. 5-6

Margaret . . . the eldest of the four, was 16, and very pretty, being plump and fair, with large eyes,

plenty of soft, brown hair,

a sweet mouth, and white hands, of which she was rather vain.

Fifteen-year-old Jo was very tall, thin and brown, and reminded one of a colt; for she never seemed to know what to do with her long limbs, which were very much in her way. She had a decided mouth,

a comical nose,

and sharp, grey eyes, which appeared to see everything, and were by turns fierce, funny or thoughtful. Her long, thick hair was her one beauty; but it was usually bundled into a net, to be out of her way.

Round shoulders had Jo,

big hands and feet,

a fly-away look to her clothes, and the uncomfortable appearance of a girl who was rapidly shooting up into a young woman and didn't like it.

Elizabeth . . . or Beth, as everyone called her . . . was a rosy, smooth-haired, bright-eyed girl of 13,

with a shy manner,

a timid voice, and a peaceful expression, which was seldom disturbed. Her father called her "Little Tranquillity," and the name suited her excellently; for she seemed to live in a happy world of her own, only venturing out to meet the few she trusted and loved.

Amy, though the youngest, was a most important person . . . in her own opinion at least. A regular snow-maiden,

with blue eyes,

and yellow hair, curling on her shoulders, pale and slender, and always carrying herself like a young lady, unmindful of her manners.[77]

Then Rachel said, "I have had a great struggle with my sister, and I have won" (Gen. 30:8).

෴

Jer. 45-47; Ps. 87; Prov. 9; Acts 16

October 10 — Something Different

A housewife called the Sanitation Department in her town to come out and please pick up a dead mule from the front of her house. The department sent out several men and a truck to do the cleanup. Then she changed her mind. She came running out to the crew and asked the men to take the dead mule upstairs and place it in the bathtub. "I'll give you $20 each for doing this little job," she said.

The crew didn't really understand. However, $20 is $20, so they began the task. After much struggle and heavy lifting they finally managed to get the mule upstairs and deposited in the bathtub. It was quite a feat. When the task had been finished and she was giving each of the crew their hard-earned $20, the foreman asked, "Ma'am, why did you want this dead mule placed in your bathtub? Thank you for the $20, but why?"

"Well," she replied, "my husband has come home every night for the past 35 years and has gone through the same routine without change. He will pull off his coat and shoes. He grabs the newspaper, sits down in his easy chair, and always asks, "What's new?" In those 35 years there has never been anything new, so tonight I'm going to tell him!" Can you just imagine what kind of a reaction that poor old guy will have to this news?

Life really is exciting! For too many of us life has been the same old routine, same old sixes and sevens, the same ho-hum, nothing different, nothing new, and that's so sad.

There's an epitaph chiseled in a gravestone some place in the New England states with this inscription: "This man died at twenty-one, but was buried at seventy-three!"

Something new or exciting in your life is not dependent upon your chronological age, either. It was my privilege to visit with a senior citizen a few years ago. At that time he was 78 years of age, and I asked him what he was planning to do. "Well," he said, with a twinkle in his eye, "this next year I'm going to learn how to become a sculptor!"

You've heard the old adage "You can't teach an old dog new tricks." Have you given it a try? You can teach an old dog new tricks with a simple technique called "behavior modification." Consider a job change or forming a new and better habit. There's excitement ahead! Plan something different. TODAY!

> *The thief comes only in order to steal, kill, and destroy.*
> *I have come in order that they [you] might have life,*
> *life in all its fullness* (John 10:10;TEV).

༄

Jer. 48; Ps. 88; Prov. 10; Phil. 1-2

October 11 — The Greatest Friend of All

Arthur Ray Ebersol had drowned! It happened on one of those beautiful beaches in southern California. Someone had called 911 and now the paramedics were frantically working over his lifeless body The frantic father was begging the paramedics to start his breathing again.

The pastor, the Rev. Jess Moody, had also been called along with the medical emergency number. When he arrived he took in this entire scene as he approached the tight circle of people around the drowned young man. He moved through the crowd and put an arm around Arthur's dad. The only sounds were the pleadings of the father and the sounds of the equipment and the whispered commands between the working paramedics.

Then . . . somewhere in the background, Pastor Moody became aware of a voice — female, soprano . . . clear as crystal, a voice ringing with hope!

All eyes turned in the direction of the song. It was Arthur's mother sitting in the cab of the paramedic's ambulance. She was looking up through the sun-roof and affirming her faith skyward in song:

> I've seen the lightning flashing
> I've heard the thunder roll,
> I've felt sin's breakers dashing,
> Trying to conquer my soul.
> I've heard the voice of Jesus
> Telling me still to fight on
> He promised never to leave me,
> Never to leave me alone.

> No! Never alone.
> No! Never alone.
> He promised never to leave me,
> Never to leave me alone! (Anonymous songwriter)

The greatest friend in all the world? Jesus Christ the Son of the living God has promised that even in the most difficult of life's circumstances . . . He is there! His promise is sure! The guarantees of His presence are promised to all who are part of the family of God. So the bottom line question to you is: Have you invited Him to be your Lord and Saviour? This is the point at which this relationship begins.

God has said, "Never will I leave you; never will I forsake you." So we say with confidence, "The Lord is my helper; I will not be afraid. What can man do to me?" (Heb. 13:5-6).

❧

Jer. 49; Ps. 89:1-18; Prov. 11; Phil. 3-4

October 12, Columbus Day — The Longest Short Cut

To the day he died, the Italian explorer Christopher Columbus tenaciously clung to his belief that by sailing westward he had found . . . not a new continent, but a short cut, a sea route to Asia which could be used for trading and commerce purposes.

Like many other explorers and geographers, Columbus underestimated the size of the earth and over-estimated the east-west reaches of Asia. A globe which dates back to the time of his first voyage in 1492 showed the distance from the Azores west to Japan as being no greater distance than the length of the Mediterranean Sea.

Therefore, when Columbus reached the Bahamas, he thought he had arrived at the Indies, which was the collective name then in common usage for India, Southeast Asia, and Indonesia. And this is why the Caribbean islands are called the "West Indies."

Not all was hunky-dory on these voyages   scurvy was rampant, disease took it's toll in other forms, mutiny occasionally happened on the high seas. Just think of the courage it took to sail off into the West on the primitive ships then in use. Sanitary conditions were deplorable.

During Columbus' second voyage, this time in 1494, the crew had to swear that the coast of Cuba, along which they sailed, was the "mainland at the beginning of Cathay." The penalties for breaking this oath depended on the rank of the sailor. Any who offended either paid a fine, had their tongue cut, or received 100 lashes at the mast.

Not only did Columbus come ashore on the North American continent . . . he also reached the Bahamas, Cuba, Hispaniola, Trinidad, Panama, and the mouth of the Orinoco River.

Think of how far we have come as people . . . from a simple sailing ship to today with the space ship Columbia, which was first launched as a re-usable space vehicle, on April 12, 1981. It has been into space a number of time and returned safely with all safe on board.

There are opportunities for all of us to explore new frontiers in personal relationships, expanded knowledge of our God and Saviour Jesus Christ. The cry of Paul the Apostle was that "I might know Him." He didn't stop there. He challenged all of us to follow his example in continuing, in searching, in living in greater dimensions of exploration.

And I pray that you, being rooted and established in love, may have power, together with all the saints, to grasp how wide and long and high and deep is the love of Christ, and to know this love that surpasses knowledge . . . that you may be filled to the measure of all the fullness of God (Eph. 3:17-19).

❧

Jer. 50; Ps. 89:19-37; Prov. 12; Acts 17

October 13 — Right of Way

An officer in the U.S. Navy had always dreamed of commanding a battleship. He had graduated from the Naval Academy, worked hard, studied diligently to make his new ranks, and been a good officer. Although he had a touch of arrogance and pride in his make-up, it was not enough to hinder his steady climb to a command.

He finally achieved that dream and was given commission of the newest and proudest battleship in the navy. What a lofty moment! He had made it!

One very stormy night, as the battleship was making its way through the choppy seas, the captain was on the bridge surveying his proud world. Off the port side, he spotted a strange light closing with his own ship. Immediately, he ordered the signalman to flash this message to the unidentified craft: "Alter your course 10 degrees to the south."

It was just a minute or two before the reply came: "Alter your course 10 degrees to the north."

Determined that *his* battleship would not take a back seat to another vessel, the captain snapped out this order to be sent: "Alter your course 10 degrees to the south — I am the CAPTAIN!"

The response was beamed right back: "Alter your course 10 degrees to the south — I am Seaman Third Class Jones."

At this reply, the captain was now infuriated. He grabbed the signal light with his own hands and fired off: "Alter your course 10 degrees to the south — I am a BATTLESHIP!"

Back came the final reply: "Alter your course 10 degrees to the north — I am a LIGHTHOUSE!"

Well, it seems that no matter how important any of us think we are, there is still a higher order. We must be subject to something more powerful than we are. That's a tough lesson for some of us to learn.

In our own little world of self-importance, there is only one thing that stands as a solid, foundational beacon for life. It's called the Word of God! You may prefer to call this book, the Bible.

By studying the Word of God, we soon discover that all other courses in life must be altered to fit this one. There is a sameness about the Word. You can read it today or ten days from now, and it will say the same things.

Every life needs a foundation. I hope and pray that you will make God's Word your unmovable lighthouse!

Thy word have I hid in mine heart,
that I might not sin against thee (Ps. 119:11;KJV).

࿇

Jer. 51; Ps. 89:38-52; Prov. 13; 1 Thess. 1-3

October 14 — Miracle Under the Hood

Often the origins of a story can't be traced. Such is this one which had been told to a nationwide TV audience by the late Howard Conatser, founder of the Beverly Hills Baptist Church of Dallas.

The names are lost, so we'll just call these two teenage sisters Cheriee and Susan. They had been shopping in a suburban mall. When they were ready to go home, it was dark, too late! From the exit they saw their car, the only one left in that section of the parking lot.

They were nervous . . . waiting, hoping some other customers would come along so they could all walk out together. They were aware of the current crime wave in area shopping malls and remembered Dad's warning: "Don't stay too late!"

"Let's get with it . . . now!" Susan shifted her packages, pushed open the door and walked as fast as she could with Cheriee following, both looking from side to side.

They just made it! Cheriee shoved the key into the door lock, got in, reached across to open Susan's door. THEN . . . they both heard the sound of running feet behind them. They turned to look and panicked — racing toward their car were two ominous looking men!

One of the men shouted, "We got you, you're not going anywhere!"

Susan jumped in and both locked their doors just in time.

With shaking hands, Cheriee turned the ignition switch. Nothing! She tried again and again . . . nothing! Click! Silence! No power! The men were ready to smash a window.

The girls knew there were scant seconds of safety left . . . they joined hands and prayed! "Dear God," Susan pleaded, "give us a miracle in the name of Jesus!"

Again Cheriee turned the key . . . the engine roared to life and they raced out of the lot!

The girls cried all the way home, shocked and relieved. They screeched into the driveway, pulled the car into the garage, burst into the house, spilling out their story to Mom and Dad.

"You're safe . . . thank God, that's the main thing. But don't do it again," Dad said. Then their father frowned, "It's strange. That car has never failed to start. I'll just check it out. I'll take a look at it now."

In the garage he raised the hood . . . in one stunned glance, he realized WHO had brought his daughters home safely that night! There was no battery in the car!

The men were amazed and asked, "What kind of man if this? Even the winds and the waves obey Him!" (Matt. 8:27).

૭

Jer. 52; Ps. 90; Prov. 14; 1 Thess. 4-5

October 15 — Two Perspectives

Jane Smith went to church on a particular Sunday morning. She heard the organist miss a note during the prelude, and she winced. When everybody was supposed to be bowed in silent prayer, she heard the teenager in the pew behind her talking. As the offering plate was passed, Jane felt the usher was watching to see how much she put in, and it made her boil! During the sermon, she caught the preacher making a slip of the tongue seven times by actual count. The choir hit an off key, and she noted that. As she slipped out through the side door during the closing hymn, she muttered to herself, "Never again. What a bunch of clods and hypocrites!"

Linda Jones went to the same church that Sunday morning. She heard the organist play an arrangement of "A Mighty Fortress" and was thrilled by the majesty of it. During the service, she was moved by a young girl's simple testimony of the difference her faith had made in her life. When the offering was taken, she was glad to learn that this church was giving a special donation to the starving in Central Africa. Linda especially appreciated the sermon that Sunday. It had answered a question that had bothered her for a long time. She thought as she walked out the doors of the church, *How can a person come here and not feel the presence of God?*

Perception is an individual and tricky thing to deal with. Correct perception is vitally important to the way you live your life.

Sweeping across Germany at the end of World War II, Allied forces searched farms and houses looking for the enemy. At one abandoned house, almost a heap of rubble, searchers with flashlights found their way to the basement. There on the crumbling wall, a victim of the holocaust had scratched a Star of David. Beneath it in rough lettering was this message:

> I believe in the sun . . . even when it does not shine;
> I believe in love . . . even when it is not shown;
> I believe in God . . . even when He does not speak!

Your individual perspective on life can make or break you! As you look at a glass with water to the halfway mark, is it half-empty or half-full? It's all in how you perceive it. How about your life — half-full or half-empty? It depends on you!

I tell you the truth, if anyone says to this mountain, "Go throw yourself into the sea," and does not doubt in his heart but believes that what he says will happen, it will be done for him (Mark 11:23).

❧

Dan. 1; Ps. 91; Prov. 15; 2 Thess. 1-3

October 16 — Strike Out

It was the fourth game of the 1954 World Series. The stands were buzzing. One more out and the New York Giants would beat the Cleveland Indians four games in a row.

The Cleveland batter hit a lazy pop fly that drifted across the third base foul line. Bill Bailey (not his real name) came running under, reached up, and grabbed it. Fellow Giants swarmed on the field to smother him with congratulations.

Not only had Bill made the last out, but he had hit in every game, batting .364 and breaking a World Series record with seven walks in four games.

Bill kept the ball of the final out as a memento of the series. But he doesn't have it now. Rules about personal property are strict in the Texas pen where he served a ten-year term for armed robbery.

Bill got only $90 from the liquor store robbery. His share of the 1954 World Series came to $11,000 (a lot in those days), and he made at least another quarter million from product endorsements.

How does a guy go from a World Series hero to a convict in less than ten years? "Liquor and bad friends," Bill told a reporter.

When Bill was a baseball player and was loaded with money, he had an infield-full of friends. They cheered Bill when he picked up the checks in restaurants and night clubs.

Players remember Bill as a "great guy with charm, except when he hit the booze." After Bill was dropped from baseball, he became a bartender. When his money ran out, he would return to the ballpark to borrow money off his former teammates. "I'm gonna get a hit pretty soon," he would tell them. "I'm gonna quit striking out."

But Bill Bailey never got his "break." Liquor and bad friends kept throwing him curves, until one day the ex-hero took a final bad pitch and was handed a prison sentence. That day none of his friends were around to see him strike out.

Today we don't know the outcome of Bill Bailey. The only thing that remains is his name on some old score books.

Life is much more than a game, but it's still up to us to play by the rules. In the Bible, God has carefully laid out the guidelines for a successful life. If you want to hit a home run, make sure you're on the right playing field.

Beware, the Lord is about to take firm hold of you and hurl you away, O you mighty man. He will roll you up tightly like a ball and throw you into a large country (Isa. 22:17-18).

ॐ

Dan. 2; Ps. 92; Prov. 16; Acts 18

October 17 — My Older Sister

During my childhood, my older sister Daryl and I shared the back seat of our parents' white Chevrolet on weekend family outings . . . but an imaginary line divided the seat into separate, hostile camps If Daryl's arm or leg strayed onto my turf, or vice versa, the car was immediately transformed into a battle zone, with bickering and shouting that even a game of States or Capitals couldn't silence.

But as clearly as I can recall these skirmishes, I can also remember quite different experiences with Daryl during these outings. Late at night, coming home from holiday dinners at our aunt's home just hours after one of our quarrels, my eyelids would become heavy and I'd snuggle next to Daryl and rest my head on her lap. The imaginary dividing line forgotten, she would gently stroke my hair and twirl my pony tail, and often I would feel so close to her that I'd try to fight off sleep to savor the moment. My big sister was taking care of me. These are among my warmest memories of childhood.

Today, three decades later, many of these elements endure in my relationship with Daryl. She is my dear friend, my ally, and although we now live a continent apart, I still look to her for support. Our personal life choices have led us down significantly different paths, but I know that Daryl will always be there when I need her, and I trust that she feels the same about me. Of course, all is not perfect . . . even though the back-seat battles are in the past, our relationship is still tested occasionally by a disagreement or crisis. But we have been strengthened . . . as individuals and as sisters . . . by what we have learned from our childhood experiences.[78]

Listen to women . . . if they have a sister, good or bad, they all want to talk about this relationship with a sister. Some will reaffirm the positive and the good while others are searching for ways to make it good while looking for answers as to why it's in such disarray.

Sisters can teach more about life than other persons. Sisters can be role models, problem solvers, challengers, and protectors. There is one thing to note about this emotional attachment . . . you meet your sister/sisters in early childhood and given good health, this relationship will outlast your spousal or parental time together. What with 80 or 90 or even more years, this relationship can be the longest lasting of any earthly relationship. Therefore, there is the compelling desire to be unconditionally accepted by one's sister.

Therefore, as we have opportunity, let us do good to all people, especially to those who belong to the family of believers (Gal. 6:10).

๛

Dan. 3; Ps. 93; Prov. 17; 1 Cor. 1-2

October 18 — The Goal Is the Goal

Bobby Dodd, the former great football coach of Georgia Tech, tells the story of a game in which his team was leading 7 to 6 with just a minute to go. He instructed his quarterback NOT to pass the ball under any conditions! He said, "Whatever you do, hold on to that football; DO NOT PASS THE BALL!"

In the next few seconds of play they moved the ball down the field to within 10 yards of the opposing team's goal line. As the quarterback began to execute the next play, with seconds ticking away, he just couldn't resist and he threw a pass!

As too often happens, the pass was intercepted by a player on the other team. This opponent began the 90-yard run toward the Georgia Tech goal line. The entire Tech team had given up the chase . . . except the quarterback who had thrown the interception. He continued to chase his opponent and somehow overtook him and tackled him, causing a fumble which the quarterback managed to recover just short of their goal line! That was the last play of the game!

Georgia Tech won the game 7 to 6. After the game, the losing coach said to Coach Dodd, "I will never understand how your quarterback was able to do what he did."

Dodd explained, "Well, it's actually quite simple . . . your man was running for a touchdown; my quarterback was running for his life!"[79]

While we're on football stories, did you hear about the coach who said, "Remember, football develops individuality, initiative, personality, and leadership. Now, get in there and do exactly as I tell you!"

Can you take one more? This coach was dejected and desperate because his team was losing 42-0. He looked down the bench at his subs and finally picked on Henderson. "Henderson, if I sent you in, do you think you could get ferocious?"

"Sure thing, coach," he said. "Just one thing. What number is this guy Ferocious?"

Oh well . . . is it possible that some of life's lessons can also be learned on the football field or in an athletic endeavor? I think so. Let's go for it!

Make it your ambition to lead a quiet life, to mind your own business and to work with your hands, just as we told you, so that your daily life may win the respect of outsiders and so that you will not be dependent on anybody (1 Thess. 4:11-12).

꿏

Dan. 4; Ps. 94; Prov. 18; 1 Cor. 3-4

I take it you already know of tough and bough and cough and dough.
Others may stumble, but not you, on hiccough, thorough, lough, and
    through.
Beware of heard, a dreadful word. That looks like beard and sounds like
    bird.
And dead . . . it's said like bed, not bead. For goodness sake, don't call
    it deed.
Watch out for meat and great and threat: they rhyme with suite and
    straight and debt.
A moth is not a moth in mother, nor both in bother, broth in brother.
And here is not a match for there, nor dear and fear and pear and bear.
And then there's dose and rose and lose . . . just look them up . . . and
    goose and choose, and cork and work, and card and ward, and font
    and front, and word and sword, and do and go, then thwart and cart.
    Come, come I've hardly made a start.
There's also click and clique, and grove and glove, and hope and soap,
    and move and love; there's sane and seine, and soup and soul,
    there's lean and lien, and fowl and bowl.
How about pear and pair and pare? There is also fear and fair and fare.
A dreadful language? Man alive . . . I'd mastered it when I was five![80]

Language . . . how wonderful it is. It's how we communicate with each other. And being a grandparent hasn't made it any easier when attempting to talk with our grandkids. We find that they are into information highways, Reeboks, CDs, roms, and rap. Many of the solid, foundational words which we grew up with are long gone from today's younger vocabulary. Just say some of the following words . . . they mean two different things to two different generations: square, gay, politically correct, grass, rock music, software, hardware, time-sharing, chip, and low-rider.

Some things are still basic, foundational . . . such as love. It's understood in any language when the actions are seen. Maybe, a grandparent is the only person available to that young life who has the patience and time to make the effort to listen, to communicate. Perhaps you may be the only one who can instill life principles into young heads. It's more than just talking . . . it's communicating, it's caring, it's loving, it's spending time, it's listening creatively, it's being available!

*The Spirit gives life; the flesh counts for nothing. The words I have
spoken to you are spirit and they are life* (John 6:63).

                 ❦

Dan. 5; Ps. 95; Prov. 19; 1 Cor. 5-6

October 20 — Real Friends

A lady writes: My sister is a police officer in Los Angeles. Before she was to be commissioned, there were all kinds of training exercises which she had to pass before she became a real policeperson. Further, they were to be trained in how to react and act as an officer. While attending the academy, where they were being trained in all kinds of procedures in every conceivable situation in which they may find themselves confronted while on duty, one procedure surprised her. They were given training and instructions about how to deal with snakebite victims.

Then this training took a more serious twist as the instructor gave them directions about what to do for oneself if bitten by a poisonous snake and unable to get to medical attention quickly. He talked about not running, but resting, about remaining calm, of preparation, and so forth. He went on to explain in great detail that in some extreme circumstances, one would have to cut the skin with a sharp knife and suck the venom out by mouth.

At this point, my sister asked, "What happens if I get bitten on my behind?"

There was a long moment of silence, then the instructor answered, "You find out if you have any friends."

KEEP HER GRIT

Hang on! Cling on! No matter what they say.
Push on! Sing on! Things will come your way.
Sitting down and whining never helps a bit;
Best way to get there is by keeping up your grit.

Don't give up hoping when the ship goes down,
Grab a spar or something . . . just refuse to drown.
Don't think you're dying because you're hit.
Smile in the face of danger and hang on to your grit.

Folks die too easy . . . they sort of fade away,
Make a little error, and give up in dismay.
Kind of woman that's needed is the woman of ready wit,
To laugh at pain and trouble and keep her grit.
(Unknown)

*A cheerful heart is good medicine, but a crushed spirit
dries up the bones* (Prov. 17:22).

❧

Dan. 6-7; Ps. 96; Prov. 20; 1 Cor. 7-8

October 21 — Years in Waiting

Did you know that most people spend an average of about five years of their lives just standing in lines? What kinds of lines? Grocery checkout, driver's license renewal, cafeteria, restaurant, ticket window, subway station, and so forth. That's not all. Most people spend a total of six months of their life waiting at stop lights!

"Most people don't realize how much time they're wasting," said Michael Fortino, president of the consulting firm, Priority Management Pittsburgh, Inc. To determine how people spend their time and where they spend their time, Priority Management researchers, often with a stopwatch and clipboard in hand, studied hundreds of people across this nation for more than a year.

The study was released in 1988, after a year's research. This time-use study estimated the average person spends six months at stop lights, eight months opening junk mail, one year searching for misplaced objects, two years attempting to return phone calls to people who never seem to be available, four years doing housework, five years in lines, and six years eating.

"The whole point is to spend time doing the things that you want to do rather than the things you dislike," said Mr. Fortino.

The study of time usage is an interesting subject because everyone of us has the same exact allotment of time. Yes, I know, perhaps not in the length of our living, but in the sense that each of us has an exact total of 24 hours in each day and 156 hours in each week. Time is also a non-renewable commodity. There is not one minute of your life that can be lived more than once.

When we were growing up as little ones, time seemed to drag . . . minutes seemed endless . . . but now the minutes flash past, but the years seem long. Have you ever given any serious thought as to how you invest your time? Perhaps a study like Priority Management's will help us think about it.

While we're on the subject, have you thought about "tithing" your time as well as your money? There are 156 hours in a week and a tithe would be 15.6 hours. If you attend church twice on Sunday that may account for about 5 hours, and throw in another 3 for a mid-week activity for church, and you still have 7.6 hours left! Where would be a good place to make this investment of your time? How about helping a neighbor or sick friend?

Be very careful, then, how you live . . . not as unwise but as wise,
making the most of every opportunity (Eph. 5:15-16).

◈

Dan. 8; Ps. 97; Prov. 21; 1 Cor. 9-10

October 22 — Horses and Water

Joseph Duveen is known as one of the world's finest art dealers. During his career, his client list read like the who's who in society and collecting. But there was one not named among his clientele, and Duveen was not content to rest until he had Andrew Mellon, the most discriminating art collector of all, to add to his list. In order to entice Mr. Mellon, Joseph Duveen carefully laid out a plan.

Patiently, over a number of years, Duveen put together a superlative collection of old masters' paintings with which he would tempt this discriminating collector. Finally, he was ready to make his move.

Duveen had his name put on the waiting list in order to lease the apartment directly beneath Mr. Mellon's in Washington, DC. He waited patiently for the call that eventually came telling of the now vacant apartment. After having each painting exquisitely framed, Duveen went to the apartment and hung the carefully selected collection from the old masters, literally covering the walls.

Then, before he returned to New York, Duveen offered the key to his apartment to Andrew Mellon and said, "Mr. Mellon, you are invited, anytime you might like, to drop in and look at the paintings." He encouraged him to feel free to view them whenever he desired.

Mr. Mellon's curiosity drew him to the pictures and the apartment. After the first visit, the financier could not stay away. He came back to the apartment night after night, and he would stay for hours admiring the pictures of the old masters. This went on for a few weeks.

Finally a call went to Joseph Duveen in New York asking if it would be possible for him to return to Washington. When that meeting took place in the apartment, Andrew Mellon proposed the purchase of the entire collection. This was a staggering transaction for Duveen who received $2 million for his paintings and Mellon as his new client!

All of us have heard the old adage that you can lead a horse to water, but you can't make him drink. But it is possible to salt the horse's hay a little to encourage the drinking to take place!

Jesus said, "No man can come to me, except the Father which has sent me draw him . . ." (John 6:44;KJV). God loves you enough to keep inviting you to accept His Son as your Saviour. What are you waiting for? The gift of eternal life is worth far more than any treasures this world has to offer.

Again, the kingdom of heaven is like unto a merchant man, seeking goodly pearls: Who, when he had found one pearl of great price, went and sold all that he had, and bought it (Matt. 13:45-46;KJV).

❧

Dan. 9-10; Ps. 98; Prov. 22; 1 Cor. 11-12

October 23 — To Be a Friend . . . Start with Yourself

The following was inscribed on the tomb of an Anglican bishop (A.D. 1100) among the crypts of Westminster Abbey located in London:

> When I was young and free and my imagination had no
> limits,
> I dreamed of changing the world.
> As I grew older and wiser, I discovered the world would not
> change,
> so I shortened my sights somewhat and
> decided to change only my country.
> But it, too, seemed immovable.
>
> As I grew into my twilight years,
> in one last desperate attempt,
> I settled for changing only my family,
> those closest to me, but alas,
> they would have none of it.
> And now as I lie on my deathbed, I suddenly realize:
> *If I had only changed myself first,*
> Then by example I would have changed my family.
>
> From their inspiration and encouragement,
> I would have been able to better my country and,
> who knows,
> I may have even changed the world.
>
> (Anonymous)

Here's the secret to change anything in life . . . be it life, friendships, relationships, concepts, life principles, or work. It all begins with ME, myself, and I!

Therefore, everyone who hears these words of mine and puts them into practice is like a wise man who built his house on the rock (Matt. 7:24).

☙

Dan. 11-12; Ps. 99; Prov. 23; 1 Cor. 13-14

October 24 — The Battle of Selfishness

A farmer's son decided to get married. When his dad heard the news he said, "John, when you get married your liberty is gone!" The son questioned this and refused to believe it. The dad said, "I'll prove it to you. Catch a dozen chickens, tie them up, put them in the wagon, and go to town. Stop at every house and wherever you find the husband is boss give him a horse. Wherever you find the woman is boss, give her a chicken. You'll give away all your chickens and you'll come back with your team of horses intact."

John accepted the proposition and drove to town. He stopped at every house and had given away 10 chickens when he came to a very nice little house. The old man and his wife were standing out in front on the lawn. He called to them and asked, "Who is the boss in your house?"

The man replied, "I am."

He turned to the lady and she said, "Yes, he's really the boss."

John was excited with the prospect of establishing the boss in this home, so he invited them to come down into the street; explained his proposition and told them to select one of the horses. The old man and his wife looked them over carefully and the husband finally said, "I think the black is the better. I choose him."

The wife said, "I think the bay horse is the better. I'd choose him."

The old man took another careful look at the bay horse and said, "I guess I'll take the bay horse."

John smiled and said, "No you won't, you'll take a chicken!"

Selfishness is a constant battle and no one can successfully master this conflict without outside help! Some of the most unselfish people I have known are in a lifelong struggle against selfishness.

A circus had a lion and a lamb in the same cage. A man asked the attendant if they got along all right. The attendant replied, "Most of the time, if we keep the lion well fed. . . . Now and then we have to put in a new lamb."

In the conflicts of life you are facing there is only one road to victory! That's found in Jesus Christ! Victory is won when we strive to be, say, and do what God wants us to be, say, and do. Then we, too, will live in victory over conflict — not in our strength, but in His strength! The bottom line will be determined in how well you handle this conflict in resolution.

I can do everything through Him who gives me strength (Phil. 4:13).

❧

Job 1-3; Ps. 100; Prov. 24; 1 Cor. 15

October 25 — Rising Above Fear

Following the success of her book, *The Joy Luck Club*,[81] the first-time novelist Amy Tan feared that she might be type-cast. "I didn't want to be the mother/daughter expert," she says. "So I tried something else until I realized that rebellion was not a good reason to write."

Then, suddenly, her mother provided inspiration for her next project. "I knew she had lived a harsh, repressed life in China. I asked about World War II and she said, 'I wasn't affected.' Then she mentioned that when the bombs fell, 'We were always scared they would hit us.' I pointed out that she had said she wasn't affected. 'I wasn't,' she replied. 'I wasn't killed.' "

That statement became a revelation. Tan's goal became to understand this difference between her perspective on life and her mother's life-perspective.

Later, during the Tiananmen Square uprising, Amy wrote the book, *The Kitchen God's Wife*,[82] based on her mother's life. Amy Tan then said, "I wanted to know what it is like to live a life of repression, to know the fear, and what you must do to rise above the fear."[83]

Did you really catch that last statement — what you must do to rise above fear! Fear is an enemy that can reduce any of us to jelly. What is the secret to overcoming fear? There is a major clue to be found in God's Word (the Bible) . . . read it through and see if you can find the 365 "fear nots." There is one for every day of the year!

Fear comes in all sizes and different kinds of packages. Now, some fear is needed to survive in life . . . without some healthy fear you'd step off the curb into the path of a speeding car or put your hand on a hot stove.

Let's try some on for size. Ailurophobia, fear of cats; algophobia, fear of pain; androphobia, fear of men; bathophobia, fear of falling from high places; ergasiophobia, dislike of work; and so on. Scientists who study human beings say there are at least 30 different kinds of fear.

Did you know that Joseph Stalin was one of the unhappiest men to ever live on our planet, as well as being a man plagued by fears? He was nearly paralyzed by his fears. He had eight different bedrooms built in the Kremlin in which he could be locked up like a bank vault. Nobody knew which of these eight he would select to spend the night in. Too much fear can cause lots of life's problems.

God says to you, "Do not be afraid!"

So do not fear, for I am with you; do not be dismayed, for I am your God. I will strengthen you and help you; I will uphold you with my righteous right hand (Isa. 41:10).

❧

Job 4-5; Ps. 101; Prov. 25; 1 Cor. 16

October 26 — Footprints

Wayne Watson has put music to the words and perhaps you've heard him or another gospel artist sing it lately. The author of these beautiful words is unknown, so we cannot give credit where it is due. Nevertheless, it conveys a timeless message that you may need to hear on a day like this. It's entitled, "Footprints In the Sand."

> One night I had a dream. I dreamed I was walking along the beach with the Lord and across the sky flashed scenes from my life. For each scene I noticed two sets of footprints in the sand. One belonged to me and the other to the Lord.
>
> When the last scene of my life flashed before us I looked back at the footprints in the sand. I noticed that many times along the path of my life there was only one set of footprints. I also noticed that it happened at the very lowest and saddest times in my life.
>
> This really bothered me and I questioned the Lord about it. "Lord, you said that once I decided to follow You, You would walk with me all the way. But I noticed that during the most troublesome times in my life there was only one set of footprints. I don't understand why, in times when I needed You most, You should leave me."
>
> The Lord replied, "My precious, precious child. I love you and I would never, never leave you during your times of trial and suffering. When you saw only one set of footprints . . . it was then that I carried you!"

What an exciting expression of God's love and care. However, a question does come to mind at this point: Is it a biblical concept, or simply the writing of an author that sounds beautiful?

Let's go no further than your own New Testament as we read, "I [Jesus] will never leave you or forsake you!" How about that for comfort in time of trouble? When you invited Him to be your Lord and Master you received a promise of His presence and power with you in all your days, good or bad, happy or sad, frustrating or wonderful! You have a Friend who will be closer than a brother. The next time you feel alone and lonely, remember this story about the footprints in the sand!

In all their distress he too was distressed, and the angel of his presence saved them. In his love and mercy he redeemed them; he lifted them up and carried them all the days of old (Isa. 63:9).

෴

Job 6-8; Ps. 102:1-10; Prov. 26; 2 Cor. 1-2

In the never-ceasing effort to attract the unchurched and to attempt to cross the bridge to football fans who don't frequent a church as often as a game . . . and to prove a certain kind of understanding of interests outside the church, you may want to intersperse these tidbits of football-speak. It might be better just to be able to express a bit of humor now and then, especially for the everlasting football season.

DRAFT CHOICE: The decision to sit close to the heating vent in the winter time and the air-conditioning vent in the summer time.

PASS INTERFERENCE: What Mama does with her eyes when she sees son, Jimmy writing notes to friends while in church.

TWO MINUTE WARNING: The Chairman of the Church Board sitting on a front pew, taking a long look at his watch in full view of the preacher.

FUMBLE: One lousy sermon.

QUARTERBACK: What church members who believe religion is free want after putting 50¢ in the offering plate.

PASSING GAME: What the ushers do with the offering plates each Sunday morning and evening.

CORNERBACKS: The people who always occupy the back pews.

ILLEGAL MOTION: Leaving before the final benediction.

PENALTY: What the church gets when its members stay at home.

HUDDLE: The weekly meeting of the church gossip team.

HOLDING PENALTY: Those who run out of and back into the sanctuary several times during a worship service.

NATIONAL ANTHEM: The choir and congregation doing their best singing of "Amazing Grace."

END RUN: Any child who successfully escaped both parents and all the ushers on his way out of the church service.

FAIR CATCH: Holding the offering plate in front of each member until money is placed in it.

CLIPPING: What the church historian is always doing.

HALF-BACK: What the choir, seated behind or beside the preacher, sees while the sermon is delivered.

NOSE GUARD: A nursery worker during the cold and flu season.

SUPER BOWL CHAMPS: Any church doing the will of God.

FINAL GUN: The benediction![84]

> *He will roll you up tightly like a ball and throw you*
> *into a large country* (Isa. 22:18).

❧

Job. 9-11; Ps. 102:11-17; Prov. 27; 2 Cor. 3-5

October 28 — The Delivery Angel

My growing-up years were wonderful and idyllic — a really happy childhood as I look back. It never dawned on me that life was tough at times. My parents at this time were struggling to establish a mission church in the town of Evansville, Minnesota, which had a population of about 850 people, not counting dogs and cats. It was not easy. Dad had to work where he could find a job to support his family . . . it was just him and Mom, my brother 1-1/2 years my junior, and myself. We had a little garden and ate well when some of the church farm families brought goodies to the parsonage. I thought everybody had to live like that . . . the memories of those years are good. It's amazing what time can do to memory.

However . . . one particular night is still a vivid memory. Mom set the table for herself and her two sons. One of us asked, "What are we going to eat tonight?" We looked around, the stove was cold, nothing was on the table except water in the glasses, nothing in the refrigerator, nothing in the cupboards. Not even a potato for watery soup. Not a cup of flour with which to make biscuits. Not even noodles for a hot dish of any kind. The house was bare and two boys were famished!

She said, "Let's sit down and ask the Lord to bless our meal." We dutifully bowed our heads and listened to her prayer. . . .

"Dear Lord, we thank you because you are so good to us. Bless Dad tonight as he's away working. And, Lord, thank you for the food we are about to partake of, in Jesus name I pray . . . " Before she got the final "AMEN" said, both of us heard a noise on the back porch. We shoved our chairs back and in one motion ran for the back door which was about six steps from the kitchen table and flung it open. There, sitting on the porch, were boxes of groceries! We ran out onto the porch and looked in every direction up and down that little dirt street in this little country town where everybody knew everybody and everybody knew everybody else's business. There was nobody! No car, nothing!

With great excitement we hauled the groceries inside, helped Mom put them away until they overflowed the cupboards and the frig! Then we sat down to a glorious feast! We asked, "Mom, who do you think brought the groceries?"

She looked back with a smile and simply said, "Let's just thank the Lord for providing!"

I was young and now I am old, yet I have never seen the righteous forsaken or their children begging bread (Ps. 37:25).

❧

Job 12-14; Ps. 102:18-28; Prov. 28; 2 Cor. 6-7

～

In addition to their shared memories
of childhood and of their relationship to
each other's children, they share memories of
the same home, the same homemaking style,
and the same small prejudices about housekeeping
that carry the echoes of their mother's voice.

Margaret Mead

～

October 29 — *Sister as a Confidante*

Consider the relationship between Terri, 34, and her sister Catherine, 37, who recently spent a quiet weekend together after Catherine's second miscarriage. During the weekend, Catherine talked about her immediate concerns, including her difficulty in getting pregnant and keeping the pregnancy, and her worry about her "biological clock" and her desire for a child. She needed the calming reassurance of a friend, and Terri had seemed like an obvious choice because she, too, had lost her own first baby when she was five months pregnant.

Initially, Terri had not been supportive of Catherine's efforts to become pregnant, because she had thought that Catherine was taking too much of a physical risk. Years earlier, she had tried to influence Catherine to have children when she was younger, before she had established her professional life. But Catherine had decided to wait, and now, although she did not regret her decision, she needed to discuss its ramifications with someone she trusted, someone other than her husband.

Fortunately, Terri proved to be the perfect choice. She listened actively and empathetically. She became a sounding board for Catherine's questions, tears, and convictions. By the end of the weekend, Catherine was sure she had found a friend in her sister . . . a reassuring listener who would ease the decision-making process for her.[85]

Communication is the life-blood of sisterhood. This has been defined in terms of the messages we send within the context of who and what we are. When sisters send messages, often it is filtered through the remembered events of childhood . . . so the response may be garbled by an event of the past. In communicating with an adult sister, it's most helpful to remember that she is no longer a little girl. Look behind the message to discover the motivation which may have prompted the current exchange. Learning to become an attentive, helpful listener may take some more time. To solve communication differences may take a greater effort to learn how to reflect, how to discover the very essence of a problem, to become an active listener, and to be non-judgmental.

Maybe your sister has leveled the accusation: "You just don't hear what I have to say!" which is a signal that all is not as it should be in this area. Make the conscious decision to commit to the effort to improve, not simply to "fake" it. Perhaps it's time for sisters to clear away some of the rubble of the past and move on to develop realistic, positive expectations from this communication interaction.

Apply your heart to instruction and your ears to
words of knowledge (Prov. 23:12).

෴

Job 15-17; Ps. 103; Prov. 29; 2 Cor. 8-9

Pastors spend quite a bit of their time in cemeteries. Here are a few epitaphs that have been collected from across the country:

Here lies Lester Moore, Four slugs from a 44, No less, no more.

Seen on the grave marker of a dentist:

Stranger! Approach this spot with gravity.

John Brown is filling his last cavity.

Taken from the grave of an editor:

Here lies an editor! Snooks if you will;

In mercy, King Providence, let him lie still!

He lied for a living; so he lived while he lied;

When he could not lie longer, he lied down and died.

Found in Ruido, New Mexico:

Here lies John Yeast; Pardon me for not rising.

From the Wall Street Trinity Church cemetery:

Remember friends as you pass by,

As you are now, so once was I.

So, as I am you soon will be,

So prepare for death and follow me.

Someplace in a Maryland cemetery:

Here lies the body of Jane Smith, wife of Thomas Smith, a marble cutter. This monument, erected as a tribute to her memory, may be duplicated for $250.

Ft. Wallace, Kansas:

He tried to make two jacks beat a pair of aces.

Middletown, Maryland:

I fought a good battle, but losted.

Connecticut:

Here lies, cut down like unripe fruit,

The wife of Deacon Amos Shute:

She died drinking too much coffee,

Anny domiuy eighteen forty. (But what was her name?)

Holly, Michigan, cemetery:

He did not reach 70 going like 60.

From the tombstone of a hypochondriac:

I told you I was sick.

For as in Adam all die, so in Christ all will be made alive. But each in his own turn: Christ, the firstfruits; then, when He comes, those who belong to Him (1 Cor. 15:22-23).

∽

Job 18-20; Ps. 104:1-17; Prov. 30; 2 Cor. 10-11

October 31, Halloween — Celebrate or Not?

You've heard the argument, "You can't take all the fun of Halloween away from the kids." To which we may agree. But do we have to concentrate on the horror, evil, and death?

Most people are unaware of the sordid history attached to Halloween. Most think of it as the eve of "All Saints Day." But All Saints Day was originally celebrated in May. In A.D. 834 the day was moved to November 1 to placate the Romans who honored Pomona, goddess of fruit and trees on this day. All Saints Day became wedded to Halloween with the same reverence for the departed dead. Halloween is considered the most important festival of witchcraft cults. The history of this day extends back to the pagan druids. Few civilizations in history have been so depraved. The druids may have been the builders of Stonehenge, those monolithic stone carvings on England's Salisbury Plain. Mass human sacrifices were performed by constructing large wicker-work figures and filling the insides with living humans . . . then, set on fire.

Some archeologists believe Stonehenge was erected to calculate the sun's movements and determine the most auspicious day to worship the earth-mother-goddess by the propitiation of human sacrifice . . . the date chosen was October 31. This was the eve of Samhain (Lord of the Dead), the Celtic new year. Demons and ghosts were believed to spring from the netherworld. To insure fertility of cattle and crops, first-born children were sacrificed to placate these evil powers. And from the folklore and demonic practices surrounding this seasonal celebration, modern society has adopted the customs associated with Halloween. For example, "trick-or-treating" is a modern form of saying "offering or revenge." Food offerings were put out to prevent the ghosts of the past year's wicked dead from taking revenge on the inhabitants of a home.

I don't want to seem over-dramatic with this information . . . but take another look at the beginnings of Halloween, even the pagan influences turning into a Christian observance such as "All Saints Day." How can anything founded on such principles bring glory to the Lord Jesus Christ? Halloween can be a fun time for kids . . . and perhaps it should be. But it can be a real source of difficulty if your child's activities are not guided by the Word of the Lord!

For our struggle is not against flesh and blood, but against the rulers, against the authorities, against the powers of this dark world and against the spiritual forces of evil in the heavenly realms. Therefore put on the full armor of God, so that when the day of evil comes, you may be able to stand your ground (Eph. 6:12-13).

Job 21-23; Ps. 104:18-35; Prov. 31; 2 Cor. 12-13

November 1 — Addicted to Activity

"See how they run, see how they run, they all run after . . ." duties, assignments, appointments, demands, deadlines! There are plans, programs, and people, so run, run, run!

How about taking a moment to sit down, let your motor idle, and take another sip from your coffee cup? Think about your pace. Are you part of the rat race? How did you get trapped? Are you being fulfilled?

James Sullivan knows exactly how you feel. Back in the sixties he blew Oklahoma City wide open, developing the world's largest "Young Life Club" — a Christian group for young people. But that's not all he blew apart. In doing it, he sacrificed his family and his health. He was a very hard man to keep up with, let alone live with.

His wife and family were tired. Life lived at full-bore was, in reality, an escape technique. He wrote the book *The Frog Who Never Became a Prince,* and we lift one line from it. "I was a man who existed in a shell . . . guilt, resentment, and hatred welled up within me. The resulting hard feeling I developed became almost insurmountable."

Wasn't James Sullivan working for Jesus Christ and the kingdom of God? Yes, but he substituted activity for living.

One Thanksgiving Day his wife, Carolyn, asked him a question as he was once more racing out the door to speak at a youth meeting, "Do you know, or do you even care, that from the middle of September until today you have not been home one night?" Not very long after that incident, she broke emotionally, while he contemplated suicide.

Does this story sound familiar? There are many churches in our land that boast, "Something every night of the week for everybody!" What a shame, and it's even worse that churches advertise it.

God's Word speaks often and loudly about cultivating a calm, peaceful inner spirit. Instead, we offer Him a life full of activity, noise, and more and more running! Could the reason we run so much be to deaden the pain of an empty life?

To change this activity, I suggest you start with admitting you are too busy; then learn the art of saying a small two letter word, "NO" — and mean it. It may take some practice. All together now, let's say it again — "NO!" And keep on saying no! There are a lot of us who are addicted to activity who would like to stop if we could. Do it before it's too late — for the sake of your wife, your children, and your relationship to God.

Be still, and know that I am God; I will be exalted among the na-tions, I will be exalted in the earth (Ps. 46:10).

❦

Job 24-27; Ps. 105:1-15; Prov. 1; Acts 19

November 2 — Getting What You Want

A man lived in a squalid tenement on a side street in East Boston. As a tailor, he worked long hours each day to barely eke out a meager existence. But he allowed himself one luxury: one ticket each year to the Irish Sweepstakes. And each year he would pray fervently that this would be the winning ticket that would bring him good fortune.

For fourteen years, his life continued in the same impoverished vein, until one day there came a loud knocking at his door. Two well-dressed gentlemen entered his shop and informed him that he had just won the Irish Sweepstakes! The grand prize was $500,000!

The little tailor could hardly believe his ears! He was rich! No longer would he have to slave away making pant cuffs, hemming dresses, shortening sleeves. Now he could really begin to live!

He locked up his shop and threw the key into the Charles River. He bought himself a wardrobe fit for a king, a new Rolls Royce, a suite of rooms at the Ritz, and soon was supporting a string of attractive women.

Night after night he partied until dawn, spending his money as if each day was his last. Of course the inevitable happened. One day the money was all gone. Furthermore, he had nearly wrecked his health.

Disillusioned, ridden with fever and exhausted, he returned to his little shop and set up business once more. And from force of habit, once again each year he set aside from his meager savings the price of an Irish Sweepstakes ticket.

Two years later, there came a second knock at his door. The same two gentlemen stood there once again. "This is the most incredible thing in the history of the Irish Sweepstakes," exclaimed one. "You have won again! Your grand prize is another $500,000!"

The little tailor staggered to his feet with a groan that could be heard by people outside his shop. "Oh, no!" he protested. "Do you mean I have to go through all that all over again?"

Getting what you want may be just as difficult to handle as having nothing in the first place. Too many people have found that living with success is much more testing than living in failure. One of the most overlooked Christian principles is to learn to be content with what we have and where we are. Dissatisfaction can drive you to real distraction.

I am not saying this because I am in need, for I have learned to be content whatever the circumstances (Phil. 4:11).

⟨∽⟩

Job 28-30; Ps. 105:16-45; Prov. 2; Acts 20

November 3 — Oldest Living Things

A careful study of tree rings in California's 4,000-year-old bristle-cone pine trees has led scientists to modify the radio-carbon dating of artifacts which has been used since 1949. These trees are the oldest known living things on the face of the earth.

This discovery is also causing a re-writing of histories which have credited the Middle East as the source of Europe's advance from barbarism to civilization. Scientifically-corrected timetables now show that many of Europe's earliest tombs, monuments, temples, and tools actually predate or are older than their counterparts in the Middle East.

For instance, chamber tombs in Brittany are now being dated 1,500 years older than the pyramids of Egypt! And it is the temples of Malta, not Mesopotamia, which must now be seen as the world's oldest free-standing stone monuments. So we are discovering that it may be later than we thought!

It's a strong possibility that we have misjudged the ancients of the European area. In the past it was thought that civilization and the advances from the Stone Age came from the Middle East and influenced the peoples of the European continent. Current discoveries are causing a re-thinking about this advance. It may well have been the other way around!

Don't such things absolutely fascinate you? I find within me an insatiable desire to learn about our past, as well as to take a look into the future.

We're really talking about time and how it's been measured. Speaking about time, did you hear about the little boy who was allowed to stay up well beyond his normal bedtime because his grandparents were visiting? The clock struck 11:00 and he listened in rapt attention, counting each strike. When the grandfather clock had finished chiming he spoke up and said, "It's later than it's ever been before."

It's so easy to get that sense in our present-day world. Times are changing, events are moving rapidly to some kind of a climax, folks are worried about issues that have not been problems before, and there's a sense of the urgent upon us.

As a person, you are older than you have ever been! This world is older than it's been. We are all aging, and we are all moving to a conclusion. Have you given any thought to your own conclusion? What of your day of dying? Have you taken care of your eternal destiny?

I have been young, and now am old; yet have I not seen the righteous forsaken, nor his seed begging bread (Ps. 37:25;KJV).

⌒⌢

Job 31-32; Ps. 106:1-16; Prov. 3; Eph. 1-2

There was an old miser who, because of his exceptional thrift, had no real friends. Knowing that he was about to die he called his doctor, his lawyer, and his accountant together around his bedside.

"I've always heard you can't take it with you, but I am going to prove that you can," he said. "I have $90,000 in cash under my mattress. It's in three envelopes of $30,000 each. When I pass on, I want each of you to take an envelope, and just before they throw dirt on me, you throw the envelope in," he instructed them.

He died shortly after. The three attended his funeral and dutifully each dropped his envelope into the casket. On the way back from the cemetery the accountant said, "I don't feel right. My conscience hurts me. I'm going to confess to you guys. I needed $10,000 badly for a new office we are building, so I took out $10,000 and tossed the remaining $20,000 into the grave."

The doctor said, "I, too, must confess. I am building a new clinic and I took out $20,000 and threw in only $10,000."

The two of them looked at the lawyer as he said, "Gentlemen, I'm surprised, shocked, and ashamed of you. I don't see how you could hold out like this. I threw in my personal check for the full $30,000!"

Taking it with you has always been a problem for people. We work and sacrifice so we can enjoy some of the material things in this world. These things are important to us and we'd sure like to take them with us.

A preacher had quite an experience during the Depression years. He was badly in need of a suit but didn't have very much money with which to purchase one. He noticed a small ad in the paper by a funeral home advertising for sale some suits they had left over, for only $5 each. He made his way to the funeral home and purchased a black "burial" suit. Quite pleased with his purchase he put it on when he got home. It looked and fit quite nice with only one problem — it had no pockets!

What will you be able to take out of this world with you? You can take some of your resources, provided you invest them into His kingdom down here. You can also take your family, provided they are also born again. Loved ones will also be there, provided they, too, have a personal relationship with Jesus Christ. You can take some of this life's goods with you, but only on conditions laid down in God's Word.

Do not lay up for yourselves treasures on earth, where moth and rust consume and where thieves break in and steal, but lay up for yourselves treasures in heaven (Matt. 6:19-20;RSV).

~❧

Job 33-34; Ps. 106:17-33; Prov. 4; Eph. 3-4

November 5 — Old Guidelines for Today's Living

More than a century ago there was a man named Robert Louis Stevenson, whom we know and remember as a famous author (*Treasure Island* and other memorable books). Among his writings were found these rules to help people so they could live happier, more productive lives. These may be more than 100 years old, but take another look. In fact, they make excellent guidelines for today's mothers. Well, these not only fit mothers, they are excellent principles to teach to children. Here they are:

1. Make up your mind to be happy . . . learn to find pleasure in simple things.
2. Make the best of circumstances. No one has everything, and everyone has something of sorrow.
3. Don't take yourself too seriously.
4. Don't let criticism worry you . . . you can't please everybody.
5. Don't let your neighbors set your standards . . . be yourself.
6. Do things you enjoy doing . . . but stay out of debt.
7. Don't borrow trouble. Imaginary things are harder to bear than actual ones.
8. Since hate poisons the soul, do not cherish enmities and grudges.
9. Have many interests . . . if you can't travel, read about places.
10. Don't hold post-mortems or spend time brooding over sorrows and mistakes.
11. Don't be the one who never gets over things.
12. Keep busy at something . . . a very busy person never has time to be unhappy.

So comes some wisdom out of our past — 100 years or more. Practical, down-to-earth, nitty-gritty, where-the-rubber-hits-the-road kind of advice. Now the problem is not so much knowing, it's putting it into practice in living.

These commandments that I give you today are to be upon your hearts. Impress them on your children (Deut. 6:6-7).

௸

Job 35-37; Ps. 106:34-48; Prov. 5; Eph. 5-6

Professors and others of the educated mind have been accused of a notorious human fault — forgetting what, where, when, direction, etc. You possibly remember the old story about the professor who was stopped by a student who had a question. When finished the prof asked which way he had been going before he stopped. The student pointed, "That way, sir." The prof replied, "Good, then I've just had my lunch." Let's hear it for the profs — they may not be the only people of the absent-mind. Read on. . . .

General Yoannes Metaxas, the dictator of Greece from 1936 to 1941, was notoriously absent-minded. Once, while flying as a passenger in a military seaplane he told the pilot that he wanted to fly it for a while. They changed places and after a short flight, Metaxas was preparing to land at the upcoming airport.

"Sir," the pilot said nervously, "this is a seaplane!"

"Of course! Of course!" Metaxas said and turned out over the adjoining bay where he brought the plane down safely. He thanked the pilot, opened the door of the cabin and stepped out into the sea!

Then there is the patient who complained, "What's the matter with me, Doctor? I can't seem to be able to remember anything."

The doctor replied, "Well, when did this problem start?"

Patient: "When did what start?"

Bill Cosby in his book, *Time Flies*, complains about absent-mindedness in this way: "I recently turned 50 . . . and I am having to learn to accept a new me; one who dials a telephone number and, while the phone is ringing, forgets whom he is calling."

The British Royal Navy likes to fondly remember its celebrated vice admiral who died with honors. When his strongbox was opened by the bank, a card inside it met the eyes of the executors of his will: "Starboard . . . RIGHT. Port . . . LEFT."

The noted Captain Frank Winston of Louisa Courthouse, Virginia, had walked the few hundred yards from his house to the railroad depot when he felt his coat pocket and exclaimed, "I do declare, I believe I've left my watch at home! I wonder if I have time to go back and fetch it?" So saying, he took his watch from his trousers pocket and saw it was still 15 minutes to train-time. "Yes, yes," he said, "Plenty of time," and returned back home.

Well, well . . . which way was I headed in this? Oh, well. . . .

Remember your Creator in the days of your youth, before the days of trouble come and the years approach (Eccles. 12:1).

Job 38-39; Ps. 107:1-22; Prov. 6; Rom. 1

November 7 — Angel Provision

Jonathan remembers well his angelic encounter even though it happened over 60 years ago. He was ten years old and the Depression was at its peak. He had younger brothers and sisters and it was one horrendous struggle simply to keep food on the table for the family.

One chore which had been assigned to Jonathan was to do the shopping for his mother every Saturday. He would hand the list to the grocer who would help pick out the items on the list. With money in such short supply this was a highly trusted job for such a little boy, but Jonathan did it with pride and a strong sense of responsibility.

On this particular Saturday, his mother gave him the grocery list and tucked ten dollars into his jacket pocket and sent him on his way. She always warned him never to buy anything that was not on the list. When he and the proprietor had loaded his wagon with the groceries from the list he stopped at the counter to pay the lady at the cash register. She asked for the money which was $9.74. He reached into his jacket pocket and no money! Frantic . . . he searched through every pocket . . . in his pants, and through his jacket again . . . no money! He pulled off socks and shoes thinking it may have been there. He looked under his cap . . . he ran back through the store hoping to see it on the floor. No money! Now filled with panic he began to cry. Nothing to do but leave the groceries and go home to tell his mother. Of course, she was angry and upset . . . to lose $10 in those days was a near catastrophe. There would be nothing to eat this week beyond what had been left in the cupboards. A bleak prospect.

With this Jonathan crept into the basement to cry. He knew what it all meant. As he was sobbing . . . he heard a voice, strong, positive, kind, coming from behind him and it called him by name, "Jonathan, just look into your jacket pocket."

How strange . . . he'd been through the jacket, the clerk at the checkout had been through his jacket, and his mother had searched through the jacket any number of times. How foolish, but he stuck his hand into the pocket once more and there he found the wadded up bills!

And to this day . . . more than 60 years later, whenever discouragement strikes, Jonathan still remembers in the basement when God heard the cries of a little boy and sent a messenger to put ten dollars into a jacket pocket!

However, as it is written: "No eye has seen, no ear has heard, no mind has conceived what God has prepared for those who love him" (1 Cor. 2:9).

෩

Job 40-42; Ps. 107:23-43; Prov. 7; Rom. 2-3

This story comes from a teacher friend of mine, and highlights in a sobering way the challenges faced by those who stand up every day in front of students.

Arriving late for school one day, "Beth" appeared more withdrawn than usual. Never an outgoing child, she always finished her work on time — quietly, of course — and seemed obsessive about remaining as inconspicuous as possible. Beth was cooperative and pleasant, but the sort of student a teacher can easily overlook in the hustle and bustle of "the daily grind."

But there was something about Beth that was definitely not right this blustery winter day. Maybe it was the subtly vacant expression. Or the mismatched socks — a first for this thoughtful sixth grader.

Breezing through a math lesson, my friend continued to keep an eye on her suddenly intriguing student. As the rest of the class groaned through the study period, my friend concocted a harmless excuse to get Beth outside. Once in the hallway, she asked Beth to tell her what was wrong.

The tears began to splatter immediately, catching the teacher a little offguard. Gathering Beth quickly, she found an empty office where they could be alone, and the story poured out.

Unknown to her mother, Beth's stepfather had been sexually abusing her for some time. Sacrificing herself for her younger sister, this terrified girl had endured a nightmare for more than two years.

That night, Beth stayed with my friend and her husband. My friend phoned home that she had to stay late for a conference, but a sheriff's deputy would be bringing Beth. Upon entering the house, Beth flinched by reflex and asked the husband if he was the only one home.

You see, one fiend had caused Beth to be afraid to ever be alone with a man again. How tragic.

Teachers see and hear our nation's most horrific stories on a daily basis. And they know that there are times when, if our children tell us they are scared of monsters, we must listen.

Then in the darkness, we have the opportunity to tell them about a man who loves them so much He sacrificed himself for us. His name is Jesus.[86]

"Because of the oppression of the weak and the groaning
of the needy, I will now arise," says the Lord. "I will protect
them from those who malign them" (Ps. 12:5).

৩৶

Ezek. 1-2; Ps. 108; Prov. 8; Rom. 4-5

November 9 — The Best

When Mary Douglas was a missionary in India, of greatest concern to her were her immediate neighbors, most of whom were Hindus.

One morning she spoke to a woman, a neighbor of hers, walking past her house pulling two of her children in a wagon. One child was clear-eyed, alert, lovely, and the picture of a healthy child. The other was quite seriously deformed and sat in the wagon with a dull stare in his eyes, no change of expression, unresponsive. In their very brief conversation the Hindu woman said, "I'm on my way to the temple by the river to make a sacrifice to the gods 'for my sins.' "

Mrs. Douglas quickly spoke of Jesus Christ and His sacrifice on the cross for all of humanity, even for Hindi women, but she would not listen and hurried on with her two children and the wagon.

Some days later she happened to see the Hindu woman coming again down the street pulling the same wagon. Mary stopped by the road and greeted the woman warmly as she approached. In the wagon on this day there was only one child, the deformed one. In an attempt to make conversation, Mary asked, "Where is your other child?"

"Don't you remember?" answered the woman. "I told you I was going to make a sacrifice. I offered my other child by throwing him into the river."

Mrs. Douglas was horrified, "How could you do that? And if you had to give up one of your sons, why didn't you sacrifice this crippled one and spare the healthy one?"

The Hindu woman squinted in the bright sunshine, then looking Mrs. Douglas in the eye said, "I don't know how it is in your religion, but in our religion, we give our best."

Sobering . . . in fact, even jarring. We don't like to think about such things. Could a person really do that? Perhaps this is the moment to stop and think it through. Where are the real priorities of living? Is it in our relationship to God or to self? In every life there has to be a bottom line, someplace. In establishing your priorities, a working thought would be, "With whom or what will I spend the longest time?" It goes without saying that, hopefully, the longest of all relationships will be with God, the Creator. The next longest will be with your own self, followed by family members, and so forth. It's a place to start, to give some serious thought. To what am I willing to give my best?

From everyone who has been given much, much will be demanded; and from the one who has been entrusted with much, much more will be asked (Luke 12:48).

❧

Ezek. 3-5; Ps. 109:1-13; Prov. 9; Rom. 6-7

November 10 — The Train Stops Just in Time

The crack British express train raced through the night, its powerful head lamp spearing the darkness ahead. This was a special run because it was carrying Queen Victoria and her attendants.

Suddenly . . . the engineer saw a startling sight! Revealed in the powerful beam of the engine's headlights was a weird figure loosely wrapped in a black coat that was flapping in the breeze, standing on the middle of the train tracks, waving its arms, a signal to stop! The engineer immediately grabbed for the brakes and brought the train to a screeching, grinding, sparks-flying halt!

Then the engineer, his assistant, the coal tender, and a couple of conductors climbed down to see what had stopped them. They looked, but they could find no trace of the strange figure. But on a hunch, the engineer walked a few yards further down the tracks. Instantly he stopped and stared into the fog in horror! The rain storm, which passed through the area earlier in the evening, had caused the bridge to wash out in the middle span and it had toppled into the storm-swollen stream! If he had not paid attention to the ghostly, weird figure, the train would have plunged into the overflowing stream . . . with, how many lives lost or bodies mangled, who knows? The engineer was so overcome with the emotion of the near miss that he sat down on the tracks for a few moments before making his way back to the idling steam engine.

Word was wired for help. And while the bridge and tracks were being repaired, the crew again made a more intensive search for the strange flagman, unsuccessfully. But it wasn't until they got to London that the mystery was solved.

At the base of the steam engine's head lamp, the engineer discovered a huge dead moth. He looked at it a few moments . . . then, on impulse, wet its wings and pasted it to the glass of the head lamp.

Climbing back into the cab . . . he switched on the lamp and saw the "flagman" in the beam. He knew the answer now, the moth had flown into the beam mere seconds before the train was due to reach the washed-out bridge. In the fog it had appeared to be a phantom figure, a flagon waving its arms signaling the train to stop!

Later when Queen Victoria was told of the strange happenings she said, "I'm sure it was no accident. It was God's way of protecting us."

Praise the Lord, you His angels, you mighty ones who do His bidding, who obey His word (Ps. 103:20).

◦~◦

Ezek. 6-7; Ps. 109:14-31; Prov. 10; Rom. 8

November 11, Veterans Day — Inclusive Love

It happened in World War II as our GIs were making their dash from the south, Italy and the Mediterranean, towards Germany. As part of this campaign, there were little side battles fought along the way. There were pockets of resistance that didn't require the entire army that Patton was leading . . . but some small platoons were dispatched to quell or recapture or liberate many towns.

One of these small squads was off into the hills of France and a small skirmish took place. Our GI's were pinned down by enemy fire. There was only one casualty. He was a favorite among the other guys . . . but he also had two very special friends. The three of them had been inseparable and had become bosom buddies.

There was a problem. They were separated from their main unit by quite a few miles and really had no way to carry the body out. They desperately wanted to give him a dignified burial, and after talking with their sergeant it was decided to do it, if possible, in the nearby village. The two friends made their way to the village and found a cemetery. It was a Roman Catholic cemetery — the only one in the village. There was a possible problem. The dead GI was a Protestant.

When the two friends managed to find the priest in charge of the cemetery they requested permission to bury their friend. The priest refused because the dead soldier was not a Catholic. When the priest saw their disappointment as they turned to leave, he called out to them to stay. He then explained that they could bury their friend outside the fence, but next to the cemetery. A simple service was held, a few words were said, and they left immediately to return to their platoon.

Later, when they had some leave coming, the two friends returned to the village and the cemetery to visit their friend's grave. They couldn't find it. Their search led them back to the same priest and, of course, they asked him what had happened to the grave of their fallen friend. The priest told them that during the night following the burial, he had been unable to sleep because he had made them bury their friend outside the fence. So, in the middle of the night, he got up and moved the fence to include their dead soldier friend.

In Jesus Christ, God has moved the fence to include all, even the undeserving. Can we follow this example and move the fence, too?

For John the Baptist came neither eating bread nor drinking wine, and you say, "He has a demon." The son of Man came eating and drinking, and you say, "Here is a glutton and a drunkard, a friend of tax collectors and sinners" (Luke 7:33-34).

᠉

Ezek. 8-10; Ps. 110; Prov. 11; Rom. 9-10

November 12 — The Switch

A young trial lawyer had developed a reputation for himself within a short time of being an accomplished and shrewd attorney. His opponents feared him; his clients loved him. He was sure to win each case. He began writing in law journals, and invitations to speak about his techniques began to appear. After a number of these he developed a standard lecture to be used for these audiences.

He traveled with his chauffeur, a bright young man who was proud to be associated with this renowned lawyer. After months of listening to the same lecture, the brash young chauffeur announced that he had heard the same speech so many times that he could give it himself.

It was agreed that the next time they were out of town and no one would recognize them, they would exchange duties. The lawyer dressed as the chauffeur while the chauffeur, dressed like the lawyer, was introduced to a room full of expectant lawyers.

The chauffeur waxed eloquent, demonstrating techniques and addressing details with precision. At the end of the speech the chauffeur was given a standing ovation. It was a magnificent talk. The moderator indicated there were still a few minutes left and asked the appreciative audience if they had any questions for their honored guest.

One lawyer ventured to ask a question concerning the legal precedents for one of the techniques referred to earlier in the speech. The lawyer, dressed as the chauffeur, in the back of the room felt his heart sink. He could easily field the question, but there was no way to let his chauffeur know the answer. They were about to be exposed!

The chauffeur asked the questioner to repeat the question. After listening to the question a second time, the chauffeur chuckled. With just a slight tinge of mockery he responded, "Why, that's such a simple and well-known precedent that all of you should know that! The common layperson should also know the answer. In fact, to demonstrate my premise, I am going to let my chauffeur give you the answer."

How's that for quick thinking on your feet? And another lesson in life-preparation. Some things look easy on the surface and can be duplicated or copied. But when the real questions come, that's where that schooling and experience pays off. That's the real thing . . . let's not take any short-cuts because sooner or later you will be found out.

But in your hearts set apart Christ as Lord. Always be prepared to give an answer to everyone who asks you to give the reason for the hope that you have. But do this with gentleness and respect (1 Pet. 3:15).

Ezek. 11-12; Ps. 111; Prov. 12; Rom. 11-12

November 13 — There's a Reason

Lou Little, the former great football coach at Columbia University, relates the following story.

This particular season the team had played through the schedule without a defeat. Now they were facing the final game of the year, and the Ivy League Conference Championship was on the line. It was winner take all. Their opponent was arch rival Harvard, also undefeated.

On Tuesday of the week in which preparation was being made, Coach Little received a phone call asking him if he would break the tragic news to one of his players that the boy's father had died and the funeral was to be on Friday. The young man was a senior on the football squad, and an unusual young man. Although he had never started a game in his four-year career, the boy had been kept on the team because of his irrepressible and contagious attitude. He was an inspiration.

After the coach called him aside and broke the news, the young man immediately left and told the coach, "I'll be back in time for the big game on Saturday."

Coach Little replied, "Son, take as much time with your family as you need. We'll just go with the team that has won so far. Don't worry."

The day of the big game arrived, and the young man, as he had promised, suited up with the rest of the team. He went over to the coach and said, "Lou, please let me start this game — even one play!" The coach kind of brushed him aside, but the young man was emotionally insistent and came back with his request again, "Please, Coach, even one play!" So Lou agreed to let him start.

Columbia won the toss and elected to kick-off. This young man was the first tackler down field and tackled the ball carrier on the seven-yard line. A great play. On the first play from scrimmage, the Harvard quarterback called for the halfback to go over his slot. The young man tackled him on the five-yard line for a two-yard loss. The next play the Harvard quarterback dropped into the end zone to pass, and this young man tackled him, scoring a safety. He played the entire game.

After the game, Little asked, "Son, what got into you today?"

The young man replied, with tears in his eyes, "Coach, do you remember that my father was blind? Today is the first time he's seen me play!"

Brothers, I do not consider myself yet to have taken hold of it. But one thing I do: Forgetting what is behind and straining toward what is ahead, I press on toward the goal to win the prize (Phil. 3:13-14).

❦

Ezek. 13-15; Ps. 112; Prov. 13; Rom. 13-14

November 14 — Friends, Brothers, and Sisters

The Bible talks about friends, and that friends are to love at all times. It also states that a brother might be/is born for adversity. And most sisters who have brothers might say that those brothers certainly have dished out lots of adversity. But have you ever thought that might not be what the Bible meant with such verses?

But what about a sister? The Bible doesn't talk very much about sisters. What are sisters born for? Why are sisters born? Caroline Burns says, "My sister was born to be the rock of our family. Even before Mother died and Daddy got old, she was the one we depended on."

Sisters are the ones who always remember to send special notes and cards on everybody's birthdays, wedding anniversaries, and all other kinds of occasions to celebrate.

Sisters are the people who love cards, intimate notes, long phone calls, holiday family gatherings, and making sure that nobody is left out.

Sisters are the people who tend to be the glue that holds families together . . . they insist on get-togethers and family reunions.

Sisters make sure that little sisters and little brothers are always included, whether it is play time when little or going as a family on a special vacation.

Sisters are the ones who show to the rest of the siblings what a lady of faith will look like and act like and be like.

Sisters put real life into those old stories we read about the women of the Bible . . . Rachel, Leah, Ruth, Mary, Salome, Deborah, Sarah, and Eve, to name just a few.

Sisters put skin and warmth into those ancient women . . . sisters give us insight into how other families and other women may have been.

Sisters are the natural leader/teachers for younger sisters about how to live life out, simply how to make life work.

Sisters make all of us proud to be family members because sisters remind us of so many things, teach us how to be human, caring, loving, compassionate, and practical.

Shirley Abbott reminds us about all these things as she writes: "Within our family there was no such thing as a person who did not matter. Second cousins thrice removed mattered. We knew . . . and thriftily made use of . . . everybody's middle name. We knew who was buried where. We all mattered, and the dead most of all."[87]

Likewise, teach the older women to be reverent in the way they live, not to be slanderers or addicted to much wine, but to teach what is good. Then they can train the younger women to love (Titus 2:3-4).

᠗

Ezek. 16; Ps. 113; Prov. 14; Rom. 15

November 15 — We Can't Come Back

Life is full of uncertainties, isn't it? Would any of us argue that point?

As humans, we understand that death is perhaps the most uncertain thing that can happen to us. We fear it, wonder at it, explore its mysteries. In the end, we hope to have wisdom and a readiness as death approaches.

A little friend of mine once reminded me of the necessity of accepting death.

One day, shortly after the sudden passing of his beloved grandfather, this little fellow, not much past three, gazed out the window of his grandmother's car. They were headed to her house — the same house that had always belonged to her and grandpa.

"Grandma," he said softly, his eyes never leaving the window, "I've been thinking about Grandpa."

"Oh . . . and what were you thinking?"

"Momma said he died and now he lives in heaven with Jesus."

"That's right, sweetheart. Grandpa is in heaven with Jesus."

The little lad then turned away from the window and faraway thoughts and finished with, "It's too bad we couldn't all go together."

Grandma couldn't say anything, as she was fighting back the tears. There was a long pause and then Jordan finished with, "But then we couldn't come back."

I can't be certain about you, but I'm not ashamed to say that story brings a tear to my eye. And a valuable lesson to my mind: God longs to have a place in eternity for each one of us, but it's up to us to make sure we know the path, and the finality of our choices.

Jesus came to the world as a perfect sacrifice for the human race. He served as our window of escape from a deserved and total punishment.

Death will reach me, and you, and everyone. We need to stop and think about our destination, because, to paraphrase a wise friend of mine: "We can't come back."

For the day will come when, as Jordan was hoping, we will indeed all go together, when Christ returns for His flock.

How about you, fellow traveler? Are you prepared to learn that supreme lesson about the road we all travel?

Then we which are alive and remain shall be caught up together with them in the clouds, to meet the Lord in the air; and so shall we ever be with the Lord (1 Thess. 4:17).

Ezek. 17; Ps. 114; Prov. 15; Rom. 16

November 16 — A Leg to Stand On

Lisa Love worked hard to win a spot on the cheerleading squad during her junior year in high school. About a month later, because of cancer, her leg was amputated above the knee. Over the summer, she was fitted with a prosthesis and worked hard in her physical therapy sessions and learned to maneuver and walk on it quite well. She then sought out and persuaded her cheerleader sponsor to let her continue as a cheerleader. The sponsor reluctantly agreed, with some doubts.

Lisa worked hard on her routines by herself before school started and joined the other cheerleaders in their first practice. They were preparing for the first pep rally in the fall football season and all went well; Lisa fit right in to all the routines, without a problem.

Then came the first Thursday pep rally; the gym was packed with high school students and faculty. The cheerleading squad began their routines. Lisa started her four-step run and into a somersault across the slick gym floor. In the middle of her somersault, her artificial leg came off and skidded across the gym floor, leaving Lisa to stumble on one leg and crash to the floor. She buried her face in her hands, cried, and thought of quitting right there.

Instead, she motioned for one of her cheerleading friends to help retrieve her leg, and helped her strap that prosthesis back on. All this in front of the bleachers packed with kids. In full sight of them, she then stood straight and tall, motioned that she was ready. The squad continued their routine and Lisa performed her part of the routine to a rousing, enthusiastic, long, standing ovation![88]

Success in life has been defined as the ability to get up one more time when you have fallen down! Everybody in life has experienced failure of some kind. The question is, what do you do after you have fallen down — lay there in your tears, have your own personal pity party, ask, "Why has this happened to me?" or get up one more time?

About 10 percent of life is composed of the things that happen to you — 90 percent is your *reaction* to what has happened to you. If you look hard enough, you can always blame somebody else for your problems . . . maturity is taking responsibility for yourself and your reactions in life. When we stumble, Jesus Christ stands ready to help us re-attach what has been lost. All of heaven is ready for your standing ovation.

Therefore, since we are surrounded by such a great cloud of witnesses, let us throw off everything that hinders and the sin that so easily entangles, and let us run with perseverance the race marked out for us (Heb. 12:1).

⟡

Ezek. 18-19; Ps. 115; Prov. 16; Acts 21

A woman was called out of town on a business trip and she asked her sister to take care of her cat for her while she was away. The cat happened to be one of those beautiful, registered, show quality Siamese cats. This cat meant everything to the woman. She made sure the cat had the very best of everything which included food, care, and exercise.

The problem was that the sister didn't really like cats at all.

The first thing the woman did upon completing her business trip was to call her sister's house and inquire about her cat. The sister was curt, blunt, and to the point when she replied, "Your cat died." And then she hung up on her sister.

For the next few hours and on into the next day, the woman was inconsolable in her grief. She called her sister back and said, "We have to talk, I'm coming right over."

When she arrived at her sister's home, obviously hurt, she pointed out, "It was needlessly cruel and sadistic of you to tell me so bluntly that my poor prize-winning cat had passed away. It was almost more of a shock than I could stand."

The sister then demanded, "Well, what did you expect me to do?"

She replied, "Well . . . you at least could have broken the bad news to me gradually. First, you could have said my cat was playing on the roof. Later you could have called to say that she had fallen off. Then the next morning you could have called and said something about the fact that one of her legs was broken. Then, when I came to get her, you could have told me how she had passed away in the middle of the night."

Her sister, nodded, understandingly, and said, "Okay, I'm getting the drift."

She went on, then, "But, it's too bad that you didn't have enough civility to treat me like your grown-up adult sister. I will, however, forgive you this time, though I don't know how I'll get along without my wonderful cat."

The sister, then, out of concern, responded, "I'm so sorry. In the future I will keep your suggestions in mind. Please forgive me."

"You're forgiven. Oh, by the way, how is Mama doing?"

Her sister pondered, thoughtfully, momentarily, then announced, "Mama is playing on the roof."

Now Sarah was listening at the entrance to the tent, which was behind him. Abraham and Sarah were already old and well advanced in years, and Sarah was past the age of child-bearing. So Sarah laughed to herself as she thought . . . (Gen. 18:10-12).

&

Ezek. 20; Ps. 116; Prov. 17; Acts 22

Richard the Lionhearted was king of England for ten years, but spent only about six months of that time at home. Why? Because he was so busy off crusading to rescue the Holy Land.

As a boy I liked the legend about Richard, based on a 13th-century romance. May I remind you of the story?

Returning from the Holy Land, Richard was captured and imprisoned by Kim Modred of Almain, or Germany. Modred's daughter Margery fell in love with him and bribed the jailer to allow him to spend his nights in her chamber. On the seventh night they were discovered.

King Modred wanted to have Richard killed there and then, but his counselors were alarmed by the idea of executing a king and preferred to arrange an "accident." The lion in the royal menagerie was to be starved for a few days and then allowed to "escape" into the captive's cell. Margery learned of the plan and begged Richard to attempt an escape but he would not hear of it.

Instead he asked her for 40 silk handkerchiefs which he then bound around his right arm. When the lion burst into his cell and leapt hungrily upon him, Richard simply thrust his hand down the lion's throat and tore his heart out!

Then, pausing only to give thanks to God, he strode up to the great hall, still bearing the warm heart in his hand. Before the astonished gaze of Modred and his court, Richard thumped the heart down on the banquet table, sprinkled salt over it, and proceeded to eat it with relish. So goes the old legend.

Some people are natural crusaders. These have a cause that is bigger than life. Occasionally they will touch home base and do some nitty-gritty work, but the cause will eventually pull them away from the humdrum.

History tells us of people like Henry Ward Beecher who stumped against slavery, and of Martin Luther King who crusaded for civil rights. There are so many causes needing crusaders today that it is a simple matter to become enchanted with a cause and become that crusader. At times it's easy to fantasize that we can take on the whole world and rip the heart out of a lion. Most of us get only a bloody arm and end up eating crow instead of heart. It boils down to this: Be careful in your crusades and keep your life in balance.

Not that I have already attained, or am already perfected; but I press on, that I may lay hold of that for which Christ Jesus has also laid hold of me (Phil. 3:12;NKJV).

⤙⤚

Ezek. 21; Ps. 117; Prov. 18; Acts 23

The woman was a famous movie star. She had come to visit her daughter at the summer gymnastics camp for girls that my husband and I run near Fresno, California. When the time came for the daily workouts, the actress watched her daughter from the sidelines. The girl was good, though not good enough to compete at a championship level. She was nervous.

When the girl finished, her mother called out, "That was awful. You looked like a sack of potatoes tumbling downhill." The girl burst into tears. My heart went out to her.

I found myself remembering the day one of my own gymnastic performances put me close to tears. I might have shed them, except for something my mother said to me then.

When my mother was carrying her first child, she was stricken with polio, and she has been confined to a wheelchair and crutches ever since. She never let that discourage her. She managed to raise five children and have a career as well.

I decided to join a gymnastics program. By 1972, I was on the U.S. Women's Gymnastic Team for the Olympic Games in Munich. I couldn't think of anything else except a gold medal.

It had become my habit, during practice and the warm-ups before a contest, to pray . . . asking God for the strength and control to get through the routine. That day in Munich, I was determined not to disgrace my country and myself. But, though I competed to the best of my ability, I didn't win a gold medal. I joined my parents in the stands, all set for a big cry. I managed a faltering, "I'm sorry. I did my best."

"You know that, and I know that," my mother said, "and I'm sure God knows that, too." She smiled and said 10 words that I never forgot: "Doing your best is more important than being the best."

Suddenly I understood my mother better than ever before. She had never let her handicap prevent her from always doing her best.

Now I went over to the sobbing girl and put an arm around her. "Honey," I said, "I've been watching you improve all summer and I know you have done your best, and doing your best is more important than being the best. I'm proud of you."

She smiled at me through her tears. Maybe somewhere, someday, she'll pass those words along.[89]

No, in all these things we are more than conquerors through Him who loved us (Rom. 8:37).

⤳

Ezek. 22; Ps. 118:1-14; Prov. 19; Acts 24

Rev. Ron Prinzing, outstanding senior pastor of the First Family Church in Whittier, California, bemoans the verbal error that hurry creates. While serving as associate pastor of Bible Assembly in South Gate, California, he created an explosion of laughter.

The Sunday night service had already been long. The choir had unexpectedly sung two songs instead of one and then the church trio sang three songs. Between each song there were testimonies, as each of the women in the trio and members of the choir wanted to thank the Lord publicly for unique events in their lives. All this was good, but very time-consuming. As the last trio song was being sung, Rev. Prinzing looked at the clock and confirmed his uneasy feeling.

A movement at the platform entrance door brought further anxiety. There stood his wife, Roselyn, and the head deacon, Frank Bunnell, violins in hand. They had prepared a special duet and were ready. Looking quickly in the direction of his wife, Prinzing shook his head no. She stared back and nodded her head yes! When the trio finished, Prinzing moved swiftly to the pulpit. "Folks, we've had a wonderful Sunday night already. I do want to preach and will be careful to watch the time. He proceeded to give the announcements and then called the ushers forward to receive the evening offering, thinking to save time by having the violin duet play for the offertory. "Friends, thank you for your faithfulness," he said. "While you're giving tonight I'm going to call on Frank Bunnell to come and fiddle with my wife."

He did not catch this embarrassing slip. The violin duet was finished and Roselyn leaned over and whispered in her husband's ear what he had said. The congregation sat silent, but an explosion of laughter was on the verge of eruption. People were covering their faces. Ron Prinzing rose and returned to the pulpit. "You all know what I meant." There was a gush of laughter. "What I meant to say," he continued, "was that Brother Bunnell was going to play with my wife." Some people jumped up and headed for the door . . . their laughter could not be stalled. He should have left well enough alone. Everyone roared a second time![90]

This is a celebration of being human! Yes, we love God and our people love God, but the words come out wrong! "To the pure all things are pure." But that doesn't stop them from being hilarious! What do you say now? Simply, the benediction, "AMEN, folks, that's all!"

For by your words you will be acquitted, and by your words you will be condemned (Matt. 12:37).

᷾᷾

Ezek. 23; Ps. 118:15-29; Prov. 20; Acts 25

November 21 — It Is Well . . .

It's 1873 and Horatio Spafford, a Christian attorney from Chicago, had booked passage for his wife and four children, all sisters, on the luxury liner *Ville de Havre* sailing out of New York to France. Spafford himself anticipated joining them on their vacation holiday in about three or four weeks, after finishing some business. Except for his wife, he never saw them again.

On the evening of November 21, in mid-Atlantic, the luxury liner was struck by another ship, the *Lochearn*, and sank in less than 30 minutes, taking most of the passengers to their death.

On being warned that the ship was sinking, Mrs. Spafford knelt with her children and prayed that they might be saved or be made willing to die, if such would be God's will. In the confusion, three of the children were swept away by the waves while she stood clutching the youngest. Then she, too, was swept from her arms. Mrs. Spafford was struck by some of the debris and knocked unconscious. She awoke later to find that she had been rescued by some sailors from the *Lochearn*. But the four sisters were gone.

Back in the United States, Horatio Spafford was waiting for news of his family. It was 10 days later, after the rescue ship had sailed to Cardiff, Wales, that the message came. "Saved alone" was his wife's message. That night Spafford walked the floor of his home in anguish. His only recourse was to pray as he shared his loss with His Lord. Later he told his friend, Major Whittle, "I am glad to be able to trust my Lord when it costs me something." Sometime later, as he reflected back on the personal disaster at sea, he wrote this hymn.

> *When peace, like a river, attendeth my way,*
> *When sorrows like sea-billows roll;*
> *Whatever my lot, Thou hast taught me to say,*
> *It is well, it is well with my soul.*
> *Though Satan should buffet, though trials should come,*
> *Let this blest assurance control,*
> *That Christ has regarded my helpless estate,*
> *And hath shed His own blood for my soul. . . .*
> *And, Lord, haste the day when the faith shall be sight,*
> *The clouds be rolled back as a scroll,*
> *The trump shall resound and the Lord shall descend,*
> *"Even so" . . . it is well with my soul.*

For God did not appoint us to suffer wrath but to receive salvation through our Lord Jesus Christ (1 Thess. 5:9).

❧

Ezek. 24-25; Ps. 119:1-16; Prov. 21; Acts 26

November 22 — Do You Still Remember?

The nation of America was electrified by the most memorable words spoken by our newly elected president, John Fitzgerald Kennedy, in his inaugural address given on Friday, January 20, 1961:

> The same revolutionary beliefs for which our forebears fought are still at issue around the globe. The belief that the rights of man come not from the generosity of the state but from the hand of God. . . . And so, my fellow Americans, ask not what your country can do for you . . . ask what you can do for your country. Let us go forth to lead the land we love, asking His blessing and His help, but knowing that here on earth God's work must truly be our own."

With those words we were ushered into an era fondly remembered as "Camelot." It was a time of innocence and excitement led by this, our youngest man ever elected president, at age 43.

JFK was known for his sharp wit and sense of history and displayed both at a White House dinner honoring Nobel prize winners in 1962 . . . and in the bargain paid graceful tribute to the third U.S. president. He told his distinguished guests, "I think this is the most extraordinary collection of talent, of human knowledge, that has ever been gathered together at the White House, with the possible exception of when Thomas Jefferson dined alone."

All of that wit and exciting leadership was cut down by an assassin's bullet on a street in Dallas, Texas, on November 22, 1963. It was a tragedy felt by a nation which was totally stunned by the suddenness and senselessness of it all. Ask anybody who was alive at that point in history and they'll likely tell you exactly what they were doing when they heard the stunning news.

Let me close with a small portion of the undelivered text of a speech which President Kennedy had planned to deliver at the Dallas Trade Mart on the day he was killed: "We ask . . . that we may achieve in our time and for all time the ancient vision of peace on earth, goodwill toward men. That must always be our goal . . . and the righteousness of our cause must always underlie our strength. For as was written long ago, 'Except the Lord keep the city, the watchman waketh but in vain.' "

I urge, then, first of all, that requests, prayers, intercession and thanksgiving be made for everyone . . . for kings and all those in authority, that we may live peaceful and quiet lives in all godliness and holiness (1 Tim. 2:1-22).

❧

Ezek. 26; Ps. 119:17-32; Prov. 22; Acts 27

DECEMBER 8: It's starting to snow. The wife and I took our hot chocolate and sat by the picture window, watching the soft lovely flakes drift down, clinging to trees and covering the ground. It was beautiful!

DECEMBER 9: We awoke to a lovely blanket of crystal white snow. What a fantastic sight. Every tree and shrub covered with a beautiful white mantle. I shoveled snow for the first time in years and loved it. Later a city snowplow came along and accidentally covered our driveway with compacted snow from the street. The operator smiled and waved. I waved back and shoveled it clear again.

DECEMBER 10: It snowed an additional eight inches last night and temperature dropped to around 2 degrees above zero. I shoveled our driveway again. Much of the snow is brownish-gray.

DECEMBER 11: Warmed up enough during the day to create some slush which soon became ice when the temp dropped again. Bought snow tires for both cars. Fell on my behind in the driveway. $175 to a chiropractor but nothing is broken. More snow and ice expected.

DECEMBER 12: Sold the wife's car and bought a 4 X 4 in order to get her to work. Slid into a guardrail anyway. Ten inches of the white crud last night. The stinking snowplow came by twice today.

DECEMBER 13: Ten degrees below zero outside. More crappy white stuff. Not a tree or shrub on our property that hasn't been damaged. Power was off most of the night. Tried to keep from freezing with candles and a kerosene heater, which tipped. I managed to put it out but suffered second degree burns on my hands and lost all my eyelashes and eyebrows. Car slid on way to emergency room and was totaled.

DECEMBER 14: Dat-gum stinking white crud keeps on coming down. Have to put on all the clothes we own just to get to the stupid mailbox. If I ever catch that jerk who operates the snowplow, I'll chew open his chest and rip out his heart. I think he hides around the corner and waits for me to finish shoveling and then comes roaring down the street about 100 mph and buries our driveway again. Power still off. Toilet froze and part of roof started to cave in.

DECEMBER 15: Eight dat-gum more stinking inches of stinking snow and stinking sleet and stinking ice last night. I wounded the snowplow jerk with an ice ax but he got away. Wife left me. Car won't start. Below zero. I'm going snow-blind. My toes are frost-bitten. Haven't seen the sun in weeks. More snow predicted. Wind chill is -38 degrees. I'm moving back south!

Have you entered the treasury of snow? (Job 38:22).

⌒⌒

Ezek. 27; Ps. 119:33-48; Prov. 23; Acts 28

November 24 — Lessons from Geese

This fall we'll again have the pleasure of watching geese heading south for the winter. It's a beautiful sight to watch their "V" formation in action as they go by. As you observe them, you might also be interested in what science has discovered about why they fly that way.

Scientific study has learned that as each of these big birds flaps its wings an uplift or updraft is created for the bird immediately following. By flying in a V formation, the whole flock adds at least a 71 percent greater flying range than if each bird flew on its own. This was a long-term study that took place in the field as well as in a wind-tunnel under very controlled conditions.

It was also discovered that when a goose falls out of formation, it suddenly feels the drag and resistance of trying to go it alone and quickly gets back into formation to take advantage of the lifting power of the bird immediately in front. When the lead goose gets tired, he or she rotates back in the wing and another goose flies point. It's a beautiful picture of cooperation and helping each other out.

Perhaps you've also noticed that there's a lot of honking going on to encourage the leader. It's also a signal to keep up to speed.

Finally, when a goose gets sick or is wounded by a gunshot and falls out of the formation, two other geese will also fall out of formation to follow the wounded or sick goose to help and protect the wounded bird. They stay with this hurting one until the sick bird is either able to fly or until it is dead, and then they launch out on their own or with another formation to catch up with their original group.

The lessons we learn from the above are at least four:

1) Christians who share a common direction can get where they are going because they can travel on the thrust of one another.

2) If we have as much sense as a goose, we will stay in formation with those who are headed the same way we are going.

3) It pays to take turns doing the hard jobs with people at church or with geese flying south.

4) If people knew we would stand by them in the church, like geese do, they would push down our church doors to get in.

You see, all we have to do to attract people to church is demonstrate to the world that we have as much sense as a goose at our church!

*If one part of the body suffers, all the other parts suffer
with it; if one part is praised, all the other parts share
its happiness. All of you, then, are Christ's body, and
each one is a part of it* (1 Cor. 12:26-27;TEV).

Ezek. 28; Ps. 119:49-64; Prov. 24; Col. 1-2

November 25 — Be Generous

Be generous! Give to those whom you love; give to those who love you; give to the fortunate; give to the unfortunate; yes . . . give especially to those to whom you don't want to give.

Your most precious, valued possessions and your greatest powers are invisible and intangible. No one can take them. You, and you alone, can give them. You will receive abundance for your giving. The more you give . . . the more you will have!

Give a smile to everyone you meet (smile with your eyes) . . . and you'll smile and receive smiles.

Give a kind word (with a kindly thought behind the word) — you will be kind and receive kind words.

Give appreciation (warmth from the heart) — you will appreciate and be appreciated.

Give honor, credit and applause (the victor's wreath) — you will be honorable and receive credit and applause.

Give time for a worthy cause (with eagerness) — you will be worthy and richly rewarded.

Give hope (the magic ingredient for success) — you will have hope and be made hopeful.

Give happiness (a most treasured state of mind) — you will be happy and be made happy.

Give encouragement (the incentive to action) — you will have courage and be encouraged.

Give cheer (the verbal sunshine) — you'll be cheerful and be cheered.

Give a pleasant response (the neutralizer of irritants) — you will be pleasant and receive pleasant responses.

Give good thoughts (nature's character builder) — you will be good and the world will have good thoughts for you.

Give prayer (the instrument of miracles) for the godless and the godly — you will be reverent and receive blessings, more than you deserve!

BE GENEROUS! GIVE![91]

Even without worldly wealth or material possessions it's possible for you to be generous!

For out of the overflow of the heart the mouth speaks. The good man brings good things out of the good stored up in him, and the evil man brings evil things out of the evil stored up in him (Matt. 12:34-35).

༺⁀༻

Ezek. 29-30; Ps. 119:65-80; Prov. 25; Col. 3-4

November 26 — Thanksgiving

THANKSGIVING is unique among holidays. It is not a religious holiday in quite the same sense as Easter and Christmas . . . but we render the day meaningless if we fail to give thanks. It does not, like Independence Day, mark the founding of our nation. Rather it marks the day of the founding of a spirit that is special in living . . . that of gratitude.

When the American colonists were being settled, they endured many privations and hardships. Being devoutly religious, they brought their problems to God on days of fasting and prayer. On one occasion when it was proposed to appoint another day of penitence and humiliation, a sensible old colonist said that he thought they had brooded over their misfortunes long enough; that it seemed high time they should remember all God's mercies toward them. He proposed that instead of another fast they should keep a feast . . . and from that time Thanksgivng Day has been an annual observance in America.

In 1795, then-President Washington asked the nation to observe a Day of Thanksgiving. He asked the people to gather in their churches to humbly and fervently pray to God that He might prolong the blessing of this nation to us; to ask God to imprint in our hearts a deep and solemn sense of our obligation to Him for these blessings. He closed his pleas with these remarkable words: "And finally to impart all the blessings we possess, or ask for ourselves, to the whole family of mankind."

It is strange how little and how seldom we thank God for being God! We think in terms of things. We think things. We thank God for what we get or are, but we rarely arrive at the point of appreciation of being grateful that God is. The average prayer of gratitude tends to run something like this: "Father, I thank thee for. . . ." What ardent "for" pray-ers we are! All too many of us thank God merely for the favors of life we experience. Not so with Jesus Christ! His gratitude was not "thing" centered . . . it was God-centered.

Thankfulness is a way of looking at life. So it is fitting that we pause in thanksgiving, in our churches, in our homes, and at our bountiful tables for the blessings of another bountiful year. We give thanks for our freedom, liberty, and the guarantee of dignity for the individual. And don't forget that celebrating THANKSGIVING DAY was not meant to be kept on one day of the year only.

Enter His gates with thanksgiving and his courts with praise; give thanks to Him and praise His name. For the Lord is good and His love endures forever; His faithfulness continues through all generations (Ps. 100:4).

Ezek. 31-32; Ps. 119:81-96; Prov. 26; Heb. 1-2

Those who tease you
love you.

Jewish Proverb

*SHE ate her jelly doughnut at lunch. You saved yours. It is now two hours later:

Sit down next to your sister on the couch. Put the jelly doughnut on a napkin in your lap. Leave it, untouched, until she asks you if you still want it. Then begin eating. "Mmmm. This is soooo good." Take a large bite and chew with mouth open so she gets a good view. Swallow and run tongue over lips. "Mmmm." Stick tongue in jelly center and wave it around in the air before pulling it back in mouth. "Don't you wish you had some?" Take tiny bites. Lick fingers in between. "Boy . . . there's nothing like having a jelly doughnut in the middle of the afternoon!" Pop last bite in mouth and pat stomach.

*WANDER into the room when she calls a friend on the telephone. Pick up a book and sit down on the couch. Pretend to read, then mimic her as she begins her telephone conversation.

Hi, how are you? *Hi, how are you?* Wha'd you do today? *Wha'd you do today?* What? Wait a minute, my sister's driving me crazy. Would you cut it out. *Would you cut it out.* You dirty creep. *You dirty creep.* Stop repeating me! *Stop repeating me!* I'll kill you if you don't stop! *I'll kill you if you don't stop!* I said STOP! *I said STOP!* STOP IT!! *STOP IT!!*

Put down book and run.

*SHE is eating peanuts. Whisper in her ear, "You can turn into an elephant if you eat too many peanuts. I read it in the *World Book*."

*FOLLOW her everywhere.

*IMITATE her best friend talking. Say that her best friend is fat.

*TALK to your mother while your sister is listening: "Do you remember Christmas when I was three years old and you gave me that stuffed animal? That was so much fun." Turn to your sister: "You weren't alive."

*YOU are in bed with the flu, watching television. She has been told to keep out of your room so that she doesn't catch it, too. As she walks by the door, stare goggle-eyed at the TV: "Oh my goodness! That's incredible! I've never seen anything like it in my life! I can't believe it! Wait till I tell the kids at school." Do not remove eyes from set, staring in amazement. "I wouldn't miss this for anything! I really don't believe it." Look at your sister. "What?" Move over on the bed. "Of course there's room for you."[92]

Isn't her younger sister more attractive? (Judg. 15:2).

⟨∽⟩

Ezek. 33; Ps. 119:97-112; Prov. 27; Heb. 3-5

Two things are in short supply — well, it could be a whole lot more, when you are a college student — sleep, and money to go home on. Margarete was away at college, a hard working, diligent, college student, a sophomore. She stayed in the dormitory where sleep was a short commodity, too. Girls being girls and studies being studies and boys being subjects of conversation, the nights are pretty short.

The Christmas holidays were soon approaching which meant the trip home was in sight. But as always, college professors haven't much heart so they schedule tests on the last two or three days preceding vacation. So again sleep was hard to come by.

As soon as class was over on that Friday Margarete made her way to the depot, loaded with luggage and a few presents she had purchased. She bought her ticket and her choice seat was available, the last seat in the back, next to the back door where she could stretch out and sleep without interruption until her destination of Mankato, Minnesota!

What luxury . . . just to stretch out. The only sounds were those of people murmuring to each other and the tires on the highway, comforting, soothing sounds to lull a tired college sophomore to sleep. As she slept the bus motion and her tossing pushed her shoulders against the back door, then more of her body weight pressed against the door.

SUDDENLY without warning, the back door sprang open with Margarete pushed against it. She tipped out the door, head and shoulders first, awakening instantly with a start to feel herself falling into the blackness of the night towards the hard concrete. Her first thought was, *I'm about to die!* She grabbed for the door frame to catch herself but missed! She prayed a three word prayer, "Jesus help me!"

And to this day, she says she can almost still feel it . . . there was a pair of huge hands that caught her and pushed her back into the bus!

The bus driver came running down the aisle to check on the problem. He came to Margarete and asked, "Are you all right? I can't understand how it happened. Did you lose anything?"

Still in shock, she answered, "No sir, no problems."

"How did you manage to hold on and not fall out?"

"I believe I had some heavenly help."

> *When you pass through the waters, I will be with you; and when you pass through the rivers, they will not sweep over you. When you walk through the fire, you will not be burned; the flames will not set you ablaze. For I am the Lord, your God, the Holy One of Israel, your Savior"* (Isa. 43:2-3).

Ezek. 34-35; Ps. 119:113-128; Prov. 28; Heb. 6-7

November 29 — The Child on the Freeway

It was a couple of weeks before Christmas in southern California a number of years back. A friend of mine, then assistant pastor in a local church, shared with me this true story that happened in his own family. His wife and her sister had been Christmas shopping and were speeding along the freeway on their way home, busily chatting in the front seat. My friend's three-year-old daughter was in the back seat by herself.

Suddenly the two adults were aware of a strange, unnatural, and horrifying set of sounds as they heard the back door open, the whistle of wind, and a sickening muffled sound. Quickly they turned and saw the child had fallen out of the car and was tumbling along the freeway!

Panic! The mother slammed on the brakes and pulled the car to a wrenching stop, jumped out, and ran back toward the child. When they arrived at her motionless body they noticed something strange. All of the traffic was stopped, lined up like a parking lot just behind her body. The child had not been hit by a car. Wonder number one!

A truck driver jumped down from his cab and was bending over the girl as they arrived at the scene. He said, "She's still alive. Let's get her to a hospital quickly. There's one nearby." He picked up the child, they all got into his large truck and sped off to a nearby hospital. The child was unconscious, but still breathing. Wonder number two!

When they arrived at the hospital they rushed into the emergency room and the doctors immediately began to check her over. Finally the doctor spoke. "Well, other than the fact that she is unconscious and scraped she appears to be in good shape. I don't see any broken bones. Her blood pressure is good. Her heart is fine. So far, so good." No apparent gross damage. She was only bruised and skinned from her vicious tumble down the freeway. Wonder number three!

The mother bent over the child. Her eyes were full of tears and her heart was filled with gratitude for such a miracle. Suddenly, without warning, the child's eyes opened, she looked up at her mother and said, "Mommy, you know, I wasn't afraid."

Startled, the mother said, "Oh, what do you mean?"

"Well," she said, "while I was lying on the road waiting for you to get back to me, I wasn't afraid, because I looked up and right there I saw Jesus holding back the cars with His arms stretched out." Wonder number four![93]

He will command his angels concerning you to guard you carefully;
they will lift you up in their hands, so that you will not strike your
foot against a stone (Luke 4:10-11).

❧

Ezek. 36; Ps. 119:129-144; Prov. 29; Heb. 8-9

November 30 — Irreverent Manipulation

Little Benjamin sat down at the desk to write a letter to God asking for a little baby sister. He started the letter like this:

Dear God, I've been a very good boy . . . .

He stopped, thinking, *No, God won't believe that.* He wadded up the piece of paper, threw it away, and started again:

Dear God, most of the time I've been a good boy . . . .

He stopped in the middle of the line, again thinking, *God won't be moved by this.* So he wadded up the letter and into the trash can it went.

Benjamin then went into the bathroom and grabbed a big terry cloth towel off the towel rack. He carried it into the living room and carefully laid it out on the couch. He smoothed out all the wrinkles. Then he went over to the fireplace mantle, reached up, and very carefully lifted down a statue of the Madonna. He had often seen his mother carefully dust the statue, and he had eyed it many times. On several occasions, his parents had told him that he could look but was not to touch the statue. Now, with all the care he could muster he had it in his possession.

Benjamin gently placed the statue in the middle of the towel, carefully folding over the edges. He then placed a rubber band around the whole thing. He brought it to the desk, took out another piece of paper, and began to write his third letter to God. It went like this:

Dear God, If You ever want to see Your mother again. . . .

What a story — this illustrates the way we attempt to manipulate God. We try to move God to intervene on our behalf by fleshly motives. If that doesn't get an answer, we go a step further and resort to begging, crying, and even move on to anger. When those tactics don't work either, we then resort to bargaining.

God does not want us to approach Him with manipulation, nor is it required to get His attention. Our loving Heavenly Father stands ready to respond and is available to each of us on the basis of an honest, trusting relationship with Him. God is as near as our heart. The Bible tells us that He knows what we need even before we ask.

> *Call to me and I will answer you and tell you great and unsearchable things you do not know* (Jer. 33:3).

Ezek. 37; Ps. 119:145-160; Prov. 30-31; Heb. 10

December 1 — The Do-It-Yourself Church

This little Lutheran Church in Idaho has an interesting history. The congregation bought an old one-room schoolhouse and prepared to move it into town and set it over a basement they would dig. Sound simple? They thought so. They had the school up on "runners" waiting for the basement when they started digging. They dug for about five inches and hit solid lava bedrock. In desperation, they started blasting the rock. This is in the middle of town. Much to their dismay, they discovered that the porous lava rock absorbed most of the blast. Each stick of dynamite only removed a small chunk of lava.

One of the farmers involved in the project said, "Golly, gee! (or words of that effect) This will take forever. Let's tie three sticks of dynamite together and set it off." The resulting explosion shattered every window on the west side of the hospital, which was a block away, and put some impressively sized boulders on their roof.

Once the hole was blasted and the basement walls poured, they realized they had forgotten to make a hole in the wall for water and sewer pipes. The same farmer suggested blasting a small hole in the wall with some of the leftover dynamite. To this day, nobody knows (a) why they let him talk them into the idea, (b) just how much dynamite he used. But he blew a hole in the east wall of the basement and blew the entire north wall of the basement into the adjoining street!

Months later, the church was complete, and a long discussion ensured concerning finishing the basement. The options seemed to be plaster, paneling, or paint. As the hour got later, tempers got shorter. Finally, the "dynamite farmer" stood up and said, "Tomorrow morning I am sending my boys into town. If the basement is not done by then, they will paint the whole thing . . . walls, floor, and ceiling . . . barn red." The other voters drank their coffee, went home, changed their clothes, and returned. By 7:00 the next morning, the basement was finished!

God works in strange ways at times, but God works, nevertheless!

Wouldn't you have loved to have been there! Reminds me of a work crew, all volunteers of course, who remodeled our first pastorate! We didn't use dynamite . . . but we did have a "dynamite" type church member who insisted on helping . . . who dumped paint on the newly sanded floor, broke out a stained glass window, mis-measured the platform. . . . If a pastor needs anything, it's probably a funny bone up his sleeve and a very tolerant spirit!

A cheerful heart is good medicine, but a crushed spirit
dries up the bones (Prov. 17:22).

⟡

Ezek. 38-39; Ps. 119:161-176; Prov. 1; Heb. 11

December 2 — How about a Good Word for Santa?

At Christmas, when calling us to be manger-people, perhaps Jesus would say:

CONSIDER IF YOU WILL, MY SERVANT, NICHOLAS. Born of wealthy parents in A.D. 280 in a small town called Patara in Asia Minor, he lost his parents early by an epidemic but not before they had given him the gift of faith. And then little Nicholas went to Myra and lived there a life which people called "Bethlehem". . . so full it was of self-offering and giving of himself, so full of sacrifice and love and the spirit of Jesus.

Nicholas lived in the mind of Christ so that when the town needed a bishop he was elected. He was later imprisoned for his faith by Emperor Diocletion and released later by Emperor Constantine.

Many stories of his generosity collected and spread — how he begged for food for the poor, of how he would give girls money so that they would have a dowry to get a husband. The story that was most often repeated told how he would don a disguise and go out and give gifts to poor children. He gave away everything he had. And everything he could gain from others.

And in A.D. 314 he died. His body was later moved to Italy. His remains are still there.

But the story of Nicholas has spread around the world.

Oh, people have done strange things to him. The poet, Clement Moore, gave him a red nose and eight tiny reindeer. And Thomas Nast, the illustrationist, made him big and fat and gave him a red suit trimmed by fur. Others have given him names . . . Belsnickle, Kris Kringle, Santa Claus.

But what's important about him is that he lived in the mind and spirit of Jesus Christ. And because he lived like that in a gentle self-offering love, he touched the whole world!

He lived what Jesus Christ taught and modeled. He caught the purpose of life. He made a difference in the spirit of Christ. And what is so exciting is that the same mind of Christ can and should be in and with us, too. The Apostle wrote, "Let this mind be in you which was also in Christ Jesus."

What a wonderful goal for this season: I will open my mind and heart and spirit so that the mind and spirit of Christ can be in me, reaching out to others to share his love![94]

Where is the one who has been born king of the Jews? We saw His star in the east and have come to worship Him (Matt. 2:2).

❧

Ezek. 40; Ps. 120; Prov. 2; Heb. 12-13

December 3 — The Christmas Gift

It was Christmas Eve, 1935. The Depression was at its height. A young widow and her six year old son prepared to try to celebrate Christmas. Supper tonight would be very plain. And the gifts . . . well, they were very simple, too. The mother had knit a pair of mittens for her son and herself.

Then just as she was going to have her son sit down for supper, he raced to the bedroom and came back proudly holding out a gift. The small gift was wrapped in an old newspaper and done as well as any six year old could hope to do. "Open it, Mommy, open it!" he urged his mother. His eyes were dancing and sparkling with excitement.

The mother carefully removed the newspaper wrappings to find an old cigar box. She then opened the cover to the contents of the gift. Inside the box was a shining copper penny and a piece of paper on which was written in crayon and terribly mis-spelled, "i luv yu mome!"

Tears welled up in her eyes as she read those words over and over again. Hugging him she cried, "Thank you, thank you, thank you. This is the best gift I have ever received!"[95]

And so . . . a bleak, dismal Christmas Eve was transformed into a joyous celebration of love. It all happened because of a gift! A pretty humble gift you'll agree but a gift which had been carefully prepared with love. A gift that was all he had to give. A gift that had been planned. A gift that was a sacrifice.

It's so easy to miss it, to blow it. Late one Christmas Day, a resident of the posh community of Hillsborough, California, accompanied by his wife and kids, set out to sing carols for the neighbors. As they were tuning up outside their first stop the lady of the house came to the door, looking distraught. "Look fella," she said, "I'm just too busy. The plumbing's on the blink, I can't get anybody to fix it, and there's a mob coming for dinner. If you really feel like singing carols, sing them someplace else."

"Yes, ma'am," replied Bing Crosby respectfully, as he herded his troop elsewhere.[96]

This Christmas, let's not any of us miss the opportunity of giving or of receiving by being too distracted. Christmas is His day!

They saw the child with his mother Mary, and they bowed down and worshiped Him. Then they opened their treasures and presented Him with gifts of gold and of incense and of myrrh (Matt. 2:11).

ҩ৶

Ezek. 41-42; Ps. 121; Prov. 3; Titus

December 4 — Free Gifts to Give for Christmas

Are you having a problem with what to give special people this season? It can be a challenge, especially when you want to give something fitting and needed and meaningful. Well here's a suggested list . . . in fact, you don't even have to go shopping for these!

1. The gift of LISTENING. . . . Why not give this valuable gift to someone who lives alone? And you must really listen! No interrupting, no daydreaming, no planning your responses. Just be there and just listen.

2. The gift of SIGNS OF AFFECTION. . . . Be generous with your hugs, kisses, and gentle squeezes of the hand. Let these tiny actions demonstrate the love inside of you.

3. The gift of a NOTE. . . . It can be as simple as "I love you" or as creative as a sonnet. Put your notes where they will surprise your loved ones.

4. The gift of LAUGHTER. . . . Just cut out a cartoon, save a clever article. Your gift will say, "I love to laugh with you."

5. The gift of a COMPLIMENT. . . . A simple "You look good in blue," or "I like your hair," or "Good supper, honey," can be of greatest value to those who may feel they are being taken for granted.

6. The gift of a FAVOR. . . . Help with the dishes, clean out the basement, mow the yard, shovel the walks, clean out the garage, fix the light, etc.

7. The gift of LEAVING ALONE. . . . There are times in our lives when we may want nothing better than to be left alone. Become more sensitive to those times and give solitude without interruptions.

8. The gift of a CHEERFUL DISPOSITION. . . . Try to be cheerful around those you love and don't add to the burden of the day.

9. The gift of a GAME. . . . Offer to play your loved one's favorite game. Even if you lose you will be a winner.

10. The gift of PRAYER. . . . Pray for those on your Christmas list and let them know that you pray for them. Praying for someone is a way of saying, "You are so special to me that I talk to God about you."[97]

There you have them — 10 free gifts you can easily give this Christmas. This list is by no means exhaustive. You could add more of these free gifts. In fact, this list may well come in handy on any day of the year. Think of the difference we could make in relationships if we were all in the giving mode on a daily basis!

Then Peter said, "Silver or gold I do not have,
but what I have I give you . . ." (Acts 3:6).

❧

Ezek. 43-44; Ps. 122; Prov. 4; Philem.

December 5 — What Did You See?

A midwestern family was struggling to make ends meet in the early days of the Depression. They were unable to afford any of the so-called luxuries of life. The father simply made enough to keep bread on the table and pay the rent on his house.

One day the news came to the community that a circus was coming to town and a ticket would cost $1.00. The little boy came running home from school excited and eager to get the money from his dad. His father, unable to provide that luxury, regretfully told his son that it would be impossible for him to attend the circus. However, he told the boy that if he went out and worked on odd jobs he might make enough money so that he could purchase a ticket on his own. His father agreed that for every nickel he earned he would match it with a nickel. Having never been to the circus before, the little boy worked feverishly and hard to earn the money to buy a ticket.

A few days before the circus came to town the boy emptied his bank and found that he had raised enough money to pay for half of the ticket price. His father gave him the other 50 cents and the boy ran off downtown to buy his very own ticket to the first circus of his life.

Excitedly, he waited for a couple of days until the circus came to town, and eagerly clutching his ticket in hand, he rushed down to the main street and stood on the curb as the circus parade went by. The clowns, the elephants, all of the performers in the circus thrilled him as he watched them go by. A clown came dancing over to him and the boy put his ticket in the clown's hand. He eagerly stood there on the curb as the rest of the parade went by on its way to the circus tent.

The little boy rushed home after the parade was over and told his father that he had been to the circus and how much fun it was. The father, surprised that he was home already, asked the boy to describe the circus to him. The boy told him of the parade that went by the main street of town.

The father, with pity and loving care, lifted his son into his arms and said, "Son, you didn't see the circus, all you saw was the parade."

This boy is typical of so many people. It's so easy to miss the real meaning of life. From the time when the first Christmas catalog arrives, all many will see is the parade of the coming season and miss the real meaning of this celebration.

For he satisfieth the longing soul, and filleth the hungry soul with goodness (Ps. 107:9;KJV).

〰️

Ezek. 45-46; Ps. 123; Prov. 5; 1 Tim. 1-2

December 6 — Courage

It was a few weeks before Christmas 1917. The beautiful snowy landscapes of Europe were blackened by war.

The trenches on one side held the Germans and on the other side the trenches were filled with Americans. It was World War I. The exchange of gunshots was intense. Separating them was a very narrow strip of no-man's-land. A young German soldier attempting to cross that no-man's-land had been shot and had become entangled in the barbed wire. He cried out in anguish, then in pain he continued to whimper.

Between the shells all the Americans in that sector could hear him scream. When one American soldier could stand it no longer, he crawled out of the American trenches and on his stomach crawled to that German soldier. When the Americans realized what he was doing they stopped firing, but the Germans continued. Then a German officer realized what the young American was doing and he ordered his men to cease firing. Now there was a weird silence across the no-man's-land. On his stomach, the American made his way to that German soldier and disentangled him. He then stood up with the German in his arms, walked straight to the German trenches and placed him in the waiting arms of his comrades. Having done so, he turned and started back to the American trenches.

Suddenly there was a hand on his shoulder that spun him around. There stood a German officer who had won the Iron Cross, the highest German honor for bravery. He jerked it from his own uniform and placed it on the American, who walked back to the American trenches. When he was safely in the trenches, they resumed the insanity of war!

Courage takes many forms. It's a human trait that we all recognize when we see it in action.

The example of Mary and Joseph is perhaps history's most important moment of courage. In a hostile time (it was King Herod's territory, don't forget!), this young couple saw a pregnancy through and helped bring the King of kings into the world. What a marvelous display of courage and love for a world that is oftentimes lacking.

He told them, "This is what is written: The Christ will suffer and rise from the dead on the third day, and repentance and forgiveness of sins will be preached in his name to all nations, beginning at Jerusalem" (Luke 24:46-47).

❧

Ezek. 47-48; Ps. 124; Prov. 6; 1 Tim. 3-4

December 7 — Is That All?

In a little Florida town there was a plain home for small, unwanted boys. The kindly matron didn't have much in the way of luxuries, but she made it up to the boys . . . she loved them, mothered them, spanked them, fed them, taught them to love God, to read their Bibles, to pray, and to become good citizens.

One day a well-to-do lady came from a distant city to see about adopting one of the boys. Everyone was so pleased and happy for the fortunate boy who would be going to live in such a fine placement home — a successful father, a beautifully dressed and coifed lady for a mother.

After going through the selection process, one particular little boy was chosen. Then the prospective mother began talking to him and asked, "Do you have a bicycle?"

Back the answer came, "No, ma'am."

She went on, "Do you have your own radio?"

The reply was "No, ma'am."

And the questioning continued . . . dress suit of clothes, personal TV set, and so on. To all of these questions about his possessions he was answering, "no."

Finally, this little boy studied her, then blurted out, "Please, ma'am, if that's all you're going to give me, I'd rather stay here!"

Yes, this is the Christmas season. For weeks and maybe longer, many of us have been planning, shopping, and preparing for the big day. Before the final rush takes place, let's pause and hear again the small boy's question, "Is that ALL you're going to give?"

Are material things worth more to you than the greater gifts? Where will you place Christ in all of this celebration, this season? Let's not miss Him like the Jewish nation missed Him when He came the first time. God had promised a Messiah for His people . . . but they weren't ready to receive Him. How about you, this Christmas?

He has filled the hungry with good things
but has sent the rich away empty (Luke 1:53).

༄

Lam. 1-2; Ps. 125; Prov. 7; 1 Tim. 5-6

December 8 — Unknown Beneficiary

One of my wealthier neighbors told me of the merriest Christmas he had ever experienced. He said, "One Christmas Eve I locked my office door and started home, feeling the spirit of Christmas had snubbed me that year. As I left the building on that bitterly cold day, I saw on the usual street corner the usual little paper boy shouting the headlines. I, slipping into my warm overcoat, noticed he had no overcoat. The dirty jacket he wore was much too large for his frail shoulders. It was also so thin he shivered with chill. On an impulse, I invited him to follow me into a nearby department store. To his surprised delight I had him fitted with a fur-lined leather coat. The shining eyes of a grinning boy excited me so I asked him if he owned a bicycle. Upon learning he did not, I accompanied him to the bicycle department and invited him to select the bicycle of his choice. Overcome with gladness, he could hardly decide, but finally settled on one of the shiniest ones. When he saw me paying for it, he jumped for joy saying, 'Just what I've been wanting! Just what I've been wanting!'

"Forgetting about his papers, he rode off into the thinning Christmas crowd shouting over his shoulder, 'Thanks! Thanks a lot! Thanks a lot, Mister.' The smile I had seen wreathed upon his face filled my heart with the true Christmas spirit. I believe that was the little boy's best Christmas. I know it was my best one," my neighbor concluded.

"What was the boy's name?" I asked.

The modest lawyer replied, "Come to think about it, I don't believe I ever asked him his name."[98]

Such a story is exactly what warms the heart. Why? It's a capturing of some of the spirit of Christ . . . freely giving to someone who cannot possibly pay back with a like gift. When we give, it has a boomerang type of effect. You can't get out of the way of the happiness which follows. Happiness is elusive . . . it cannot be captured if you set out to seek it . . . but it hits you like a surprise reaction when you give in an honest act of love! Yes, the boy was happy to be the recipient . . . but for my money, the lawyer got the better portion of happiness.

When looking at the Christmas story, think in terms of giving . . . Mary gave her body, Joseph gave a name and relationship, the shepherds came to give, the wise men came with gifts . . . but most of all, the Heavenly Father gave a Son to this world so desperately in need of the love, grace, mercy, and happiness this special Son provided.

Give to him that asketh thee, and from him that would borrow of thee turn not thou away (Matt. 5:42).

⟨◆⟩

Lam. 3; Ps. 126; Prov. 8; 2 Tim. 1-2

December 9 — Trouble at the Inn

For years now, whenever Christmas pageants are talked about in a certain little town in the Midwest, someone is sure to mention the name of Wallace Purling. Wally's performance in one annual production of the Nativity play has slipped into the realm of legend.

Wally was nine that year and in the second grade, though he should have been in the fourth. Most people in town knew that he had difficulty in keeping up. He was big and clumsy, slow in movement and mind. Still, Wally was well liked by the other children in his class.

Wally fancied the idea of being a shepherd with a flute in the Christmas pageant that year, but the play's director, Miss Lumbard, assigned him a more important role — that of the innkeeper.

And so it happened, a large audience gathered for the town's annual extravaganza. No one was more caught up in the magic of that night than Wallace. They said later that he stood in the wings and watched the performance with such fascination that Miss Lumbard had to make sure he didn't wander on stage before his cue.

Then came the time . . . Joseph appeared slowly, tenderly guiding Mary to the door of the inn. Joseph knocked hard on the wooden door set in the painted back-drop. Wally the innkeeper was there, waiting.

"What do you want?" he asked brusquely.

"We seek lodging."

"Seek it elsewhere." Wally looked straight ahead but spoke vigorously, "The inn is filled!"

"Please, good innkeeper, this is my wife, Mary. She is heavy with child and needs a place to rest."

For the first time, the innkeeper relaxed his stance and looked at Mary. There was a long pause.

"No! Begone!" the prompter whispered from the wings.

"No!" Wally repeated automatically, "Begone!"

Joseph sadly put his arm around Mary and she laid her head on his shoulder and they started to move away. The innkeeper stood there watching the forlorn couple. His mouth was open, brow creased with concern, eyes filling with tears. Suddenly this Christmas pageant became different! "Don't go, Joseph," Wally called out. "Bring Mary back!" His face grew into a bright smile, "You can have MY room!"[99]

And she gave birth to her firstborn, a son. She wrapped Him in strips of cloth and placed Him in a manger, because there was no room for them in the inn (Luke 2:7).

༺ஓ༻

Lam. 4-5; Ps. 127; Prov. 9; 2 Tim. 3-4

December 10 — Missing Christmas

George Mason's life centered on his business. He lived alone and on this Christmas had refused all invitations, even to his brother's home. On Christmas Eve, after his employees had left, he went into the office vault to get a little extra cash. Soundlessly, on newly oiled hinges, the great door swung shut behind him.

Desperately he pounded on the door. Then he realized no one could hear him. Everyone was gone, even the cleaning woman. Surely he could make it overnight, he consoled himself. Then he remembered that the next day was not a working day, it was Christmas! His heart pounding with fear, he wondered if he would have enough air. It was a new vault. Hadn't he heard something about a "safety air hole?" Feeling around in darkness he finally located it at the bottom of the wall; he could feel a gentle breeze coming in.

Christmas Eve and then Christmas Day passed. He was alone as he had planned. But he was uncomfortable, hungry, and thirsty in darkness so dense he could almost feel it brushing his face. He tried to sleep . . . anything to pass the time. He thought of friends and family and how they must be enjoying Christmas. He wondered if they had missed him.

The day after Christmas the chief cashier arrived early and unlocked the vault but did not open the door. Without anyone seeing him, George Mason staggered out and tottered to the water cooler. Then he took a taxi to his lonely apartment to freshen up. Back at the office, no one suspected a thing.

Physically, he had missed Christmas, but friends and family hadn't given him a thought, so in a way, he hadn't missed anything. After that lonely experience, he wrote on a little card these words: "To love people, to be indispensable, somewhere, that is the purpose of life. That is the secret of happiness." He then taped it to a wall high up in the vault to always remind himself of what had been missed.[100]

I really think that there are a lot of ways in which we can miss Christmas. It may take an extra special effort on your part to not miss the impact of this season. I for one, want to remember and be remembered on this upcoming holiday season. Let's decide together that we will not miss this Christmas!

Thus there were fourteen generations in all from Abraham to David, fourteen from David to the exile to Babylon, and fourteen from the exile to the Christ (Matt. 1:17).

⌐⌐

Nah.; Ps. 128; Prov. 10; 1 Pet. 1-2

December 11 — A Christmas Hymn Story

Phillip Brooks was a young minister of 30 when he visited the Holy Land in 1865. It was Christmas Eve when Brooks and several friends rode on horseback from Jerusalem to Bethlehem. It must have been exciting for that young minister to walk the streets of Bethlehem and think on those events which occurred so many years ago on the night when Christ was born.

Shortly before sundown, Brooks and his friends rode a short distance east of Bethlehem to the fields thought to be where the shepherds were keeping their flocks. And later that Christmas Eve, they attended services in the Church of the Nativity, built in A.D. 326 by Constantine over the place where it is believed Jesus was born.

Three years after this Christmas tour of Bethlehem, Phillip Brooks wrote this carol for the children in his church's Sunday school:

> O little town of Bethlehem,
> How still we see thee lie!
> Above thy deep and dreamless sleep
> The silent stars go by;
> Yet in thy dark streets shineth
> The everlasting Light;
> The hopes and fears of all the years
> Are met in thee tonight.

Familiar words and music which we have sung many, many times at Christmas. But have you really read them, grasped their meaning? Read with me the fourth verse of this song:

> O holy Child of Bethlehem,
> Descend to us, we pray;
> Cast out our sin and enter in,
> Be born in us today.
> We hear the Christmas angels
> The great glad tidings tell,
> O come to us, abide with us,
> Our Lord Emmanuel.[101]

Not only is this a beautiful poem, there's some great theology in it. But that last verse is really a prayer . . . a prayer that is as contemporary today as it was when written.

The beginning of the gospel about Jesus Christ, the Son of God.
It is written in Isaiah the prophet: "I will send my messenger
ahead of you . . ." (Mark 1:1-2).

༺ఇఞ༻

Ezra 1-2; Ps. 129; Prov. 11; 1 Pet. 3-5

December 12 — Watch That Step

There was a small country church having the yearly Christmas cantata. Part of the ritual of their cantata was that they always marched in singing "O Come, All Ye Faithful" and then at the end they proceeded out singing, "Hark, the Herald Angels Sing." This small country church had a large floor furnace that heated the building. The grating for that furnace was right in the center of the aisle.

As the choir began their processional, they marched precisely up the aisle, each person three pews behind the other. Just as the last alto got middle way up the aisle, she stepped on the grating of the floor furnace.

Unfortunately, the pencil-thin heel of her shoe went through the grating and stuck there. Hardly breaking stride, she shook her foot hard several times, but, unfortunately, the shoe was stuck. The man in line behind her was getting close. She slipped her foot out of the shoe and went limping up the aisle with only one heel on.

The man coming behind looked down and realized what had happened. He knew if the shoe was left sticking there, it would break up the congregation. Thinking quickly, he reached down, grabbed the shoe and gave it a strong twist.

To his amazement, the entire floor grate came up with the shoe. He went into a mild state of shock and dazedly marched up the aisle in time with the music, with the floor grate and shoe in hand.

You guessed it! The next man in line fell in the hole![102]

I'll be willing to wager that that was one Christmas program never forgotten, at least by those who participated and those who observed!

In the Christmas story, fear fills the hearts of the shepherds. Now and then something introduces a bit of fear into Christmas. Everyone present at the Newbiggin (England) Middle School Christmas Pageant, December 23, 1991, was engrossed in the presentation and enjoying their kids. Midway through, a field mouse popped out from a bale of straw, sat on its hind legs, and began grooming itself.

According to headmaster Alan Symmonds, "The 130 children on stage were fairly good . . . they were only in mild hysterics . . . but the people in the audience jumped out of their seats and screamed."[103]

When we think about it . . . jumping and shrieking are more appropriate than yawns!

An angel of the Lord appeared to them, and the glory of the Lord shone around them, and they were terrified. But the angel said to them, "Do not be afraid . . ." (Luke 2:9-10).

༺ঌ

Ezra 3-4; Ps. 130; Prov. 12; 2 Pet.

December 13 — Need to Be Hugged

In the fall of the year, Linda, a young woman, was traveling alone up the rugged highway from Alberta to the Yukon. Linda didn't know you don't travel to Whitehorse alone in a rundown Honda Civic, so she set off where only four-wheel drive vehicles normally venture.

The first evening she found a room in the mountains and asked for a 5:00 a.m. wake-up call so she could get an early start. She didn't understand why the clerk looked surprised at that request but as she awoke to early morning fog shrouding the mountaintops, she understood.

Not wanting to look foolish, she got up and went to breakfast. Two truckers invited Linda to join them and since the place was so small, she felt obliged.

"Where are you headed?" one of the drivers asked.

"Whitehorse."

"In that little Civic? No way! This pass is dangerous in weather like this," the other chimed in.

"Well, I'm determined to try," was Linda's gutsy, if not very informed response.

"Then I guess we're just going to have to hug you," the trucker suggested.

Linda drew back. "There's no way I'm going to let you touch me!"

"Not like that!" the truckers chuckled. "We'll put one truck in front of you and one in the rear. That way we'll get you through the mountains."

All that foggy morning Linda followed the two red dots in front of her and had the reassurance of a big escort behind as they made their way safely through the mountains.[104]

Have you ever been caught in the fog of life? Visibility is almost non-existent. Then, there's not only the fog to contend with, but you're faced with a mountain pass as well. The combination can be deadly. What do you do? You need help. Hopefully at a time like that you have some mature Christian friends upon whom you can call to "hug" you through such a life-situation. Someone who can lead the way as well as someone who can follow behind with gentle encouragement.

But it doesn't stop with receiving such help. How about you? Are you willing to help someone else through the treacherous passes of life? We are to be a part of each other's life needs. Give someone a "hug" of care.

Two are better than one . . . for if they fall, one will lift up his companion. But woe to him who is alone when he falls, For he has no one to help him up (Eccles. 4:9-10;NKJ).

⁖

Ezra 5-6; Ps. 131; Prov. 13; 1 John 1-2

December 14, Hanukah — The Eight-Day Wonder

Have you ever wondered what the "Hanukah" celebration which the Jewish people observe is all about? Perhaps this will be of some help.

One of the best-known of the Jewish emblems is the seven-stemmed candelabrum known as the "menorah" in Hebrew. It commemorates the seven lamps of Solomon's Temple. This golden candlestick was first a part of the furnishings of the Tabernacle in the Wilderness, to specifications given by God. It was to stand on the left side of the Holy Place and to be made of beaten pure gold. It was minutely detailed in Exodus 25:31-40 and 37:17-24. Why this candlestick? Because all natural light was shut out from the tabernacle. It was symbolic of Jesus Christ, the light of the world, bringing us the full radiance of divine life.

But once a year, the Jews use a larger, nine-stemmed menorah to commemorate an important victory in their history. In 164 B.C., the Jewish leader Judas Maccabeus defeated the Syrian king Antiochus Epiphanes and occupied Jerusalem. When the Jews entered the temple, they discovered that there was only enough oil left to keep the lamps lit for one day. Miraculously, however, the oil lasted for eight days.

This episode is now celebrated in the eight-day "Festival of Lights" called "Hanukkah" in Hebrew, which begins on December 14. On the first evening of the festival a single branch of the menorah is lit. Each subsequent evening another branch is lit, until by the end of the festival all the branches are lighted. The ninth branch of the memorah is a pilot light and is kept burning throughout the festival. Special cakes similar to pancakes, called "latkes," are eaten, and children play with a top bearing four Hebrew letters standing for the words "a miracle happened here." This festival starts on the eve of the 25th day of the Hebrew month of Kislev . . . which translates to December 14th.

This festival is distinctly Jewish and not normally kept by the rest of the world. When thinking of festivals and feasts and special days, think of how many have been given to us by the Jewish people. Christmas, which we celebrate this month is in honor of a Jewish child . . . Jesus Christ. Easter is celebrated because of the birth, death, and resurrection of a Jewish man. The Bible, from which we read and follow as a pattern for life, was brought to us by Jewish people. And we could go on and on in expressing our thanks. . . .

They made the lampstand of pure gold and hammered it out, base and shaft; its flowerlike cups, buds and blossoms were of one piece with it . . . they made the lampstand and all its accessories from one talent of pure gold (Exod. 37:17-24).

Ezra 7-8; Ps. 132; Prov. 14; 1 John 3-5

December 15 — The Night Christmas Arrived

Marge had been a member of our church study group for several years. Now she was terminally ill with cancer. The rest of our group gathered to go caroling. It was a cold night with snow in the air. We visited people who were house-bound and would sing two or three carols at each house. We all were looking forward to singing to Marge. She was feeling fairly well that evening and came to the door to hear us. We sang two or three carols and were about to leave when, on impulse, I asked if there was any particular carol she would like to hear.

"There is," she said, "but I suppose it is too much to ask. During the Second World War, I was a nurse in a prison camp for German soldiers in Arizona. I remember on Christmas Eve when they sang 'Silent Night, Holy Night' as one of the most moving experiences in my life. I would really enjoy hearing that sung in German again."

My heart sank. There was no way we could do that. Suddenly, behind me, I heard a voice, "I can do that." Ed, a member of our group who sang in our church choir, began to sing. The rest of us began to hum along with him.

I never knew what prompted Marge to ask for that particular carol. Perhaps she was reviewing her life experiences, trying to make sense of her life before she died. None of us knew that Ed had majored in languages and had been a German language teacher earlier in his life. All of us knew that, in the God-given serendipity of that moment, Christmas had arrived![105]

Serendipity is the aptitude for making desirable discoveries by accident . . . and God specializes in these moments, lots of them. Co-incidence has been described as an event in which God chooses to remain anonymous. Do you think that each of us could have a role in providing such a moment for someone else at this season?

Here's another one of those special moments: To show the splendor of the newborn Saviour in the church Christmas pageant, an electric light bulb was hidden in the manger. All the stage lights were to be turned off so only the brightness of the manger could be seen, but the boy who controlled the lights got confused and all the lights went out.

It was a fairly tense moment broken by a little shepherd's loud whisper, "Hey, you just turned off Jesus!"[106]

Be prepared, let it happen, and let's share the moment!

Anna . . . coming up to them at that very moment, she gave thanks to God and spoke about the child to all who were looking forward to the redemption of Jerusalem (Luke 1:38).

❦

Ezra 9-10; Ps. 133-134; Prov. 15; 2, 3 John

December 16 — The Better Gift

During World War II, at the Christmas season, Miss Kathryn Drummond was passing through a small Minnesota town. She observed a Red Cross bloodmobile parked before the schoolhouse and stopped to contribute a pint of blood.

Among the workers was a middle-aged handy-man who waited on the nurses by fetching supplies, washing utensils, and so forth. Meeting this man in the hall and assuming him to be the janitor, she commented upon the fine new school building. "No doubt you find it a great improvement over the old one," she said.

He blushed like a freshman but smiled, too. "I'm a stranger here," he said. "I live in Minneapolis and travel around with this unit. You see, I'm too old to fight and too unskilled to help these doctors and nurses in any other way than this. I have a great interest in collecting blood for Europe, as all my people are imperiled there."

His light complexion and sensitive features suggested to her that he was Nordic. "Are you from Denmark?" she asked.

"Oh, no," he replied, "I'm a Greek. You know, some Greeks are very fair complected."

The following winter Miss Drummond was in Minneapolis. Friends took her to hear the renowned Minneapolis Symphony Orchestra. And when its great conductor stepped to the podium she recognized him at once! He was the handy-man she had mistaken for a school janitor. He was the world-famous musician/conductor, Dimitri Mitropoulos!

This story has been shared with you in order to ask this question: What are you giving this year? There are a lot of things that are impossible for any of us to give . . . but by the same token there are a number of things we can give.

None of us could give a blind child sight this Christmas, but how about giving a few minutes of companionship? We can't give a father or mother back to a child who may have lost a parent, but we could give interest and a bit of time! It's impossible to restore to health a person who may have lost the use of any of their limbs, but how about time spent with them to give purpose and meaning? Have you caught the concept? Let Jesus Christ so fill you with His birthday spirit this year that you will give something of real value, lasting value in His name!

If my people, which are called by my name, shall humble themselves, and pray, and seek my face, and turn away from their wicked ways; then I will hear from heaven, and will forgive their sins, and will heal their land (2 Chron. 7:14).

༄

Zech. 1-3; Ps. 135; Prov. 16; Jude

December 17 — He's More Alive

A small country church had set up a Nativity scene on the front lawn of their church for the Christmas season. The pastor happened to be watching through his study window when a young family drove up to get a better look at the scene. Out of the car piled Mom and Dad and three little ones. They scurried about looking at the entire setting.

The pastor reached for his coat to walk outside to greet the family. As the pastor made his way toward the family, he noticed the smallest of the children, a little girl standing and looking a long time at the manger scene. She looked at the figures of the shepherds, then at Mary and Joseph, but particularly she was drawn to the face of the doll that had been laid in the straw to represent the Baby Jesus.

The pastor spoke with the parents and greeted the children. All the while the little girl stood glued at the manger scene.

When the family was finished, she was still standing at the manger scene. The mother called, "Come on, honey, we must go."

Then in a voice of finality and quite loudly to the others who were in the snow getting ready to leave, she turned and said, "HE'S A LOT MORE ALIVE THAN THAT!"

Smart little girl. She said it for me! She saw what I wish all of this world could see in the great Christmas story — that Bethlehem is now and that He is here just as much as He was in the stable of the inn that night, waiting for us to come . . . to give of ourselves . . . to acknowledge Him and to receive Him.

The angels made the birth announcement to the shepherds on the hillsides, "Peace, good will. . . ." And again, this year, the worldwide prospects for peace seem a bit remote. But that still doesn't take away from the purpose of His coming . . . to bring peace into the living and lifestyle of all people and nations.

Will standing armies be reduced this year? Will people start to live in harmony with each other? We want to capture this feeling of peace at Christmas. So then, why does it wear off about two days following the celebration of His birth? Will this year be any different? Christmas is in step with some of the deepest longings of humanity. Christmas says we can change! This year, let's allow the benefits of this season to be ours all year through.

Suddenly a great company of the heavenly host appeared with the angel, praising God and saying, "Glory to God in the highest, and on earth peace to men on whom His favor rests" (Luke 2:13-14).

༄

Zech. 4-7; Ps. 136; Prov. 17; Rev. 1

December 18 — Childlike

As Christmas approached, each student was asked to create a Christmas banner. The best creations were to be selected for the "Children's Mass" on Christmas Eve. The day the selections were made, Vivian came home from school in tears. Her heart was breaking. Not only had the teacher rejected her banner but she told her she didn't have the proper respect for the project. And certainly she didn't know what Christmas was all about. To make matters worse, the rest of the kids had laughed at her.

"Viv, dear," her mother asked, "what did your banner say?"

Through her tears, Vivian, managed to blurt out, "My banner said, 'Mary had a little lamb. His name was Jesus.' "

Her mother paused for a moment or two. Then, with tears welling up in her own eyes, she took her daughter in her arms and gave her a long, tight hug. "I think you made a lovely banner, Viv. Bring it home. We'll put it up right over our family creche."

Vivian's banner became a prominent part of the family creche every year thereafter, proclaiming to all visitors their love for Jesus.[107]

Joseph Ng tells it like this: On Christmas Eve of 1986 a package was found stuck between the gates of my rented house. When my wife asked me to check the package, I was hesitatant for there had been bombings in Manila. I managed to open the package and found two toys for our two sons (ages three and five). According to our maid, her daughter had no money to buy toys, so she had gone caroling, singing Christmas songs from door to door. People in Manila sometimes give money to kids in such circumstances. In this way she was able to gather a few coins for presents.

End of a beautiful story of love expressed. There is so much about Christmas that we fail to capture in a few sentences on a page like this. My prayer for you this year is that this season will bring you new insights into God's fantastic love for us. It really makes no difference as to how that insight may come . . . be it through a child, from the Word of God, as expressed by loved ones, or a new pattern of thinking. Maybe the best approach is to read and re-read the biblical account as though we had never read it before. Take a fresh look, perhaps reading it from a different translation. Whatever it takes, let it come alive again.

This is how the birth of Jesus Christ came about. His mother Mary was pledged to be married to Joseph, but before they came together, she was found to be with child through the Holy Spirit (Matt. 1:18).

❧

Zech. 8-9; Ps. 137; Prov. 18; Rev. 2

December 19 — Fourth Wise Man

The story is told of the "Fourth Wiseman" named Artaban. He, too, set out to follow the star and he took with him a sapphire, a ruby, and a pearl beyond price as his gifts for the newborn King. He was riding hard to meet his three friends, Jasper, Melchior, and Balthasar at the agreed upon place. Time was running out when he came upon a traveler stricken with fever.

If he stayed to help he would miss his friends. He stayed, he helped, and nursed the man back to health. But now he was alone. He needed camels and bearers and a guide to help him cross the desert. Because of his act he had missed the caravan of his friends. He had to sell the sapphire to get the needed supplies and camels and bearers, and he was saddened because the King would never have this special gem.

He finally reached Bethlehem only to find Joseph and Mary and the Baby gone. While at the home where they had been staying, soldiers from Herod's army came by to kill all the boy babies in the house. The mother wept behind Artaban as he stood in the doorway. To save the child from certain death he paid the captain with the ruby so he would not so much as enter the home. One boy child was saved and the ruby was gone — now one less gift for the King.

For years he wandered, looking in vain for the King until some 30 years later he found Him in Jerusalem during His crucifixion. He thought just maybe he could use the pearl to buy His freedom. On the way to the hill a girl came running from a band of soldiers who were chasing her. She cried out, "My father is in debt and they are taking me to sell me as a slave to pay the debt. Please . . . help me, save me!"

Artaban hesitated . . . then, sadly, he took out his pearl, offered it to the soldiers, and bought the girl's freedom and cleared the debt.

The sky went dark and . . . the King died.

Now . . . think . . . did not the wiseman, Artaban, give his gifts to the King because he had cared for those who needed his gifts?

Christmas is soon upon us. Have you given any thought about your gift giving this year? Will it be exchange time . . . giving to people who are able to give back to you? Or will it be an honest act of real giving? How about giving to people who can't give back? I know of a family who pool their "gift" giving money every other year, and give it to a needy family as their Christmas. Just a thought.

The King will reply, "I tell you the truth, whatever you did for one of the least of these brothers of mine, you did for Me" (Matt. 25:40).

∽

Zech. 10-12; Ps. 138; Prov. 19; Rev. 3

The early part of December is the time of year when Christmas plays and pageants are being planned and practiced and prepared. It's such a big time of the year for little ones.

Well, it seems that a small boy in his Sunday school was bitterly disappointed at not being given the role of "Joseph" in their upcoming Nativity play. Instead he was given the minor role of playing the innkeeper. All during the weeks of preparation and rehearsal, he brooded and planned how he could get some kind of revenge on his more successful rival. Finally, the day of the performance came. The play was moving on quite nicely.

Then it was time for the Joseph and the Mary to make their entrance. They moved across the stage setting and knocked on the door of the inn. The innkeeper opened it a fraction, as he had been told to do, and eyed them coldly, for it was now his big scene.

"Can you give us board and lodging for the night?" pleaded Joseph. He then stepped back for the awaited rebuff and rejection.

But the innkeeper had not planned for all those weeks and practices for nothing. He flung the door wide open, beamed genially and in a loud, happy voice said, "Come on in . . . come right in! You shall have the very best meal and the best room in this hotel! It's yours! I'm pleased and delighted to welcome you to our inn. It's my privilege! Please step in and be my guests!"

There was a pause . . . the audience caught their collective breath. This was certainly a change in plot and definitely not in the script!

Then with great presence of mind, the youthful Joseph turned and said to Mary, loud enough so all could hear, "Hold on. I'll take a look inside first." He walked in past the innkeeper, who still stood with door flung open, looked all around at the inn, and came back out. He shook his head firmly at the innkeeper who was grinning broadly and announced: "No. I'm not taking my wife into a lousy place like that. Come on, Mary, tonight we'll be sleeping in the stable out in back!"

And the plot and play was back on course. It's not too early to be thinking about Christmas and how it will be celebrated this year. It's become an overly-commercialized holiday and gotten off track too often. Let's take a moment or two to make plans to get back on track. Give thought to the significance of His coming.

And this shall be a sign unto you; Ye shall find the babe wrapped in swaddling clothes, lying in a manger (Luke 2:12;KJV).

☙

Zech. 13-14; Ps. 139; Prov. 20; Rev. 4-5

Though Christ a thousand
Times in Bethlehem be born
If he's not born in thee
Thy soul is still forlorn.

Angelus Silesius

We recently heard a story, the true account of a child born with more birth defects than you can imagine: only one lung, one kidney, misshapen nose and ears, a cleft palate so deep that speech was incredibly difficult, almost totally deaf, and destined to become blind!

Cruelly teased by other children and depressed by parental neglect, Helen became so desperate about her situation that a friend took her to church where she learned to pray, to have faith in a God whose loving arms would hold her safe in spite of everything.

Her church friends found doctors to perform surgery on her eyes and ears. But the operations failed. So she went to a school for the blind to prepare for a life of total darkness.

Years passed and communication steadily became more difficult for Helen. One Christmas Eve at the midnight service back in Helen's friendly church the minister was offering communion. A young woman approached the table. There was a pause as she did not seem to hear the invitation to accept the bread and wine.

Then, with a gasp of astonishment, the minister recognized Helen, noticed her white cane and understood why she did not see the Christ gift in front of her, and had not heard the minister's voice offering it. Deeply moved, he leaned forward to kiss her and a tear fell on her cheek. But it was not Helen's tear. You see, she was born without tear ducts. Even the comfort of having a good cry had been denied her!

Later, in the minister's office, struggling to express her emotions through her cleft palate, Helen's words tumbled out. She told her pastor that although what little vision she'd had was gone, her faith was stronger than ever before. She said that she was the luckiest one in her class for the blind. In her halting words: "I'm so blessed to have had what I had, because I'm the ONLY one in the class who REMEMBERS what it was like to SEE!"[108]

I don't know what a story like that does to you. It makes me want to pause and count the many blessings of life that are enjoyed. There are many. There are blessings which we don't even know about. If any kind of an attitude should mark our celebration . . . it should be one of gratitude. Let it begin with an expression of gratitude for this season, for the fact that God did send His only Son to this world that so desperately needs Him.

In the beginning was the Word, and the Word was with God, and the Word was God (John 1:1).

⚬⚬

Hag.; Ps. 140; Prov. 21; Rev. 6-7

December 22 — Christmas Eve Tears

Christmas Eve, late afternoon, I believe I was seven and Mother, bless her, was making something special instead of the traditional jello, whipped cream, and bananas. She was baking a towering pie. I stood at her elbow, as small boys always will, as she peaked for a moment through the partially opened oven door.

"Perfect, perfect. The meringue is just right!"

In color and consistency, the moment had arrived. Carefully, so cautiously, she drew it out, when suddenly a slip of those sure hands and the capsized tower slithered across the floor, never to be a pie again! And Mother, not a weeper (I can count the times), covered her face with her apron and cried.

She was disappointed that God would let it happen! No one, but no one, cries on Christmas Eve. Why did she do it, prepare this gift for hungry little gluttons . . . jello was enough. I know! It was her language for telling us we were special.

More than 60 years have come and gone, 60 Christmases, and I remember that one the best and its gift of tears.[109]

Memories of family are wrapped around this season for many of us. I can clearly recall some of my childhood Christmas celebrations without too much effort. And it's so easy to lose the impact and import of the season.

A military "expert" was asked to deliver a speech in St. Louis, Missouri. It was during World War II and he had a difficult time getting a seat on the plane. However, he secured it and departed from his home town of Boston. Enroute he was "bumped" in Washington, DC by an army general who had a higher priority. Disgruntled and frustrated the lecturer cooled his heels while his plane left for Missouri.

His disappointment was nothing, however, compared to the general's disgust when he arrived in St. Louis only to discover that the speaker had to cancel out. The general's dismay was complete when he was told that the speaker was the man whose plane seat he had pre-empted in Washington!

We've worked around this theme before in this book . . . but here it is again. Are our presents to each other crowding out His presence? Where are the top priorities this season? Just for this year . . . let's get it right! Right? Right!

> *The light shines in the darkness, but the darkness*
> *has not understood it* (John 1:5).

❧

Neh. 1-2; Ps. 141; Prov. 22; Rev. 8-9

December 23 — Christmas Eve, 1915

It was cold and it was Christmas Eve 1915, and World War I raged. Please come with me to the Western Front in Europe.

The men on both sides of the line, Germans on the one side and British on the other, were in their trenches trying their best to keep warm against the bitter cold. There was snow on the ground, a moon in the sky, and stars were shining down on that particularly icy night.

Great guns were rumbling up and down the line . . . tracer shells leaped across the trenches. You must remember, at this time warfare was in the trenches.

Even though Christmas Day was coming, the war went on. Then along about the very special time of midnight on Christmas Eve an incredible thing happened. Gradually the noise of guns and cannons grew less and less. Deep silence lay over that Western Front. It was almost mystic, the noise of battle had given way to peace.

In the silence, suddenly, there came from the trenches the sound of voices singing, German voices. It grew in volume until it was all up and down the line, an old song of Christmas: "Stille Nacht! Heilige Nacht! Alles schlaft, einsam wacht. . . ." Then it died away.

Soon the sound of English voices singing the same song: "Silent night, holy night. All is calm, all is bright. . . ." The antiphonal singing was taken up by the Germans, again, this time: "Oh little town of Bethlehem, how still we see thee lie. . . ." and the Scotch and English soldiers sang it back.

Finally, some of the Germans became so excited that they burst from their trenches. Their officers tried to restrain them but nothing could stop them as they came running across "no-man's-land," reaching out their hands to the British in greetings. This lasted for two or three hours as they fraternized. No longer were they soldiers. They were Germans from the Rhineland and Bavaria. Allies were from the Scottish Highlands, from London, and the English countryside.

"Let the war stop," they were saying, "it is Christmas Eve!" It continued the next day in celebration, playing soccer, and sharing rations. On the 26th, when fighting was to re-commence, no one wanted to and no one did. Fighting on the Western Front didn't continue until new troops were sent to that front.

She will give birth to a son, and you are to give him the name Jesus, because He will save His people from their sins (Matt. 1:21).

❧

Neh. 3-4; Ps. 142; Prov. 23; Rev. 10-11

December 24 — What Do You Have?

A surgical magazine tells the story of a hard-pressed, irritable, nervous, overworked surgeon in a busy New York City hospital. He was ready to perform another emergency operation. He was in a hurry, it was Christmas Eve, December 24, and it had been quite a day in the surgical suite.

The patient was a beautiful girl of 17 who had been seriously injured in an auto accident. The nurse, about to give the anesthetic, said kindly, "Relax — breathe deeply and the pain will be gone."

The girl said, "Would you mind if I repeated the 23rd Psalm from the Bible, before you operate?"

The nurse looked at the surgeon and he nodded; the girl began: "The Lord is my shepherd, I shall not want. . . ."

The surgeon continued with his preparations, but everyone else stood still, listening. They had heard these beautiful words many times in church but they had never sounded so moving. Here in that surgical suite, they had another meaning, a deeper kind of meaning to them.

The girl went on, "Though I walk through the valley of the shadow of death, I will fear no evil: for Thou art with me. . . ."

The nurse held the cone above her to begin with the anesthetic.

"Hold it," said the doctor. "Let her finish." Then he moved over and looked down at her and said, "Go on, honey, say it to the end and say it for me, too, won't you?"

They all stood quietly and listened as her heart, full of faith, filled the operating room that Christmas Eve day. They heard some of the most moving words ever written:

"Thy rod and thy staff they comfort me," she paused, catching her breath, then went on to the finish, "and I will dwell in the house of the Lord forever."

The surgeon looked down at her. He was relaxed, his sense of irritation was gone. There was no feeling of other duties pressing in on him. He and his patient and the operating room crew were at peace and ready for the surgery.

Everybody in that room had been lifted by that girl's faith. It's soon Christmas, once more. What will you be giving this year, beyond the usual? Plan to give something of a spiritual value to others this Christmas!

And Mary said: "My soul praises the Lord and my spirit
rejoices in God my Saviour" (Luke 1:46-47).

❧

Neh. 5-6; Ps. 143; Prov. 24; Rev. 12-13

December 25, Christmas Day, —
That First U.S. Christmas

It was December 25, 1776, and destiny was in the making. We were at war for our freedom from the British. The cities were in the hands of the British . . . only the woods, the snow, and cold were ours.

On that night, the town of Trenton, New Jersey, was ablaze with light. Houses were filled with German troops. Who cared about the ragged, tattered, starving, and dying roustabouts under George Washington's command? To these professional soldiers, Washington's soldiers were simply a "rabble-in-arms."

There hadn't been much to change these professional military minds. They had seen these Yankees run at Long Island when the Hessians had come out of the fog. General Sullivan and his men had been chased and caught, with bayonets driven into the backs of the Yanks. There was drinking and boasting about how they would catch that rebel, Washington, and take his head back to England!

On this Christmas Day, Colonel Rall lay at Trenton with three Hessian regiments, 50 Jagers, 20 British dragoons, and a detachment of artillery. At midnight, Rall gathered his officers about him and shouted, "Noch einmal! Glory to Gott and to the Foxhunter, freezing in the hills across the river!" It was a night of revelry.

But the despised Foxhunter was on the move. Drawing his coat tighter, Washington peered ahead into the darkness. He sat there thinking. It was the "fulness of time" for him, the enlistments of 2,400 men still left to him were up on New Year's Day. It was now or never!

At 6:00 p.m. on December 25 his men assembled at the river and somehow they got horses, cannon, and men into the barges. Just after midnight, with nothing but chunks of frozen soup to gnaw on for rations, they pushed across the river. It was a good clean plan for dedicated men.

Suddenly Washington struck! He could have chosen no better moment! They wiped out the defeats of the past. Washington drove Ralls and his 1,400 men out into the cold. It was the turn of the war — every post along the Delaware River had been cleared of the enemy! Christmas Day meant war, good against evil, just as it did on the very first Christmas Day!

Then Simeon blessed them and said to Mary, his mother: "This child is destined to cause the falling and rising of many in Israel, and to be a sign that will be spoken against . . ." (Luke 2:34).

∽

Neh. 7-8; Ps. 144; Prov. 25; Rev. 14-15

December 26 — The Letter

Dear Innkeeper:

I was a guest at your inn a few weeks ago. My visit to your city was most unpleasant. The Romans were enrolling me for another of their miserable taxes. And the stay in your hostel did not improve matters.

I am a patient man, innkeeper. One must be if he is to be a merchant. I can forgive you for many inconveniences. I can overlook the fact that your wine was poor and your bread stale.

But, innkeeper, there are several things I cannot forgive. For my private room, you charged an unreasonable price. And it was about as private as the market place. The stench from the stable was unbearable.

No sooner had I fallen asleep when I was awakened by shouts of "Hallelujah, the King is born!" I saw a group of shepherds in front of the stable. I could see them by the light of bright stars. I ordered them to be quiet, but they paid me no mind. At long last, they disappeared into the stable and it became relatively quiet again.

Five minutes later, I was awakened again, this time by the crying of an infant. Strangely enough, the cries came from the stable. I looked out again and, through the open stable doors, could see the infant and its mother. I yelled down to keep the baby quiet but apparently they didn't hear me.

I could not sleep for the rest of the night. It was the most miserable night of my life . . . and all because of those people in the stable.

If you are going to permit your high-paying guests to be disturbed by those who pay less and are less, then I hope you are prepared to suffer great financial loss. You will never get anything from shepherds and a family which had to be housed in a stable.

> With great displeasure,
> I remain,
> SILAS OF JERUSALEM[110]

That must have been some kind of a night! Awesome! Let's just think a moment . . . the Son of God takes the form of a human baby and is born in the most humble of circumstances! My hope is that heaven has a video of this entire scene!

Today in the town of David a Saviour has been born to you; he is Christ the Lord (Luke 2:11).

❧

Neh. 9-10; Ps. 145; Prov. 26; Rev. 16-17

Warden J. Scudder tells of a friend riding on a train next to an obviously troubled and anxious young man. Finally the boy blurted out the story that he was a convict returning from prison. His crimes had brought shame on his poor but proud family, and they had never visited or written him during the years he was away. He had hoped this was only because they were too poor to travel the long distance and too uneducated to write. However, he could not be sure they had forgiven him.

The youth went on to explain he had wanted to make it easy for them. He had written them a letter asking them to put up a signal when the train passed their little farm near the outskirts of town. If they had forgiven and wanted him to return home they were to tie a white ribbon in the big apple tree near the tracks. If they did not want him back they were to do nothing and he would stay on the train, go West, and lose himself forever.

Nearing his home town, the youth's suspense and discomfort grew to the point where he could not look. His new-found friend offered to watch for him so they traded places. A few minutes later he put his hand on the young former convict's shoulder and whispered in a broken voice, "Look, it's all right . . . the whole tree is white with ribbons!"

Later, this friend told Warden Scudder, "I felt as though I had witnessed a miracle!"

There is something exciting and miraculous about a forgiving kind of love. This is the love that somehow manages to bridge over the troubled waters of a broken past. It's always amazing.

My understanding is that this story was also the inspiration for a very popular song of a few years back. Perhaps you also remember the words and melody of the song, "Tie a Yellow Ribbon 'Round the Old Oak Tree."

There is a tremendous cry from humanity for a forgiving kind of love. You seem to hear this wistful cry coming from all kinds of sources. The question may not be articulated, but the unspoken refrain goes like this: "Does anyone care enough about me to love me with an unconditional kind of love? Can I be forgiven?" I'm most delighted to tell you that that kind of love is yours for the taking from Jesus Christ! Just ask Him. So, this holiday season, forgive someone you should have forgiven long ago.

And now these three remain: faith, hope and love. But the greatest of these is love (1 Cor. 13:13).

❧

Neh. 11-13; Ps. 146; Prov. 27; Rev. 18

December 28 — One Solitary Life

How does one explain the greatness of the Man whose birthday we celebrate each year on December 25? Let's make a humble attempt:

He was born in a stable, the child of a peasant woman. He grew up in an obscure village; worked as a carpenter until He was 30; and then became an itinerant preacher for three years.

He never went to college;

He never wrote a book;

He never held an office;

He never owned a home;

He never had a family;

He never had a lot of money;

He never traveled farther than 200 miles from His place of birth;

He never accomplished any of the things that usually mark greatness;

He had no credentials but himself.

Although He spoke with great authority; taught with unusual wisdom; and was widely accepted by the people, the religious leaders of His day opposed Him. While He was still a young man, the tide of popular opinion turned against Him. He was betrayed by a friend; abandoned by His associates; and turned over to His enemies. He was falsely accused; endured the mockery of a trial; and was unjustly condemned to die.

He was crucified between two thieves, and while He was dying His executioners gambled for the only piece of property He had on earth, and that was His clothing. When He was dead, He was buried in a borrowed grave through the pity of a friend.

Nineteen centuries have come and gone, and today He is the central figure of the human race, and the cornerstone of world progress.

And all the armies that ever marched;

And all the navies that ever sailed;

And all the parliaments that ever sat;

And all the kings that ever reigned, put together. . . .

Have not affected the life of man upon this earth as has that ONE SOLITARY LIFE![111]

Therefore, let all . . . be assured of this: God has made this Jesus whom you crucified both Lord and Christ (Acts 2:36).

᳘

Esther 1-3; Ps. 147; Prov. 28; Rev. 19

December 29 — Winding Down

General Douglas MacArthur evaluated his life on his 75th birthday, saying, "Nobody grows old merely by living a number of years. People grow old by deserting their ideals. Years may wrinkle the skin, but to give up interest wrinkles the soul. In the central place of every heart, there is a recording chamber; so long as it receives messages of beauty, hope, cheer, and courage, so long are you young. When the wires are all down and your heart is covered with the snows of pessimism and the ice of cynicism, then are you grown old."

Benjamin Disraeli, former prime minister, expressed it like this in a letter to Lady Bradford: "I am certain there is no greater misfortune than to have a heart that will not grow old. The wisdom of the heart is its growing old in experience, recollected in tranquility, and digested in grace, humility, and love. What other wisdom is worth seeing and having? If people are rightly aging, they are growing in that wisdom, and as their years increase so does this wisdom."

G.K. Chesterton tells us that his old Victorian grandfather grew more silent as he grew older. One day his grown-up sons were complaining about a portion of the "General Thanks-giving" in the *Book of Common Prayer.* It is wicked, they were saying, to thank God for creation when so many people have little reason to be thankful for their miserable existence. The old man broke his silence to say, "I would thank God for my creation if I knew I was a lost soul."

Simcox wrote, "I love people more, because now I can dare let myself love them for their own beauty of being instead of what I can get from them. This change in the focus and the very nature of my loving is a change of the command of myself from eros to agape, from loving others for my sake to loving others for theirs."

William Saroyan said while dying of cancer in his seventies, "I am growing old. I'm falling apart. And I find it VERY INTERESTING when it was most painfully coming apart."

Sir W. Grenfell reportedly wrote this while in his twenties: "As for the life to come, I know nothing about it, but I want it, whatever it is."

Paul the Apostle, in the second letter to the church in Corinth, tells us that nature is winding down, petering out, while the inner self is being renewed. It's this new being which is composed of what remains of the old disintegrating self. Aging beautifully is a decision!

Therefore we do not lose heart. Though outwardly we are wasting away, yet inwardly we are being renewed day by day (2 Cor. 4:16).

⁂

Esther 4-7; Ps. 148; Prov. 29; Rev. 20

December 30 — Part of the Gift

A missionary was sent to Africa to be part of a ministry already in the works. This man had been raised on the Pacific Coast of the United States and loved the ocean. He had hoped that when sent to Africa he would be stationed in an area next to the ocean. His wish was not fulfilled, and upon his arrival he found his mission station was about 85 miles inland from the coast.

He determined to make the best of his assignment. Part of his responsibilities involved teaching in a Bible school in the area. It had been set up to provide ministerial training for the natives so that they could be effective evangelists to their own people.

In his teaching, many times this missionary-teacher would draw upon the ocean for his illustrative material. Often he talked of his great love for the ocean which he missed being this far inland. His students made note of his affection for the sea.

He began to teach about the fact that much of the Christian life is one of giving. He spoke about Christ being given as a special gift to this earth when He came as a babe in a manger. He shared with the native students about Christmas. He wasn't at all sure that the concept had been picked up, but he did the best he knew how about giving.

Then there was time for a break in the school year as the students were dismissed for a two-week period.

One day during this break there was a knock on his door. The missionary went to the door to see one of his students standing there with a huge smile on his face. Upon taken a closer look he noticed that the young man had scratches on his face, arms, and legs. His clothes looked like he had been on a long trek through jungle and formidable terrain. There was a tiredness about the young man.

However, in his hands this black man was holding a basketful of sea shells. Obviously they were not to be found locally. Then it dawned on the missionary — this young man had walked to the ocean to bring them back.

"Here is a gift from the ocean," the young man beamed.

The missionary was almost overcome with emotion as he replied, "But you have walked almost 170 miles to do this!"

His black face showed surprise and delight. He pulled himself to his full height and said, "Long walk is part of the gift!"

But just as you excel in everything — in faith, in speech, in knowledge, in complete earnestness and in your love for us — see that you also excel in this grace of giving (2 Cor. 8:7).

Esther 8-10; Ps. 149; Prov. 30; Rev. 21

December 31 — One Success Formula

There is one absolute principle if you really want your life to count, if you want to live with enthusiasm, if you want to make friends. *FIND A NEED AND FILL IT! Only* six words but what a powerful concept! I would venture to say that every enterprise that has been successful has been built on this formula. Every true friendship is based on this foundation. Find people's needs and fill them! Love people! Love this wonderful world! Love God.

To see how this works in real life, let's stop at Ed's Place . . . nothing but a little diner in a big city — greasy spoon, plain and simple, stools at a counter. Let's sit down.

Consider Ed . . . resting his big hands on the counter he asks, "Okay, brother (sister), what'll you have?"

"Are you Ed?"

"Yep."

"They tell me you have good hamburgers here."

"Brother, you never ate such a burger."

"Okay, let me have one, everything on it."

Then we notice, also at the counter sits an old man who looks miserable. He is hunched over, hands shaking. After Ed puts the burger in front of us, he places his hand in a friendly way on the old man's shoulder. "That's all right, Bill," we hear him say, "everything is all right. I'll get you a bowl of nice hot soup right away."

Another old man shuffles up to pay. Ed says, "Now Mr. Land, watch the cars out there. They're pretty fast at night." Then he adds, "Have a look at the moonlight on the river. It's pretty tonight."

When we pay our check . . . one of us remarks, "I like the way you talked to those old men. You made them feel that life is good."

"Why not?" Ed asks. "Life is good. Me, I get a kick out of living. Our place is sort of like home to them. Anyway, I kind of like 'em."

Believe in yourself, believe in life, believe in people, believe in God. Practice the principle of our concept! Practice these principles and discover that real enthusiasm becomes a part of your life! Believe that your life can be improved, believe that your job can be improved, believe that you can become a better person, believe that you can help others by finding their needs and helping to fill them! What a way to live! Go for it!

A cheerful heart is good medicine, but a crushed spirit dries up the bones (Prov. 17:22).

୭

Mal.; Ps. 150; Prov. 31; Rev. 22

Endnotes

[1] James S. Huett, *Illustrations Unlimited* (Wheaton, IL: Tyndale House Publishers, 1988).

[2] Billy Graham, *Angels: God's Secret Agents* (Irving, TX: Word, Inc., 1991).

[3] AP, *News Leader,* Springfield, Missouri, 3/19/94.

[4] *Newsweek,* 2/10/92.

[5] Eric W. Johnson, *Humorous Stories about the Human Condition* (Del Mar, CA: Prometheus Books).

[6] Kelli Anderson, *Sports Illustrated,* 2/21/93.

[7] Leslie R. Smith.

[8] Jan Winebrenner, *Steel in His Soul: The Dick Hillis Story* (Milpitas, CA: Overseas Crusades, 1985).

[9] Don Shelby sermon, "Where God Can Be Seen," adapted by Jeff Meaney.

[10] Anonymous, *Parables, Etc.,* 10/93.

[11] Corrie ten Boom, *Not I, But Christ* (Nashville, TN: Thomas Nelson Publishers, 1983), p. 61.

[12] E. Paul Hovey, *Treasury for Special Days* (Westwood, NJ: Fleming H. Revell).

[13] Yvonne S. Thornton, *The Ditchdigger's Daughters* (New York, NY: Birch Lane Press, Carol Publishing Group, 1995), as it appeared in *Reader's Digest,* September 1995.

[14] Abigail Van Buren, "Dear Abby" column, 2/14/93, adapted.

[15] Robert Fulghum, *All I Really Need to Know I Learned in Kindergarten* (New York, NY: Ivy Books, 1989), p. 4-5.

[16] *Newsweek,* 8/3/92.

[17] Alice Kalso, "World," from *Parables, Etc.,* 9/88.

[18] Amy Hill Hearth, *The Delany Sisters' Book of Everyday Wisdom* (New York, NY: Kodansha International, 1994).

[19] Rose Hodgin, *Parables, Etc.,* 5/92.

[20] Hope MacDonald, *When Angels Appear* (Grand Rapids, MI: Zondervan Publishing House, 1995), p. 41-42.

[21] Jeff Letofsky, *Daily Sentinel*, Grand Junction, Colorado, 7/17/88.

[22] William Goodin (Lima, OH: CSS Publishing Co., 1990).

[23] J. Allan Petersen, *The Myth of the Greener Grass* (Sherman, TX: Bible Believers Evangelical Assn., 1983).

[24] Robert J. Strand, *Love 101* (Green Forest, AR: New Leaf Press, 1993).

[25] Elmer Bendiner, *The Fall of Fortresses.*

[26] Chuck Mylander, *Parables, Etc.,* 11/89, adapted.

[27] *News Leader*, Springfield, Missouri, 4/2/94.

[28] Kenneth Nordvall; James S. Hewett, editor, *Illustrations Unlimited* (Wheaton, IL: Tyndale House Publishers, 1988).

[29] Steve Wulf, *Sports Illustrated,* 2/21/94, condensed.

[30] Barry & Joyce Vissell, *Chicken Soup for the Soul* (Deerfield Beach, FL: Health Communications, Inc., 1993).

[31] Paul Brand and Philip Yancey, *Fearfully and Wonderfully Made* (Grand Rapids, MI: Zondervan, 1980), p. 201-203, condensed and adapted.

[32] Walter Lord, *A Night to Remember* (New York, NY: Henry Holt and Company).

[33] Charles R. Hembree, *Pocket of Pebbles* (Grand Rapids, MI: Baker Book House, 1969), p. 65.

[34] Raymond Coffey, *Pasadena Star News*, 11/3/85.

[35] Charles Treptow, *Parables, Etc.,* 12/95.

[36] Helice Bridges, chairperson of the Board for Difference Makers, Inc., Del Mar, CA, condensed.

[37] Richard Selzer, *Mortal Lessons*, p. 45-46.

[38] Russell Conwell.

[39] David Goerzen, *The Pastor's Study File*, 5/93, adapted.

[40] Rev. Billy D. Strayhorn, *The Pastor's Study File*, 7/93.

[41] Erma Bombeck, adapted and condensed.

[42] Jack Canfield and Mark Hansen, quoting Art Buchwald, *Chicken Soup for the Soul,* p. 32-34.

[43] Joan Webster Anderson, *Where Miracles Happen* (New York, NY: Ballantine Books, Random House, Inc., 1994), p. 104-106.

[44] Norman Vincent Peale, *Treasury of Joy and Enthusiasm* (Old Tappan, NJ: Fleming H. Revell, 1981), p. 61.

[45] George H. Reavis.

[46] Dear Abby, *The News Leader,* Springfield, Missouri, 9/93.

[47] John B. Wilder, *Stories for Platform* (Grand Rapids, MI: Zondervan Publishing House, 1963), p. 48.

[48] Norman Schwarzkopf, *Ministry Advantage*, Nov./Dec. 1992, Fuller Institute.

[49] "News Digest," *Pentecostal Evangel,* 8/23/87.

[50] Ernest Campbell, *Campbell's Notebook*, 10/88, adapted.

[51] Jack Canfield and Mark Hansen, *A 2nd Helping of Chicken Soup for the Soul* (Deerfield Beach, FL: Health Communications, Inc., 1995).

[52] Brian Cavanaugh, *The Sower's Seed* (New York, NY: Paulist Press, 1990).

[53] Margaret Atwood, *Family Portraits: Remembrances of Twenty Celebrated Writers* (New York, NY: Bantam, Doubleday, Dell Pub. Group, Inc., 1989).

[54] Jo Ann Larsen, *Desert News,* condensed.

[55] G. Geauchamp Vick.

[56] Charles Colson, from his 1986 commencement address at Reformed Theological Seminary, Jackson, Mississippi, condensed.

[57] *Moody Monthly.*

[58] Tim Kimmel, *Little House on the Freeway* (Sisters, OR: Multnomah Books, 1987).

[59] Gary Smalley, *If Only He Knew* (Grand Rapids, MI: Zondervan Publishing House, 1988).

[60]Josh McDowell and Norm Wakefield, *The Dad Difference* (Nashville, TN: Here's Life Publishers, 1992), p. 61.

[61]M. Hirsh Goldberg, *The Blunder Book* (New York, NY: Quill/Wm. Morrow, 1984).

[62]John Hersey, *The Wall*

[63]Norma Copley, *The Pastor's Story File*, 7/86.

[64]Charles R. Swindoll, *Laugh Again* (Dallas, TX: Word Publishing, 1992), p. 20-21.

[65]John Schlatter, motivational speaker, Cypress, California.

[66]Carl Johnson, *Parables, Etc.*, 7/91.

[67]*Fortune*, 4/11/88, p. 88.

[68]Howard Hendricks, *Say It with Love* (Wheaton, IL: Victor Books, 1989).

[69]Sylvia Porter, *Focus on the Family*, 1/92, p. 7.

[70]Gary Smalley and John Trent, *The Blessing* (Colorado Springs, CO: NavPress, 1988).

[71]Chad Miller, *The Pastor's Story File*, 7/86.

[72]Russell Chandler, *The Overcomers* (Old Tappan, NJ: Revell, 1978).

[73]Debbi Smoot, *The Pastor's Story File*, 2/92.

[74]Zig Ziglar, from a motivational talk.

[75]John D. Gondol, *Responding in Gratitude.*

[76]Brian Cavanaugh, *More Sower's Seeds* (Mahway, NJ: Paulist Press, 1992), p. 31-32.

[77]Louisa May Alcott, *Little Women.*

[78]Dale V. Atkins, *Sisters* (New York, NY: Arbor House Publishing Co., 1984), p. 13-14.

[79]George Maronge Jr., *Parables, Etc.*, 2/93.

[80]Gene Sikkink, *Parables, Etc.*, 11/91.

[81]Amy Tan, *The Joy Luck Club* (New York, NY: Ivy Books, 1989).

[82]Amy Tan, *The Kitchen God's Wife* (New York, NY: G.P. Putmans Sons, 1991).

[83]Mervyn Rothstein, *New York Times*, adapted.

[84]William Ellis and Earl Banning, Religious Broadcasting, 1/93, selected and condensed.

[85]Atkins, *Sisters*, p. 67.

[86]Camille Shirah, *Teachers in Focus*, 1/95, p. 13.

[87]Shirley Abbott.

[88]Larry Pillow, *Parables, Etc.*, 12/90, adapted.

[89]Cathy Rigby, *The Guideposts Treasury of Love* (New York, NY: Guideposts, 1978), p. 24-25.

[90]Sam Sasser, *Let Us Continue to Hold Sister Smith's Leg Up in Prayer!* (Shippensburg, PA: Treasure House, 1993), p. 39.

[91]W. Clement Stone, *A Treasury of Success Unlimited* (New York, NY: Hawthorne Books, 1966), p. 9-10.

[92]Delia Ephron, *How to Eat Like a Child* (New York, NY: Penguin USA, 1988).

[93]James S. Huett, ed., *Illustrations Unlimited* (Wheaton, IL: Tyndale House Publishers, 1988), p. 101.

[94]Bruce Thieleman, chaplain, Grove City College.

[95]Vernal Anderson, St. Matthews-Bethany Lutheran Church, Evan, Minnesota.

[96]Herb Caen, *Personal Glimpses.*

[97]Impression Printing.

[98]Perry Tanksley, *I Call You Friend* (Jackson, MS: Allgood Books).

[99]Dina Donohue, *The Guideposts Christmas Treasury* (Carmel, NY: Guideposts Magazine, 1972), adapted and condensed.

[100]*Moody Monthly*, adapted.

[101]Phillip Brooks, *Hymns of Glorious Praise* (Springfield, MO: Gospel Publishing House, 1969).

[102]Billy D. Strayhorn, *The Pastor's Story File*, 12/92.

[103]*LaGrange Daily News*, LaGrange, Georgia, 12/24/91.

[104]Don Graham, Moose Jaw, Saskatchewan.

[105]J. Stuart Wells, *The Pastor's Story File,* 12/92.

[106]Donald O. Maddox, *The Pastor's Story File,* 12/92.

[107]Myles Colgan.

[108]*Guideposts* fundraising letter, approx. 1980.

[109]Gerhardt Frost, *Blessed Is the Ordinary, Reflections of Gerhardt Frost,* from a Charles Swindoll sermon, 12/9/84.

[110]Michael Daves, "Letter to an Innkeeper," *Together.*

[111]Phillip Brooks, as adapted by George Clarke Peck.

Moments to Give series

Moments for Christmas
Moments for Each Other
Moments for Fathers
Moments for Friends
Moments for Graduates
Moments for Grandparents
Moments for Mothers
Moments for Pastors
Moments for Sisters
Moments for Teachers
Moments for Teens
Moments with Angels

$9.95 each

Available at bookstores nationwide or write
New Leaf Press, P.O. Box 726, Green Forest, AR 72638